CHRONICLE OF THE ROMAN REPUBLIC

PHILIP MATYSZAK

CHRONICLE OF THE ROMAN REPUBLIC

THE RULERS OF ANCIENT ROME FROM ROMULUS TO AUGUSTUS

With 293 illustrations, 98 in color

Thames & Hudson

CONTENTS

Author's note
My thanks to Adrian Goldsworthy for his help and advice. Also to my wife Malgosia for her constant support, and to the staff at T&H for their energy and enthusiasm. A particular debt is due to Barbara Levick for her excellent work on reading the text, and correcting my many errors.

(*Half-title*) Coin showing the twins Romulus and Remus being suckled by the she-wolf.

(*Frontispiece*) A statue of a prosperous Roman holding the busts of two of his ancestors: possibly of Augustan date, the busts are in first-century BC style.

First published in hardcover in the United States of America in 2003 by Thames & Hudson Inc., 500 Fifth Avenue, New York, New York 10110

thamesandhudsonusa.com

First paperback edition 2008

Library of Congress Catalog Card Number 2002111074

ISBN 978-0-500-28763-7

Printed and bound in Singapore by Craft Print International Ltd

Numa Pompilius

Claudius Marcellus

Pompey the Great

Mark Antony

Preface: Republican Virtues

Rome gained most of its empire while it was still a republic. The leaders of the Republic were a military aristocracy who governed with the consent of the people. They were hard men – prudish, superstitious, brutal and utterly uncompromising. And they were also unflinchingly, sometimes suicidally, brave. Yet theirs was one of the most civilized societies in the ancient world. Once established, the Roman Republic was led not by monarchs ruling by divine right or heredity, but by elected executives whose power was checked by a constitution so well crafted that it inspired the founding fathers of the United States of America. In theory, even the weakest and poorest Romans had the protection of the law, and by and large their rights were respected.

Political battles were vicious, but for most of the Republic they were fought in the legislature and the courtroom. Exile, disgrace and the confiscation of lands and money awaited the unsuccessful statesman of the early to mid-Republic, but the Roman aristocracy did not kill its own. This did not mean that life as a Roman aristocrat was either comfortable or safe. The Roman élite led from the front, and the armies that marched from Rome to conquer Italy and then the rest of the Mediterranean world were led by people such as the Fabians, Scipios and Claudians – scions of Rome's greatest houses. They fought and died with their soldiers, and sometimes their casualties were horrific. Contrary to popular belief, defeated Roman generals did not fall on their swords. Rather they fought to the last, and, in the words of one writer, it was necessary not only to kill them, but to push them over afterwards.

Who were these men? In this history we see the best and worst of the Roman élite – men such as Marcus Licinius Crassus, a kind father and loving husband, who crucified captured slaves in their thousands; or Cato the Censor, upright and incorruptible, xenophobic and misogynistic. Some families make numerous appearances – the proud Claudians, the cultured Scipios, the noble Valerians. Others, such as Quintus Sertorius or Atilius Regulus, make but a single appearance. As a backdrop to their stories are the true builders of Rome – the common people. The *plebs romana* were not a passive mass, obediently following their leaders. They insisted on choosing their leaders themselves, and took an active part in political debate and the framing of legislation. And when they took to arms they formed the finest fighting machine in antiquity.

The Romans, plebs and patricians, shared a common outlook. They were intolerant of weakness, exploiting it in others and despising it in themselves. They won their wars simply because, to this arrogant nation, the concept of defeat was literally unthinkable. But their pride did not lead to exclusivity. The Romans originated from what might reasonably be described as the scum of Italy – including bandits, mercenaries and escaped slaves. Until late in the history of the Republic, conquered peoples and freed slaves were welcomed into the ranks of citizens. When this policy of inclusiveness changed, the consequences led directly to the fall of the Republic.

A marble bust of Scipio Africanus, the victorious general who finally defeated the Carthaginians led by Hannibal. Despite many military achievements, he died in exile.

(*Above*) A bust of an anonymous elderly Roman, a good example of the 'warts and all' veristic style of Republican portraiture. A first-century AD copy of a portrait of the mid-first century BC.

(*Right*) The forum of Rome: a view through the Arch of Titus to the three remaining columns of the Temple of Castor and Pollux, with the Temple of Vesta on the left.

THE SITE OF ROME

How could Romulus have acted with more divine wisdom than by placing his city on the banks of a river which flows with a never-failing current towards the sea; having all the advantages of being near the sea, and none of the drawbacks? That which the city lacks it can import from the sea, and it can export back there that which it has in excess. But yet the city depends not only on what it gets from the sea, but also the land can be cultivated to maximum effect. To me then, it appears that Romulus had from the outset the divine inspiration to make his city the seat of a mighty empire. No city placed in any other part of Italy could so easily have maintained our power and dominion.

Cicero, *De Republica* 2.10

INTRODUCTION: THE RISE OF ROME

ACCORDING TO LEGEND, THE TROJAN WAR ended in 1184 BC when the victorious Greeks finally sacked Troy, which had defied them for ten years. As the city burned, the aged Anchises was carried to safety by his son. It was unsurprising that the gods should see to the welfare of Anchises – he had been the lover of the goddess Venus herself. The gods also had plans for the son, Aeneas – he was to become the father of the Roman race.

Like his contemporary Odysseus, Aeneas was destined to wander far before he found a home. His travels took him to the shores of Africa, where he met and loved the Carthaginian queen, Dido. But destiny drove Aeneas on, and he abandoned Dido, who was so distraught that she killed herself; thus, according to the legend, sowing the seeds of future conflict between Carthage and the descendants of Aeneas.

Aeneas himself settled in Italy and married an Italian princess. His son, Iulus, founded the city of Alba Longa, from where, 400 years later, Romulus and Remus set out to found the city that became Rome. Iulus was claimed as an ancestor by the Julian clan, and because Iulus' grandmother was Venus, Julius Caesar was able to claim divine descent. The Julians were undoubtedly of great antiquity, but in this they were not unique. It is one of the features of early Rome that power was shared among the members of some 50 or so families whose names appear over and over again in the roll of office holders (the *Fasti*). Many of them, such as the Iunian Bruti, the Julians and the Ahenobarbi, span the centuries between the birth of the Republic and its bloody death.

Roman names

Roman men (there was a different system for women) were known by the famous *tria nomina*: the 'triple name'. The first name was the one by which a man was known to his family. This was followed by the name of the *gens*, the extended clans to which most élite Romans belonged. As these clans were so extensive, most Romans also had a *cognomen*, a nickname which was often idiosyncratic or unflattering. (Some sound like American gangsters: Pretty boy Claude, Lenny the Limp, Chick-pea Tullius and Curly are not unreasonable, if loose, translations of Claudius Pulcher, Lentulus Crux, Tullius Cicero and Caesar respectively.)

The Romans had the habit, which has infuriated historians for centuries, of preserving family names intact down the generations. Thus the son of, say, Publius Licinius Crassus, would probably be none other than Publius Licinius Crassus. This has led to considerable confusion as to exactly which scion of a great house held which office, as the *Fasti* often give just the name, or sometimes helpful information such as 'Metellus, son of Metellus, grandson of Metellus'. The Romans themselves were not immune from this confusion – history has recorded

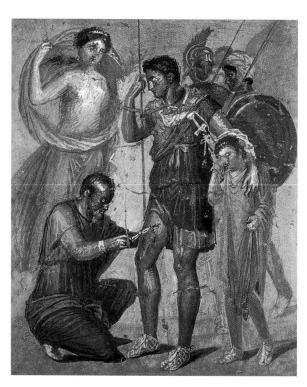

Aeneas having a wound attended to, while comforting his son Ascanius (Iulus). This wallpainting from Pompeii (first century AD) shows the Roman view of their own origins, but how close these legends are to fact is disputed.

The eagle of Rome: just as the Athenians adopted the owl as the symbol of their patroness Athena, so the Romans adopted the eagle as the bird of their principal deity Jupiter. This onyx cameo dates to the late first century BC.

Like all Roman statesmen, Julius Caesar was expected to lead his countrymen not just in the senate but also on the field of battle. Roman politicians who declared war on an enemy were obliged to share in the risks of fighting that war. This statue, possibly of Julius Caesar, is from Otricoli, near Rome.

a debate between Cicero and Metellus Scipio as to which particular Publius Cornelius Scipio is commemorated by a statue in the city.

With women the situation is even worse. Roman daughters took the feminine form of the father's family name. Thus the daughter of Julius Caesar would be Julia, of Tullius Cicero, Tullia, of Cornelius Scipio, Cornelia. Where a father had more than one daughter, they all had the same name, distinguished only by an ordinal addition. The father of Publius Clodius had three daughters, called Clodia, Clodia and Clodia. One of these was an enemy of Cicero, another is believed to have been the lover of the poet Catullus, and another was wronged by an aristocrat called Caelius. Historians have since had to work out which was which.

Builders of empire

It is often forgotten how closely the great families of Rome were linked by blood, friendship and marriage. Livia, wife of Augustus, was a descendant of Livius Drusus. Tiberius Gracchus was killed in a riot incited by his maternal cousin Scipio Nasica. Cicero was distantly related to Marius, who married the aunt of Julius Caesar, who was related to Mark Antony, who was one of the closest relatives of his nemesis, Augustus. Thus it was a small, tightly knit aristocracy which drove Rome to dominate the Mediterranean world. Yet it was not totally exclusive. *Novo homines*, men whose ancestors had not held a consulship, were not uncommon, and the lower ranks of the senate were constantly replenished by rising families.

The legacy of the Republic

What these people achieved is little short of incredible. Rome started almost from nothing and faced powerful enemies who were often better armed. Agriculture was barely above the subsistence level, communication was slow, all forms of technology were primitive. Yet Rome built an empire that stretched from the English Channel to the Red Sea, and ruled it with an executive body the size of an average city council.

This empire was not built on military might alone. Those the Romans conquered became not subjects, but citizens. Citizens had their rights protected, not only by patronage and favour, but by a code of law so solid and sensible that it still underpins the legal systems of many modern states.

The fall of the Republic brought in the Imperial era. The Rome of the Caesars was built on foundations laid in the Republic, and many Republican traditions and offices lingered on. Imperial Rome surpassed the Republic in many ways – yet in the one way that mattered most, the Romans of the Republic could count themselves superior. *They were free men.*

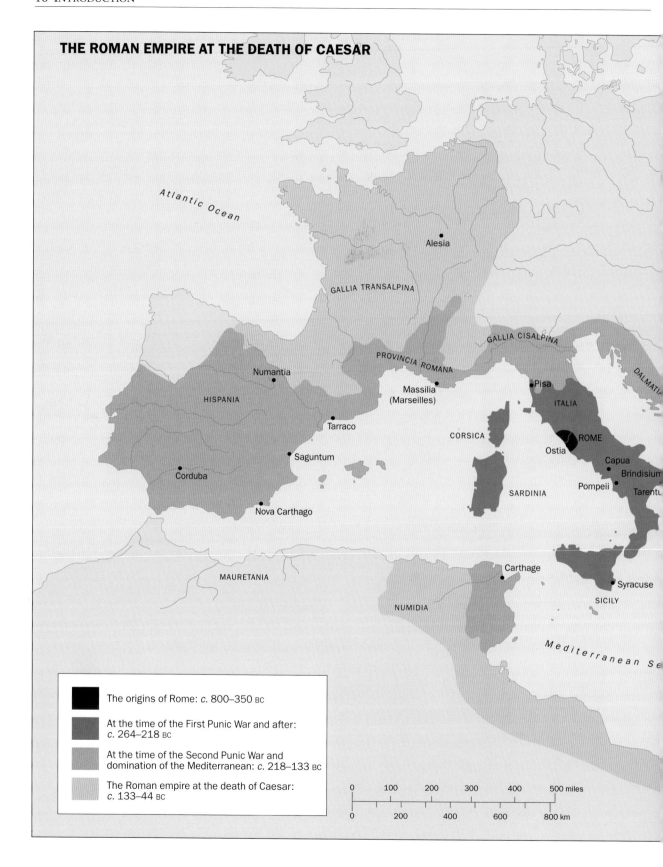

THE ROMAN EMPIRE AT THE DEATH OF CAESAR

Atlantic Ocean

Alesia

GALLIA TRANSALPINA

GALLIA CISALPINA

PROVINCIA ROMANA

DALMATIA

Numantia

Massilia
(Marseilles)

Pisa

HISPANIA

ITALIA

Tarraco

CORSICA

ROME

Saguntum

Ostia

Capua

Corduba

Brindisium

Pompeii

Tarentum

Nova Carthago

SARDINIA

MAURETANIA

Carthage

Syracuse

NUMIDIA

SICILY

Mediterranean Sea

■	The origins of Rome: *c.* 800–350 BC
▨	At the time of the First Punic War and after: *c.* 264–218 BC
▨	At the time of the Second Punic War and domination of the Mediterranean: *c.* 218–133 BC
▨	The Roman empire at the death of Caesar: *c.* 133–44 BC

0   100   200   300   400   500 miles

0   200   400   600   800 km

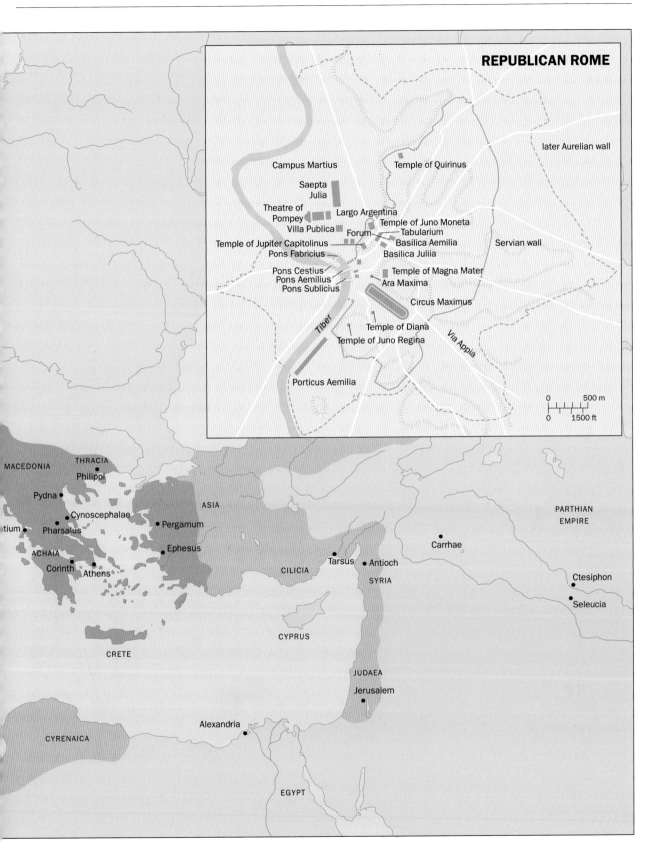

REPUBLICAN ROME

later Aurelian wall

Campus Martius

Temple of Quirinus

Saepta Julia

Theatre of Pompey

Largo Argentina

Villa Publica

Temple of Juno Moneta

Forum

Tabularium

Temple of Jupiter Capitolinus

Basilica Aemilia

Servian wall

Pons Fabricius

Basilica Juliia

Pons Cestius

Temple of Magna Mater

Pons Aemilius

Ara Maxima

Pons Sublicius

Circus Maximus

Tiber

Temple of Diana

Temple of Juno Regina

Via Appia

Porticus Aemilia

0   500 m

0   1500 ft

MACEDONIA

THRACIA

Philippi

Pydna

ASIA

PARTHIAN EMPIRE

Cynoscephalae

Pergamum

tium

Pharsalus

Ephesus

Carrhae

ACHAIA

CILICIA

Tarsus

Ctesiphon

Corinth

Athens

Antioch

SYRIA

Seleucia

CYPRUS

CRETE

JUDAEA

Jerusalem

Alexandria

CYRENAICA

EGYPT

THE PRINCIPAL SOURCES

Unlike the well-documented period of the early Empire, much of the history of the Roman Republic is a murky mixture of myth, legend and propaganda. Rome was more than 300 years old before its first histories were written, and these are now lost. Most of what we know of the Roman Republic comes from histories written in the Imperial period, and these must be considered unreliable at best.

Recently, archaeology and epigraphy (the study of inscriptions) have helped to throw more light on the picture, and what has been found is generally reassuring. When not pursuing their own agendas (for instance the glorification of a particular family, or brushing over a disgraceful event), the Romans have proved rather good at reporting their own history.

Towards the end of the Republic, our sources grow increasingly rich. We have the writings of the protagonists, such as Sallust, Caesar and Cicero. Biographers such as Suetonius and Plutarch are writing of events nearer their time, and the increasing wealth of the Empire created a greater architectural and artistic tradition for archaeology to unearth.

What follows is by no means a comprehensive account of the ancient sources for this book, but all of them are recommended to readers who want to hear from writers who knew ancient Rome at first hand.

POLYBIUS c. 200–c. 118 BC

His work is the earliest history of Rome to have come down to us in anything like complete condition. Polybius was a Greek politician who was brought to Rome as a hostage at the time of the Macedonian wars. He was a contemporary of Cato the Censor (pp. 109–13) who had the decisive word on allowing Polybius to return to Greece. Polybius was a client of the Scipio family, and part of

Polybius was born in Greece and was brought to Rome as a captive; his work is intended to explain to his fellow Greeks what it was about the Roman state that enabled it to conquer the known world.

that family's glorious military reputation is due to his public relations work on their behalf.

CICERO 106–43 BC

Cicero's letters, orations and philosophical works are mainly concerned with the late Republic, but they provide us with a wealth of intimate detail. Cicero was closely involved with the affairs of his day, and was personally acquainted with all the leading figures. He was vain, insecure and boastful, but he is a first-rate reporter, and our knowledge of the crisis of the Republic would be infinitely poorer without him.

LIVY 65 BC–AD 17

Livy was the greatest of all the historians of the Republic. Unfortunately only the earlier part of his monumental work *Ab Urbe Condita* ('from the founding of the city', or *History of Rome*) now survives. In his preface Livy complains that the official records have been lost or corrupted, and that frequently he had to resort to the private, often contradictory records kept by the great families of Rome.

From the birth of Romulus and Remus to the defeat of Hannibal and the conquest of the Mediterranean world, Livy is essential reading for all who are interested in the history of the Republic.

VALERIUS MAXIMUS (*dates unknown*)

Very little is known about this writer, who compiled his handbook in AD 31–37, during the reign of the emperor Tiberius. In nine volumes, the work, entitled *Memorable Doings and Sayings* or properly the *De Viris Illustribus* ('about famous men'), gives us a fascinating insight into how the Romans thought and acted in different situations.

PLUTARCH c. AD 40 – c. 125

Writing later than the others, in about AD 75, Plutarch was more interested in the character than the deeds of his protagonists. Though a Greek, he used Roman sources. Much in his biographies, the *Lives*, is undoubtedly myth or falsehood, yet Plutarch assembled the facts as best he could – and at worst gives us a unique insight into how the Romans saw their own history.

Our knowledge of early Rome is very fragmentary, and a mix of myth, legend and propaganda; without Livy's histories, the situation would be much worse.

OFFICES OF THE ROMAN CONSTITUTION

The constitution of Rome famously balanced the powers of the ruler, the aristocracy and the people. It did this by giving each of the offices of state different functions and powers, and making some checks on others, and by limiting the duration of all elective positions (apart from the censorship) to one year. This system was codified into the *cursus honorum* – the 'course of honours'. The following is the order in which an aspiring Roman politician might hold these honours.

There was considerable overlap between the various offices, and personality was all-important. A powerful censor, such as Cato, could easily cow the consuls, and a tribune such as Gaius Gracchus could almost literally re-design the state.

MILITARY TRIBUNE

This office was a forerunner to the *cursus honorum* itself. Members of the Roman aristocracy had to serve eight years in the army before holding any other office, and the first time we hear of many of the men described in these pages is when they took service with one of the great commanders of the day. Thus Valerius Maximus Corvus was a military tribune to the great Furius Camillus, and Marius to Scipio Aemilianus.

QUAESTOR

The quaestorship was the most junior rank which qualified its holder for membership of the senate. Quaestors were essentially financial officers. They could serve with the treasury (as Cato the Stoic did with great distinction), or with a commander in the field. Since a high proportion of the work of a general involved money – payments to troops and for supplies and equipment, and handling and distributing booty, as well as possibly administering the usual financial affairs of a Roman province at the same time – it was essential that there was a strong bond between quaestor and commander.

TRIBUNE

Properly speaking, this office was outside the regular *cursus* as it was not an office of the senate at all, but of the Roman plebs. Patricians, who originally dominated the senate, could not hold this office, though plebeians who were aristocrats could, and often did. Tribunes were not elected by the whole Roman people, but by the plebeians alone in a special council called the *concilium plebis*. A tribune could veto and propose legislation, and even, if he felt the situation demanded it, arrest other officers of state, including the consuls. He had no power outside the city of Rome, but within the city, a citizen to whom he extended his protection was untouchable. In reality, tribunes knew well that the senate could take vindictive revenge at leisure after their year in office, and most tended to be circumspect. But a tribune from an aristocratic family with popular support could be a truly formidable political force.

AEDILE

These were the officers charged with the care of the city of Rome itself – its public buildings, streets, bridges and aqueducts. Aediles also had the task of staging the *ludi Romani*, Rome's great public games. This was of crucial importance, as the electorate tended to reward well-presented games with election to higher office – this is less illogical than it may seem, since the organization of these spectacles required considerable logistical and management skills. Patricians originally had a type of aedileship reserved for them – the curule aedileship.

PRAETOR

This was one of the oldest offices of the Republic, and it only became obsolete in modern Italy in 1999. A praetor could command a province, lead an army or sit as a judge in a criminal case. Some praetors, such as the *praetor peregrinus*, had special tasks – in this case the care and supervision of foreigners in Rome. After his praetorship, the office holder would probably serve at least another year as a *propraetor*, as commander of an army or governor of a small province. These offices were called *provinciae* which originally meant 'area of responsibility' and only later became a geographical description.

CONSUL (abbreviation cos.)

The number of lesser offices changed with time, but Rome always had two serving consuls. Though the office was originally restricted to the patricians, plebeian aristocrats later succeeded in having the consulship shared between the two orders, so there was often one patrician and one plebeian consul. Consuls were legislators and generals. Originally, they commanded Rome's principal armies, but as time went on they tended to remain in Rome and spend their consular year in civil activities, afterwards commanding abroad as *proconsuls*.

CENSOR

This represented the final office of a political career, and it was usually awarded only to the most distinguished politicians. Censors were not elected every year, but when they were, their responsibilities were broad. They oversaw the allocation of public contracts for everything from the maintenance of sewers to the gathering of taxes from foreign provinces. They also had the responsibility for maintaining the voters' rolls, and counting the number of Roman citizens (hence the modern term 'census'). Censors also maintained the senatorial roll, and could strike off senators whom they felt did not qualify for the honour on either financial or moral grounds.

Romulus
(r. *c.* 753–*c.* 716 BC)

Remus
(*c.* 770–753 BC)

Numa Pompilius
(r. *c.* 715–*c.* 673 BC)

Tullus Hostilius
(r. *c.* 673–*c.* 641 BC)

Ancus Marcius
(r, *c.* 641–*c.* 616 BC)

Tarquin the Elder
(r. *c.* 616–*c.* 579 BC)

Servius Tullius
(r. *c.* 579–*c.* 535 BC)

Tarquin the Proud
(r. *c.* 534–*c.* 495 BC)

Lucius Iunius Brutus
(*c.* 545–509 BC)

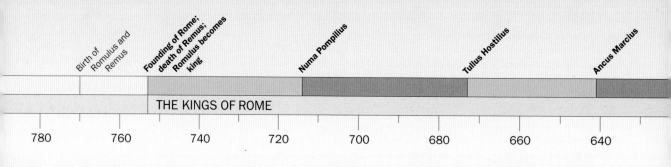

Birth of Romulus and Remus

Founding of Rome; death of Remus; Romulus becomes king

Numa Pompilius

Tullus Hostilius

Ancus Marcius

THE KINGS OF ROME

780   760   740   720   700   680   660   640

Romulus

Ancus Marcius

Servius Tullius

Lucius Iunius Brutus

THE AGE OF KINGS
753–509 BC

IN THE EIGHTH CENTURY BC, civilization was centred on the eastern Mediterranean kingdoms of Persia and Egypt. The Phoenician states of the Levant had given birth to the city-state of Carthage on the North African shore, while further north and west of Phoenicia were the dynamic and inventive states of Greece, and their colonies in Sicily and southern Italy. In the rest of Italy, the Etruscans were the leading civilization, but counted for little in comparison to the glittering cultures of the east.

Italy was a backwater in which the occupation by a group of landless men of a deserted hill in Latium went completely unremarked. Yet so was Rome born. It is an indication of the size and power of the fledgling state that under Tarquin the Proud, Rome's last king, the entire city-state measured less than 30 miles (48 km) from east to west, and 15 miles (24 km) from north to south.

It was hardly the sort of place that people wrote histories about, and as the Romans were largely illiterate they wrote no histories of their own. Thus the story of early Rome is a mixture of oral tradition, confused folk memories, myth and outright lies. Yet it cannot be altogether ignored. Traditional tales often preserve a kernel of truth, and the little archaeological evidence we have from this period tends to support the Roman version of events. But even the more implausible of these foundation legends are deeply significant, as they tell us how later generations of Romans saw their origins.

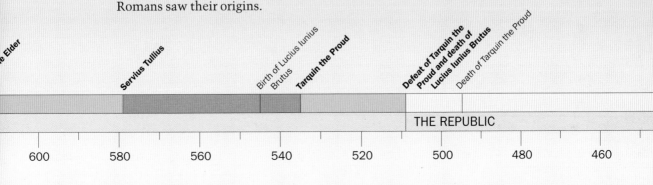

the Elder

Servius Tullius

Birth of Lucius Iunius Brutus

Tarquin the Proud

Defeat of Tarquin the Proud and death of Lucius Iunius Brutus

Death of Tarquin the Proud

THE REPUBLIC

600   580   560   540   520   500   480   460

Romulus
(r. *c*. 753–*c*. 716 BC)

Remus
(*c*. 770–*c*. 753 BC)

A denarius of the mid-first century BC with the head of Romulus, the legendary founder of Rome. His mother Rhea Silvia was a Vestal Virgin of the town of Alba Longa, where, according to tradition, Aeneas had settled after fleeing from Troy. In this way the Romans traced their ancestry to Aeneas and the Trojans.

ROMULUS

Born	*spolia opima,*
c. 770 BC	became the god
Famous ancestors	Quirinus
Aeneas, Venus	*Wife*
Mother	Hersilia
Rhea Silvia	*Children*
Father	Son: Aellius
Mars (or uncle,	(Abillus); step-
Amulius)	daughter (?), Prima
Positions held	*Death*
King of Rome,	Taken up to heaven,
c. 753–716 BC	or assassinated
Achievements	*c*. 716 BC
Founded Rome, won	

REMUS

Born	*Death*
c. 770 BC	Killed by Romulus
Famous ancestors	*c*. 753 BC
Aeneas, Venus	

But Romulus has, first of all, one great plea, that his performances proceeded from very small beginnings; for both the brothers, being thought servants and the sons of swine-herds before becoming free men themselves, gave liberty to almost all the Latins, obtaining at once all the most honourable titles. Romulus, indeed, obtained himself lands, a country, a kingdom, wives, children and relations. And, in so doing, he killed or destroyed nobody, but benefited those that wanted houses and homes and were willing to be of a society and become citizens.

As to Remus, it is doubtful by whose hand he fell; it is generally imputed to others. His mother he clearly retrieved from death, and placed his grandfather, who was brought under base and dishonourable vassalage, on the ancient throne of Aeneas. He did his grandfather many good offices, but never did him harm even inadvertently.

Plutarch, *Life of Romulus*

THE STORY OF THE FOUNDERS OF ROME begins in the nearby city of Alba Longa, where according to tradition Aeneas had long before settled after his flight from Troy. A Vestal Virgin of the city, Rhea Silvia, became pregnant, and the punishment for such sacrilege was to be buried alive. But

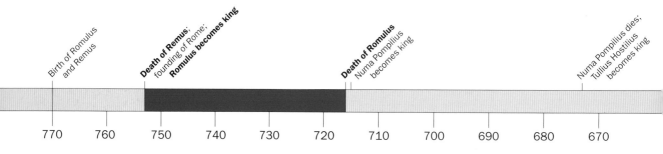

Birth of Romulus and Remus

Death of Remus; founding of Rome; **Romulus becomes king**

Death of Romulus Numa Pompilius becomes king

Numa Pompilius dies; Tullius Hostilius becomes king

770   760   750   740   730   720   710   700   690   680   670

The Capitoline wolf, a bronze statue of the mid-fifth century BC of the she-wolf which rescued Romulus and Remus after they had been cast into the river Tiber. The figurines of the twins were added in the fifteenth century AD by Antonio Pollaiuolo.

Rhea Silvia, mother of Romulus and Remus, depicted in a statue by Jacopo della Quercia (1371–c. 1438). A Vestal Virgin, Rhea Silvia claimed divine parentage for the twins, saying that their father was the god Mars.

Rhea Silvia claimed in her defence that the father of the unborn children was the god Mars. Seduction by a god was almost the only defence it was possible to offer.

Rhea's death would have suited Amulius, the king of Alba Longa. He had usurped the throne from his brother Numitor, and Rhea Silvia was Numitor's daughter; Amulius had made her a Vestal Virgin to prevent her from having children of royal blood. The people would not allow her to be killed, however. (The less superstitious even suspected that Amulius had raped Rhea, and this gained her a lot of sympathy.) But as soon as Rhea had given birth to twins, the children were taken by the king's men and flung into the flooded River Tiber.

Fortunately, the children were washed up on the river bank, still in their cradle. A passing she-wolf, who had lost her cubs in the flood, came to investigate and she suckled the twins until they were found and adopted by the shepherd Faustulus. The children grew up among shepherds and other riff-raff, unaware of their noble, possibly divine, ancestry. Following a skirmish involving stolen cattle, Remus was brought before Numitor. While questioning the young man, Numitor realized that he might be his grandson. Seeing the chance to regain his throne and re-establish his line, Numitor set about initiating a rebellion against Amulius. Romulus, meanwhile, had gathered a mass of men from the country and was marching on the city to rescue his brother.

Surprised by these internal and external attacks, Amulius had no time to organize a defence. He was killed, and Numitor resumed his throne. But the twins, having tasted power, decided to found a city of their own.

The birth of Rome

Such is the story given to us by the historian Plutarch. He took his account from the historian Fabius Pictor, who was writing in about 235

'THE SACRED SPRING'

Whenever the population of any city increased to such a degree that the produce of the land was no longer enough for them all, or whenever the earth was damaged by changes of the weather so it would fail for fruit and bear less abundantly than usual, or for any occurrence such as years, either excessively good or bad which made it necessary for them to lessen their numbers, they would dedicate to some god or the other all the men born within a certain year, and giving them weapons, would send them out of the country.... Those who departed, feeling that they had no share in the land of their fathers but must get another land for themselves, looked upon any place that received them in friendship, or which they conquered in war, as their country thereafter.

Dionysius of Halicarnassus,
Roman Antiquities 1.17

The Lapis Niger or 'black stone' is one of the oldest Roman inscriptions, dating from the sixth century BC. So antique is it, that some Romans believed it marked the grave of Romulus. The text runs boustrophedon – left to right, then right to left, 'as an ox ploughs a field'.

BC; Fabius Pictor apparently got the details from a yet earlier historian, one Diocles of Peparethus, of whom we know nothing else. Obviously, much of the story is myth. It is suspiciously similar to legends about Cyrus, the Persian king. Also, archaeology has found settlements on the Roman hills dating to long before Rome was supposedly founded, on the very precise date of 21 April, 753 BC. (The Romans themselves measured dates *ab urbe condita* – from the founding of the city in year 1 A.U.C.)

However, Roman tradition stresses that the Roman hills had a religious function even before the city was founded, so the archaeological evidence is not incompatible with the legend. And the story of the she-wolf exchanges romance for credibility when it is remembered that *lupa* can also mean 'prostitute'. Further, the Latin people (who, despite their alleged Trojan descent, included the people of Alba Longa) had a tradition known as 'the sacred spring'. By this, if a settlement grew too large, the first-born – both animal and human – were dedicated to a god and sent out to found a new city. The name 'sacred spring' is thought to mark the season when the dedication took place. Perhaps then, historical tradition may be surprisingly accurate. After all, the legendary home of the Romans – Troy – was not believed to have actually existed until archaeologists dug it up in the nineteenth century.

The founding of Rome was bloody – the twins quarrelled over which hill to build on, and Remus was killed when he contemptuously leapt over Romulus' rising walls. Once more, there is some agreement with the archaeological evidence: the Palatine – Romulus' choice – was the first hill to be settled. Having created his new city, Romulus then needed people to fill it. He opened a temple within the walls, and decreed that anyone who entered it was safe from arrest or seizure. From the protection given by this temple, we get the word 'asylum' (from the Greek '*a*' – 'without', plus '*syle*' – 'right of seizure'). As a refuge, the temple attracted more men than women, and the inhabitants of the new city found themselves short of wives.

The rape of the Sabine women

Romulus asked their nearest neighbours, the Sabines, for women; the Sabines insultingly refused. But they did accept when Romulus invited them (and their families) to a festival. Halfway through the festival, the Romans descended on the unmarried women and seized as many as they could. This was the famous 'rape of the Sabine women', though in this context 'rape' means 'seize', from *rapere*, rather than 'rape' in the modern sense. To symbolize the fact that their first brides did not come willingly, later Roman men carried their brides into their new homes – a tradition continued in Western countries today.

Romulus himself married a Sabine woman called Hersilia, who helped to negotiate a peace between her new husband's people and their outraged fathers-in-law. Eventually, the Sabines were reconciled and some even agreed to move to Rome, with Tatius, the Sabine king, ruling jointly with Romulus.

THE PALATINE

In the continuing debate about exactly when Rome was founded, there is general agreement on one point – that the first settlement in the city was probably on the Palatine hill. Archaeology has shown that there were settlements in this area even before the traditional date of the founding of Rome in 753 BC. Indeed, some of the earliest burials in the area date back to the tenth century BC.

The Palatine seems to have had a religious function from the earliest times. Numa, the second king of Rome (pp. 22–25), was said to have communed with a nymph at one of the springs on the hill's south side. In historical times, the temples of Victory and the Magna Mater (the Great Mother) stood there. Later, Augustus added a temple to Apollo.

Excavating the earliest occupation of Rome is an enormously challenging task as the Palatine has been settled continuously for the best part of 3,000 years, and many of the oldest remains lie under sites of prime historical importance. However, two cisterns for the collection of rainwater have been found which almost certainly date back to the archaic period, and holes cut into the rock were probably post-holes for Iron Age huts, such as the famous hut of Romulus which stood on the Palatine for much of the Republic.

Legend has it that Remus, the twin brother of Romulus, was killed when he mockingly leapt over the fortifications which Romulus was constructing on the Palatine, and traces of fortifications dating to about that period have indeed been found.

From Romulus onwards, the Palatine was one of the best addresses in Rome. Those known to have lived there included Lutatius Catulus, Aemilius Scaurus (whose house has been found and excavated), Livius Drusus, Cicero, Crassus and Mark Antony. As the emperor Augustus, Octavian made his home on the hill, which gradually became the seat of imperial government – and was the origin of the word 'palace'.

(Above) A ceramic Etruscan hut-urn of the seventh century BC, from Vulci. The earliest huts of the Romans probably looked something like this.

(Below) Aerial view of the Palatine hill. According to legend, it was on this hill that Romulus founded his new city of Rome, and archaeology has shown that there was human occupation here at the time of the traditional founding of Rome in 753 BC, and even earlier.

Hersilia intervenes to bring peace between her husband, Romulus, and her father, a Sabine, in a painting by Jacques-Louis David (1799), *The Sabine Women.*

As one who was subject to divine favour, Romulus was a very religious man and was appalled at the sacrilegious murder by friends of Tatius of ambassadors from a nearby town. So when Tatius was himself killed in revenge, Romulus did not react, saying one murder had caused the other.

Becoming a god

Romulus was certainly no mean soldier when he did fight. By each of his campaigns, Rome grew larger and more powerful. In Romulus' last campaign, legend states that he killed 7,000 of the enemy single-handed – a claim that even Roman historians rejected with scorn.

Romulus became increasingly arrogant and arbitrary, and was widely disliked. One day he was sacrificing by the river when there was a sudden storm. The people fled for cover, but the senators, the leading men of the state, remained standing around Romulus. After the storm, Romulus had vanished. The superstitious believed that he had been taken directly to heaven. The cynical thought that he was taken by the senators – having killed him, each one removed a bit of his body hidden under their cloaks. It was a suitably ambiguous end for Romulus. He met his end aged 54; a foundling, a fratricide and the father of the greatest empire in antiquity.

THE VESTAL VIRGINS

Originally there were four virgins who served the goddess Vesta. They were chosen by the king in accordance with the regulations which Numa established. Because of the numerous sacred duties which they perform, their number was increased to six, and six it has remained up to our own time. The virgins live in the sanctuary of the goddess, and no one can be prevented from entering there in the day if he so wishes, but it is forbidden for any man to stay there at night.

The priestesses remain pure and unmarried for 30 years, offering sacrifices, and performing other religious rituals in accordance with the law. They learn these rituals in the first ten years, and for the second ten years they perform them, and during the remaining ten years they must teach them to their successors. When the 30 years have been completed, nothing prohibits those who want to from putting aside their headbands and other insignia of their service and getting married. But only a few have done that, and their lives for their remaining years were neither enviable nor very happy. Therefore, taking what has happened to those unhappy few as a warning, the rest of the virgins remain in service to the goddess until their deaths, at which time another virgin is appointed by the priests to take the place of the one who has died.

They receive many splendid honours from the city, and therefore they do not want children or marriage. And anyway, there are heavy penalties for misbehaviour. Misdeeds are investigated and punished by priests according to the law. They whip those who have committed some lesser offence, but those who have lost their virginity are sentenced to a shameful and pitiful death. While they are still alive they are carried in a funeral procession. Their friends and relatives join the procession and mourn for them as though for someone deceased. They are taken as far as the Colline gate, and interred (alive) in an underground cell which has been built within the walls of the gate. They are dressed in funeral clothes but they receive no monument or funeral offering or any of the other rites which are customary at funerals.

There are said to be many clues which indicate that a priestess who is performing a holy ritual is no longer a virgin, but the principal clue is that the fire goes out, something which the Romans fear more than all catastrophes, since they believe that whatever was the cause of the fire going out, it warns of the destruction of the city. They reintroduce the fire with many rituals of atonement.

Dionysius of Halicarnassus,
Roman Antiquities 2.67

(Above) A fragment of a relief of the first century AD, showing the six Vestal Virgins seated at a table. The Vestal Virgins originated in Alba Longa but the order was brought to Rome by Numa Pompilius.

(Below) The remains of the Temple of Vesta in the forum, Rome.

Numa Pompilius

(r. *c.* 715–*c.* 673 BC)

An antique bust depicting the king Numa Pompilius as a priest, as shown by the shawl draped over his head. Numa established a regular sequence of religious rituals and reorganized the calendar to ensure that they were performed on time.

NUMA POMPILIUS	
Born	*Wife*
c. 750 BC	Tatia
Famous ancestors	*Lover*
None	Nymph Egeria
Mother	*Father-in-law*
Unknown	Tatius, the Sabine
Father	king
Pomponius	*Children*
Positions held	Sons: Pompo,
King of Rome,	Pinus, Calpus,
c. 715–673 BC	Mamercus;
Achievements	daughter: Pomponia
Established Roman	*Death*
religion	Old age c. 673 BC

It is true he waged no wars, but he was no less beneficial to the state than was Romulus, for he established Rome's laws and customs. The Romans, because of the frequency of their battles, had by then become regarded by their neighbours as bandits and semi-civilized barbarians … but Numa established in Rome numerous religious rituals and temples.

Eutropius, *Compendium of Roman History* 1.3

THE ROMAN PEOPLE, SUSPECTING THE SENATE of being involved in Romulus' disappearance, were deeply uneasy about the senators' future intentions. Then one Julius Proculus claimed that Romulus had appeared to him and announced that he was now the god Quirinus and that the Romans should find a new king. The superstitious were pacified. The more cynical noted that Julius promptly applied to fill the vacant position. (This Julius marks the first appearance in the chronicles of Rome's famous Julian line.)

The Sabines in Rome pointed out that since the death of King Tatius, they had been ruled by Romulus, so it was now time for a Sabine king. The Romans accepted this, on condition that they could choose which Sabine became king. In fact, the choice was obvious – Numa Pompilius, the son-in-law of old King Tatius.

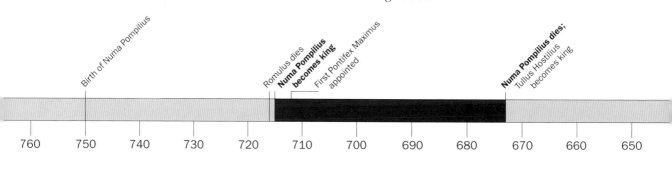

Birth of Numa Pompilius

Romulus dies
Numa Pompilius becomes king

First Pontifex Maximus appointed

Numa Pompilius dies; Tullius Hostilius becomes king

760   750   740   730   720   710   700   690   680   670   660   650

A silver denarius showing the Sabine king Titus Tatius, minted in 88 BC. Numa Pompilius was his son-in-law, and so was chosen to become king of Rome after the death of Romulus.

A reluctant king

Numa lived outside Rome, in a village in the woods, so a delegation went to fetch him. To their astonishment the new king refused to go – he preferred a life of contemplation and philosophy, and the little of Rome that he had seen was not conducive to either. The delegates had to work hard to persuade their prospective king to take the job. As sometimes happens, even those who were lukewarm about the idea were convinced by their own arguments. So when Numa finally agreed to be king, there was a national outpouring of joy and relief. As the Romans became accustomed to happy outcomes to such crises, they began to realize that this was due not to good fortune, but to Numa's shrewd political instincts.

Numa saw his mission as bringing civilization to Rome, where the people were still strongly divided along tribal lines. The Romans distrusted the Sabines, and both were united against the runaway slaves and fugitives who had joined the citizen body. Since Rome was founded by the dispossessed, many Romans were destitute and desperate, and even the better-off tended to covet their neighbour's lands. Finally, Rome was not really yet a city, but a gathering place for those with nowhere else to go. Each group retained the customs and traditions of their home city.

Divine assistance

When his wife died, Numa reputedly indulged in a highly elevated romance as the lover of the nymph Egeria, whom he would meet on the south side of the Palatine, by the spring which bore her name for centuries thereafter. Egeria allegedly passed Numa advice from the gods about how to govern the new state. But Numa never attributed any of his actions to divine counsel, so people were unsure whether any particular initiative was Numa's, or came from Jupiter himself. Numa did once divulge a spell given to him by Jupiter for controlling thunder and

A painting (1624–27) by Nicolas Poussin of a landscape with Numa Pompilius and the nymph Egeria. Legend has it that through this source Numa received advice from the gods on how best to govern Rome.

EARLY ROMAN RELIGION

We do not discover a great deal about the religion of the early Romans in the literary tradition because later Romans were reluctant to believe that their beliefs had undergone a shift with the Hellenization of their culture. Many of their writings reinterpret ancient religious practice in a more contemporary manner, and there are a number of stories which seem to have been created to explain certain aspects of Roman religious behaviour.

The early Romans were both religious and superstitious. Their religion was pantheistic, meaning that they had many gods; animistic, in that they believed that some minor gods or goddesses were embodied in particular objects or places; and patriarchal, in that their principal gods and priests were men.

For the early Romans, the gods were not distant creatures, only remotely interested in the affairs of humans. Their gods lived with them and around them, watching their moves, demanding their dues, and guiding, warning and punishing. It is

The engraved back of a bronze mirror of the fifth/fourth century BC depicting a soothsayer examining a liver for omens.

an example of the Roman intimacy with their gods that there was no punishment for blasphemy. It was believed that the gods were well aware of insults, and could avenge themselves as they saw fit.

Much of early Roman religion came from the Latin peoples among whom they lived. Another major influence on the Romans was their neighbours the Etruscans, whom the Romans believed to be experts in divining and interpreting the will of the gods. They adopted from them the practices of taking the auspices – interpreting the will of the gods from certain natural phenomena – and priests called *haruspices*, who read the will of heaven through analysing the liver of a sacrificed animal.

The Romans were constantly on the watch for signs and portents. Thus Romulus was confirmed in his choice of where to build the city through the flight of birds – their number, type and direction were all favourable – and when work started, a severed head was found, still bleeding, which signified great things for the new city.

The religious rites of Rome became embedded in the system very early in the life of the Republic, and persisted long after the significance of the acts was lost. Indeed, for the Romans of the late Republic even the meaning of some of the words they chanted at their religious rituals was unknown, but they dutifully performed the ceremonies.

Chief of the ancient orders of priests was the *Flamen Dialis*. His life was surrounded by apparently meaningless rituals. He was not permitted to look on anything which was dead or bound, which meant that even his clothing could not have knots in it – a major disadvantage in the days before buttons became common. He wore a pointed hat, and had special eating and sleeping arrangements. His life was so circumscribed by ritual that, when the last *Flamen Dialis* died in 87 BC, no one could be found to take up the burden of office until it was reinstituted by the emperor Augustus.

The Largo Argentina in Rome, where the foundations of four Republican temples have been uncovered. Archaeology helps to fill in the patchy picture of early Roman religion known from the literary sources.

lightning. The conjuration required an onion, human hair and live pilchards. Various historians have speculated on the significance of these ingredients without considering that the Romans might enjoy a good joke as much as anyone else.

Religious organization

To unite his people, Numa divided them up into smaller groups. He established the boundaries of Rome (something Romulus never dared to do in case his neighbours saw exactly how much land he had grabbed) and established communities of peasant farmers on the land. These were called *pagi*, a word which has mutated in modern English to 'parish'. Those remaining in the city proper were divided into professional guilds. Guild rivalries soon overcame tribal rivalries, and ethnic differences in Rome were gradually forgotten.

In Numa's reorganization of the Roman calendar he added the month of January, named after Janus, god of beginnings, depicted on the coin above. He also built a temple of Janus, the doors of which stood open during times of war, and were closed in peacetime. In the whole of Numa's reign, which lasted 43 years, the doors remained closed, as shown on the coin below.

Numa established a routine of religious rituals and various religious orders. He brought the order of the Vestal Virgins from Alba Longa to Rome, and established a priesthood called the *Fetiales*. Their function was to curb the warlike instincts of the Romans by mediating in disputes, especially with Rome's neighbours. The Romans would send the Fetiales to anyone they felt had wronged them, and the priests would explain the nature of the offence and ask for compensation. If the reply was unsatisfactory, the *Fetiales* would declare war. Only they could do this, though matters thereafter rested with the commander of the army.

So that the religious ceremonies were performed on time, Numa also reorganized the calendar. Up to that point there had been ten months in the year. Extra days were assigned more or less at random, the only requirement being that they added up to 360. Numa added January (from Janus, god of beginnings) and February (from *febrare*, to clean and purify). In consequence the later months were no longer consistent with their names. Even now, September, October, November and December mean, but do not equate with, the months seven, eight, nine and ten.

The legacy of Numa

Numa had a daughter and four sons and these went on to establish great Roman dynasties. Calpus founded the Calpurnian line and Mamercus – nicknamed Aemilius, which means a smooth and fluent speaker – was claimed as ancestor by the great Aemilian family. Indeed, even hundreds of years later one family name was Rex, or king – a reference to their illustrious forebear.

Numa's deeds passed into legend, and truth is now inseparable from fiction. A thousand years later the Romans still showed visitors 'Numa's house' on the Quirinal hill. Roman tradition used Numa's reign for the origin of hundreds of the obscure rituals and superstitions which filled Roman life. Perhaps the best testament to Numa is the Temple of Janus, which he founded. The temple's doors were open in wartime and closed in peacetime. During Numa's 43-year reign the doors were never open. In all the subsequent history of the Republic they were closed, briefly, once.

Tullus Hostilius
(r. *c.* 673–*c.* 641 BC)

Ancus Marcius
(r. *c.* 641–*c.* 616 BC)

A coin with the head of Ancus Marcius of *c.* 56 BC. The fourth king of Rome, Ancus Marcius was the grandson of Numa Pompilius and therefore a Sabine. Legend records that he was the first king to build an aqueduct to bring water into the city.

TULLUS HOSTILIUS	
Born c. 710 BC *Famous ancestors* Hostius Hostilius (grandfather) *Mother* Unknown *Father* Hostilius (?) *Positions held* King of Rome, c. 673–641 BC	*Achievements* Conquered Alba Longa; built senate house *Wife* Unknown, possibly Hersilia *Death* Killed by lightning bolt from Jupiter c. 641 BC

TULLUS HOSTILIUS

Neither the tiredness of the army nor the great reluctance of his soldiers deterred the bellicosity of the king. He even professed to believe that it was healthier for the young men to be under arms rather than becoming soft and lazy at home. When he fell ill himself, the long sickness changed his mind ... his proud spirit was broken, so that he seemed to have become another man.

Livy, *History of Rome* 1.31

THE NEXT KING OF ROME was a very different proposition. Numa had been a Sabine, so this time a Latin king was chosen. Though unrelated to the previous two kings, Tullus Hostilius had as near to an illustrious pedigree as the new state possessed. His grandfather, also called Hostilius, had been a distinguished warrior who had fallen in the war which followed the abduction of the Sabine women. Numa had practised the arts of peace while his new state took shape, but Hostilius was a man of war. This was fortunate, since he had serious conflicts to deal with.

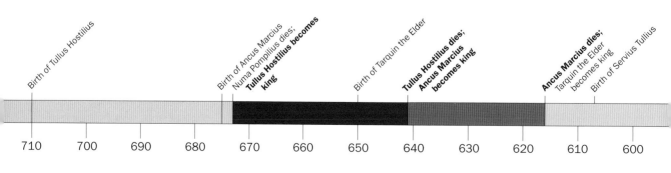

Birth of Tullus Hostilius

Birth of Ancus Marcius
Numa Pompilius dies;
Tullus Hostilius becomes king

Birth of Tarquin the Elder

Tullus Hostilius dies; Ancus Marcius becomes king

Ancus Marcius dies;
Tarquin the Elder becomes king
Birth of Servius Tullius

| 710 | 700 | 690 | 680 | 670 | 660 | 650 | 640 | 630 | 620 | 610 | 600 |

The Oath of the Horatii, a painting of 1784 by Jacques-Louis David. To settle the dispute between them, the Romans and the city of Alba Longa each chose a group of three brothers to fight on their behalf. The Romans – the Horatians – were victorious.

This ruined tomb at the site of Alba Longa is known as the Monument of the Horatii. Alba Longa had ancient historical ties with Rome – it was from here that Romulus set out to found his new city – but there were also hostilities between the two states.

Conflict with Alba Longa

It was not long before Hostilius came up against the area's other major power – Alba Longa. The two city-states had adjoining borders, and a long tradition of cattle-raiding across them. Usually, after each phase of raiding, envoys were dispatched and matters were negotiated. Now, however, the Roman envoys were more truculent, and Hostilius would not speak to those sent to him. War was declared.

Alba Longa clearly had close historical ties with Rome. To avoid what was almost a civil war, Hostilius and the Alban king, Mettius, found an alternative. Each side chose a group of three brothers to represent them (some legends say they were triplets), and the nation of the losing brothers would be subordinate to the victors'. The two kings swore a solemn oath to this effect, administered by the high priest Valerius. (This is the first mention of the Valerian family who appear repeatedly in Roman history for the next 600 years.) The Roman brothers were Horatians, a family which became a distinguished ally, and occasionally rival, of the Valerian clan.

The Horatians won, and Alba duly swore allegiance to Rome. King Mettius was deeply disgruntled by the defeat, but he did not want to break his oath – and neither did he want to face the Romans in battle. So instead he provoked Rome's other neighbours, the Fidenates, into war.

EARLY ENEMIES OF ROME

The **Sabines** were close neighbours of the Romans. Their lands began only a few miles to the northeast of Rome, and extended to the central Apennines. From the very earliest days they interacted with the Romans, as is shown by the legend of the rape of the Sabines (p. 18).

Tatius, who ruled jointly with Romulus, was the first of three Sabine kings of Rome, another being the legendary law-giver Numa. There was a constant unforced migration of Sabines to Rome, the most famous immigrant being Attus Clausus, patriarch of Rome's formidable Claudian line (p. 51).

Other members of the Sabine tribe remained opposed to Rome, and fought a long series of campaigns against the expanding city. The last Sabine strongholds were only conquered in 290 BC, and by 260 the Sabines were full Roman citizens.

The **Aequians** were a tribe from central Italy who moved north

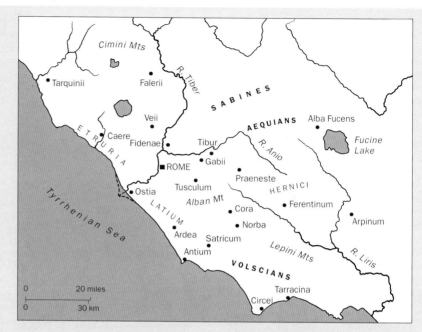

(Above) Coin depicting the abduction of the Sabine women.

(Above right) Map of early Latium.

towards Tibur and Praeneste in about 500 BC. They were a mountain people, and were never very numerous. But what they lacked in numbers, they made up for in ferocity. They often made common cause with another invading people, the Volscians, against Rome. During the fifth century BC they entrenched themselves in the Alban hills, and it took a series of Roman campaigns, ending in 431 BC, to push them out.

Rome pacified the area held by the Aequians with a string of colonies, including Alba Fucens, and the surviving members of the tribe were absorbed into the growing Roman state by 250 BC.

The **Volscians** were another Italic tribe from central Italy. They seem to have overrun south Latium – the traditional home of the Latins – some time soon after the founding of Rome.

(There is a distinct change in the archaeological pattern at this time, suggesting the arrival of a different people.) The only record of their language is a bronze tablet called the Tabula Veliterna which seems to confirm their Italic origins.

The Romans fought a number of campaigns against them, at first defensive in nature (as shown in the legend of Coriolanus (pp. 53–55), when they were pushed back to Rome itself); but later they took the initiative and established a colony at Satricum, the former Volscian principal city.

The Volscians were broken in a major battle in 338 BC, and their lands were occupied in 304 BC. After this, they seem to have become completely Romanized. Certainly there is nothing particularly Volscian about Marius and Cicero; yet both were from Arpinum which was a major Volscian centre.

Alban treachery

As the armies closed in for battle, the Alban contingent withdrew to the hills on the Roman flank, exposing the Romans to attack from that direction. Hostilius immediately understood that the Albans intended to rejoin the battle when they saw which side was winning. It was too late for the Romans to redeploy, so Hostilius shouted to his men that the Albans were withdrawing to strike the enemy in a flanking manoeuvre

The Roman soldiers believed him, and so too did the enemy, who were close enough to overhear. They started to fall back in some disorder. The Romans fell on them and broke them, winning the battle. At this point Mettius rejoined the fight on the Roman side. Hostilius pretended to believe in the Alban king's loyalty, but overnight the Albans found themselves surrounded by the rest of the Roman army. Hostilius denounced Mettius, and had him torn apart between two chariots driven off at speed in opposite directions.

The Albans were now combined with the people of Rome. The amalgamation was on equal terms, with the Alban nobility joining the Roman senate and the people becoming full Roman citizens. The city of Alba Longa was destroyed, except for its temples. In Rome, the Albans settled mainly on the Caelian hill, and to encourage their integration Hostilius built a new palace and lived among them. With this sudden increase in the city's population, the meeting house of the senate was too small, so Hostilius constructed another. His building, known as the Curia Hostilia, stood in the corner of the Forum Romanorum, and this remained the site of the Roman senate house thereafter. Today, the parliament of modern Italy stands just a few hundred metres away.

Changed by the plague

Hostilius took his people to war again, this time against those Sabines who had not come to Rome under King Tatius. Some Roman merchants had been abducted, and Hostilius settled the matter by defeating the Sabines in battle. Not long after this signs of divine disfavour began to appear. A shower of stones from heaven fell on the Aelian hill, and a great voice from the sky denounced the transplanted people of Alba Longa for abandoning the ways of their ancestors.

Despite such dire warnings Hostilius continued to campaign, but was stricken with the plague. Soon the whole Roman people were debilitated by this terrible disease, and Hostilius was unable to wage war even if he so desired. But this was no longer the case. Having previously scorned religion as unsuitable for a warrior, he threw himself into the service of the gods, hoping to avert their anger from Rome. In studying the books of Numa, Hostilius discovered a rite of Jupiter; he performed it so maladroitly that the palace was immediately struck by lightning. The thunderbolt killed Rome's warrior king in the 36th year of his reign.

Hostilius – a myth?

Most historians consider the story of Hostilius to be nothing more than a Roman foundation legend. They admit that the Roman senate house was probably constructed in the late seventh century, but claim that it is more likely that it gave the legendary king his name, rather than the other way around.

Certainly, his reign seems rather long. Indeed, all the kings of Rome supposedly enjoyed reigns suspiciously longer than average, even for modern monarchies. If Hostilius did exist, the major event of his reign, the destruction and absorption of Alba Longa, is probably fiction. But the Romans revered their ancestors, and this made it necessary for their history to relate the relatively peaceful absorption of the city of their founders, no matter what had happened in reality.

ANCUS MARCIUS

ANCUS MARCIUS	
Born	*Achievements*
c. 675 BC	Founded Ostia
Famous ancestors	*Wife*
Numa Pompilius	Unknown
(grandfather)	*Children*
Mother	Two sons, names
Pompilia	unknown
Father	*Death*
Marcius (?)	Natural causes
Positions held	c. 616 BC
King of Rome,	
c. 641–616 BC	

Ancus Marcius, grandson of Numa on his mother's side, received the kingship. He fought the Latins, and added the Aventine and Janiculan hills to the city. He founded a city on the coast [Ostia] sixteen miles from Rome at the mouth of the Tiber. He died a natural death in the twenty-fourth year of his rule.

Eutropius, *Compendium of Roman History* 1.5

WITH ANCUS MARCIUS, a grandson of Numa, the Romans once more rotated the kingship from a Roman to a Sabine. But by now the old distinction between Romans and the Sabines of Rome had almost disappeared. Rome was increasingly influenced by the Etruscan civilization to the north, now at its peak of power and culture.

War with the Old Latins

After decades under the warlike Tullus Hostilius, the Roman people longed for a respite from campaigning. They hoped that the new monarch would emulate his illustrious grandfather, and bring a second era of peace and prosperity. However, Rome's neighbours had also decided that Rome's new king was no soldier and they had wrongs suffered at Roman hands to avenge. The first to open their account were peoples who had been on the plain of Latium even before Aeneas arrived in Italy. This ancient people were called the Old Latins or *prisci Latini*. They shared their language and much of their culture with the Romans, but they wanted to check the hybrid vigour of the fledgling state. Now they began raiding over the border.

Marcius' envoys were sent back empty-handed, so he responded by calling out his troops, understanding that this was a test. Had he done nothing, all his neighbours would have attacked *en masse*. In the event, the Latins found that they had bitten off more than they could chew. The Romans attacked one of their leading city-states and conquered it. As seems to have been Roman policy at this time, they demolished the city and absorbed its defeated citizens into Rome.

Improving the city

Another of Rome's seven hills was settled, this time the Aventine. The Janiculum hill was also fortified and brought within the walls. The Janiculum is to the north of the city, so this was probably done with the cities of Etruria in mind, as these were Rome's nearest neighbours in that direction.

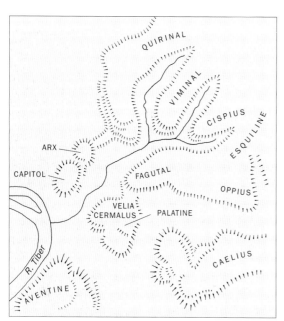

The major hills of Rome: these were gradually occupied and brought within the walls as the city grew.

DECLARING WAR

To ensure that they had the support of the gods, the Romans did not go to war lightly. First they sent envoys to the other side, explaining their precise grievance, and what reparations they required.

War was not declared by king or senate, but by special priests called *Fetiales*. When they had established that the war was just, they went to the enemy's lands, and ceremonially threw a spear over the border. The prosecution of the war was then handed over to the Roman commander.

This ceremony continued until the end of the Republic, when Rome's borders were far distant. The problem of travelling to the frontier was solved by dedicating a piece of land in the Roman forum to the enemy, and throwing the spear into that.

By his actions, Marcius gave the city another strong point, at the same time denying it to the enemy.

Popular legend records that Marcius was the first king to bring water to Rome by aqueduct. One of the earliest known Roman aqueducts, the later Aqua Marcia of 144 BC, was probably named after this supposed achievement. An old aristocratic family, the Marcian clan, claimed to be his descendants, and their involvement with the later aqueduct reflects this.

The growth of Rome's territory and population allowed Marcius to expand the city. Tradition says he gave Rome its first salt-water port, at Ostia, about 16 miles (26 km) from the city proper. Ostia Antica (not the modern port of Ostia, which is further away because of changes in the Italian coastline) has been largely undisturbed over the centuries and much of the Roman city, including temples and theatre, can still be seen today. Archaeologists have not precisely dated its foundation, so it is unknown whether Ancus Marcius was in fact its founder.

A good king

Like Numa, Ancus Marcius was religious, and he further refined the Roman religious system. More particularly, he developed an elaborate system for declaring war. He reigned 25 or 26 years, depending on which account is followed, and later historians judged him a good king. (The annalist Ennius called him exactly that – *bonus*.) He was calm and temperate, equally skilled in the arts of peace and war. Whether or not he himself was legendary, the main events of his time are certainly true – Rome rose to prominence among the Latins and the Etruscans were a growing power.

Etruscan ascendancy is demonstrated clearly by the fact that the next king on the throne of Romulus was neither Roman nor Sabine, but from an Etruscan town from which he took his name – Tarquin.

A reconstruction showing some of the later aqueducts that brought water to Rome. The Aqua Claudia/Anio Novus cuts through a loop of the older and lower Aqua Marcia, which dates back to 144 BC and was probably named after Ancus Marcius, traditionally the first king to build an aqueduct to bring water to the city.

Tarquin the Elder
(r. *c.* 616–*c.* 579 BC)

Servius Tullius
(r. *c.* 579–*c.* 535 BC)

Tarquin the Proud
(r. *c.* 534–*c.* 509 BC)

Servius Tullius, from the François Tomb, Vulci: although he is supposed to have instituted many important political reforms, in particular the census, the fact that he was not elected and may have had servile origins meant that his position was never secure.

TARQUIN THE ELDER	
Born c. 650 BC	*Achievements* Built Circus
Original name Lucumo	Maximus *Wife*
Famous ancestors None	Tanaquil *Children*
Mother Unknown	Sons: Arruns, Lucius and adopted
Father Demaretus of Corinth	Servius Tullius; daughter: Tarquinia
Positions held King of Rome, c. 616–579 BC	*Death* Assassinated c. 579 BC

TARQUIN THE ELDER

He showed himself an excellent man, sharing his money with those in need and offering himself readily to any one who required his assistance.... But upon the death of Marcius he behaved without honour to the latter's two sons and got the kingdom for himself.

Cassius Dio, *History* 2.9

WHILE ANCUS MARCIUS WAS STILL KING, a remarkable prodigy occurred. An eagle swooped from the heavens, and plucked off the cap of a man entering Rome for the first time. Hardly had the surprised man realized what had happened when the eagle returned, and put the cap back on his head again. This was clearly a portent of some substance, and fortunately the man's wife could interpret it. Her husband would reach the head of affairs by his own efforts, but once he was there, his position would be confirmed by divine favour.

The truth behind the legend

The wife, named Tanaquil, was an Etruscan, a people famous for their understanding of augury and prophecy. She was from one of the leading

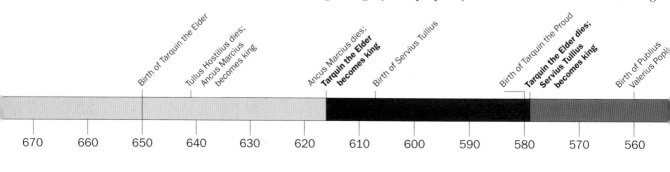

Birth of Tarquin the Elder

Tullius Hostilius dies;
Ancus Marcius
becomes king

Ancus Marcius dies;
**Tarquin the Elder
becomes king**

Birth of Servius Tullius

Birth of Tarquin the Proud

**Tarquin the Elder dies;
Servius Tullius
becomes king**

Birth of Publius
Valerius Popl

| 670 | 660 | 650 | 640 | 630 | 620 | 610 | 600 | 590 | 580 | 570 | 560 |

A view of the site of Gravisca. It served the Etruscan city of Tarquinii as a port and archaeology has revealed that the Greeks built a sanctuary there. Tarquin the Elder was supposedly of Greek origin, but married a woman from Tarquinii before moving to Rome and becoming its fifth king.

families in the ancient city of Tarquinii (modern Tarquinia) but had married an outsider, Lucumo the Corinthian. As a result, they found themselves shunned by the inner circle of the local élite. Undaunted, the pair decided to try their luck in the rising city of Rome. Thus, according to legend, Rome's fifth king arrived in the city.

Inevitably, time has distorted the story and it is difficult to know how much, like the story of the eagle, is pure invention. The Etruscan city of Tarquinii was real. It lay 56 miles (91 km) north of Rome, 6 miles (10 km) from the sea. The mention of Corinth is significant, because Etruria had trading links with that city. Archaeology shows that there were indeed Greeks in Tarquinii, who built a sanctuary in Gravisca, which served the city as a port, much as Ostia served Rome. It is also apparent from inscriptions that élites often moved about the cities of Etruria, so a couple translocating to Rome was not greatly unusual. There is an unlikely tradition that Lucumo's father, Demaretus, was driven from Corinth by the tyrant Cypselus. But since the grandson (or great-grandson) of Demaretus was allegedly the last king of Rome, the dates cannot be made to fit. Increasing Etruscan influence on Rome is clear from archaeology – so much so that some historians consider Rome in the late sixth century BC almost as much an Etruscan as a Latin city.

The rise to power

Lucumo and Tanaquil settled in Rome, where Lucumo took the name Lucius Tarquin. The name 'Priscus' ('the Elder'), was attached at some point to distinguish this Tarquin from his son of the same name. Tarquin

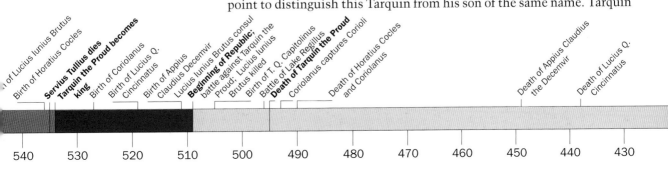

540   530   520   510   500   490   480   470   460   450   440   430

THE ETRUSCANS

The Romans had much in common with the other people of the plain of Latium, with whom they traded, fought and intermarried. To a large extent, in fact, Roman culture was one particular strand of Latin culture, though it did possess a number of unique features. Nevertheless, Rome could be described as a Latin city until it came under the sway of the Tarquins. The Tarquins were Etruscans, and their influence was to have far-reaching consequences on the new city-state.

A mysterious people

The Etruscans were not Latins, and there has been considerable controversy over exactly who this enigmatic people were. The debate began in antiquity, with a report by the Greek historian Herodotus that the Etruscan people were from Lydia in Asia Minor. He quoted an account that rather than submit to the expanding Persian empire, the Lydians under Tyrrhenus put all their possessions on to ships and fled to the west. From Tyrrhenus comes the alternative name for his people, the Tyrrheni, or Tuscans, and the modern name of the country to which they fled – Tuscany.

The language of the Etruscans is as mysterious as much else about this people. It resembles no other European language, and its nearest relative is found among the pre-Greek peoples of Lemnos in the eastern Mediterranean. Studies of Etruscan have made great strides since the discovery of a book written in Etruscan on linen, the so-called *Liber Linteus*, containing some 1,500 words. The linen was later used to wrap an Egyptian mummy (now in Zagreb), and the text was found among the bindings.

Modern historians have come to the conclusion that another ancient historian, Dionysius of Halicarnassus, was right when he said that the Etruscans were autochthonous – that is, native peoples of the region. On the whole, the Etruscans seem from the evidence to have been a Villanovan Iron Age people; though strongly influenced by Greek culture.

A dynamic civilization

Etruscan civilization was not a mere imitation of the Greek, however, but a dynamic culture in its own right. The Etruscans were great builders, and it is to them that the Romans owed their talent for aqueducts, not to mention one of early Rome's saving graces as a city – its magnificent network of sewers.

The Apollo of Veii, one of the terracotta figures that once adorned the roof of the Portonaccio temple at the city of Veii, built towards the end of the sixth century BC. The use of such figures on temple roofs was a characteristic Etruscan feature.

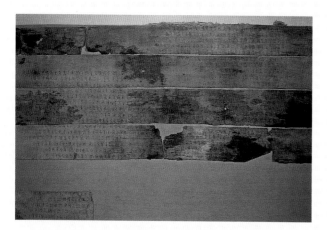

(Above) The Liber Linteus *of Zagreb. An Etruscan text written on linen, it was later re-used as the wrappings for an Egyptian mummy. While the Etruscan script can be read, the Etruscan language is still a mystery.*

Etruscan nobles were buried in single chamber tombs, and from paintings and vases in these tombs we get a picture of a people who enjoyed hunting, banqueting, athletic events and chariot races.

At their peak, the Etruscans were the dominant people of Italy, and their influence was felt right across the peninsula. However, the Etruscans were never a unified nation, despite their shared language and religion. They were capable of forming short-lived leagues and alliances, but their city-states were as prone to warring with each other as were the Greek states of the same period.

In the end, this lack of unity proved fatal. The Etruscans found themselves trapped between two expanding and aggressive peoples, the Romans in the south and the Gauls in the north. Of the two, it was the Romans who were to prove the greater threat, as their expansion assimilated the Etruscan culture and eventually destroyed it almost entirely. By the end of the Republic, the Etruscans were already becoming a remote and mysterious people. The last speaker of the language that we know of was the emperor Claudius, and even in his time the study of Etruscan culture was regarded as a task for historians.

(Right) The so-called Sarcophagus of the Married Couple, from the Banditaccia necropolis, Cerveteri, late sixth century BC. They would originally have held separate objects in their hands, such as fruit, eggs or vessels.

(Below) A lively painted scene of servants and musicians from the Tomb of the Leopards, Tarquinia, first half of the fifth century BC.

A life-size Italic statue of a warrior, sixth century BC, from Capestrano, in a style typical of the art of central Italy of this period. Tarquin had to campaign against several of the indigenous populations of the peninsula, and was usually successful.

A coin showing the Temple of Jupiter Capitolinus. The construction of this temple may have begun under Tarquin the Elder and been completed by Tarquin the Proud, though it is possible that later tradition was simply uncertain which Tarquin to attribute it to.

the Elder became famous for his shrewdness and generosity, and soon came to the attention of King Ancus Marcius. The two men became great friends immediately; in fact they became so close that Ancus made Tarquin the guardian of his two sons.

When Ancus died, Tarquin suggested to the king's sons that they go hunting for a few days while he took care of things. With the sons gone, Tarquin immediately proposed himself for election as king of Rome. He pointed out that the Roman kingship was not hereditary, and that the Romans had previously selected a king born outside the city. Tarquin had a reputation for generosity and fair dealing, and by the time the sons returned from hunting, they found him in an unassailable position.

However, Tarquin had still to deal with Rome's external enemies, who usually became more aggressive at a change of monarch. He fought the Latins, and if the historian Dionysius of Halicarnassus is correct, he campaigned very successfully against the Etruscans themselves. But his most severe military test came from the Sabines. Unlike their relatives, these Sabines had not joined Rome, and now were preparing to destroy it. Their attack caught the Romans unprepared. There were several bloody battles before the Romans prevailed, partly because Tarquin had doubled the size of the cavalry.

Tarquin's reign

Tarquin originally intended to add another three squadrons of cavalry to those established by Romulus. This ran into religious objections, though we cannot now be certain what they were. Like the good diplomat that he undoubtedly was, Tarquin gave way, and left the number of squadrons at three. But he doubled the size of the squadrons and divided each into two parts, thus getting the six squadrons he wanted.

He also increased the size of the senate – to the great nobles who made up its number, he added 100 of the petty nobility. This made the senate more representative of the Roman people and, not incidentally, gave Tarquin a solid nucleus of supporters.

Tarquin may have begun building the Temple of Jupiter Capitolinus on the Capitoline hill, which tradition says was completed by his son (or grandson). More probably, tradition was uncertain which Tarquin was responsible for the building, and so the work was simply divided between them. The two Tarquins are also credited with identical activities in draining marshes and building the city walls.

Tarquin the Elder's success aroused the envy of the sons of Ancus. They perhaps originally hoped to succeed Tarquin in their turn, but as his reign entered its 38th year, time was running out. Furthermore, Tarquin now had two young sons of his own, Lucius and Arruns, so if the Romans decided to adopt dynastic principles, the sons of Tarquin would have more claim than the sons of Ancus. The final straw was a protégé of Tanaquil, Tarquin's wife – a man called Servius Tullius. Tullius was of obscure origin, but Tanaquil claimed that he was divinely favoured; and she had a good track record in these matters.

Assassination

Accordingly, the sons of Ancus hired a pair of assassins who approached the king posing as litigants in a dispute. As the first presented his case, the second crept up behind Tarquin. Taking an axe from his robes, the assassin struck Tarquin in the back of the head, killing him instantly.

Bizarrely, the reign of Tarquin the Elder was not quite over. Realizing that someone had killed Tarquin in order to exploit the turmoil resulting from his death, Tanaquil claimed that he had only been wounded. While he was recovering, the regent would be Servius Tullius, who was to be obeyed as if he were the king himself. Thus Tanaquil span out the transition of power, and by the time the Romans found out that Tarquin was dead, they were already accustomed to Servius Tullius as their leader.

SERVIUS TULLIUS	
Born	*Achievements*
c. 607 BC	Created Roman
Famous ancestors	legislative assembly
None	*Wife*
Mother	Tarquinia
Ocrisia	*Children*
Father	Daughters: Tullia
Unknown	Prima; Tullia
Positions held	Secunda
King of Rome,	*Death*
c. 579–535 BC	Assassinated
	c. 535 BC

SERVIUS TULLIUS

The inevitable course of fate overwhelms the wisest of human intentions. The jealousy that Servius had aroused by ascending the throne pervaded his household, and hatred and disloyalty were rife even among his own family.

Livy, *History of Rome* 1.42

BEFORE SERVIUS TULLIUS, Roman kings were elected by the people. Servius Tullius had no such mandate, and this affected his rule from the start. Tullius became king through the machinations of the woman who had also been behind his predecessor – Tanaquil, the wife of Tarquin the Elder.

Fated to be king

The origin of Servius Tullius is uncertain. One story assumes his name to be a corruption of *servus*, 'slave', and according to this, Servius was the son of a household slave. One night his parents were astounded to see his

A battle of Etruscan heroes: a scene from the life of Mastarna (Servius Tullius), from the François Tomb, Vulci, c. 300 BC. Vulci was one of the twelve great cities of Etruria.

head covered with flame while the boy slept on, unharmed. Tanaquil immediately realized that he was marked by destiny.

The child was groomed as Tarquin's successor and he married the daughter of Tarquin and Tanaquil. Later Romans could not countenance a free people voluntarily becoming subjects of a former slave, so the historian Livy suggests that the boy was a captive prince of Corniculum, a city recently conquered by the Romans. This neatly allows Servius to be of noble blood, but at the same time not free. In fact, Servius was never to escape the imputation of slavery, and ultimately it proved his downfall.

However dubious his status, Servius got off to a good start. Having failed to gain the throne by assassination, the sons of Ancus retired into exile. This left the sons of Tarquin, Lucius and Arruns. Hoping to win over the young men, Servius married them to his daughters. By coincidence or design, the more ambitious daughter was paired with the less ambitious of the two new sons-in-law.

Nevertheless, what saved Servius Tullius' position was not his dynastic arrangements but an external threat. The Etruscans of the city of Veii noted the turmoil in Rome, and since their treaty with the Romans had expired, they declared war. Servius turned out to be a very competent commander. His brisk and successful campaign was so convincing that he did not need to take the field again for the remainder of his 44-year reign.

The basis of the constitution

Roman tradition has used the rest of Servius' reign as a convenient catch-all for those elements of the Republic which pre-dated its foundation. Thus the division of the people into tribes for tax purposes (hence the relationship between 'tribe' and 'tribute') is attributed to Servius, as is the introduction of coinage to Rome – the better to facilitate payment.

The 'tribes' were not ethnic groups but were organized by residence. Though others were created later, the first tribes may genuinely date back to the time of Servius. The tradition that he built the defensive structure still today called the 'Servian' wall is false, since archaeology dates it to the fourth century BC; and coinage was only introduced another century later, so Servius was not responsible for that either.

Archaeology gives some support to the claim that Servius was the builder of the Temple of Diana, which was constructed in the sixth century BC. This temple emulated the first Temple of Artemis/Diana at Ephesus, later one of the Seven Wonders of the ancient world. The significant feature of the Roman temple was that it was built by the combined peoples of Latium, and the choice of Rome as its site shows explicitly that Rome was the recognized Latin capital. Servius' greatest creation, however, was the census. The people were divided into classes, the first five of which were ranked according to their property. The more property a man had, the more expensive the armour and weapons he brought into battle, and therefore the higher his class rating.

Remains of the Servian wall in Rome. Though attributed to Servius Tullius, this wall has recently been dated to the 370s BC. It was made from tufa, and was probably about 25 ft (8 m) high originally. Markings on the wall suggest that Greek workmen were employed on its construction.

Perhaps Servius Tullius' greatest constitutional innovation was the creation of the census, which divided the Roman people into classes according to their property. This scene from the so-called Altar of Domitius Ahenobarbus (first century BC) is thought to show an official recording the census on tablets.

There were 80 centuries (40 senior and 40 junior) of first-class citizens, and 20 centuries (senior and junior) each of second-, third-, fourth- and fifth-class citizens. The remainder of the people, too poor to own weapons, were excused military duties and were lumped into a single century. They were called the *Capite Censi*, the 'head count' as they were counted by their heads rather than by their possessions.

For the equites, or knights – the richest people in Rome – there were 18 centuries. These brought not only personal armour into battle but they came on horseback. The knights and the first class voted first, followed by the other classes in order. A majority of centuries carried the day, so if the knights and the first class were in agreement they could outvote the rest of the population.

This re-organization of the Roman people created a timocratic state (office based on a property qualification), in which the wealthy and powerful took responsibility for financial and military affairs in return for a privileged political position. Whether or not this system was created by Servius, it certainly lasted for the life of the Roman Republic.

The first census numbered 80,000 Roman citizens capable of bearing arms. To accommodate them Servius brought the Quirinal and Viminal, and later the Esquiline hills into the city; he made the Esquiline fashionable by moving there himself.

A palace revolution

Amidst all this success, trouble was brewing. Servius' daughter Tullia wanted to emulate Tanaquil as a king-maker, and her brother-in-law Lucius Tarquin was equally ambitious. The pair disposed of their respective spouses, passing rapidly from widower and widow to husband and wife. Tarquin began to repeat the old calumnies about Servius' slave origins, and also undermined his position with Rome's leading men by claiming that Servius had favoured the lower classes in his land distributions.

Finally, in a bid for power, Tarquin dressed in royal regalia and went to the senate house. The senators were summoned to attend King Tarquin. Servius, now an old man, hurried to the senate where Tarquin accused him of being a slave and a usurper, and physically threw him out. The senate was in chaos, but Tarquin prevailed by sheer force of character. Servius was returning to the palace when assassins sent after him killed him on the street which was called the Street of Crime thereafter.

Legend alleges that Tarquin's impious act was compounded by Tullia. She had been to the senate to salute her husband as king and returned by the same street as her father had. Without noticing, she drove over his corpse, splattering her carriage with his blood. It was an inauspicious, but appropriate, start to Tarquin's reign.

Tullia driving over her father, by Jean Fouquet (c. 1420–81). Respect for parents, especially fathers, was ingrained in Roman tradition. To call a Roman a parricide was one of the worst insults imaginable, so Tullia's conduct reveals her as utterly depraved in Roman eyes.

TARQUIN THE PROUD

Born	Achievements
c. 580 BC	Extended Roman
Famous ancestors	territory, built
Tarquin the Elder	Temple of Jupiter
(grandfather?)	Capitolinus
Mother	*Wife*
Unknown	Tullia Secunda
Father	*Children*
Arruns or Lucius (or	Sons: Sextus,
Tarquin the Elder?)	Arruns, Titus;
Positions held	daughter: Tarquinia
King of Rome,	*Death*
c. 534–509 BC	Old age c. 495 BC

TARQUIN THE PROUD

He always kept himself protected by armed men, for he had taken the throne by force – neither people nor senate had consented to his usurpation. He accepted that there was no hope of his being accepted into the hearts of his subjects, so he ruled by fear.

Livy, *History of Rome* 1.49

TARQUIN HAD NO REAL CLAIM TO THE THRONE – kingship in Rome was not hereditary, so being the son of a previous king did not give him any legitimacy. (In any case, modern research suggests that he was more probably a grandson of the older Tarquin.) Having neither the support of the senate, nor the mandate of popular election, Tarquin decided that his reign would have to be based on awe and fear.

First, he gave himself the right to try capital cases without the assistance of the senate, which allowed him to remove dangerous enemies – and to expropriate their money and lands. The Romans came to believe that he intended to reduce the senate to an enfeebled rump incapable of serious opposition. Interestingly, this receives some support from recent discoveries. At the temple site in St Omobono in Lombardy, various terracottas show that at this time, kingship in central Italy was becoming more flamboyant and was modelled on the tyrannies then flourishing in the city-states of Greece. And it was to Greece that Tarquin sent his own sons to consult the oracle at Delphi on at least one occasion.

Success in foreign policy

While the Romans suffered under Tarquin's conduct of internal affairs, in foreign relations he was undeniably a good leader. By diplomacy and threats he rearranged the Latin League to make Rome its official head. The other Latin states now supported the Roman military machine, with each Latin unit having a counterpart Roman unit, the two parts being under Roman command. Again, this 'Treaty of Ferentina' is probably not entirely fiction. Rome had come into contact with the powerful Phoenician city-state of Carthage, and a treaty made at about this time between the two states confirms that the Latin League was organized more or less as tradition has it. As the treaty is reported by the Greek historian Polybius, who had every opportunity to see it personally, there is little reason to doubt this.

Tarquin put his new system to the test in a campaign against the warlike neighbouring tribe of the Volscians. The immediate capture of one of their towns netted him a large sum of silver. Another town, Gabii, resisted. Unable to storm the place, Tarquin used guile. His son Arruns pretended to be estranged from his father and went over to Gabii, where he was given a military command against the Romans. The soldiers of Arruns (thanks to co-operation from the Roman troops they were supposedly fighting) were immensely successful and soon Arruns was the military leader of the Gabians.

The Cloaca Maxima – the arch in the river wall visible in the centre – was some 2,000 ft (600 m) long, and was designed to drain the forum and run off from the surrounding hills. Attributed to Tarquin, it is certainly of sixth-century Etruscan construction, though later amended and improved by Agrippa in the time of Augustus.

This ivory plaque from Palestrina, dating from the third century BC, gives a good idea of the equipment of a soldier of that era. Though much of his equipment is Hellenistic, the soldier appears to be holding a Roman-type oval shield.

At this point he asked his father what to do next. Tarquin did not trust the messenger, and simply walked through the field where they had met, swinging his stick at the tallest poppies. The messenger went back to report this, and said that Arruns' question had not been answered. But Arruns understood well enough, and disposed of the town's leading men through treason trials, assassination and exile. Consequently Gabii fell to the Romans without a fight.

Building in Rome

Tarquin had also been busy in Rome. He used the booty from his conquests to build (or complete) a great temple to Jupiter Capitolinus. This temple, to Jupiter Optimus Maximus, 'best and greatest', was to be the focal point of Roman religion for almost a thousand years, until the empire became Christian. The poor of Rome, the *Capite Censi*, were excused military duty, but Tarquin believed that an idle proletariat was a restless one, so they were set to work on a major building programme. This included not just the new temple, but also improvements to the roads and city defences, and the construction of the Cloaca Maxima. This great Roman sewer was one of the least conspicuous but most important works of civil engineering in the city's history.

With the plebs chafing under such oppression, and the aristocrats alienated by constant purges, the city was ripe for revolution. Tarquin was away on campaign when it happened. The spark was provided not by the tyrant, but by one of his sons, Sextus.

The rape of Lucretia

Sextus was obsessed with a beautiful young woman named Lucretia, who was married to one of his friends, Lucius Tarquinius Collatinus. Unable to seduce the honourable Lucretia, Sextus took a direct approach. He threatened to kill Lucretia and one of her slaves, and swear that he had taken the pair in adultery, unless she surrendered herself to him. Faced with no choice between dishonour or death, since Sextus was offering either the one or both, Lucretia submitted to the lesser evil. As soon as she could, however, she revealed the truth to her father and her horrified husband and then committed suicide.

This rape of an innocent girl was the final straw for the people of Rome and they rose in rebellion, led by Lucius Iunius Brutus. When Tarquin left his army to try to impose order on Rome, the rebel leaders brought the soldiers over as well. Tarquin was forced into exile.

But Tarquin did not give up without a fight and he began to rally his powerful friends to his cause. First, he turned to the Etruscan cities. A league of these, including Veii and Tarquinii, met the Romans in battle in around 509 BC, when both Brutus and Tarquin's son Arruns were killed. The Etruscans, united under Lars Porsenna, king of Clusium, then forced the Romans back to their city walls, though entry to the city itself was famously denied them by Horatius' defence of the bridge (p. 52) in 506 BC. Frustrated in their attempt to capture Rome, the Etruscan alliance lost its cohesion and dissolved. The Romans preferred to believe it was the heroism of their people, including Mucius Scaevola and the family of Valerius, which had forced Porsenna to withdraw.

Still Tarquin did not give up. He turned to his son-in-law, Octavius Mamilius, the leader of the Latin League he had so recently reorganized. The Latins finally took up his cause only after many years during which relations with Rome had deteriorated. The two sides met at Lake Regillus in 496 (or 497) BC; the battle was evenly balanced and ferocious. Tarquin himself was wounded, and many leaders on both sides were killed. These included Octavius Mamilius, Valerius and Herminius, the companion of Horatius on the bridge. Rome won the day, however, and Tarquin, now an old man, retired to spend his few remaining days as an embittered exile in Tusculum. Thus ended the rule of kings in Rome. It had lasted for 244 years, and had seen Rome rise from a quasi-bandit encampment to stand among the foremost cities of Italy.

The Rape of Lucretia (c. 1570), by Titian. The beautiful Lucretia was the virtuous wife of Lucius Tarquinius Collatinus. Sextus, the son of Tarquin the Proud, raped her and she committed suicide as a result. Led by Brutus, the outraged Roman populace rebelled against the Tarquins. They drove the tyrant out in 509 BC and the Republic was instituted as a result.

Lucius Iunius Brutus

(*c.* 545–*c.* 509 BC)

An archaic bust believed to depict Lucius Iunius Brutus. Although it is unlikely to have been taken from life, this statue well represents the qualities of high principle and severity which Brutus stood for.

LUCIUS IUNIUS BRUTUS	
Born c. 545 BC *Famous ancestors* Tarquin the Elder *Mother* Tarquinia *Father* Marcus *Positions held* Tribunus Celerum, c. 515 BC; Consul 509 BC	*Achievements* Overthrew monarchy, established Republic *Wife* Unknown (Vitellian family) *Children* Sons: Titus, Tiberius *Death* In battle c. 509 BC

That ancient Brutus was a severe and inflexible character, like steel tempered too hard, for his character had never been softened by contemplation and education, and he let himself be so carried away by his rage and hatred of tyrants that he executed his own sons for conspiring with them.

Plutarch, *Life of Marcus Brutus* 1.1

THE FEW FACTS WE KNOW about the kings of Rome have been painstakingly sifted from myth and checked against archaeological remains. But for those who claim that the 'real' history of Rome begins with the Republic, Lucius Iunius Brutus is a disappointment. Confusion and ambiguity surround him no less than they do the line of kings he brought to an end.

A perilous childhood

The story as we have it is this: when Tarquin the Proud seized power, a certain Marcus was among the richest men in Rome. He married the sister of the tyrant and died not long thereafter. Tarquin's various building projects needed money and the fact that Marcus had left his fortune to his two young sons – Tarquin's nephews – was not allowed to stand in the way. The tyrant soon found an excuse to have the older son murdered

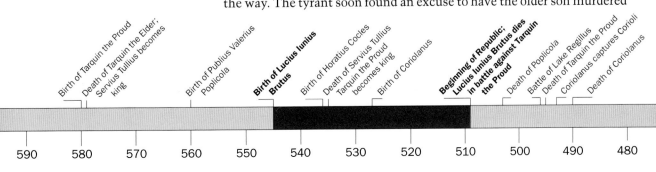

Birth of Tarquin the Proud

Death of Tarquin the Elder; Servius Tullius becomes king

Birth of Publius Valerius Poplicola

Birth of Lucius Iunius Brutus

Birth of Horatius Cocles

Death of Servius Tullius Tarquin the Proud becomes king

Birth of Coriolanus

Beginning of Republic; Lucius Iunius Brutus dies in battle against Tarquin the Proud

Death of Poplicola

Battle of Lake Regillus

Death of Tarquin the Proud

Coriolanus captures Corioli

Death of Coriolanus

590   580   570   560   550   540   530   520   510   500   490   480

Delphi in Greece was the premier oracle of the Mediterranean world. The priestess of Apollo spoke the truth as it was revealed to her in a trance, and her cryptic pronouncements were sought not just by the Greeks (the Spartans sought the opinion of the oracle before the Peloponnesian War against Athens), but by also Croesus of Lydia, and Tarquin, the last king of Rome.

and he then seized the estate. The younger brother was unable to object, being apparently simple-minded. His *cognomen* (nickname) was 'Brutus', which has the same root as the word 'brute', in the sense of lacking the higher faculties of a civilized creature.

This unfortunate young man was raised with the king's sons, and was the butt of their jokes. When the king sent his two older sons, Titus and Arruns, with a question to the oracle at Delphi in Greece, Brutus was taken along to relieve the monotony of the journey. At the oracle, they asked their question: 'What was the significance of a snake that had appeared in the pillars supporting the palace?' Then one of the princes put a question of his own. 'Which of us will rule in Rome after my father?'

The oracle's reply to the second question was: 'Whoever is the first to kiss his mother will have supreme authority in Rome.' The two brothers agreed to draw lots, and thought nothing of it when on the way home Brutus fell on the narrow and slippery path. However, Brutus was more intelligent than the others, and was feigning stupidity to save his life. He had realized the true intent of the oracle, and in falling had kissed the earth, Gaia, mother of all things.

The founding of the Republic

Back in Rome, Brutus was made Tribunus Celerum, which meant that in military terms he was the tyrant's second-in-command. Either his feigned stupidity was more transparent than legend suggests, or the tyrant was unwilling to give this powerful position to anyone he considered more competent. If the latter, Tarquin made a bad miscalculation. Brutus raised the Roman aristocracy to revolt after Lucretia's rape and personally brought the army over to the cause of the new Republic. Henceforth the Romans were to elect their leaders by an assembly of the whole army, the *Comitia Centuriata*. As a protection against further tyranny, the person elected would rule for only one year, and with a colleague. These two rulers would be metaphorically yoked together for their year in office like oxen at the plough – as co-ploughers, or *consules*. Brutus was one of the first consuls; the other was Lucius Tarquinius Collatinus, the husband of Lucretia, whose rape had sparked the revolution.

Brutus restored the numbers of the senate which had fallen sharply under the despotism of Tarquin. To 'fathers' of the senate, Brutus added 'conscripts' from the leading non-aristocrats. According to legend, this divided the senate into patricians and plebeians, though others maintain that plebeians only entered the senate later.

Conspiracies

As Tarquin was rallying his allies, the Romans began to have reservations about Lucius Tarquinius. Though a leader of the liberation, he was also a Tarquin and so not to be trusted. Finally, Brutus brought matters to a head. In an open assembly he told his fellow consul of the people's doubts. For the sake of Rome, he urged Tarquinius to quit his office and leave the city. Tarquinius protested his innocence, but when even his own father-in-law joined those against him, Tarquinius agreed to go into exile.

Brutus too was closely related to the Tarquins, and this was brought home in a very unpleasant fashion. Tarquin had sent envoys to discuss the return of his personal property and these envoys took the chance to spread sedition where they could. They found an audience in the family of the Vitellians, among whom was a daughter who had married Brutus and borne him two sons. The sons were on the verge of adulthood, and they joined the conspiracy.

The plotters were betrayed, and Brutus had to choose between his family and his principles. He chose the latter, and his sons were executed with the other conspirators, while he, their father, looked on in his official capacity. He blamed the Tarquins for leading his sons astray, and thereafter he hated the Tarquins with as much vehemence as they hated him. So when Tarquin's Etruscan allies marched on Rome in 509 BC, Arruns, son of Tarquin, and Brutus sought each other out on the battlefield. They rode at each other with no thought for personal safety, and each managed to kill the other. Brutus, founder of the Republic, did not see out its first year.

Flaws in the story

The story has its weak points. Tarquin allegedly reigned for 25 years, beginning when Brutus was an under-age youth. Yet at the end of the 25 years Brutus has sons who are themselves almost adults. Also, being of royal blood, Brutus was an aristocrat, a patrician. Yet the *gens Iunia*, the family supposedly descended from Brutus, are plebeian. Furthermore, how did this descent come about? The record states categorically that Brutus' sons were executed and he himself died soon after. The Roman grammarian Festus pointed out that in Archaic Latin *Brutus* meant 'heavy'. Brutus' name might be more comparable with Severus (another Roman name) as a description of character, and the story of feigned idiocy pure invention.

Brutus was given a father's farewell by the women of Rome, with a year of mourning. His role in the move from kingdom to Republic was recognized by later generations. They placed his statue on the Capitoline hill, and for the life of the Republic Brutus stood among them, his sword unsheathed in his hand.

The Lictors Bringing Brutus the Bodies of his Sons. In this painting of 1789, Jacques-Louis David associates the new republicans of revolutionary France with the stern self-sacrifice and high principles of the founder of the Roman Republic.

Publius Valerius Poplicola
(*c.* 560–503 BC)

Horatius Cocles
(*c.* 536–*c.* 490 BC)

Coriolanus
(*c.* 527–*c.* 490 BC?)

Titus Quinctius Capitolinus Barbatus
(*c.* 505–*c.* 430 BC)

Lucius Quinctius Cincinnatus
(*c.* 519–*c.* 438 BC)

Appius Claudius the Decemvir
(*c.* 510–*c.* 449 BC)

Marcus Furius Camillus
(*c.* 447–*c.* 365 BC)

Valerius Maximus Corvus
(*c.* 386–*c.* 285 BC)

Appius Claudius Caecus
(*c.* 350–*c.* 271 BC)

Lucius Cornelius Scipio Scapula
(*c.* 337–*c.* 270 BC)

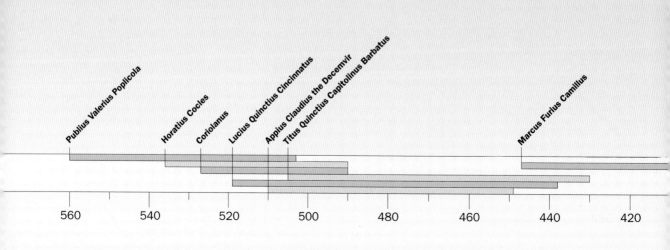

Coriolanus

Horatius Cocles

Lucius Quinctius
Cincinnatus

FOUNDERS OF THE REPUBLIC
509–264 BC

THE INFANT REPUBLIC OF ROME had been born into dangerous times. Even without the threat from the Tarquins and their allies, central Italy was a perilous place. Rome was threatened by wild mountain tribes and the mounting threat of the Volscian peoples, while at the same time the state was racked from within by violent class conflict between the common people and the land-holding aristocracy.

Somehow the institutions of the Roman state withstood usurpation, tyranny and secession, and despite internal conflicts, Rome continued to conquer and absorb its external enemies. Then, just after Rome's triumph over its neighbour and rival, Veii, the Gauls swept down from northern Italy, shattering the power of Etruria, and capturing and looting Rome itself.

Not for the last time, the Romans demonstrated doggedness in adversity. They shook off this crushing defeat, retook Rome and forced the Gauls on to the defensive. All that saved the Gauls from total defeat was that Rome had to repulse an invasion by Pyrrhus, the most warlike of the generals who succeeded Alexander the Great, and then fight a sustained war against the numerous and powerful Samnites in south-central Italy.

Through it all Rome triumphed and grew strong. Yet if the early years of the Republic had taught one thing, it was that victory brought not peace, but new and greater challenges.

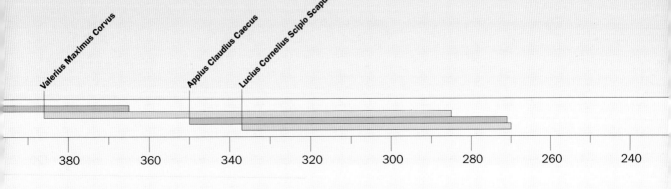

Valerius Maximus Corvus

Appius Claudius Caecus

Lucius Cornelius Scipio Scapula

380   360   340   320   300   280   260   240

Publius Valerius Poplicola
(*c*. 560–503 BC)

Horatius Cocles
(*c*. 536–*c*. 490 BC)

Coriolanus
(*c*. 527–*c*. 490 BC)

Given the nature of the Coriolanus legend, it is perhaps unsurprising that there are no contemporary portraits of him – he was, after all, a renegade and a dangerous enemy of Rome. (Detail of p. 55.)

PUBLIUS VALERIUS POPLICOLA	
Born c. 560 BC *Famous ancestors* Valerius the Mediator *Mother* Unknown *Father* Unknown *Positions held* Consul: 509, 508, 507, 504	*Achievements* First Consul, first Triumphator *Wife* Unknown *Children* Daughter: Valeria *Death* Old age c. 503 BC

(Opposite above) This stone, the Lapis Satricum, from the city of that name in southern Latium, was found in the temple of Mater Matuta. The surviving part of the inscription, in antique Latin, can be translated as 'the comrades of Publius Valerius dedicated this to Mars'. This dedication is quite possibly to Poplicola, or a very close relative.

PUBLIUS VALERIUS POPLICOLA

'Can you find no man worthy enough to be above your suspicion? I am the bitterest enemy of the kings, yet I must fear your suspicion of wanting to be one myself. Does my reputation among you really hang on so light a thread?'

> Publius Valerius, to the Roman people: Livy, *History of Rome* 2.7

WITH BRUTUS DEAD, THE LEADERSHIP OF ROME fell to the consul who had replaced Lucius Tarquinius Collatinus – Publius Valerius. The Valerians were one of Rome's most distinguished families – it was a Valerius who helped to reconcile the Romans and Sabines under Romulus.

Taking command

Valerius assumed command while the Romans were still locked in battle with Tarquin's Etruscan allies. The battle raged until evening without either side gaining the advantage. However, the Romans were fighting for their homes and liberty, whereas the Etruscans were fighting only to change the leadership of another state. Finding the price too high, they withdrew during the night to avoid further casualties.

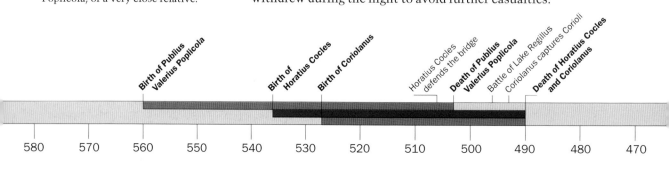

Birth of Publius Valerius Poplicola

Birth of Horatius Cocles

Birth of Coriolanus

Horatius Cocles defends the bridge

Death of Publius Valerius Poplicola

Battle of Lake Regillus

Coriolanus captures Corioli

Death of Horatius Cocles and Coriolanus

580   570   560   550   540   530   520   510   500   490   480   470

THE FASCES

Dating from at least the seventh century BC, the fasces symbolized the authority of Rome over her citizens and subjects. So powerful a symbol were they, that they were adopted by the Italian fascists (hence the name) some 2,000 years later.

The fasces consisted of a bundle of rods, about 5 ft (1.5 m) long, tied together with red cords; sometimes an axe was bound into the middle. The fasces demonstrated the power of unity, for while any individual rod could be broken in two, together the rods were virtually unbreakable. They also symbolized the power of magistrates to enforce the will of Rome. In fact the fasces were more than symbols – if unbundled they could be used to beat or execute criminals. For this reason, the axes were not carried with the fasces within Rome, indicating magisterial respect for *provocatio*, the Roman citizen's right of appeal. And to show respect for the assemblies of the Roman people, the fasces were lowered when a magistrate entered.

The fasces were carried by lictors, special attendants to the magistrate. The rank of a magistrate was indicated by the number of lictors. For instance, a consul or proconsul had 12, and a dictator probably had 24.

The fasces carried by the lictors who accompanied Roman magistrates were not mere symbols, but were used to punish or even execute wrongdoers. Detail of a relief of the first century BC/AD.

The Romans attributed this success to divine intervention, and Valerius led his army home in triumph. He rode to the Capitol in a chariot, an act that is supposedly the origin of the Roman Triumph, when a leader led his conquering army through the city to the acclaim of the populace. *Triumphatores* were honoured men, and Romans of later generations contended fiercely to be among them.

For Brutus' funeral, Valerius adopted the Greek tradition of the eulogy, whereby a leading man gives praise to the deceased. Valerius then tried to win over Tarquin's powerful ally, the Etruscan king Lars Porsenna who was now at the gates of Rome. Valerius argued that Tarquin had been justifiably deposed, and invited Porsenna to adjudicate. However, Tarquin lived up to his sobriquet of 'the proud', and denied that any man could sit in judgment on him. He thus lost the argument by default, and Porsenna decided that the Romans made better friends than enemies. He withdrew from the siege, and ordered his men to take only their weapons, and leave everything else as a gift to the Romans. (Thereby also showing that he was not giving up because he had run out of supplies.)

Establishing the Republic

Valerius now had authority and power to such a degree it was feared he might throw off the trappings of republicanism and become king in his own right. Tarquin's palace had been demolished, but Valerius' house on the Velia was as palatial as Tarquin's had been, and the rods and axes carried by his lictors, which symbolized his right to scourge and behead, made him no less royal.

Realizing the danger of adverse public opinion, Valerius acted swiftly and dramatically. He collected a host of workmen, and in the dead of night levelled his house to its foundations. In the morning the amazed populace was greeted by the sight of Valerius, homeless, begging accommodation from his friends.

Valerius then separated the rods and axes, and had them lowered in respect whenever he entered the assembly – thus establishing another lasting tradition. Lucretius, father of the martyred Lucretia, was chosen as consul to replace Brutus, and Valerius happily gave him the status of senior consul. Lucretius died soon after, and was replaced by Marcus Horatius, of Rome's heroic Horatian family.

Historians are unsure whether it was Valerius or Brutus who restored the numbers of the senate. But it was at this time that the senate assumed the role which it kept for the rest of the Republic – an unelected body, without constitutional power, yet wielding immense influence; and from which the Roman electorate selected their magistrates.

A ROMAN TRIUMPH

Whenever a great and noteworthy victory had been achieved, the general was immediately hailed by the soldiers as imperator. He would tie sprigs of laurel about the fasces and give these to runners to carry to the city and announce the victory. When he returned home, he would assemble the senate, and ask it to have a triumph voted for him. If he obtained a favourable vote from the senate, and from the popular assembly, the title of imperator was then ratified. If he was still in office when he won the victory, he remained in that office for the celebration of the triumph. However, if his term of office had expired, he assumed some other title appropriate to the office, because it was forbidden to allow a triumph to a private citizen.

Dressed in triumphal clothing, and wearing bracelets on his arms and crowned on his head with laurel, and holding a branch in his right hand, he summoned the people together. Then he would praise the soldiers who had served under him, both collectively, and in some cases individually. Some he gave gifts of money, and honoured them also with military decorations, presenting arm bracelets to some and spears (but without iron tips) to others, he gave crowns, some gold, some silver, and each crown had the name of the honoured individual and a representation of his particular brave deed. If he was the first over the wall, for example, his crown bore the likeness of a wall. A man who won a sea battle received a crown adorned with ships ... but the soldier who had saved the life of a fellow citizen in battle or in some other danger, or in a siege, won the greatest praise, and received a crown of oak leaves, which was considered a much greater honour....

A large amount of the booty was also distributed to the soldiers who had served in the campaign. Some triumphant generals also gave it to the entire populace and defrayed the expenses of the triumph and made the booty public property. If any was left over, they spent it on temples, porticoes and other public works.

When these ceremonies had been completed, the triumphant general mounted his chariot. This chariot did not resemble a racing chariot or a war chariot, it was constructed to look like a round tower. And the general did not stand alone in the chariot. If he had children or relatives, he took the girls and the male infants in the chariot with him and put the older male relatives on the chariot horses. If there were many relatives, they rode in the procession on the horses, as out-riders for the general. No one else in the triumph was mounted, they all marched along wearing laurel wreaths. However, a public slave rode in the chariot with the

Pompey in triumph, on a coin struck possibly around the time Pompey entered into an alliance with Caesar and Crassus to form the first triumvirate.

general, holding above his head a crown with precious gems set in gold, and the slave kept saying to him, 'look behind!'; warning him to consider the future, and events yet to come, and not to become haughty and arrogant because of present events.

Arranged in this way, they entered the city. At the head of the procession were the spoils and trophies, placards with the representations of captured forts, cities, mountains, rivers, lakes, and seas, indeed, all the things they had captured. And if one day was sufficient for the exhibition of these things, this was good. If not, the exhibition continued for a second, or even for a third day. When all the men that ahead of him had reached the concluding point of the procession, the general, who was at the back of the procession, was finally escorted into the Roman forum. The general ordered some of the prisoners to be taken to the prison and executed, and then he went to the capitol, performed a certain religious ritual, and made offerings.

Zosimus, *Epitome* 7

Triumph of the consul Sosius, on a marble relief from the Temple of Apollo, dating to the end of the first century BC. It was customary to exhibit captives in triumphs, who were often executed afterwards.

The Temple of Saturn in the Roman forum was first erected in about 496 BC. It was the centre of festivities to mark the Saturnalia, one of the most important festivals in the Roman year. The Romans also called the building the Aerarium, because it held the national treasury. These granite columns, from the late fourth century AD, and the podium (42 BC) are all that remain of the temple today.

Valerius also considered how to store the monies which Rome was rapidly accumulating through its equally efficient military campaigns and tax system. The money would be a public menace in the hands of any one person, so Valerius entrusted it to the god Saturn, and Saturn's temple in the Roman forum became the Roman treasury. A new magistracy, the quaestorship, was created for officials with financial responsibility.

Valerius and the Sabines

Valerius' year as consul was so successful, and the fear of tyranny had so far receded, that the grateful people hailed him as Poplicola or 'the people's friend'. They further endorsed their faith in him by electing his brother, Marcus Valerius, as consul. Poplicola accompanied Marcus as an advisor when he went to war with the Sabines. The pair won resounding victories and finished the war by the end of the year, when Poplicola again became consul. He was consul four times, the last occasion being 504 BC.

Poplicola befriended one of the most powerful Sabine leaders, Attus Clausus of the city of Regillus. He persuaded Clausus to move to Rome with his family and dependants – all 5,000 of them. The family of Attus Clausus was to remain a dominant force in Rome long after the Valerian glory had faded. Two members of the Claudian line rose to be sole masters of Rome – as the emperors Tiberius and Claudius.

The remainder of the Sabines attacked again – and were again crushed by Valerius. The campaign over, at the peak of his fame and popularity, Valerius died. He was afforded the rare honour of being buried within the city walls, on the Velia, where his beloved house had once stood. This honour of burial within the walls became an ancestral privilege of the Valerians, though the family adopted the practice of performing a burial within the walls, but at the last moment removing the corpse and interring it outside the city. Thus they exercised their privilege, but remained true to the populist tradition of their family's greatest member.

HORATIUS COCLES	
Born	*Achievements*
c. 536 BC	Held the bridge
Famous ancestors	against the
Horatius the	Etruscans
Sororicide	*Family*
Mother	Unknown
Unknown	*Death*
Father	c. 490 BC
Unknown	
Positions held	
Guard commander	
506	

HORATIUS COCLES

Then out spake brave Horatius,
The Captain of the Gate:
'To every man upon this earth
Death cometh soon or late.
And how can man die better
Than facing fearful odds,
For the ashes of his fathers,
And the temples of his gods?'

Thomas Macaulay, *Lays of Ancient Rome*

THE CLAN (IN LATIN, *GENS*) HORATIA was Latin and patrician. The Horatians were among the first families of Rome in both eminence and antiquity. When King Tullus Hostilius (pp. 26–30) was fighting the Albans, three brothers (or triplets, depending on the source) of the Horatian family were matched against three brothers from the Curiatian family on the Alban side, representing the armies of each state. The Horatians were victorious – just. The sister of the Horatian brothers was the fiancé of one of the Curiatii. When she saw her brother enter in triumph with her fiancé's cloak over his shoulders, she wailed in grief. Her brother, furious, stabbed her on the spot. Only his recent military success and the appeals of his father saved him from the death sentence.

With this record, the Horatians were naturally among the leading defenders of the new Republic. They contended with the Valerian family for honours in battle and politics. As the Valerians were Sabellians, this rivalry might have contained a touch of the old tribal tensions.

Holding the bridge

The Valerians gave Rome a superb leader in Poplicola, and they later distinguished themselves in the Battle of Lake Regillus in 496 BC. However, the fighting spirit of the Horatians eclipsed them with the famous stand on the bridge in defence of Rome itself. The Horatius in question was called Cocles (from Cyclops), apparently because he had only one eye.

The story (first mentioned by Polybius several centuries later) is that in 506 BC the Etruscans under Lars Porsenna attacked Rome so suddenly that they seemed about to enter the city through the Sublician gate, approached over a bridge of the same name. Horatius, whom tradition gives only two companions, held the enemy from the bridge until it was destroyed behind him, and then swam to safety over the Tiber.

The appeal of the Horatian legend has endured for millennia: this painting is entitled *Horatius Cocles Defending the Bridge* (1642), by Charles LeBrun. Even today, Horatius remains one of the best-known figures of the early Republic.

The remains of the Pons Aemilianus (now called the Ponte Rotto, the 'Broken Bridge). It was the first stone bridge in Rome, constructed in 179 BC. The Romans had long been capable of building stone bridges, but it was not until 179 that they felt secure enough to build a bridge that could not be easily demolished for defensive reasons.

The tale has passed into legend, as shown by the quote above from the Victorian poet Macaulay. It is very possible that the Romans did carry out a fighting rearguard action to slow the Etruscans, who could easily have pushed as far as the bridge itself. But it is highly doubtful that the actual stand could have taken place as described. Even the historian Livy described Horatius' feat as 'more famous than credible'. Nevertheless, a one-eyed man did distinguish himself in that period. An archaic bronze statue, claimed by later Horatians to be of Cocles, stood in the assembly house for centuries thereafter.

CORIOLANUS

CAIUS MARCIUS CORIOLANUS	
Born	*Achievements*
c. 527 BC	Won the oak
Famous ancestors	garland; won title
King Ancus Marcius	Coriolanus
Mother	*Wife*
Veturia or Volumnia	Volumnia or Veturia
Father	*Death*
Unknown	Assassinated(?)
Positions held	*c.* 490 BC
Volscian	
commander	

Therefore, be it known,
As to us, to all the world, that Caius Marcius
Wears this war's garland: ... and from this time,
For what he did before Corioli, call him,
With all the applause and clamour of the host,
Caius Marcius Coriolanus! Bear
The addition nobly ever!

William Shakespeare, *Coriolanus*

CAIUS MARCIUS, as the young Coriolanus was known, belonged to the Marcian clan, which was descended from Ancus Marcius, one of the early kings of Rome (pp. 30–31). Caius' father was dead, and the youth had been raised by his mother. Plutarch calls this woman Veturia, while other Roman historians give this name to Coriolanus' wife, and call the mother Volumnia. For many modern historians the question is somewhat irrelevant, as Coriolanus is probably fictional.

Many of the figures of early Rome may indeed be foundation legends. However, each of these legends is probably based to some degree on fact.

Coriolanus is less probable than most, but the Romans believed that he existed, and this tells us something about the Romans.

A promising youth

Caius Marcius won his spurs in the Battle of Lake Regillus in 496 BC against the Latin League. This was a significant victory for the Romans as it both secured their dominance in Latium and finally ended the hopes of Tarquin the Proud. It is also notable for the fact that before the battle two men on shining horses met the Roman senator Domitius. They informed him that they were the divine twins Castor and Pollux, and that victory would go to the Romans. To show that they were speaking the truth they touched his beard, changing its colour to bronze. The Domitii Ahenobarbi ('Domitians of the bronze beards') reappear frequently throughout Roman history, ending with the most famous Ahenobarbus of all, the emperor Nero.

During the battle, Caius Marcius killed an enemy who was about to slay a fallen Roman. For saving a citizen's life, Marcius received a crown of oak leaves, the Roman equivalent of a medal – oak trees were sacred to Jupiter, the patron god of Rome.

Marcius then went on to serve in several more campaigns. Rome's principal enemies were now the Volscians, a warlike neighbouring tribe. Like others who encountered the Roman military machine, the Volscians quickly discovered that Rome was no pushover. They soon found themselves under siege in the city of Corioli by a Roman army which included Caius Marcius.

When the Volscians sallied out of the town to destroy the Roman siege works, they were met by Marcius and a few companions who had anticipated the move. Though greatly outnumbered, this group drove the Volscians back into the city. For his heroism Marcius was given the name of Coriolanus (a Roman who performed a heroic action was sometimes allowed to append the location of his act to his name).

Patricians and plebeians

After this success Coriolanus returned to Rome, but found it a divided and troubled city. The aristocratic patricians had forced many plebeians into debt or even slavery, and exploited their cheap labour for their own profit. The plebeians were fighting back, and had won the right to their own representatives in government – the tribunes. These had the power to veto or propose legislation, and could shield citizens from injustice or bring them to justice as the situation demanded. They were also declared inviolate – no one could lay hands on them.

The patricians, including Coriolanus, refused to surrender what they regarded as their rights under the law. Finally the plebs had had enough, and they seceded from the Roman state. Menenius Agrippa, a patrician moderate, persuaded them to return, but though reunited, the Roman people were far from reconciled, and Coriolanus was among the patricians whom the plebeians chiefly distrusted.

Remains of the Temple of Castor and Pollux, the twin divinities who inspired the Romans before the crucial Battle of Lake Regillus in 496 BC. They were special patrons of the Roman cavalry, and the annual review of knights was held before their temple.

Consequently, when Coriolanus stood for the consulship he failed to be elected. Such electoral defeat amounted to a public humiliation for Coriolanus and his patrician hard-line faction. The young aristocrat wanted revenge, and his opportunity soon came. Rome was in the grip of a famine and a friendly Sicilian prince sent a substantial gift of corn. Coriolanus proposed that the grain be withheld from the plebs until they renounced their right to have tribunes – a controversial idea, to say the least. More moderate senators refused to starve their fellow-citizens into submission and Coriolanus lost the argument.

In exile

Unrepentant, he refused to answer the treason charges which the tribunes levelled against him. His heroic military record saved him from death, but he was expelled from Rome. In exile, Coriolanus was contacted by the leader of the Volscians, Attius Tullius. The Volscians were chafing over their losses in the previous war, and they invited Coriolanus to join them in their attempt to win back lost cities. Coriolanus accepted.

This part of the legend is quite credible. As shown by the elder Tarquin and his father, and also by Attus Clausus, members of the élite class of central Italy were apparently able to transfer themselves and their allegiance from city to city. Similar cases can also be found in the better-documented history of contemporary archaic Greece.

Coriolanus was a very successful general and the Romans were driven back against their city walls. They sent delegation after delegation pleading with Coriolanus to return to his former allegiance, but he refused them all. He was holding out for the Volscian cities to be restored and the Volscians to be made citizens. Finally, the Romans sent a delegation which included Coriolanus' wife and mother. Unable to resist this moral persuasion, Coriolanus withdrew his army. The story of subsequent events is confused. Some claim Coriolanus was assassinated when he returned to the Volscians, others that he lived to an old age. Certainly he never returned to Rome.

How much of Coriolanus' story is true? The German historian B. Niebuhr (1776–1831) points out that events that took place 10 years later fit the story more closely than the traditional dates. At that time there was indeed a famine in Rome, and Hiero, tyrant of Syracuse, might have sent grain to Rome to spite the Etruscans with whom he was feuding. The Volscians, despite Plutarch's protestations, seem to have joined the Roman state on terms rather like those Coriolanus was demanding. Quite possibly the Romans, weakened by famine, were defeated by the Volscians. Rather than admit losing a battle to foreigners, the Romans attributed the Volscian success to a Roman exile, and one who might have been descended from King Ancus Marcius.

Volumnia before Coriolanus: this painting by Giovanni Francesco Barbieri (Guercino) of 1643 shows the appeal of the Coriolanus legend at a time when the established order in Europe felt threatened. It is uncertain how much of Coriolanus' story is true, however.

Titus Quinctius Capitolinus Barbatus

(c. 505–c. 430 BC)

Lucius Quinctius Cincinnatus

(c. 519–c. 438 BC)

Cincinnatus, the Roman general called from the plough to save a Republic which did not deserve it. This legend of great-hearted public service inspired the founding fathers of the American city of Cincinnati in Ohio. (Detail of p. 60.)

TITUS QUINCTIUS CAPITOLINUS BARBATUS	
Born c. 505 BC	Positions held Consul 471, 468,
Famous ancestors None	465, 446, 443, 439; Proconsul 464
Mother Unknown	Achievements Triumphator
Father Unknown	Family Unknown
	Death Old age c. 430 BC

TITUS QUINCTIUS CAPITOLINUS BARBATUS

In the senate, it seemed as though Titus Quinctius alone upheld the majesty of Rome. The leading senators declared his speech to have been in the finest tradition of consular authority. It was worthy of a man who had been consul so many times, and who had lived a life replete with honours, and yet deserved more.

Livy, *History of Rome* 3.69

TITUS QUINCTIUS CAPITOLINUS BARBATUS was the first of the Quinctian family to achieve great distinction in Rome. Like many great Romans, from Romulus to Julius Caesar, he was both statesman and soldier. His birth date is uncertain, but his name suggests that his family lived on the Capitoline hill of Rome.

A leader in war and peace

Capitolinus first appears in history as consul in the year 471 BC. His colleague in office was Appius Claudius, the son of the Attus Clausus whom Poplicola had invited to Rome (p. 51). The class struggle between the plebs and the aristocracy was still raging on, unresolved, and Appius

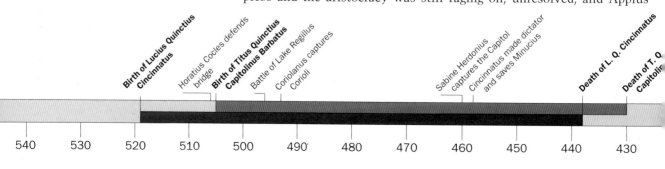

Birth of Lucius Quinctius Cincinnatus

Horatius Cocles defends bridge

Birth of Titus Quinctius Capitolinus Barbatus

Battle of Lake Regillus

Coriolanus captures Corioli

Sabine Herdonius captures the Capitol

Cincinnatus made dictator and saves Minucius

Death of L. Q. Cincinnatus

Death of T. Q. Capitoli

540   530   520   510   500   490   480   470   460   450   440   430

Remains of the harbour at Antium (modern Anzio). Antium went from being a Volscian stronghold against Rome to a strategic port to a pleasure resort. It was the birthplace of the emperors Nero and Caligula.

Claudius was a fervent partisan of the patricians. Capitolinus tried to keep the peace between the factions, but with mixed results. Once, when Appius was haranguing the mob which was threatening to tear him to pieces, Capitolinus ordered Appius Claudius removed from the forum – by force, if need be.

Rome was also still under attack by the Volscians, and these were now joined by the ferocious warrior tribe of the Aequians. As consul, Capitolinus conducted his campaign against them competently and returned to popular acclaim. Appius Claudius, meanwhile, had to contend with mutinous troops who hated him almost as much as he hated them.

Capitolinus was re-elected consul for 468 and successfully campaigned against the Volscians. Having captured Antium, on the Italian coast, he was one of the commissioners who chose new settlers for the town. The number of Romans was growing rapidly: the citizen body – that is free males of voting age – now numbered over 104,000, a substantial state in ancient times.

Between campaigns Capitolinus continued to try to calm the volatile political situation in Rome. He was one of the few men trusted equally by the aristocrats and the common people. Once, when a rumour got about that the enemy had slipped past the army and was marching on a virtually undefended Rome, Capitolinus stemmed the panic and maintained order until the report was proved groundless. On another occasion, the consul Furius was advancing into Aequian territory when, meeting only light resistance, he pushed too far. Suddenly, he found himself besieged in his camp by a huge Aequian army. Receiving the call for help, Capitolinus gathered a scratch force of such Roman soldiers as were available. Assisted by loyal allies from the Hernician tribe, he fell on the rear of the Aequian army and soundly defeated them.

Trials and treason

In Rome Capitolinus found himself having to use his authority to defend a relative and son of his friend Cincinnatus, Caeso Quinctius. Caeso was a youth of great promise, but a wild and lawless character who led a group of young aristocrats in acts of violence and intimidation against the common people. When Caeso was eventually brought to trial, only the pleas of the veteran general allowed the young man to escape into exile.

When a further crisis arose in 439, Capitolinus was elected consul for the sixth time, the previous occasions being in 471, 468, 465, 446 and 443. Now a man called Spurius Maelius was plotting to seize supreme power. The people suspected his intentions and voted for Capitolinus to sort things out. Capitolinus was, as Livy puts it, 'a difficult man for a revolutionary to deal with'. He and his colleague Menenius Agrippa rapidly established that Maelius was planning a *coup d'état*. Capitolinus called on the senate to elect Cincinnatus as dictator before matters went too far. As dictator, Cincinnatus was not constrained by the same delicacy as the consuls, and Maelius' career came to an abrupt and bloody end.

Though by now probably well over 60 years old, Capitolinus – soldier and statesman – remained in the service of Rome. He took to the field once more a year or so later under a military tribune, Mamercus Aemilius, to do battle with the Etruscans. Aemilius commanded the right wing, his second-in-command the centre, and Capitolinus the left. The second-in-command was his friend Lucius Cincinnatus, another Quinctius, and by no means the last of that family to lead Romans into battle.

LUCIUS QUINCTIUS CINCINNATUS

Quinctius Cincinnatus, who, possessing only four acres of land, and cultivating them with his own hands, was taken from the plough to be made dictator – an office more honourable even than that of consul – and after having won great glory by conquering the enemy, he preferred notwithstanding to continue in his poverty.

St Augustine, on Christians of his time who boasted of their
righteous poverty, *The City of God* 5.18

LUCIUS QUINCTIUS CINCINNATUS	
Born c. 519 BC	*Achievements* Triumphator
Famous ancestors None	*Children* Sons: Caeso, Lucius
Mother Unknown	*Death* Old age c. 438 BC
Father Unknown	
Positions held Consul 460; Dictator 458, 439	

IN THE MID-FIFTH CENTURY BC the Quinctian family was a major force in Rome. This was a phenomenon of the Roman Republic: if certain people performed well in office, the Romans tended to elect other members of the same family. (Rather as the voters of the United States seem to have a predilection for people called Kennedy, Clinton or Bush.)

Thus Titus Quinctius Capitolinus Barbatus was to bring several generations of Quinctians to high office. As we have seen, Capitolinus himself was consul six times. And now Lucius Quinctius Cincinnatus was to be made dictator, the supreme, sole leader of Rome, not once, but twice.

The life of Cincinnatus was filled with triumphs and disasters, a fact which partly reflected the turbulent struggle between the nobility and the common people. As a patrician Cincinnatus supported the aristocratic faction, and his fortunes rose and fell with his party.

The trial of Caeso

As already mentioned, Capitolinus' great authority and experience were needed to defend Cincinnatus' son, Caeso. Strong, hot-headed and an excellent soldier, Caeso used forthright military tactics on his political opponents. The tribunes, when pressing for legislation favourable to the common people, were often driven from the forum by young Caeso's gang of aristocratic bully-boys. Finally Caeso was brought to trial on a capital charge. Allegedly, a man he had attacked subsequently died of his wounds. The nobility of Rome queued up to give character testimonials for young Caeso; Cincinnatus himself argued that though his son had been headstrong and rash, he was developing a steady character and would be a great asset to the city. Despite this, it became evident that Caeso would be sentenced to death. It was only when Capitolinus intervened that Caeso was bailed from prison, and he fled into exile before he was sentenced. The tribunes demanded that Cincinnatus pay every penny of the bail which Caeso had forfeited. Cincinnatus did this, though the expense ruined him. He had to sell everything, including his house. Finding an abandoned cottage near the city, he set up home in that.

We must take this drama with a pinch of salt. Cincinnatus very probably did move to a more modest house as the record says – not because he was destitute, however, but because the Romans loved dramatic gestures, and this was pure political theatre. Cincinnatus escaped true hardship. He was a member of a powerful family with influential friends, as demonstrated the following year. In 460 BC a Sabine called Herdonius, taking advantage of Roman distraction with party strife, captured the Capitol with a band of slaves and exiles. The consul, another Valerius, retook the hill at the cost of his life, and his chosen replacement was Lucius Quinctius Cincinnatus.

Consul and dictator

The new consul publicly reprimanded the tribunes before getting on with state business. Some complex political manoeuvrings followed, with consuls and tribunes deadlocked. At the end of the year, the tribunes presented themselves for re-election so that they could pass the reformist legislation that Cincinnatus had blocked.

The senate duly prepared to re-elect Cincinnatus also, but he flatly forbade it. Bad enough that the tribunes held office year after year, he said, but for the senate to imitate these political delinquents was disgraceful. He stepped down, and new consuls were elected.

Externally, Rome was still fighting its perennial enemies, the Volscians and Aequians. Then the Sabines joined the attack, and the situation became serious. One consul was fully committed, and the other, Lucius Minucius, was besieged in his camp. The Romans stood to lose an army, and as usual in such circumstances, they decided to appoint a dictator.

The saviour of Rome

Cincinnatus was chosen and a delegation went to summon him. They found him on his farm, a tiny plot which he had acquired after his financial ruin. Legend says Cincinnatus was at the plough, though Livy only mentions farm work, and suggests he may have been digging a ditch.

Within 15 days Cincinnatus had raised a levy, surrounded and destroyed the enemy, and returned for a triumph in Rome, pausing only to give the unfortunate Minucius a tongue-lashing for putting his army into such a predicament. He then laid down his office, though not before he saw the witness most responsible for his son's exile condemned for perjury and expelled from Rome.

Cincinnatus and Capitolinus were both subsequently excluded from being elected decemvirs by Appius Claudius the Decemvir (p. 63). Appius' eventual downfall was followed soon after by Capitolinus' fourth consulship – the Quinctians were once more back in power. Cincinnatus was now over 80, but Capitolinus urged that he be made dictator again in 439 to put down the conspiracy of Maelius. When Maelius refused to answer the summons of Cincinnatus, he was killed, and the incipient coup perished with him.

Capitolinus and Cincinnatus worked together one last time when another son of Cincinnatus was put on trial for military incompetence. Cincinnatus did not attend the trial, and Capitolinus asked who would tell the aged hero, now near the end of his life, that his son was condemned. The jurors relented – Cincinnatus junior was acquitted.

Cincinnatus Receiving the Deputies of the Senate, a painting by Félix Barrias, which won the Prix de Rome in 1844. Barrias began using themes from classical sources to add historical significance to his paintings, as his earlier compositions had been criticized as too lightweight.

Appius Claudius the Decemvir

(*c.* 510–*c.* 449 BC)

APPIUS CLAUDIUS THE DECEMVIR	
Born	*Positions held*
c. 510 BC	Consul 471(?), 451;
Famous ancestors	Decemvir 451, 450
None	*Achievements*
Mother	The Twelve Tables
Unknown	*Family*
Father	Unknown
Attus Clausus (?)	*Death*
	Suicide or murder
	c. 449 BC

'You have stripped away the two pillars of our liberty – the aid of the tribunes and the right of appeal. But you still have no right to make our wives and children the victims of your lust. You can use up your cruelty on our backs and necks, if only female honour remains safe. Violate that, though, and I shall call on the the aid of every true Roman.'

Icilius, the fiancé of Verginia, to Appius Claudius in Livy, *History of Rome* 3.45

THE EXPULSION OF THE KINGS had brought no peace to Rome. The city was constantly at war with its neighbours, and internally there was strife between aristocrats and the people, often embodied in disputes between their elected representatives – the consuls and the tribunes.

The need for law

One major grudge of the people was that the laws of Rome were not codified, and that the interpretation of the law – even the nature of the laws themselves – was determined by the consuls. This allowed unscrupulous aristocrats to use the law as an instrument of oppression; and the people could not appeal because no one knew exactly what the law was. Finally, in the middle of the fifth century BC, it was agreed that the laws of Rome

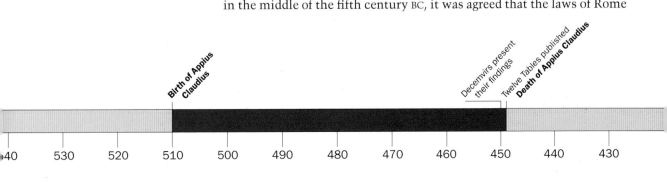

Birth of Appius Claudius

Decemvirs present their findings

Twelve Tables published

Death of Appius Claudius

540 | 530 | 520 | 510 | 500 | 490 | 480 | 470 | 460 | 450 | 440 | 430

Family tree of the early Claudians. It is possible that the consuls of 471 and 451 may in fact be the same person.

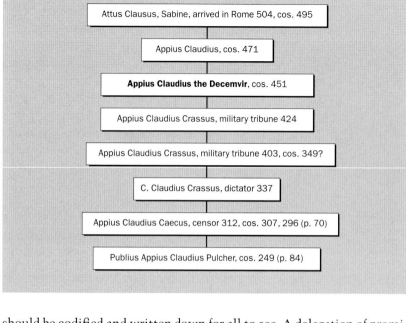

Attus Clausus, Sabine, arrived in Rome 504, cos. 495

Appius Claudius, cos. 471

Appius Claudius the Decemvir, cos. 451

Appius Claudius Crassus, military tribune 424

Appius Claudius Crassus, military tribune 403, cos. 349?

C. Claudius Crassus, dictator 337

Appius Claudius Caecus, censor 312, cos. 307, 296 (p. 70)

Publius Appius Claudius Pulcher, cos. 249 (p. 84)

THE *FASTI*

The Romans kept track of the years by two different methods – events could be measured from the founding of the city (A.U.C. from *ab urbe condita*) or by the names of the consuls in a given year.

This last fact has been of immeasurable benefit to historians, since lists of consulships were maintained by the Romans for dating purposes. Though often controversial, especially for the early period of Roman history, the list of Roman consuls for the Republican period is almost complete.

The list is called the *Fasti Consulares* (*fasti* are lists of days connected with public or legislative events), and was assembled from a number of different *fasti*. The first definitive list of modern times was the *fasti consulares et triumphales* compiled by A. Degrassi in 1947.

should be codified and written down for all to see. A delegation of prominent Romans travelled to Athens to study that city's laws as codified by the lawmaker Solon. Returning to Rome three years later, in 451, they presented their findings. It was agreed that for one year, instead of consuls a board of ten men (*decemviri*) would be appointed, who would run the state and make its laws. At the end of the year the laws would be presented to the people for approval.

The three emissaries who had been sent to Athens were chosen to be decemvirs, as were the men who would have been consuls for that year. Another decemvir was Gaius Julius – a rare mention of the Julian family in this period. The man who became the most influential decemvir was Appius Claudius Inregellensis Sabinus Crassus, known today as Appius Claudius the Decemvir.

The Decemvirs

This Appius Claudius was either the son or grandson of the Attus Clausus who had brought his family to Rome (p. 51). A son of Attus Clausus called Appius Claudius was consul in 471, and later Roman historians assumed that the man taking office 20 years later was that consul's son, but the Capitoline *Fasti* state explicitly that it was the same man.

The decemvirate's year was a great success. Despite Appius' (or his father's) earlier clashes with the people, the decemvirate tried hard to appear impartial and just. In theory, there was no appeal from the verdict of a decemvir, but if a claimant's appeal was heard by another decemvir, the first decemvir would usually overturn his own judgment.

At the end of the year, ten of the 'tables' of law were presented for approval, and were voted in by the full assembly of the Roman people in the *Comitia Centuriata*. The decemvirs then asked for a new board to be appointed to codify a further two tables of law which remained. The first board had been so successful that there was no resistance to the decemvirate taking another year to finish its work.

Everyone on the first board stepped down, except Appius Claudius. He began to campaign seriously for re-election and courted the popular vote. This would have been preposterous, except that the common people were so enthusiastic about the decemvirate's work to date. Other aristocrats were now more interested in becoming decemvirs, and among those seeking election were Quinctius Capitolinus and Cincinnatus, and the uncle (or brother) of Appius, Gaius Claudius.

To ensure that Appius was not re-elected, the Quinctians arranged for him to preside over the election. It was unprecedented for someone in this position to be a candidate – there would be a huge conflict of interest, which could result in the entire election being manipulated. Indeed, Appius coolly engineered the election so that the only prominent candidate elected was Appius himself. The others were nonentities, though one family name – Sergius – would be made infamous later in Roman history by the conspirator Catiline (p. 213).

The Twelve Tables (see p. 65) and the decemvirate are historical fact, but historians are deeply sceptical about the second decemvirate (450–449), and the role of Appius in subsequent events.

Tyranny

With the second decemvirate firmly under Appius' thumb, a new order began. Roman magistrates now appeared in public with lictors – men who carried the rods and axes of office, and who executed the magistrate's judgments. In the first decemvirate, only the decemvir actually on court duty on a particular day had lictors, but the members of the second board immediately appeared with a full retinue of lictors each.

Rome was in the grip of a tyranny against which there was no appeal. The decemvirs' justice was arbitrary, and often biased towards their own friends and supporters. The aristocrats could escape to their estates in the country, but the common people were at the mercy of Rome's new rulers.

Before long, Appius and his cronies faced problems. Rome's perennial enemies, the Sabines and Aequians, were attacking. The army was ably commanded by a member of Rome's leading military family, the Fabians; but the soldiers were the same people that the decemvirs were tyrannizing at home. They refused to fight, or put up only feeble resistance

Within Rome, opposition to the tyranny centred around Horatius and Valerius, two members of families which had done most to liberate Rome from the Tarquins. The other leading Claudian, Gaius, was also a force for moderation. The political skills of Appius were equal to the situation, however, until his own sexual appetite let him down. He became obsessed by a schoolgirl called Verginia who was engaged to be married to a man confidently expected to become tribune once the office was restored. Her father, Verginius, was a centurion in the army.

Three Scenes from the History of Verginia, by Filippino Lippi, fifteenth century AD. The story of Verginia and her father's choice to kill her rather than face dishonour were also very relevant to the people of the medieval era. Chaucer gives over one of his Canterbury Tales (the Physician's Tale) to the subject.

The fall of the decemvirs

Appius persuaded one of his dependants to claim that Verginia was in fact a slave who was smuggled from his household while an infant. When this dependant, one Marcus Claudius, made his claim, there was uproar. Appius gave judgment on the case, and to no one's surprise, announced that she was indeed a slave, and Marcus Claudius was her true master. Verginia's father decided that death was better than dishonour for his daughter, and killed her on hearing the verdict. This man – with considerable support from the people – then fought his way out of the city, and raised the army in revolt. The people, in disgust, also withdrew from the city, and camped on the Janiculum hill across the Tiber. The wives and daughters of free citizens could not be treated in this way they said, and demanded that the decemvirs step down.

There was no reason why they should not. The last two tables had long been completed, and the appointed year had expired. The decemvirs were now a tyranny, pure and simple. Faced with a total lack of support, their period of ascendancy was over. They surrendered, asking only that they should not be given over to the people, who were understandably eager to get hold of them.

Their terms were granted, and the crisis was resolved. Now a private citizen, Appius Claudius appeared brazenly in the forum as though nothing had happened. He was promptly seized by Verginius, who accused him of breaking one of the laws so recently codified – that no man should bring a free person falsely into slavery.

Appius appealed, but not a single person vouched for him. He was thrown into the prison he had mockingly called 'the working men's quarters'. When an impassioned plea delivered on his behalf by Gaius Claudius failed, Appius took his own life. (Or so says Livy. A separate tradition, by the historian Dionysius of Halicarnassus, says that the tribunes killed Appius while they had the chance.)

Appius Claudius the Decemvir came to symbolize the arrogance and violence of the Claudians. He also showed the excellent work which his family could do for the state, as demonstrated by the lasting contribution of the Twelve Tables.

THE TWELVE TABLES

Though all the world exclaim against me, I will say what I think: that single little book of the Twelve Tables, if anyone look to the fonts and sources of laws, seems to me, assuredly, to surpass the libraries of all the philosophers, both in weight of authority, and in plenitude of utility.

Cicero, *De Oratore* I.44

While the Twelve Tables are too long to reproduce here in their entirety, here are some of the most significant points.

Table I

If anyone summons a man before the magistrate, he must go. If the man summoned does not go, let the one summoning him call the bystanders to witness and then take him by force. If he shirks or runs away, let the summoner lay hands on him.

When the litigants settle their case by compromise, let the magistrate announce it. If they do not compromise, let them state each his own side of the case, in the *comitium* of the forum before noon. Afterwards let them talk it out together, while both are present. After noon, in case either party has failed to appear, let the magistrate pronounce judgment in favour of the one who is present. If both are present the trial may last until sunset but no later.

Table II

He whose witness has failed to appear may summon him by loud calls before his house every third day.

Table III

One who has confessed a debt, or against whom judgment has been pronounced, shall have thirty days to pay it in. After that forcible seizure of his person is allowed.

Table IV

A dreadfully deformed child shall be quickly killed.

If a father sell his son three times, the son shall be free from his father.

As a man has provided in his will in regard to his money and the care of his property, so let it be binding. If he has no heir and dies intestate, let the nearest agnate [descendant from a common male ancestor] have the inheritance. If there is no agnate, let the members of his *gens* [extended family] have the inheritance.

If one is mad but has no guardian, the power over him and his money shall belong to his agnates and the members of his *gens*.

A child born after ten months since the father's death will not be admitted into a legal inheritance.

Table V

Females should remain in guardianship even when they have attained their majority.

Table VI

When one makes a bond and a conveyance of property, as he has made formal declaration, so let it be binding.

Usucapio [full legal rights over] of movable things requires one year's possession for its completion; but *usucapio* of an estate and buildings two years.

Any woman who does not wish to be subjected in this manner to the hand of her husband should be absent three nights in succession every year.

Table VII

Should a tree on a neighbour's farm be bent crooked by the wind and lean over your farm, you may take legal action for removal of that tree. A man may gather up fruit that was falling down on to another man's farm.

Table VIII

If one has maimed a limb and does not compromise with the injured person, let there be retaliation. If one has broken a bone of a freeman with his hand or with a cudgel, let him pay a penalty of three hundred coins. If he has broken the bone of a slave, let him have one hundred and fifty coins. If one is guilty of insult, the penalty shall be twenty-five coins.

If a man is slain while committing theft by night, he is rightly slain. It is unlawful for a thief to be killed by day … unless he defends himself with a weapon; even though he has come with a weapon, unless he shall use the weapon and fight back, you shall not kill him. And even if he resists, first call out so that someone may hear and come up.

A person who had been found guilty of giving false witness shall be hurled down from the Tarpeian Rock.

No person shall hold meetings by night in the city.

Table IX

There shall be capital punishment for a judge or arbiter legally appointed who has been found guilty of receiving a bribe for his decision.

Treason: he who shall have roused up a public enemy or handed over a citizen to a public enemy must suffer capital punishment.

Putting to death of any man unconvicted, whosoever he might be, is forbidden.

Table X

No one is to bury or burn a corpse in the city.

Table XI

Marriages should not take place between plebeians and patricians [this law was in abeyance soon after it was pronounced].

Table XII

Whatever the people have last ordained should be held as binding by law.

Marcus Furius Camillus
(c. 447–c. 365 BC)

Valerius Maximus Corvus
(c. 386–c. 285 BC)

Appius Claudius Caecus
(c. 350–c. 271 BC)

Lucius Cornelius Scipio Scapula
(c. 337–c. 270 BC)

MARCUS FURIUS CAMILLUS

The populace and all those who were somewhat jealous of his reputation – and even his best friends and his relatives – felt such envy towards him that they did not even attempt to hide it. When he asked some of them to support his cause and others to vote for his acquittal, they refused to assist him with their vote.

Cassius Dio, *History* 6.24

MARCUS FURIUS CAMILLUS	
Born	Dictator 396, 390,
447 BC	389, 368, 367
Famous ancestors	*Achievements*
None	Triumphator four
Mother	times; conquered
Unknown	Veii; saved Rome
Father	from the Gauls
Unknown	*Children*
Positions held	Sons: Spurius,
Censor 403;	Lucius (another
Military tribune	died in infancy)
401, 398, 394,	*Death*
386, 384, 381;	Plague c. 365 BC

THE FORTY YEARS SINCE THE DEATH OF CAPITOLINUS has been hard ones for Rome. As well as the unending feud with the Volscians, Rome had suffered both a plague and a famine so severe that the tyrant Dionysius I of Sicily supposedly sent relief supplies of grain. Through it all, Rome remained a democracy, though a dictator was elected in times of crisis when a single firm hand was required. Marcus Furius Camillus was to be elected military tribune repeatedly, and dictator five times. Camillus' first military success was to defeat Rome's ancient enemies from the neighbouring Etruscan city of Veii. Since Veii was too strong for a direct attack to succeed, Camillus and his second-in-command, Cornelius Scipio, settled for a siege. By undermining the city walls, Camillus

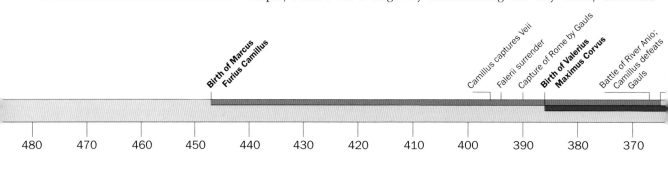

Birth of Marcus Furius Camillus

Camillus captures Veii

Falerii surrender

Capture of Rome by Gauls

Birth of Valerius Maximus Corvus

Battle of River Anio; Camillus defeats Gauls

480   470   460   450   440   430   420   410   400   390   380   370

Head of a terracotta statue from Veii. The city of Veii was architecturally and culturally superior to Rome, and after they had conquered it, many Romans wanted to abandon their own settlement and re-site the capital at Veii.

finally brought the city under Roman control. This was a considerable achievement, as Veii was a large and handsome city, perhaps the foremost in that part of Etruria, and culturally and architecturally superior to Rome.

In the city was a large statue of Juno Regina, the queen of the gods. Camillus brought this to Rome and placed in a purpose-built temple. However, he then undid this act of piety by celebrating his triumph in a chariot pulled by four white horses – almost sacrilege, since this form of transport was used by the gods themselves.

In 394 BC Camillus was again at war, this time against Falerii. A teacher of the children of Falerii's principal citizens saw a chance to put himself on what he reckoned would be the winning side. He handed over his pupils to the Romans as they were preparing to besiege the city and told a stunned Camillus that with these children hostage, the Falerians would surrender. Camillus sent the treacherous schoolteacher back to Falerii under the guard of his students. These took a message that the Romans intended to win by fair rather than underhand methods. In fact, the schoolteacher's actions did avert the war, though not as intended. The Falerians were so impressed by Camillus' honourable dealing that they surrendered on the spot.

Into exile

Camillus' soldiers were not happy with this outcome, as many were hoping for plunder from the campaign. Since Camillus had also mishandled the distribution of plunder from Veii, he now became deeply unpopular. It was only a matter of time before some demagogue attacked him, and he duly found himself charged with expropriating state booty and was forced to leave Rome and go into exile.

There is a legend that as he left, he said a prayer that if his expulsion was unjust the gods should arrange that the Romans would need him again. That day soon came. The Gauls, expanding south through Etruscan lands, arrived at Clusium, where Lars Porsenna had once been king. The Clusians asked the Romans to mediate with the Gauls for the sake of their ancient friendship. Rome accordingly dispatched three ambassadors, all from the Fabian family.

The Gauls were intent on conquest and the peace negotiations came to nothing. One of the Fabians, Quintus Ambustus, therefore felt free to join the Clusians in fighting the Gauls. Such behaviour by someone who was supposed to be an ambassador outraged the Gauls, and they sought

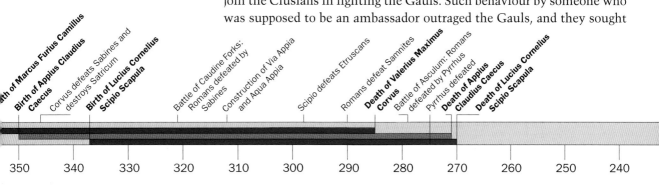

350 340 330 320 310 300 290 280 270 260 250 240

MILITARY TRIBUNES

Military tribunes, or to give them their official title – *Tribuni Militum cum Consulari Potestate* – came about in 444. The powers of the consuls were divided between two new magistrates – the military tribunes and the censors. They could be chosen from both patricians and plebeians, and the system was a compromise to the idea that the consulship should be open to both orders.

In any year, the people could choose to elect either consuls or military tribunes, and while there were always two consuls in a year, (if consuls were elected) there could be two, three or even six military tribunes. (Sometimes their colleagues, the censors, were also described as military tribunes, making the number even higher.) The system lasted until 367 and was abolished by the Licinian Law.

redress from Rome directly. Their protests were ignored, and the Romans added insult to injury by making Quintus Ambustus military tribune for the next year.

The fall of Rome

War with the Gauls was now inevitable, and the two sides met at the Allia, just 11 miles (18 km) from Rome, in 386 BC. Faced with an unfamiliar foe, the allies of the Romans deserted (according to the face-saving tradition in Livy). The Roman flank was turned and the Romans were massively defeated. Rome, in the 121st year of the Republic, 367 years after its foundation, fell into enemy hands.

Roman legend maintains that a small Roman garrison remained on the Capitoline hill, under siege. The Gauls launched an attack at night, and this would have succeeded but for the hissing of the sacred geese in the temple of Juno which alerted the Romans.

Camillus was duly recalled and appointed dictator. He rounded up an army from the scattered Roman contingents and set out for Rome. Meanwhile the Romans in the Capitol had reached an agreement with the Gallic chieftain Brennus to ransom the state for a huge sum of gold. While the the ransom was being weighed, it was discovered that the Gauls had shamelessly fixed the scales. To the Roman complaints, the Gallic chief bluntly replied '*Vae victis*' – 'woe to the conquered'. At this point Camillus arrived with his troops and brought the shameful affair to an abrupt halt, telling the Gauls that Rome would pay in steel, not gold.

The challenge was accepted, and the two armies met in battle. This time the Romans triumphed, and drove the Gauls from their land. Before reconstruction of the ravaged city could begin, however, the Latins and the Volscians took advantage of Rome's weakened condition to invade. Camillus drove back these invaders as well.

Rome restored

After the victory, a large proportion of the population wanted to emigrate to the relatively undamaged city of Veii, which Rome still held. Camillus and other patriotic Romans campaigned to prevent this and they prevailed. The Romans thereafter attributed the narrow, irregular streets of their capital to the hurried and unplanned rebuilding which followed.

Rome had fully recovered when the Gauls returned in 367. Camillus was now an old man with several more successful campaigns to his credit. He had studied Gallic weapons and devised tactics to cope with their headlong charge; the close-combat technique he taught the Romans distinguished their military machine thereafter. He destroyed the Gallic army in a battle at the River Anio, not far from Rome.

Still dictator, Camillus was called on to resolve the long feud that still bitterly divided people and aristocrats. He forced the senate to accept proposed legislation that henceforth the consulship should be shared

Fragment of a marble relief showing the sacred geese, second century AD. Later Romans held a festival in which the geese, and their patroness Juno Moneta, were honoured for warning the garrison of the capital of the attack by the Gauls at night.

between one patrician and one plebeian. This brought domestic strife to an end – at least temporarily. Camillus proposed building a temple to Concord to celebrate this reconciliation, but died from the plague before it was built.

It is tempting to believe that many of Camillus' feats were invented to salve Roman pride after their defeat by the Gauls. Archaeology shows that the Temple of Concord was built later, and Camillus' arrival just in time to save the Romans from paying ransom is too fortuitous to be true. But Rome was undoubtedly conquered by the Gauls; somehow it shook off this crushing blow to regain its former prominence in less than a generation. Marcus Furius Camillus, justly or unjustly, gets much of the credit for this.

VALERIUS MAXIMUS CORVUS

VALERIUS MAXIMUS CORVUS	
Born	*Achievements*
386 BC	Triumphator four
Famous ancestors	times
Valerius Poplicola	*Children*
Mother	Unknown
Unknown	*Death*
Father	Old age *c.* 285 BC
Unknown	
Positions	
Consul 348, 346,	
343, 335, 300,	
299; Dictator 342,	
302, 301(?)	

It is recorded that M. Valerius Corvus lived up to his hundredth year, and after his public service was done he lived on his farmstead and improved it. Between his first and sixth consulships there was an interval of forty-six years.... Furthermore, that last period of his old age was more felicitous than his middle life, for he had greater influence on the conduct of affairs of state and less labour. For the crown of old age is influence.

Cicero, *Essay on old age* 17

ONCE RE-ESTABLISHED, ROME ENTERED into a period of escalating wars against ever more powerful enemies. Fortunately it had generals of exceptional ability and heroism, chief among whom was another of Rome's great Valerian line, Valerius Maximus Corvus. This man's long life was filled with such fame and achievement that he became a paradigm for later generations.

Help from a raven

As a member of the Valerian family, Maximus was destined for high office. His first post was with Camillus in his final campaign of 367 against the Gauls. Before the decisive battle a gigantic Gaul stepped forward and challenged the Romans to single combat. Valerius volunteered to take on this Goliath. In the fight, he was apparently assisted by a raven (*corvus* in Latin) which repeatedly struck the Gaul in the face. Aided by this distraction, Valerius slew his opponent, and took the name Corvus in recognition of his unexpected ally.

He was consul in 348, and again in 346, when he defeated Rome's old enemies the Volscians. On taking the town of Satricum, he burned it to the ground to remove it forever from enemy hands.

Like most of his family, Valerius was an easy-going and popular general, who took part in the athletic contests that the soldiers held when not in action. It was his popularity that led to his being made dictator in 342 when a section of the army mutinied. Valerius was mindful

Gallic helmet of the third century BC. Helmets and shields were as much protection as many Gallic warriors carried – indeed some Celtic peoples preferred to fight naked. A higher-ranking Gaul, such as the owner of this elaborately worked helmet, might also have had chain-mail armour, and a bodyguard.

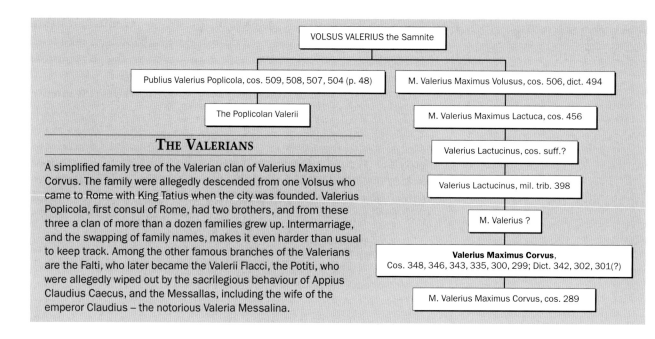

VOLSUS VALERIUS the Samnite

Publius Valerius Poplicola, cos. 509, 508, 507, 504 (p. 48)

The Poplicolan Valerii

M. Valerius Maximus Volusus, cos. 506, dict. 494

M. Valerius Maximus Lactuca, cos. 456

Valerius Lactucinus, cos. suff.?

Valerius Lactucinus, mil. trib. 398

M. Valerius ?

Valerius Maximus Corvus,
Cos. 348, 346, 343, 335, 300, 299; Dict. 342, 302, 301(?)

M. Valerius Maximus Corvus, cos. 289

THE VALERIANS

A simplified family tree of the Valerian clan of Valerius Maximus Corvus. The family were allegedly descended from one Volsus who came to Rome with King Tatius when the city was founded. Valerius Poplicola, first consul of Rome, had two brothers, and from these three a clan of more than a dozen families grew up. Intermarriage, and the swapping of family names, makes it even harder than usual to keep track. Among the other famous branches of the Valerians are the Falti, who later became the Valerii Flacci, the Potiti, who were allegedly wiped out by the sacrilegious behaviour of Appius Claudius Caecus, and the Messallas, including the wife of the emperor Claudius – the notorious Valeria Messalina.

that the mutineers were also Roman citizens, and he brought them back to their loyalty by sheer force of character. He then fought hard to have them pardoned since they had voluntarily returned to their allegiance.

A long and distinguished life

Valerius Corvus was consul six times and dictator twice (possibly three times); he also held 21 other magistracies. Much of his later life was spent on campaign, as Rome was embroiled in a serious war with the Samnites – a hardy mountain people who were to trouble the Romans for centuries. At the age of 70, Valerius was leading his troops against the Marsi, a warrior tribe who were usually Roman allies. After their defeat, the Marsi returned to the Roman side, though in a more subordinate position.

Valerius Corvus retired from public life soon after, though he remained fit and healthy for another 30 years, dying before the First Punic War, sometime after his 100th birthday.

APPIUS CLAUDIUS CAECUS	
Born 350 BC	*Achievements* Built the Appian
Famous ancestors Attus Clausus, Appius the Decemvir	Way; resisted Pyrrhus; first Latin prose writer
Mother Unknown	*Children* Sons: Appius, Publius, Caius,
Father C. Claudius Crassus	Tiberius; daughters: Claudias Prima,
Positions held Censor 312; Consul 307, 296; Dictator year unknown	Secunda, Tertia, Quatra, Quinque *Death* Old age *c.* 271 BC

APPIUS CLAUDIUS CAECUS

Appius Claudius used to say that the Roman people were better trusted with trouble than with leisure. Not because he thought it unpleasant to enjoy a state of tranquillity, but he saw how powerful empires are roused by disturbance to energetic action but slip into idleness with too much peace and quiet.

Valerius Maximus, *De Viris Illustribus* 7.2.1

APPIUS CLAUDIUS STARTED HIS POLITICAL CAREER at the top – as censor in 312. At this early stage of the Republic, the order in which offices were held – the *cursus honorum* – was not yet fixed. Later, the censorship

The Via Appia, the Appian Way, was the first of the great Roman roads which were later to spread across Europe. Like all Roman roads, its principal purpose was military – in this case to move the legions quickly to trouble spots in Campania.

Detail from *Blind Appius Claudius in the Senate*, by Cesare Maccari (1840–1919). Appius Claudius Caecus, who built the Appian Way, was a typical Claudian – high-handed and selfish, yet a man who enriched the state and strengthened its resolve against enemies. Here he is shown being led into the Senate to debate the offer of peace from Pyrrhus, which Appius Claudius strongly opposed.

marked the end of a long and distinguished political career.

A controversial censor

The Claudians never feared controversy, and Appius Claudius' censorship was predictably controversial. The censor had the power to chose who went on the voters' rolls and who should join the senate – or be expelled from it. Appius Claudius bypassed better-qualified candidates in favour of his own supporters, including, the historian Livy indignantly says, the sons of freed slaves. Lower-class voters were distributed among different constituencies, which made it harder for Appius Claudius' opponents to gain a majority in any one of them.

Next, he transferred the custodianship of the ancient cult of Hercules from the Potitian family to public slaves. For relinquishing their sacred trust, however involuntarily, the Potitian clan died out within a generation. And for his sacrilege, the same vengeful god allegedly struck Appius Claudius with blindness, which gave him his distinguishing cognomen (Caecus means 'blind'). If so, Hercules took his time, as Appius was blind only in his old age.

Appius did achieve two feats of construction during his censorship. Roman engineering excelled at building roads and aqueducts, and Appius supervised a major example of each. His aqueduct, the Aqua Appia, brought water to Rome; while his road to Capua, the Via Appia, or the Appian Way, is perhaps the most famous highway of antiquity.

A marble bust of Pyrrhus, king of Epirus in Greece, from Herculaneum. The question of what would have happened if Pyrrhus, a very capable general and one of the successors of Alexander the Great, had managed to conquer Rome is one of the most fascinating 'what-ifs' in ancient history.

As with all Roman magistracies, each censor had a colleague. That colleague, C. Plautius, resigned in disgust at Appius' manipulation of the electoral rolls. By tradition, this meant that Appius should have resigned also. He did not, and neither did he go when the 18 months that were the usual tenure of the censorship had expired. The tribune Sempronius (an ancestor of the Gracchi) tried to arrest him for this, but Appius blocked the move.

Further honours

He finally stood down after four years in office, to become consul soon after. He was consul in 307 and again in 296. In 296 he fought the Samnites, continuing this campaign the next year as a praetor. An indifferent general, he had little faith in his troops, while they had even less in him. He was helped to his only significant victory in these campaigns by the fortunate arrival of his fellow consul Volumnius, who inspired Appius' army with a brilliant speech. Afterwards, Appius remarked sourly that Volumnius, previously a poor speaker, had improved from listening to Appius himself. 'It is a pity', Volumnius responded viciously, 'that you learned nothing about warfare from me.' Nevertheless, the battle was won and Appius vowed and dedicated a temple to the goddess Bellona.

By 280 Appius was old and blind. Yet he still had the pride and stubbornness of a true Claudian. Rome was now fighting Pyrrhus, the king of Epirus who was among the successors to Alexander the Great. Pyrrhus had invaded Italy but Roman resistance was taking a terrible toll on his army. After a particularly bruising battle at Asculum, Pyrrhus commented 'one more victory like that, and I'll be ruined.' (From which comes the term 'a Pyrrhic victory'.) Following a victory at the Battle of Heraclea, Pyrrhus sent an embassy to Rome to negotiate peace. The Romans wavered until old Appius delivered a speech which inspired them to reject the peace and drive Pyrrhus from Italy.

Appius Claudius is one of the first known Roman writers, though none of his works has survived. He wrote some prose (including a book of moral essays) and a legal treatise. Three of his four sons became consuls in their turn.

LUCIUS CORNELIUS SCIPIO SCAPULA	
Born	*Positions held*
c. 337 BC	Consul 298; Censor
Famous ancestors	(?) 280
None	*Achievements*
Mother	Took Aquilonia
Unknown	*Children*
Father	Sons: Lucius
Gnaeus Cornelius	*Death*
Scipio	c. 270 BC

LUCIUS CORNELIUS SCIPIO SCAPULA ('BARBATUS')

It is noticed in the histories that hardly any other general ever appeared in such high spirits while in battle. This was either because of his fearless temperament or because he felt completely confident of final success. It was this same fearlessness and resolution which prevented him from abandoning all idea of fighting when the omens were challenged.

Livy, *History of Rome* 10.42

TOWARDS THE END OF THE FOURTH CENTURY BC, two shameful events occurred in Rome. One disgraced a particular family, and the other the

ROMAN ROADS

Even today, few people in Europe live far from a Roman road. These roads are an enduring testament to the engineering genius of the Romans, and it is not surprising that in the Dark Ages some people believed them to have been built by giants. In one way at least, they were correct.

There was nothing revolutionary in the principles behind Roman roads. They were laid with care, on gravel foundations which allowed the soil beneath the surface to drain, and they were often paved on top with stone flags. Ditches along the sides helped drainage, and Roman roads had a tendency to follow the ridges of river valleys, which had the additional effect of helping to prevent erosion on the slopes. Most of these principles were known to the Greeks, and the Romans picked up others from the Etruscans, who were no mean road-builders themselves.

What distinguishes the great Roman roads is their relationship to the landscape. Most roads, including modern ones, accommodate themselves to the land, curving with its contours and following a line of least resistance to their destination. Roman roads, on the other hand, were straight, often quite unnecessarily so, making as few concessions to the landscape as was humanly possible. This was because the Roman road was not only a means of communication, though it fulfilled this function superbly, it was also a propaganda statement.

Roman roads were one way that the Romans assimilated conquered peoples into the state. In the first place they showed that the Romans did things differently – and better. Secondly, the straight edges of the roads made it easy to divide the land between them into equal-sized plots of land for settlers. This process was called centuriation and it was one of the distinguishing features of Roman settlement.

The roads also had a military purpose. The Appian Way was built in

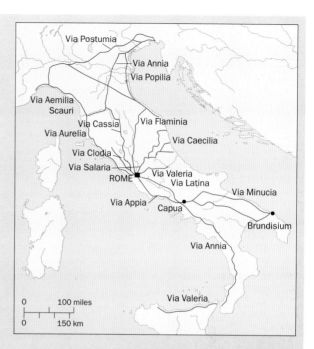

(Right) Map of Roman roads in Republican Italy. Despite the huge expense involved, Roman aristocrats were keen to be associated with these projects, which were often named after them. Also, the work gave employment to hundreds of engineers and labourers who considered the man who commissioned the work as their patron.

(Below right) A stretch of the Via Appia, built in 312 BC by Appius Claudius Caecus.

312 on the initiative of the Roman censor Appius Claudius Caecus (pp. 70–72), making it easy for Roman troops to move between Rome and their new conquest of Capua. Initially 152 miles (211 km) long, his road was later extended to Brundisium, and is still the most famous of Italian roads. Later roads, such as the Via Aemilia, remain as a testament to the great Roman families who inspired their creation.

Monuments were built along the side of the most important roads, and religious rites were performed at milestones. Milestones were another device which the Romans did not invent, but which they applied more methodically than anyone had done before. As a reflection of the military purposes of the roads, the stones marked 1,000 (*mille*) paces of a Roman legionary. The Romans measured a double pace. This is the interval between the first foot leaving the ground to when the second touches it again. The Anglo-Saxons who later came to Britain used the single pace, the yard, and, as they were taller, this accounts for the idiosyncratic 1,760 yards in a British mile.

entire Roman state. The man connected with both in one way or another was Lucius Cornelius Scipio Scapula, also known as Barbatus.

Scipio was a Cornelian – a clan so widespread in Rome that people divided the family into its various branches – the Cinnas, Sullas, Dolabellas and Scipios. The origin of the name Scipio is uncertain. A *scipio* was a small rod of office which distinguished a magistrate. Cornelian was also a type of wood, so a Cornelian magistrate might have acquired the nickname Scipio, and Roman nicknames often had the habit of sticking.

A 'disease' and a disaster

In 331 BC, a strange disease had afflicted the upper classes of Rome. It was generally fatal, and apparently struck at random. Finally a slave girl revealed to the senior statesman of the day, a Quintus Fabius Maximus, the source of the mysterious sickness. She led investigators to a group of women, led by a Cornelia and a Sergia, who were preparing potions. The women claimed that the potions were healthy herbal remedies for their families. If so, the magistrates inquired, would the women object to drinking them? After conferring, the women agreed – a tactic which proved not their innocence but the opposite, as it was a means of escaping justice through suicide. It turned out the women had chosen this means of winnowing the ranks of rival families. The poisonings were the first episode of this type in Rome, and since Cornelia had been the Cornelian matriarch, the family reputation suffered accordingly.

Ten years later, in 321, a far more disastrous episode affected the nation. The second war against the Samnites had been dragging on, with neither side able to inflict a decisive blow. But then the Samnites trapped an entire Roman army at the Caudine Forks, south of Rome between Capua and Beneventum. The Romans had to submit to a humiliating peace, and their army passed under the yoke – a ritual indicating total submission, with each unarmed soldier having to bow under a frame constructed for the purpose, while the victorious enemy jeered at them. The Romans later repudiated the peace using some specious arguments, and war resumed. The Samnites were bitter and uncompromising enemies, and the Roman disgrace was unavenged in the battles which followed.

Scipio became consul in 298. He won a victory against the Etruscans, allies of the Samnites, outside Volaterrae, but was unable to take the city, and plundered the countryside instead. In later years he fought the Samnites, campaigning with distinction under the command of Fabius.

Victory in battle

Scipio's major contribution in the third Samnite war came outside the city of Aquilonia. The Samnites had an élite corps called the Linen Legion, which took its name from a huge linen tent into which each man selected for the legion was conducted. The soldier swore an oath that he would fight to the last, and kill any of his colleagues who did not show the same spirit. The legion contained the best fighters in the Samnite nation, and had a formidable reputation.

Samnite warriors from a fourth-century BC wallpainting in the Tomb of the Warriors, Paestum. The Romans fought many wars against the Samnites, and later a type of gladiator in the Roman arena was called 'Samnite' in recognition of this people's prowess in battle.

Entrance to the Tomb of the Scipios, Rome. At the beginning of the second century BC, the Romans were returning to their earlier practice of burying rather than cremating their dead, which is why Lucius Cornelius Scipio was the first of his line to be buried in this tomb.

The sarcophagus of Lucius Cornelius Scipio Barbatus. A rough translation of his epitaph reads: 'Lucius Cornelius Scipio Barbatus, son of Gnaeus, a valiant and wise man, whose fine body matched his great bravery. Aedile, consul and censor to the Romans; he took Taurasia and Cisauna, in fact Samnium; he subdued Lucania and brought hostages from there.'

When the Romans learned that this force was opposing them at Aquilonia, they were eager to meet it in battle and so clear the disgrace that had hung over the army for a generation. This eagerness spread to the keepers of the sacred chickens, who reported that the omens for the coming battle could not be better. However, the general, Gaius Papirius, heard rumours that this report was fabricated and he ordered one of the men who had given it to be brought to the front of the battle line. The false prophet was promptly transfixed by a javelin.

This convinced the Romans that their gods were watching; they fell on the Samnites and broke them after a bitter battle. Lucius Scipio was in command of the left wing, and he pursued the fleeing Samnites back to Aquilonia. Seeing an opportunity to capture the city, which had opened its gates to admit the retreating soldiers, he ordered his men to charge.

The men were reluctant – there were not many of them, and it was a large city. But Scipio himself formed the leading contingent into a *testudo* and led it against the walls. A *testudo* was a tight formation of soldiers all holding their shields so that they overlapped forming an impenetrable barrier; the men in the middle held their shields above their heads, so the formation resembled a tortoise – *testudo* in Latin.

An offer to Jupiter

In times of crisis, Roman generals vowed to build temples to the gods should things work out well. Scipio was trying to persuade his men that the charge was not seriously dangerous, so the bemused soldiers heard him promising Jupiter that if the day turned out successfully, he would offer a cupful of honey and wine before he had a drink for himself.

Evidently the god was pleased with the offer, for the Romans stormed the gates. The rest of the consular army followed and the city was taken.

In the battle the Samnites lost over 20,000 men, with a further 3,500 or so taken prisoner.

We know slightly more about Lucius Cornelius Scipio Scapula than about earlier members of his family because his mausoleum became the family tomb. His sarcophagus, the oldest in the tomb, is inscribed with a verse about his early campaigns in Etruria. With a certain bombast it says he 'subdued Lucania'. Later, the Scipios were to surpass the Valerians, and even the Fabians, as Rome's greatest generals.

Marcus Atilius Regulus
(*c.* 310–*c.* 250 BC)

Gnaeus Cornelius Scipio Asina
(*c.* 310–*c.* 245 BC)

Publius Appius Claudius
Pulcher
(*c.* 288–247 BC)

Gaius Lutatius Catulus
(*c.* 291–*c.* 220 BC)

Gaius Flaminius
(*c.* 265–217 BC)

Publius Cornelius Scipio
(*c.* 260–211 BC)

Quintus Fabius Maximus
Verrucosus
(275–203 BC)

Claudius Marcellus
(*c.* 265–208 BC)

Publius Cornelius Scipio
Africanus
(236–185 BC)

Titus Quinctius Flamininus
(*c.* 229–174 BC)

Marcus Porcius Cato
(237–149 BC)

Aemilius Paullus
(229–160 BC)

Servius Sulpicius Galba
(*c.* 190–136 BC)

Scipio Aemilianus
(*c.* 184–129 BC)

Tiberius Sempronius Gracchus
(*c.* 210–*c.* 150 BC)

Gnaeus Servilius Caepio
(*c.* 181–112 BC)

Tiberius Gracchus
(*c.* 163–133 BC)

Gaius Gracchus
(*c.* 153–121 BC)

Marcus Aemilius Scaurus
(*c.* 163–89 BC)

Quintus Caecilius Metellus
Numidicus
(*c.* 150–91 BC)

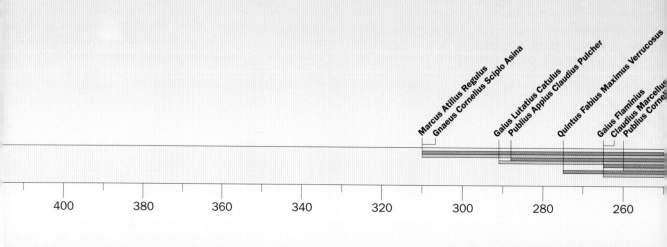

400   380   360   340   320   300   280   260

Marcus Atilius Regulus

Claudius Marcellus

Scipio Africanus

Titus Quinctius Flamininus

ROMANS OF THE MID-REPUBLIC
264–100 BC

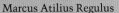

ROME AND CARTHAGE FOUGHT each other to exhaustion during the First Punic War, yet a generation after her victory, Rome was fighting against a renascent Carthage, led by Hannibal, perhaps the finest tactician in antiquity. Rome's final victory came after sixteen years of war, and cost hundreds of thousands of lives. Some of Rome's greatest families were almost wiped out, and whole tracts of countryside were devastated.

Yet as the war with Carthage ended, Rome promptly embarked on the great overseas adventures that were to push her dominion across the Mediterranean. In Greece the Romans generally fought with distinction and conducted themselves with honour. In Spain they displayed savagery, venality and incompetence in equal measure.

Victory encouraged arrogance, and the wealth flowing from Rome's new conquests undermined the famous probity of the Roman élite. Rome's government urgently needed overhauling to cope with the new circumstances, yet vested interests were set resolutely against change.

The Republic was at the height of its glory. Rome was supreme from Gibraltar to the Hellespont, and historians such as Polybius praised the statesmanship which kept the constitution in balance. But the first fatal flaws were already evident, and Rome's great success story was about to go dreadfully wrong.

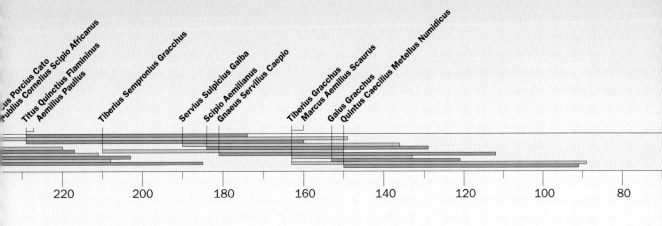

Marcus Atilius Regulus
(*c.* 310–*c.* 250 BC)

Gnaeus Cornelius Scipio Asina
(*c.* 310–*c.* 245 BC)

Publius Appius Claudius Pulcher
(*c.* 288–247 BC)

Gaius Lutatius Catulus
(*c.* 291–*c.* 220 BC)

The story of Regulus came to typify the unflinching self-sacrifice expected of a Roman aristocrat: one of the interesting features of the Roman aristocracy of the third century BC is the degree to which they seemed genuinely to put country above personal interest.

MARCUS ATILIUS REGULUS	
Born c. 310 BC	*Achievements* Victory against Carthaginians in First Punic War
Famous ancestors None	
Mother Unknown	*Children* Son: M. Atilius Regulus
Father Unknown	*Death* In prison c. 250 BC
Positions held Consul 267, 256	

MARCUS ATILIUS REGULUS

'I know, to be sure, that manifest destruction awaits me, for it is impossible to keep the Carthaginians from learning the advice I have given; but even so, I esteem the public advantage above my own safety. If any one shall say, "Why, then, do you not run away, or stay here?" he shall be told that I have sworn to them to return, and I will not transgress my oaths, not even when they have been given to enemies. My reasons for this attitude are various, but the principal one is that if I abide by my oath, I alone shall suffer disaster, but if I break it, the whole city will be involved.'

Speech of Regulus, quoted by Zonaras

THE STORY OF REGULUS is one of the most inspiring Roman legends. It is also among the least probable.

The legend

According to the story, Regulus was consul during the First Punic War against the Carthaginians. While campaigning in North Africa he was captured by the enemy and his army destroyed. Believing they had cowed

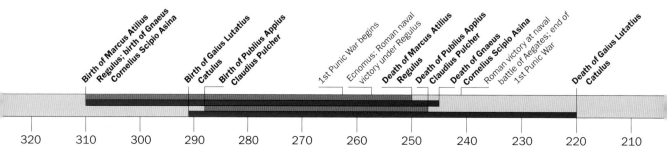

Birth of Marcus Atilius Regulus; birth of Gnaeus Cornelius Scipio Asina

Birth of Gaius Lutatius Catulus

Birth of Publius Appius Claudius Pulcher

1st Punic War begins

Ecnomus: Roman naval victory under Regulus

Death of Marcus Atilius Regulus

Death of Publius Appius Claudius Pulcher

Death of Gnaeus Cornelius Scipio Asina

Roman victory at naval battle of Aegates; end of 1st Punic War

Death of Gaius Lutatius Catulus

320 310 300 290 280 270 260 250 240 230 220 210

The Departure of Regulus for Carthage, by Jacques-Augustin Pajou (1793). Though this event is probably fictional, there is no doubt that the Carthaginians did use torture, even crucifying their own unsuccessful generals.

True coins only began to appear in the late fourth century, probably as a result of Roman interaction with Greek cities. Above is a relief of a coin-striker at work, below is the Santa Marinella Treasure, fourth–third century BC.

the Romans, the Carthaginians sent Regulus back to Rome under two conditions. First, Regulus had to argue in favour of peace on Carthaginian terms. Second, if the terms were not accepted, Regulus would return to Carthage.

The Romans were as demoralized as the Carthaginians had supposed. The senate was inclined to accept the Carthaginian terms, although this represented a major Roman setback. Regulus, however, delivered a stirring speech against the proposed treaty. Inspired by his oratory and example, the Romans redoubled their efforts and eventually won the war. But Regulus paid a terrible price. True to his word, he returned to Carthage, and the Carthaginians brutally tortured him to death.

This is one of the most celebrated episodes in Roman history – it is also mostly Roman propaganda.

The real Regulus

Regulus did exist. He was of the family Atilius – distinguished enough, but not among the great families of Rome. For this information we have to thank Polybius, the earliest historian of Rome whose work still survives and whose chronicles now begin to move Roman history from the shadows of legend into the light of fact (p. 12). We also have the Capitoline *Fasti*, which tell us that an ancestor of Regulus was consul in 335 BC.

In 267 Rome was consolidating its grip on the Italian peninsula. Regulus, then in his first consulship, defeated the Sabellian tribe and captured the port of Brundisium (Brindisi). Carthage had long been the dominant regional power in the western Mediterranean, and it resented the growing strength of Rome. In 264 war was declared: the Romans were in need of experienced generals, and in 256 Regulus was consul again.

THE EARLY ROMAN ARMY

The army that faced the Carthaginians was rather different from the armies of the early Roman Empire. Above all, it differed in being a citizen army of non-professional soldiers. Instead of making a career in the army, most of those who served had been called up by the levy, and looked forward to retiring to their family farms, preferably with some booty picked up in the wars.

The aristocracy served in the cavalry. While prestigious, at this time cavalry was not a particularly effective arm of warfare. Stirrups were unknown, so the cavalryman had to hold on with his thighs, making weapon play difficult. Furthermore, even the most determined cavalry could not break a line of formed infantry, since the horses sensibly refused to hurl themselves on to the thicket of spears facing them. Cavalry were best against scattered, disorganized or light troops.

The Roman legions were none of these things. They were mostly close-formation, heavy infantry, and their organization was second to none. The soldiers of Regulus did not wear the famous 'lobster-plate' armour of the Imperial legions (the *lorica segmentata*), but chain mail (*lorica hamata*). Their helmets were higher and steeper, since they were designed to deflect the downward swing of a Gallic broadsword on to the wearer's well-padded shoulders. The Roman soldier's first line of defence was an oval shield, and he used a heavy javelin (*pilum*) as his main throwing weapon.

In battle the legions were arranged in quincunx formation, the centuries arranged rather like the black squares on a chess board. At the front were the *hastati*, young men in their first campaign and therefore full of energy with their valour untempered by experience. Behind them were the more seasoned *principes* and in the third line the veteran *triarii*. Unlike the first two ranks, the *triarii* were armed with long spears. They did not take part in the early engagements, and if the front two ranks were beaten back in the fighting, the *triarii* provided a hedge of spears for the others to rally behind. Long after they had ceased to exist as a unit in the Roman army, the expression 'it's come to the *triarii*' was used to describe a desperate situation.

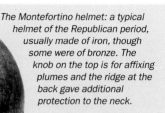

The Montefortino helmet: a typical helmet of the Republican period, usually made of iron, though some were of bronze. The knob on the top is for affixing plumes and the ridge at the back gave additional protection to the neck.

For light troops and skirmishers, the Romans relied on their allies, the *auxilia*. As a part of each ally's settlement with the Roman authorities, it was agreed how many troops, and what type, they would contribute to the Roman forces. Some of the poorer communities furnished slingers or archers, while the more wealthy cities provided soldiers armed and equipped much as the Roman legions were themselves. These allies made up between a third and a half of the army.

An army commanded by a consul was usually two legions strong, that is about 16,000 men with the *auxilia*. These, together with their supplies and camp followers, presented the general with a formidable logistical problem, and keeping an army in the field was usually only possible in the summer months.

(Left) Legionaries on the Altar of Domitius Ahenobarbus. They have plumes, chain-mail armour and shields with a long central boss, all features of Roman army equipment from the Punic wars to the time of Caesar.

(Right) Figurine of a soldier carrying the eagle standard into battle. While the eagle was the most famous of the Roman army symbols, during the Republic a number of other devices were also used.

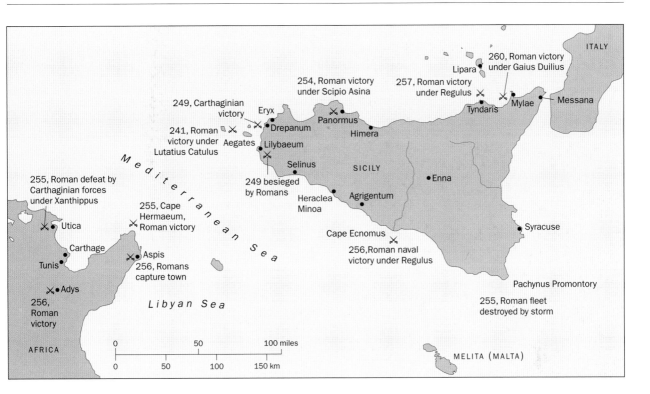

Map showing the major sites in Sicily and North Africa and battles of the First Punic War. The battles in Africa mark the campaigns of Regulus, and those in Sicily were Roman assaults on Carthaginian positions. It can be seen that there were no major clashes in the heartland of Sicily, confirming that this war was unique in being fought by Rome as a mainly naval campaign.

The Romans decided to bring the war to the Carthaginians. They prepared an invasion force of 140,000 men and 330 warships under Regulus and his fellow consul, Manlius Vulso Longus. The Carthaginians came to meet them, confident of victory – though they had the same number of ships, theirs were faster and better manned.

The *corvus*

The two fleets met off Sicily at Ecnomus. The Romans, with their ships equipped with a secret weapon, the *corvus* (the 'raven': see *The Romans at Sea* p. 88), were victorious and sailed on to Africa. Regulus immediately attacked and captured the city of Aspis before Carthaginian reinforcements could arrive.

Longus was recalled to Rome with the fleet, while Regulus continued campaigning in Africa, defeating Carthaginian reinforcements for Aspis at a place called Adys. The Carthaginians fell back while the Romans went on to take Tunis, plundering the countryside.

Final defeat

Regulus' career had so far been a series of unbroken successes, and he wanted to finish his consular year with yet another. He invited the Carthaginians to surrender, and his terms were harsh. The Carthaginians were to release all Roman prisoners while ransoming their own. They would pay an indemnity and be deprived of all their ships save one. To add insult to injury, the Carthaginians had to agree to build 50 ships for the Romans at any time that the Romans needed them.

The terms were indignantly rejected. The Carthaginians now realized that their commanders were no match for the more seasoned Roman general and they hired a Spartan mercenary called Xanthippus, who promptly brought into play two neglected strengths of the Carthaginian army: cavalry and elephants. Xanthippus crushed the Romans in battle in 255, and Regulus and the remnants of his army who did not manage to escape were captured. A Roman fleet was sent to rescue those of Regulus' soldiers who had fled; on the way back to Italy 184 of 264 ships were wrecked in a storm off Sicily and thousands of men died. Polybius describes this as the greatest Roman naval disaster.

For Polybius, the story ends there. There is no mention of a heroic return or self-sacrifice. Polybius implies that Regulus died of natural causes in captivity. The historian Diodorus Siculus adds the information that the wife of Regulus tortured two Punic prisoners to death to revenge her husband.

The legend of Regulus was perhaps invented to explain this woman's barbaric behaviour. In the war, dark and bloody deeds were done by both sides, but with Regulus the Carthaginians seem to have been more sinned against than sinning.

GNAEUS CORNELIUS SCIPIO	
Born	*Positions held*
c. 310 BC	Consul 260, 254;
Famous ancestors	Proconsul 253
Scipio Barbatus	*Achievements*
(uncle?)	Triumphator
Mother	*Children*
Unknown	Son: Publius
Father	*Death*
Unknown	c. 245 BC

A silver denarius of Q. Nasidius, 38–36 BC, depicting a naval battle between four galleys, with rostra projecting below their prows. Rome's main enemy at sea was not the Carthaginians but the weather, and they lost many more ships in storms than in battle.

GNAEUS CORNELIUS SCIPIO ASINA

Who would have believed that he would pass from the consulship to Carthaginian chains? Again who would have thought that he would pass from being a Carthaginian captive to the emblems of highest command? All the same, from consul, he became prisoner, and from prisoner, consul.

Valerius Maximus, *De Viris Illustribus* 6.9.11

ASINA'S CAREER SPANS THAT OF REGULUS. The first events related here took place at the beginning of the Punic War, and those at the end of the narrative came after the death of Regulus.

Rome at sea

Before the first Carthaginian war, the Romans knew little of naval warfare, having had no need of it while they expanded along the Italian peninsula. Now they faced an enemy from the other side of the Mediterranean and the focus of the conflict was Sicily – an island.

Fortune favoured the Romans. A Carthaginian warship harrying the crossing of Roman troops to Sicily became stranded on a lee shore. This handed the Romans a prize piece of Carthaginian naval technology, and they built a fleet of ships modelled on their capture. The commander of the fleet was one of the consuls of 260 – a Cornelius from a branch of that clan fast developing a military reputation, the Scipios.

Though Scipio's fleet was not yet ready, he began training the crews immediately. The sailors sat on benches on dry land and practised rowing in the air while their ships were assembled in the dockyards behind them. The training was necessary, for the Romans had no experience of anything larger than a trireme, which has three banks of oars with one rower to each oar, whereas many of the new ships were quinqueremes, with five rowers manning the oars (hence the name – *quinque* means 'five' and *remus* means 'oar').

Once fully equipped, the new fleet set sail for Sicily. Scipio took an advance party of 17 ships to Messana (Messina) to arrange the logistics – a fleet of some 200 ships and several thousand men required a huge amount of material to keep it operational.

Seizing an opportunity

While Scipio was at Messana, word came to him that the town of Lipara (modern Lipari), on the island of the same name, was lightly garrisoned, and that garrison might be persuaded to switch its allegiance. Lipara was in the Aeolian islands, just to the north of Sicily, and within the Carthaginian sphere of influence.

Scipio swiftly took his 17 ships to capture Lipara, where he found conditions as he had been informed. What he had not been told was that the main Carthaginian fleet of some 150 ships was in the area, at their base at Panormus on the north coast of Sicily. The admiral was called Hannibal (a fairly common Carthaginian name).

Hannibal sent 20 ships, commanded by one Boödes, to find out what Scipio was planning. These ships, whether by luck or design, arrived during the night, so that the Romans woke to find the enemy blocking the harbour. The hastily trained crews panicked and collapsed without resistance. Some sailors beached their ships and escaped on to the island, but many were captured – among them Scipio, whom the historian Polybius says was as panic-stricken as his men.

A late – face-saving – tradition holds that Scipio was betrayed while negotiating with Boödes. This is improbable, not least because this ill-advised military escapade gained Scipio his sobriquet of 'the ass'. To make it worse, the Romans chose *asina* – the feminine form rather than the masculine *asinus*.

Scipio would surely have taken a certain gloomy satisfaction at what happened next – Hannibal, curious as to where the rest of the Roman forces were, went up the coast with 50 ships. As he rounded a headland, he found the Roman fleet in its entirety. He lost most of his ships and almost his life.

Return from disgrace

Asina's family did not suffer from his fall. The consul for the next year was also a Scipio – the son of Scipio Scapula (p. 72). At some point in the following years the Carthaginians exchanged or ransomed Scipio Asina, perhaps hoping that he would repeat his earlier exploits. And despite his unfortunate reputation, Asina again became consul in 254, following the destruction of the fleet sent to rescue the survivors of Regulus' expedition to Africa, when hundreds of ships and thousands of men were lost.

A nineteenth-century reconstruction of the triumphal column of Gaius Duilius in the forum, with prows of captured Carthaginian ships. Gaius Duilius took over as commander when Scipio Asina was captured, and is credited with the invention of the *corvus*, which helped in his naval victory at Mylae in 260 BC.

The Romans, with that dogged determination which was one of their most frightening, and perhaps greatest, qualities, promptly built another 220 ships, which they placed in the hands of Asina and his fellow consul. Presumably they believed that Asina had something to prove.

Prove it he did. He surrounded the Sicilian city of Panormus, disembarked his soldiers, and conducted a model siege operation. He quickly destroyed one of the towers of the city and took the part called the New Town. With its defences irreparably breached, Panormus surrendered. Scipio regained his pride but did not lose his nickname. Asina he remained for the rest of his life – and for the two millennia after that.

PUBLIUS APPIUS CLAUDIUS PULCHER

I don't know whether Appius Claudius was a greater affront to religion or his country, seeing that he neglected the time-honoured practices of the former, and lost a fine fleet for the latter.

Valerius Maximus, *De Viris Illustribus* 8.1.6

THE ROMAN NAVY DID SURPRISINGLY WELL against the Carthaginians, winning as many battles as they lost. But they took massive casualties, and lost entire fleets simply through being bad sailors.

Bad admirals

It was the consul Marcus Aemilius Paullus who was responsible for probably the greatest naval disaster in antiquity by taking his fleet, which was carrying the remnants of Regulus's army from North Africa – against expert advice – past a lee shore off Sicily while a storm was brewing. Scipio Asina's mishaps have also already been recorded, but yet greater naval incompetence was achieved by Publius Appius Claudius Pulcher.

Publius was the son of one of the greatest Claudians – Appius Claudius Caecus, 'the Blind', whose prodigious family probably included three sons and five daughters. This Appius was the second son, and the first with the cognomen 'Pulcher', meaning 'good-looking'.

Like all Claudians, Publius was destined from birth for high office. Both his brothers became consuls, as did Publius in 249, when the war with Carthage was focused on the Roman siege of the Carthaginian naval base at Lilybaeum. Casualties in this siege left Publius in command of a fleet which was undermanned and not completely seaworthy.

Publius had some 40,000 men under his command. He set out for battle by night, intending to attack the enemy at dawn in the harbour at Drepanum (Trapani) before they discovered that the Roman fleet had been reinforced. It was typical of Publius that instead of leading from the front, he put his flagship at the rear to keep an eye on any laggards.

Bad omens

The Romans invariably consulted the gods before a battle – in this case, they used sacred chickens. If the birds ate enthusiastically, the gods were

PUBLIUS APPIUS CLAUDIUS PULCHER	
Born	*Positions held*
c. 288 BC	Consul 249
Famous ancestors	*Achievements*
Appius Claudius	Lost Roman fleet
the Decemvir	*Children*
Mother	Sons: Appius
Unknown	Claudius (cos.
Father	212)
Appius Claudius	*Death*
Caecus	Probably suicide
	c. 247 BC

Drepanum, modern Trapani, scene of one of Rome's more humiliating naval encounters with the Carthaginians. As this photograph shows, Trapani is still a thriving port, though the harbour where the Romans were defeated has almost vanished with changes in the coastline.

on their side; but in fact the birds refused to eat at all. But Publius did not intend his naval strategy to be dictated by chickens. Hearing that they would not eat, he snapped 'Well, let them drink!' and had the unfortunate birds thrown overboard, becoming the first casualties of the battle.

The Carthaginians had a competent admiral called Adherbal. As soon as he heard that the Romans were approaching, he took his ships out to sea. Publius, at the rear of the Roman fleet, was unaware of this. So the Roman fleet kept pouring into the harbour even as their first ships were already trying to get out again after the enemy. There were collisions, snapped oars, and general confusion.

The situation got worse: with the Romans backed against the shore without room to manoeuvre the Carthaginians attacked from the open sea. A battle begun in confusion was set to end in disaster. As a modern naval expert has remarked 'those chickens knew their consul'.

The price of incompetence

The Romans lost 93 ships out of 120. Publius survived, and it surprised no one that he was recalled to Rome. He was uncowed by the disaster, though his fellow citizens felt that it was severe enough to require a dictator to take charge in Rome. With true Claudian arrogance, Publius attempted to use his consular position to force the Romans to appoint one Claudius Glicia, the son of one of his former slaves.

The outraged people brought Publius to trial for *perduellio* – an elastic term with overtones of sacrilege, but which was basically a charge of treason by incompetence. Though the death penalty was a possibility, it is likely that Publius got off with a huge fine, although others claim that the trial was postponed because of a sudden thunderstorm. (As followers of Jupiter the thunderer, the Romans were very superstitious about thunder.)

Before the trial could resume (or soon after it), Publius was dead. Quite possibly he took his own life. He left a posthumous footnote in Roman history thanks to his sister Claudia. She, returning home from the games some years later and finding it slow going because of the crowds, remarked loudly that it was a pity that her brother Publius was not alive to lose another fleet, since the Roman plebs was evidently in need of further culling.

This crass statement did not pass unpunished, and Claudia too picked up a heavy fine from the magistrates.

GAIUS LUTATIUS CATULUS

GAIUS LUTATIUS CATULUS	
Born	*Achievements*
c. 291 BC	Triumphator; ended
Famous ancestors	First Punic War
None	*Children*
Mother	Son: Lutatius
Unknown	Catulus (cos. 220)
Father	*Death*
Unknown	c. 220 BC
Positions held	
Consul 242	

Lutatius never lost sight of the main objective of his expedition – that it was only by victory at sea that the war could be decided. So he wasted no time, and kept his men active. The crews were rehearsed and drilled every day in the manoeuvres they would need in battle. Lutatius also paid great attention to the training and discipline of his sailors. By these methods he raised them in a short time to the conditions of athletes trained for a contest.

Polybius, *The Rise of Rome* 1.59

IN THE YEAR 242 THE LUTATIAN CLAN achieved the consulship for the first time with Gaius Lutatius Catulus. According to one interpretation, 'Catulus' has the same root as the English word 'cautious', suggesting wisdom, care and shrewdness. If this is so, this Catulus certainly suited his description.

A new fleet

In 242 the war with Carthage was in its 22nd year. After the defeat of Publius Appius Claudius at sea, the Romans had doggedly raised another fleet, only to have it once more dashed to pieces in a storm. Even the indomitable Roman spirit was daunted by such repeated massive losses. The Romans had abandoned the sea to Carthage and concentrated on the land war in Sicily.

But by 242 they were ready to try the sea again. Catulus must have advocated this, for as consul he would command the fleet. Indeed, he may have succeeded in getting elected because other possible candidates decided to wait for another year rather than risk a watery grave. It is interesting to note that the other consul, Albinus, was a priest of Mars, and as such forbidden to leave the city. Catulus too had problems connected with religion – he had intended to consult the oracle at Praeneste concerning his naval campaign, but as consul of Rome he was allowed to deal only with the gods of the city.

The new fleet had been funded by Rome's aristocrats from their own resources, as the treasury lacked money. Catulus' colleague in command was the senior praetor for the year, a Falto of the Valerian clan. The two men proceeded rapidly to Sicily, where the Romans were besieging the

Denarius of C. Considinus Nonianus, *c.* 63–62 BC, thought to show the Temple of Venus Erycina at Eryx, Sicily. The temple was an important religious shrine and was excavated in the 1930s. The town, near the mountain of the same name, was destroyed by Carthage during the First Punic War.

DEATH AND THE ROMANS

As in all ancient societies, death was something that the Romans associated more with the young than the old. The average adult Roman aged between 40 and 60 was about as likely to die as someone of the same age in the twentieth century – but these Romans had survived a terrifying array of illnesses and afflictions which killed off a high percentage of babies and young children. It has been estimated that a Roman woman needed to bear six children simply for the population replacement rate to remain stable.

Consequently, while dead infants were often disposed of with what we would regard as brutal callousness,

Relief depicting a Roman funeral procession on a sarcophagus from Amiternum, first century BC. Note that the body is reclining on cushions as though at a banquet, as was the usual Roman custom.

adult funerals were relatively rare events, carried out with due solemnity and reverence. Death itself brought a sort of blemish on the household, which had to be cleansed with certain rites and purifications.

The actual disposal of the body would take place about a week after death. In the early Republic, inhumation (burying the body) was the usual practice, but by the late Republic this had been replaced by cremation. The Cornelians, conservative in many ways, were among the last to abandon inhumation in 78 BC.

It is not certain at what point it became common for eulogies of the dead to be spoken at funerals, but it was certainly the practice by the late Republic. (The lack of archaeological evidence for burials in the Republican period in Rome suggests that most funerals were simple, straightforward affairs.) After the eulogies had been spoken – usually by the senior member of the family – the cortège would proceed to the city gates.

Burial within the city walls was a privilege rarely granted. Most tombs were outside the city, lining the roads leading in. Though several generations might be deposited in a single tomb, it has been truly said that travellers generally had to pass through a city of the dead before they reached that of the living.

The deceased would be accompanied on their last journey by actors wearing the funeral masks of distinguished ancestors, and dressed in their magisterial robes. If the dead person had been of particular distinction, the senate would permit his family to take a wax mask of him, which would thereafter be displayed in the atrium of the family house as an example to future generations.

The unburied dead were believed to be restless, and to haunt and disturb the living. The properly interred, on the other hand, provided a spiritual source of strength for individuals and the city as a whole.

only three parts of the island still under Carthaginian control – Drepanum, Lilybaeum and fortifications on Mt Eryx, the latter under the command of the highly capable Hamilcar Barca. The Carthaginians were being supplied through their ports and so Catulus took immediate steps to close these off. He was involved in the fighting personally, and took a severe wound in the thigh.

The Romans at Sea

The Romans were not a naturally seafaring people – they took to the sea only when forced to do so. In antiquity sea travel was a risky business. Sudden squalls brought tragedy to many craft, for the Mediterranean is famously changeable. In fact the poet Horace compares a temper tantrum of the girl Pyrrha to a storm in the Adriatic, fierce one moment, gone the next. Horace, like many Romans, had little time for 'ungodly ships'.

Nevertheless, sea travel was sometimes inescapable. It took five days to go by ship from Italy to Spain with a favourable wind, yet more than a month by land. Africa was unreachable almost any other way, yet it was just two days sailing away. With the high cost of land travel, much commerce of the ancient world was by sea, and from relatively early in its history, Rome was dependent on grain imported from Sicily and, later, from Egypt.

Without sophisticated navigational tools, sailors were reluctant to venture far out to sea, and many smaller merchant fleets beached their ships at night. Pirates were another problem – both Clodius (pp. 198–99) and Julius Caesar were captured by pirates; and they were far from being alone in this. Even a century later, the philosopher Seneca asks 'if I am captured by pirates, and ransomed by an unworthy man, ought I yet be grateful to him?'

In naval warfare, the battle was principally between the Romans and the sea, with the sea generally coming off better. When a Roman fleet did manage to stay afloat long enough to encounter the enemy, the navy generally acquitted itself well. This was partly because the Romans regarded their vessels as floating fighting platforms, and the most vital skill of an admiral in battle was to bring his ship to a position where the soldiers on board could engage with the enemy.

During the first Carthaginian war, the Romans took this measure to a logical extreme by mounting a heavy spiked plank, the *corvus* ('raven') on their ships. This impaled the enemy vessel, which could not disengage, and provided a bridge for the troops to cross. The combination of naïve seamanship and ships made top-heavy by the *corvus* caused such mayhem, however, that the idea had to be abandoned, though it was a success when used in battle.

Incompetent sailing caused the loss of several

Republican coin of a ship: the rowers sitting at the benches were probably not the slaves of popular imagination – in antiquity most ships were rowed by free men.

hundred ships and the death of thousands of men in a series of shipwrecks that wiped out whole fleets. If the figures are accurate, Roman naval casualties in the first Carthaginian war far outnumber those of any naval campaign since, including those of the Second World War and the Napoleonic wars.

With Carthage's final defeat, the Romans gladly abandoned the sea, leaving it to client states such as the Rhodians to police. When the Rhodian fleet fell foul of Roman politics, it was destroyed, releasing swarms of pirates on marine trade. Eventually the necessity of sea power forced the Romans to take to the sea again in the late Republic. Despite losing several fleets to the weather and Sextus Pompey, Octavian finally won the empire through the last great sea battle of the Republic, at Actium in 31 BC. At the end of the campaign, Octavian had some 700 warships, few of which were ever to see action again.

An illustration of the corvus *in action. Although successful in combat, the* corvus *had to be abandoned as it made the ships carrying it too unstable in bad weather.*

Warships in a wallpainting from Pompeii. Sea battles were rare after the First Punic War and non-existent after the Battle of Actium in 31 BC, but such battles continued to have a fascination for the Roman public.

Hostilities died down while Catulus recovered. His wound prevented activities at sea and Catulus refused to allow his sailors to be frittered away in siege actions on land. Instead, Catulus threw his energies into honing his men's skill in naval warfare. His intention was that when they met the Carthaginians again, the Romans would be their equals in skill. In this, as it happened, he was wrong – they were better.

The Carthaginian response

News of the resurgent Roman fleet came as a thunderbolt to Carthage. Believing the war at sea to be won, they had laid off crews and decommissioned ships which they could no longer afford. Now, they stretched their resources to match the Roman effort and raised a new fleet.

Under the general Hanno the fleet set sail for Sicily to re-supply the besieged troops there. Hanno intended to slip past the Romans, unload his supplies, and strengthen his raw recruits with Hamilcar Barca's veteran marines. But Catulus, unlike Claudius, had a good intelligence service, and he intercepted the fleet at Aegates (Aegusa), near Lilybaeum on 10 March, 241. There was a heavy sea, and this put Catulus in a dilemma. The Carthaginians intended to run past the Romans under sail and rendezvous with Hamilcar. If Catulus waited, he would fight a reinforced enemy with lightened ships and veteran troops on board. But if he attacked now, his fleet would be caught in a strong wind off a hostile shore.

Ending the war

In the end, he put his faith in his crews and ordered the fleet into battle. Events totally justified his decision. The Romans coped with the challenge of the elements far better than the Carthaginians coped with the challenge of the Romans. The Carthaginian ships were heavily loaded, undermanned and crewed by raw recruits who had just completed a long crossing. The Romans sank 50 ships and captured another 70. Probably the only disappointment for Catulus was that, being incapacitated by his wound, he had to allow Valerius Falto to command the ships at sea.

This last defeat proved one too many for the Carthaginians. They crucified Hanno, the unsuccessful admiral, and sent ambassadors to Catulus to arrange peace terms. Unlike Regulus before him, Catulus did not miss this opportunity to bring the war to a close. The terms he imposed were made slightly more severe by a commission from Rome, but Catulus had the honour of taking the Carthaginian surrender. The war was over.

Back in Rome, there was an unsightly quarrel with Valerius Falto, who claimed the victory because he had commanded the fleet in the battle. Catulus had the better claim, as he was the overall commander and the victory was won by his careful preparation. But the name of Valerius had its own arguments, and in the end both admirals were granted a triumph. It was a small price to pay for finally having a fleet that could beat both the Carthaginians and the weather.

A Carthaginian votive stela carved with the prow of a Carthaginian ship. The Carthaginians were great sea traders and competent sailors, but the First Punic War was ended when the Roman fleet finally defeated the Carthaginians in the naval battle at Aegates. Stelae (a type of stone pillar) were a common feature of the ancient world and were used to mark graves, land boundaries or to carry public declarations such as decrees.

Gaius Flaminius
(c. 265–217 BC)

Publius Cornelius Scipio
(c. 260–211 BC)

Quintus Fabius Maximus Verrucosus
(275–203 BC)

Claudius Marcellus
(c. 265–208 BC)

Claudius Marcellus belonged to a generation of Romans whose entire lives were spent in the struggle against Carthage – this profoundly changed the Roman aristocracy, and the Roman state.

GAIUS FLAMINIUS	
Born c. 265 BC	*Achievements* Triumphator; built
Famous ancestors None	Via Flaminia and Circus Flaminius
Mother Unknown	*Wife* Unknown
Father C. Flaminius	*Children* Son: Gaius
Positions held Tribune 232; Praetor 227; Consul 223, 217; Censor 220	Flaminius (cos. 187) *Death* Killed at Battle of Lake Trasimene 217 BC

GAIUS FLAMINIUS

A few days after Flaminius took office, he was sacrificing a calf. The animal, after being struck with the knife, escaped from the hands of those officiating, and splattered those standing around with blood. There was consternation everywhere ... most people took the incident as a sign of coming disaster.

Livy, *History of Rome* 21.63

ACCORDING TO ROMAN HISTORIANS, Gaius Flaminius was a demagogue of an insignificant family who led a Roman army to a massive and unnecessary defeat. Modern opinion is more favourable. Being a self-made man now carries no stigma, while an inclination towards democracy is not considered a sign of being a radical. Flaminius was actually a successful politician and general. He was defeated by Hannibal, but was hardly unique in this.

A man of the people

Flaminius first enters the historical record as tribune of the plebs in 232. While in office he succeeded in having land recently captured from the

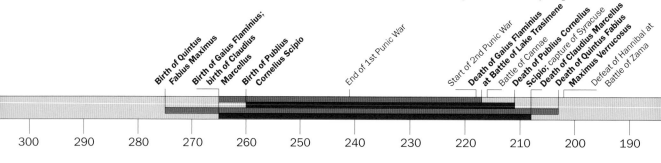

Birth of Quintus Fabius Maximus

Birth of Gaius Flaminius; birth of Claudius Marcellus

Birth of Publius Cornelius Scipio

End of 1st Punic War

Start of 2nd Punic War

Death of Gaius Flaminius at Battle of Lake Trasimene

Battle of Cannae

Death of Publius Cornelius Scipio; capture of Syracuse

Death of Claudius Marcellus

Death of Quintus Fabius Maximus Verrucosus

Defeat of Hannibal at Battle of Zama

300   290   280   270   260   250   240   230   220   210   200   190

Gauls distributed among the plebeians of Rome, earning him the lasting enmity of the senators, who at one time threatened to declare him a public enemy. His principal opponent was Quintus Fabius Maximus (pp. 96–99), who was later to be one of the few generals Hannibal was unable to defeat.

A popular story relates an occasion when Flaminius was haranguing the mob from the Rostra. This was Rome's principal speakers' platform and was decorated with the rams (*rostra*) of captured warships; it is the ancestor of every speakers' rostrum today. Flaminius' father, aghast at his son's radicalism, begged him to stop. The turbulent tribune dutifully halted the proceedings for the day.

In 227, Rome's extended possessions – Sardinia had recently been annexed, to the impotent fury of the Carthaginians – required the creation of two more praetors. Flaminius, with popular support, was elected praetor of Sicily. He discharged his duties so well that the province still fondly remembered him 30 years later when his son became aedile.

Enemies in the senate

Flaminius became consul in 223. His colleague was an aristocrat, a Furius of the family of Camillus (pp. 66–69) and a man with a military pedigree, elected because Rome was at war with the Gauls – in fact the historian Polybius blames the war on Flaminius' earlier land legislation. The senate, not wanting Flaminius to gain any military glory, 'discovered' omens which meant that the consuls had to be recalled to Rome. But the consuls were about to begin a decisive battle with the Gauls. They had literally burned their bridges and there was no option but to fight, leaving the letters of recall unopened. After the Roman victory Furius returned to Rome. Flaminius followed after devastating the lands of the enemy. The biographer Plutarch reports that Flaminius returned to universal disapproval; but he celebrated a triumph, which would hardly have been possible without popular support. Having made a point by celebrating his victory, Flaminius laid down his office.

There is a tradition that he was nominated as second-in-command to a dictator, who may even have been Quintus Fabius Maximus, in 221. Once more the senate would not have it, and dissolved the dictatorship on the grounds that an ill-omened mouse had squeaked during the nomination. Flaminius must have had his supporters (one theory suggests the Scipios were among them), because he became censor with one of the ancient Aemilian family soon after. As censor, Flaminius initiated two great civil engineering projects: an amphitheatre in Rome called the Circus Flaminius, which survived for centuries, and the Via Flaminia, a road that ran north through Etruria and Umbria to Ariminum, parts of which can still be walked today.

The feud with the senate continued. In 218 Flaminius supported a measure that prevented senators from owning more than one or two modest-sized cargo ships. He argued that senators who determined the political course of Rome should not be influenced by their own trading interests. The people knew their senators, and agreed. The senators, who

Coin showing the speaker's Rostra, with prows (*rostra*) of ships below. Silver denarius of Lollius Palikanus, *c.* 47 BC. Though the Rostra was the foremost platform for speakers in the forum in Rome, some chose to orate from the steps of the nearby temples, or even on the steps of the senate house itself. Cicero's preference for the Rostra was shown by the fact that Antony had his head and hand displayed there.

The Via Flaminia, built by Gaius Flaminius, looking towards the north gate at Carsulae. Carsulae in Umbria is one of the prime archaeological sites of the area, having also a well-preserved temple, baths and amphitheatre. Both Tacitus and Pliny the Younger refer to the town in their writings.

had disliked Flaminius before, now loathed him.

Ambushed by Hannibal

The people elected Flaminius consul again for 217. Flaminius did not wait for his formal investiture because he was sure the senate would almost certainly find something inauspicious about it and have his command revoked.

More importantly, Rome was now at war with Hannibal, and it was going very badly. So Flaminius hurried to take over from Tiberius Sempronius Longus (an ancestor of the famous brothers Gracchus). Hannibal was devastating Roman land in Etruria, and Flaminius wanted to bring him to battle. The Carthaginian led him on, until, on the ill-omened morning of 21 June, 217 BC, he turned and ambushed the Roman army at Lake Trasimene. Flaminius died fighting, along with 15,000 of his men.

When word reached Rome there was confusion, until a praetor mounted the Rostra and addressed the Roman people in typically blunt Roman fashion: 'We have been defeated in a great battle.' This would not be the last such announcement in the dark days to come.

LAKE TRASIMENE

At Lake Trasimene, near modern Passignano in Italy, the misty morning of 21 June, 217 saw the consul Flaminius hastening in pursuit of Hannibal along the narrow road between the lake and the nearby hills. Unknown to the consul, his enemy was nearer than he thought.

Suddenly the Romans found their way blocked by Hannibal's Spanish and African troops. As they attempted to form line of battle, hordes of Celts poured down the hillsides on to the Roman flank, and cavalry attacked the rear. Flaminius desperately tried to organize his lines, but his troops were cut into isolated groups and massacred before they could form a consolidated defence. Some

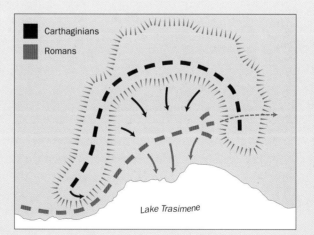

Carthaginians
Romans

Lake Trasimene

The disposition of the Roman and Carthaginian forces in the Battle of Lake Trasimene. These dispositions have had to be worked out from later accounts, and it is not now certain exactly where on the lakeside the battle actually took place. The shoreline of the lake has also changed.

Romans were driven into the lake and drowned, while others managed to fight their way through to the hills and safety. The consul was not among them. He, and more than half of his army of 25,000 men, died at the lakeside in one of the largest and most famous ambushes of ancient times.

PUBLIUS CORNELIUS SCIPIO	
Born	*Achievements*
c. 260 BC	Defeated Hasdrubal
Famous ancestors	in Spain
Scipio Barbatus –	*Children*
grandfather	Son: Scipio
Mother	Africanus
Unknown	*Death*
Father	Killed in battle
L. Cornelius Scipio	211 BC
Positions held	
Consul 218;	
Proconsul 216–211	

PUBLIUS CORNELIUS SCIPIO

'They are ghosts, shadows of men. Beaten, weakened and broken among the Alps by hunger, cold, dirt and neglect. They are shrivelled up with frost, muscles wasted by snowstorms, limbs frozen with cold, their horses are lame and their weapons damaged.... This is not an army, it is the remnants of one.'

Scipio on the army that was about to defeat him on the Ticinus and the Trebia in 218, Livy, *History of Rome* 21.40

PUBLIUS SCIPIO WAS THE BROTHER OF GNAEUS SCIPIO, the consul who, with Claudius Marcellus, took Milan from the Gauls (p. 100). He was also the father of Scipio Africanus, the man who finally defeated Hannibal.

Hannibal's opponent

Scipio was consul in 218 when war with Carthage again broke out (the Second Punic War). At first, the Romans intended to fight Hannibal in Spain, where the Carthaginians had built a considerable empire in the inter-war years. However, Scipio's planned departure for Spain with two legions was interrupted by an uprising of the northern Italian Gauls which required fresh troops to be raised.

Scipio had reached the River Rhone when he discovered that Hannibal had already crossed it going in the other direction. His brother Gnaeus continued on to fight in Spain while Publius Scipio returned to Italy. He caught up with Hannibal at the River Ticinus (the modern Ticinio, near Pavia). There he was wounded in a cavalry action and forced to retire to Placentia (Piacenza). Scipio avoided capture only through the gallant actions of one soldier; legend has it that this was his son, the future Africanus, who was campaigning with him, though Livy suggests that it was one of Scipio's Ligurian servants.

The consul Tiberius Sempronius Longus joined Scipio, and, against his advice, took the combined consular armies into battle at the Trebia, where the Romans lost at least half their force. Most of the discredit fell on Sempronius, since he was in command and Scipio was still wounded. Recovering from his wound, Scipio went to Spain, where his brother Gnaeus was already campaigning with some success. His ships had taken on the Carthaginian navy at the mouth of the Ebro and won a resounding success. He had also defeated the Carthaginian commander in battle at a place called Cissa.

The 'Thunderbolts of War'

With the arrival of Publius Scipio, the war in Spain became something of a family affair. On the Roman side were the two Scipios, who were nick-named the 'Thunderbolts of War'; on the Carthaginian side there was Hasdrubal, brother-in-law of Hamilcar Barca, and Hamilcar's sons, Mago and Hasdrubal Barca. (Hamilcar's other son, Hannibal, was already in Italy). The Carthaginian senate now ordered Hasdrubal to join Hannibal

Carthaginian coins, minted in Spain, of Mago and Hasdrubal Barca. The younger brothers of Hannibal were formidable generals in their own right, and helped Carthage to carve out an empire in Spain.

in Italy. If he were to succeed in this, it would mean calamity for Rome, which was being strained to the limit to contain the one army already on Italian soil.

The Scipios stopped Hasdrubal in a battle fought near the town of Ibera in 216 or 215. The Carthaginian army was routed, and their camp plundered. For the moment this ended Carthaginian hopes of a second invasion of Italy.

The Scipio brothers then set out to conquer Spain. It was not going to be easy – the Carthaginians were well prepared to fight to defend their empire, while Rome, in its extremity, could send precious little in the way of men or supplies. To make matters worse, crooked contractors sometimes embezzled what little there was, creating scandal in Rome.

Despite this, the brothers achieved a series of successes, which at least did something to raise morale in Rome while Hannibal was winning battle after battle. Gnaeus was probably the more experienced campaigner of the two brothers. Both were moderate men who won the support and sympathy of the native Spaniards. This was important, as the loyalty of the local population balanced the better knowledge of the land which the Carthaginians had built up during their long occupation of Spain.

Carthage strikes back

By 212 the Scipios were tying down valuable resources which the Carthaginians wanted to use in Italy, and they were also denying the enemy a valuable recruiting ground for fresh troops. In an attempt to rid Spain of their annoying presence for good, the Carthaginians sent in three armies, under Hasdrubal, Mago and Hasdrubal Barca. They also sent formidable Numidian light cavalry under a young prince called Masinissa.

Meanwhile, the Scipios had recruited some 20,000 Celtiberians – the fiercest fighters in Spain. Publius Scipio took these out to blunt the enemy attack. But the Carthaginians bribed the Celtiberian leaders to withdraw from the war, leaving Publius Scipio badly outnumbered. He attempted to re-join his brother, but there were three Carthaginian armies between them. Harassed by light cavalry, Publius attempted to head off one of the enemy armies by a night march. This desperate expedient failed and he and his men were killed. Outnumbered and outmanoeuvred, Gnaeus fortified a hillside for a last stand, but his tiny army was crushed soon after.

In a single month, the Romans had lost two of their best generals, along with any chance of conquering Spain in the near future. An enterprising knight called Marcius was elected commander by the remnants of the army. He managed to stabilize the situation north of the Ebro, but to the south the Carthaginian victory was complete.

Relief of a Celtiberian warrior from Osuna, Spain, fourth century BC. Celtiberian fickleness in supporting different sides in the Spanish war was probably due to their understanding that neither of the opposing armies had their best interests at heart.

HANNIBAL

Of all the enemies who stood against the growing power of the Roman Republic, none impressed the Romans as much as Hannibal the Carthaginian. While others might threaten Rome's wealth or power, Hannibal threatened the state's very existence.

Hannibal was born in 247 BC, the oldest son of Hamilcar Barca. Hamilcar had been one of Carthage's greatest generals in the First Punic War, a drawn-out campaign which the Romans had finally won through superior sea-power. Hamilcar never forgave Rome for inflicting this defeat, and he made his young son swear a solemn oath never to be friends with the Romans. It was an oath that Hannibal was to keep.

Hannibal's family, the Barcids, were in the process of creating a new empire for Carthage in Spain, and while still young, Hannibal went there and learned the basics of generalship in campaigns against the tough Spanish hill tribes. In 221 he took supreme command in Spain. He soon recognized that the main impediment to Carthaginian expansion was Rome's allies in the region, and in 219 he decided to attack Saguntum, a city allied to Rome. He took the city after a siege of eight months.

There was no doubt of the consequences – Carthage was now at war with Rome. Hannibal took the war to his enemy. He led his army from Spain and crossed into Italy over the Alps. The crossing of the Alps took two weeks and Hannibal's feat in bringing his army through intact is among the wonders of military history.

In Italy, Hannibal went on to win a string of victories. His first was in a cavalry action at Ticinus near Pavia in 218. This was followed by a more testing challenge when he defeated the Roman armies at the battle of the Trebia. He then rampaged through Etruria, killing the consul Flaminius and 15,000 of his army in an ambush at Lake Trasimene in 217 BC.

The Great St Bernard pass over the Alps. Not only did Hannibal have to contend with the weather to keep his troops and elephants warm and fed, but also hostile mountain tribes, who were implacably opposed to him.

The year 216 brought a renewed effort from Rome. Near Cannae Hannibal faced two consular armies, each larger than normal, and he defeated them in a classic envelopment manoeuvre. Another consul, Aemilius Paullus, was killed, and Rome suffered perhaps the greatest casualties received in a single battle until the First World War two millennia later.

Hannibal received no reinforcements from Carthage and he was unable to persuade significant numbers of Rome's allies to defect. In 211 he was in danger of losing Capua, one of the largest cities he now controlled. He led his army to Rome in an effort to dislodge the Romans from their siege of the city. But the Romans refused to be drawn.

Hannibal was pushed ever further southwards, and in 207 he received the crushing news that an army sent to reinforce him had been defeated at the Metaurus, and his brother killed. In 202 he was recalled to Africa to deal with the threat from Scipio Africanus, who had landed an army there. The two sides met at the battle of Zama, and Hannibal was finally defeated.

Carthage was forced to surrender, and Hannibal turned to politics. He became the leader (sufete) of Carthage, and re-arranged the state finances to pay for the huge indemnities Rome demanded. His enemies accused him of conspiring against Rome, and he was forced to flee to Antiochus of Syria in 195. Five years later, still in the service of the king, Hannibal was defeated at sea by the Rhodians, and when

Bust, thought to be of Hannibal, found in Capua. After the defeat of Hannibal it would be over 600 years before anyone else came as close to threatening the existence of the Roman state.

Antiochus made peace with Rome, Hannibal had to flee again, this time to Bithynia, near the Black Sea. When Roman ambassadors demanded his surrender, Hannibal commented 'Let us free Rome of her dread of one old man' and committed suicide.

Rightly considered one of the greatest generals of antiquity, Hannibal was a superb tactician, but a flawed strategist. And he certainly left his mark on the Roman psyche.

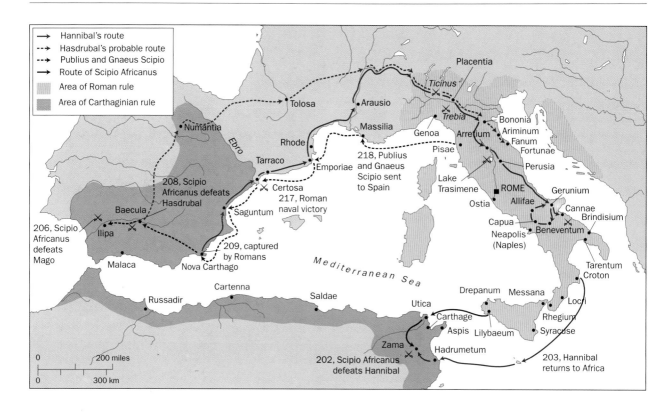

Map showing the movement of the main protagonists and major battles of the Second Punic War. Over 18 years, Hannibal began his war in Spain, fought his way through Italy and finally met with defeat in Africa. Unlike in the previous war, the Romans had the luxury of being able to move their troops by sea without a serious threat from the Carthaginians.

QUINTUS FABIUS MAXIMUS VERRUCOSUS

Hannibal found that he was no match for Fabius in either character or generalship, so tried to destroy his character, by sparing his lands while he was plundering all others. To counter this move, Fabius transferred his lands to the possession of the state, and so, by his high principles he saved his honour from suspicion from his fellow countrymen.

Frontinus, *Stratagems* 1.8.2

THE FABIANS, ONE OF THE OLDEST of the great Roman families, feature several times in this history. Their name was believed to be a corruption of 'wolf-trapper', and there was a tradition that it was bestowed on them by Remus, the brother of Romulus.

A quiet beginning

Fabius Verrucosus was the third in his line to bear the name Maximus, inherited from his illustrious grandfather, the consul of 322. The young Fabius' placid, unexcitable nature led to his nickname 'Ovuncula' or 'little sheep'. An alternative nickname for him was 'Verrucosus' or 'warty' from a wart on his upper lip.

Fabius joined the priesthood of Augurs when young, perhaps even in 265 when he was still in his early teens. In 233, during the first of his five consulships, he campaigned against the Ligurians and won a triumph. A natural conservative, he opposed the demagogic Gaius Flaminius (p. 90).

QUINTUS FABIUS MAXIMUS VERRUCOSUS	
Born 275 BC	Censor 230; Dictator 221, 217;
Famous ancestors Fabius Ambustus, Fabius Rullianus	Chief Augur and Pontifex Maximus *Achievements*
Mother Unknown	Capture of Tarentum *Children*
Father Quintus Fabius	Son: Fabius Maximus (cos. 213)
Positions held Legate to Carthage 218; Consul 233, 228, 215, 214, 209;	*Death* Old age 203 BC

He was censor in 230 and consul again in 228. In 221 he was probably elected dictator, possibly to supervise elections.

So by 218, Fabius had already had a distinguished career. A young man at the end of the First Punic War, he was moderately elderly now, at the start of the Second. When Hannibal attacked Rome's ally, the city of Saguntum in Spain, Fabius led a delegation to Carthage to ask whether Hannibal's actions represented the policy of the Carthaginian state.

The Carthaginians refused to disavow Hannibal. Finally Fabius stood, clutching his toga to his chest. With the Roman talent for theatre, he said 'I have two folds in my toga. Which shall I let drop – that holding peace, or that with war?' The Carthaginians casually told him to drop whichever he pleased. Fabius let fall war.

When Hannibal erupted into Italy and Fabius' old opponent Flaminius was killed, along with most of his army, at Lake Trasimene in 217, Fabius was elected dictator. Perhaps aware of his tactical defects, but with great strategic vision, Fabius did not meet Hannibal in battle; rather he harassed his army and prevented him from gathering supplies. Through a steady erosion of men and supplies, he hoped the Carthaginian threat could be reduced to nothing.

The long year 217

Fabius' very un-Roman approach made him unpopular, and earned him another nickname – Cunctator, 'the Delayer'. Hannibal, who knew and thoroughly disliked what Fabius was doing, increased the popular outrage by pillaging the area where Fabius lived, but scrupulously leaving all Fabius' lands intact, even posting guards on his property to prevent looting.

This prompted the Romans to promote Fabius' second-in-command to joint commander. On getting independent command, this man, Minucius, immediately led his part of the army into battle. Fabius watched the inevitable ambush with a jaundiced eye, commenting 'He's too reckless and impulsive, but he's brave and loyal. Perhaps we should remember his faults another day'. He led a timely sortie saving Minucius and giving Hannibal a strong rebuff. Afterwards Hannibal remarked wryly 'I always thought that the cloud that follows us along the mountain tops could carry a vicious storm.'

Fabius did once manage to trap Hannibal's army in a valley, and for a while Hannibal seemed finally to be bottled in. He escaped by the famous ruse of tying fire-brands to the horns of his camp oxen and driving them in the opposite direction. This fooled Fabius into moving the army which was preventing the Carthaginians from escaping. By the time Fabius discovered his mistake, the enemy had slipped away.

Quintus Fabius Maximus before the Carthaginian Senate, by Giambattista Tiepolo, *c.* 1730. This is one of a series of ten paintings which Dionisio Dolfin, Patriarch of Aquileia, commissioned on themes from military history for his palace in Venice, known as the Ca' Dolfin.

THE BATTLE OF CANNAE

Cannae (modern Canne) is in Apulia on the right bank of the River Ofanto. It was here in 216 that the Romans decided to take the war to Hannibal, abandoning the Fabian strategy of containment that they had followed until then.

The Romans assembled a huge army of over 85,000 men, under the command of both consuls – Aemilius Paullus and Terentius Varro – with the objective of destroying Hannibal once and for all.

Hannibal did not attempt to meet the legions head on. Instead, his Spanish troops managed the most difficult manoeuvre on an ancient battlefield – a fighting withdrawal which sucked the legions into the centre while Hannibal's heavy African troops enfolded their flanks, and the cavalry attacked the Roman rear. Tactically, the battle was then over, with the Romans doomed to certain defeat. Nevertheless the Romans went down fighting, and the killing went on for most of the day.

The consul Aemilius Paullus was killed, along with all but a few thousand of his men. Casualties on this scale were never seen again in a single day's fighting in Europe until the battles on the Western Front in 1916.

Steadying the state

In 216 the Romans tried again to defeat Hannibal in open battle. The result was the battle of Cannae, one of the most famous battles of all time. The Romans were literally decimated. In fact, it has been estimated that the Hannibalic war claimed the lives of one in every three Roman males. The casualties among the Roman generals in this chronicle reflect this. Flaminius, Marcellus, and the two Scipios all died, as did yet another consul at Cannae – Lucius Aemilius Paullus. The surviving consul, Varro, who was largely responsible for the disaster, returned to Rome. The Romans, led by Fabius, did not criticize him, but instead thanked him for showing by his return that he still had faith in the Republic.

Fabius became chief Augur and such was his authority that he was also made Pontifex Maximus – a combination of major religious offices that was not repeated until the time of Caesar. Fabius was consul again in 215 and 214. In 213 Fabius was legate to the new consul, his son Fabius Maximus. There is a legend that the old Fabius once approached his son on horseback. The son told a messenger 'tell my legate that if he wants to approach the consul, he should show proper respect, and do so on foot.' The consul's retainers waited in horror as the old man approached, but Fabius merely embraced his son, and said that he obviously understood the prerogatives of his position.

Fabius was elected consul for the fifth time for 209, the year in which he recaptured Tarentum, in the very south of Italy. Hannibal had taken it in 212, but the citadel had held out under the city's Roman governor who now claimed responsibility for the town's liberation. 'Indeed,' Fabius agreed, 'without you, we would never have lost it, so I couldn't have retaken it.'

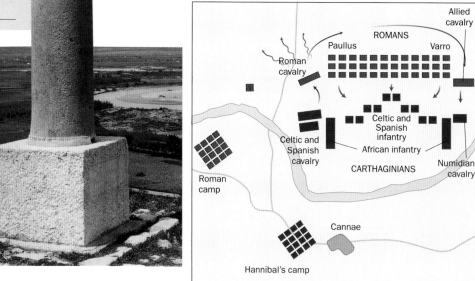

Marker column and plan of the Battle of Cannae. The legions that were encircled by the Carthaginian forces did not break but resisted to the last. Those forces which survived the massacre, the 'Cannae legions', suffered the disgrace of losing the battle for years thereafter, although it was not their fault that their leaders had been comprehensively out-generalled.

A boy, possibly Taras, astride a dolphin; stater of Tarentum, *c*. 380–345 BC. Like many cities in southern Italy, Tarentum was a Greek colony. When the Romans took it from Hannibal in 209, some 30,000 Tarentines were enslaved by their captors.

Although Claudius Marcellus is shown in this statue in a toga, he was happier on the battlefield than in the senate, and had it not been for the Hannibalic war he would probably have passed his life in obscurity.

Fabius strongly resisted Scipio Africanus' idea of taking the war to the enemy in Africa. He died in 203, before Scipio was successful. The people of Rome contributed willingly to his funeral, not because Fabius lacked money, but as members of a family in duty to a father.

One story sums up the Roman spirit of Fabius. In 211 when the Romans were besieging Capua, Hannibal tried to draw them away by marching on Rome. The campfires of his army were visible from the Capitoline hill. Fabius advised calm, and that the siege of Capua should continue. At the time, the state was selling off land to raise money. This included the land Hannibal's army was currently camped on. It got the usual market price.

CLAUDIUS MARCELLUS

Besides the monuments raised to him in Rome, there was a wrestling arena dedicated to him in Catana in Sicily. Statues and pictures ... were set up in the temple of the Cabiri in Samothrace, and of Athena in Lindos, this statue having the inscription:

> *'This, stranger, was Rome's divine star,*
> *Claudius Marcellus, of Rome's great family.'*

Plutarch, *Life of Marcellus*

THE FORTUNES OF THE GREAT ROMAN FAMILIES ebbed and flowed. Some families fell from popular favour and remained in the shadows for generations. Others, such as the Horatians, seem simply to have died out.

A plebeian Claudius

The massive Roman casualties in the war against Carthage raised to prominence the Marcelli, a branch of the Claudian clan. The Claudian Marcelli were plebeians, and thus only tenuously related to the aristocratic Appii Claudii. The first consulship in their branch had been Claudius Marcellus, consul in 331, the year when Cornelia and her accomplices poisoned many of the other likely candidates (p. 74). This Marcellus was the great-grandfather of our Marcellus.

Marcellus was born in around 265. Apart from training in warfare, he was poorly educated – in fact some claim he was illiterate. He fought with distinction in the first war with Carthage, and was decorated for saving his brother's life. This military record did not help him politically, and in 226 he had only reached the rank of curule aedile. While aedile, Marcellus accused his colleague, Scantinius Capitolinus, of indecently assaulting his son. The senate fined Scantinius heavily, and Marcellus had the money dedicated to the gods to show that he had not made the accusation for gain.

Marcellus supported the aristocratic faction in politics, and perhaps in recognition of his loyalty he was made a priest in the prestigious college of Augurs. In 222 he became consul. He prepared to campaign against the Gauls, who had just been soundly beaten by Gaius Flaminius

CLAUDIUS MARCELLUS

Born c. 265 BC	*Achievements* Spolia Optima; Triumphator; Ovatio
Famous ancestors C. Marcellus (cos. 331)	*Children* Son: Claudius Marcellus (cos. 216)
Mother Unknown	*Death* Killed in battle 208 BC
Father C. Marcellus	
Positions held Consul 222, 215, 214, 210, 208; Augur	

and P. Furius (p. 91). The Gauls wanted peace, but Marcellus and his colleague Gnaeus Cornelius Scipio Calvus (literally 'Cornelius the Bald') would have none of it.

In an action near the Alps, Marcellus defeated a Gallic army and killed the leader in single combat. This, one of the rarest and most prized achievements possible to a Roman general, earned him the *spolia opima* (as recognition of this feat was called). Marcellus was the last of the four men who managed it. Marcellus and Scipio captured the Gallic capital of Milan, and returned to Rome in triumph.

Marcellus and Sicily

In 216 Marcellus, as praetor, was en route to Sicily when the terrible news came from Cannae of the greatest defeat in Roman history. Rome elected a dictator, a descendant of Lucius Iunius Brutus, Iunius Pera, with Sempronius Gracchus as his second in command. Marcellus, as the man nearest the scene, was told to restore order where possible. In 215, with yet another consul dead in action, Marcellus was elected in his place. This election was annulled, however – perhaps because of an inauspicious peal of thunder, perhaps because it was felt impolitic to have two plebeian consuls at one time.

Marcellus became consul the following year with Quintus Fabius Maximus. The pair recaptured the strategic town of Casilinum, in Campania, and Marcellus brutally massacred its garrison, even though they had surrendered to Fabius. In the following year, 214, Marcellus was posted to Sicily, which though at peace, was restless. To quell the unrest Marcellus went to Leontini and captured one of the main anti-Roman conspirators; he also killed some 2,000 Roman deserters he found there. His severity prompted a full-blown rebellion.

An eighteenth-century engraving showing Archimedes' claw in action in the siege of Syracuse. (J. C. de Foland, *Histoire de Polybe*, 1727–30.) Although it is not known exactly how the claw worked, Archimedes' defence of the city was a permanent reminder to later generations of the importance of science in warfare.

Next, Marcellus took charge of the fleet besieging Syracuse, a Greek city now effectively under Carthaginian control and essential to Roman success in Sicily. The defence of the city was masterminded, in the most literal sense of the word, by Archimedes, the foremost inventor of antiquity. His infernal machines dragged Marcellus' ships under water, or hoisted them high into the air. Once Marcellus attacked with a complex siege apparatus called a *sambuca* (it resembled a gigantic musical instrument of the same name). Archimedes had it smashed to pieces before it reached the walls. With his troops too terrified to approach the city, Marcellus had to resort to a blockade, remarking ruefully, 'Archimedes dips my ships under water like wine glasses into a bowl, and when I

Mosaic depicting the death of Archimedes, once believed to have been made in ancient times, but now thought to be much later, possibly 16th or 18th century. By the end of the Republic Syracuse had so forgotten its most famous scientist that Cicero (who was in Sicily as quaestor) had to search for his tomb, which he found neglected and overgrown.

send a *sambuca* band to the party, it is kicked off the premises.' Eventually Syracuse did fall, but only through treachery. Marcellus spared the citizens' lives, but comprehensively looted the city. Archimedes was slain by a vengeful soldier, much to Marcellus' displeasure.

Confronting Hannibal

Marcellus was consul for the fourth time in 210, with a Valerius as his patrician colleague. His return to Sicily was averted by the horrified protests of the Sicilians, and he went to the Italian front instead. Hannibal was still ensconced in central Italy, holding off the Romans but unable to strike any decisive blow. Marcellus fought three battles against Hannibal, with mixed results. Hannibal remarked that Fabius was a schoolmaster, and Marcellus an adversary: one punished his mistakes, the other tried always to harm him.

The battles left Marcellus' army exhausted and incapable, while Hannibal remained a dangerous threat. Marcellus was recalled to Rome to explain himself, which he managed to do so competently that he returned to the war as consul for the fifth time. Soon after, while he was reconnoitring a hill near Venusia (Venosa), Hannibal's Numidian cavalry ambushed and killed him.

The Romans said that Fabius was their shield and Marcellus their sword. Future generations continued to hold the Marcellans in high regard. Among the last of the line was Gaius Marcellus, brother-in-law to Augustus himself.

Publius Cornelius Scipio Africanus

(236–185 BC)

Scipio Africanus finally defeated Rome's great enemy, Hannibal, at the Battle of Zama in 202 BC. Despite such success, Scipio ended his life in exile at Liternum. Highly intelligent, humane and cultured, Scipio was also one of the first Romans to be captivated by Greek civilization. This bronze statue was found at Herculaneum.

PUBLIUS CORNELIUS SCIPIO	
Born 236 BC	*Achievements* Defeated Hannibal; Triumphator
Famous ancestors Scipio Scapula	
Mother Unknown	*Wife* Aemilia
Father Publius Scipio	*Children* Sons: Publius, Lucius; daughters: Cornelia Prima, Cornelia Secunda
Positions held Consul 205, 194; Censor 199	
	Death Died in exile 185 BC

Scipio was in Spain when a captive was brought to him. She was a maiden of noble birth, whose beauty drew all eyes to her. Scipio had this woman returned to her fiancé ... and made the couple a marriage gift with the gold which her parents had brought as a ransom. The tribe was so overwhelmed by his conduct that they gave themselves over to the cause of the Roman people.

Frontinus, *Stratagems* 2.9.5

THE YOUTH AND EARLY MANHOOD of Publius Scipio were set against the grim background of the Hannibalic war. Legend has it that his first experience of combat was rescuing his father from Hannibal's cavalry at the battle of Ticinus (p. 93). We next hear of Scipio as a military tribune, rallying survivors after the Battle of Cannae in 216. He was curule aedile in 213, and two years later he received the devastating news that both his father and uncle had been killed in action in Spain (p. 94). At the age of 24, Scipio became the head of Rome's powerful Cornelian family.

Command in Spain

The war in Italy, if not exactly going well was at least a stalemate, so the senate raised two new legions to retrieve the situation in Spain. These

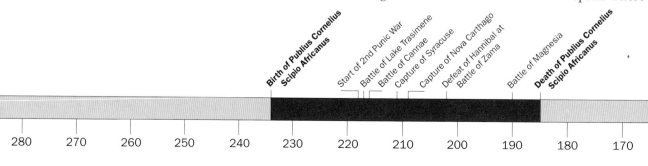

were at first commanded by Claudius Nero, a solid but uninspired general descended from Appius Claudius Caecus (pp. 70–72). Then Claudius was replaced by Scipio.

This move was dramatic, unprecedented and imaginative. Dramatic, because Scipio was sent to avenge his father and uncle. Unprecedented, because Scipio had proconsular *imperium*, a power usually granted only to consuls after their year in office, and occasionally to distinguished praetors, whereas Scipio's highest office so far had been curule aedile. Imaginative, because the name of Scipio was well regarded in Spain and would bring some Spanish tribes back to their loyalties, especially as Scipio had an inspiring personality.

Scipio may have wanted the post, but Livy reports that not many others did. Armies in Spain received few reinforcements or supplies, and victories in Italy were more easily converted into electoral success. Scipio started planning his campaign early. In a letter written later to Philip, King of Macedon, he said that he arrived knowing his strategy – what remained were the details. Polybius reports that when Scipio arrived in 210, he questioned everyone he met about the country and its people, and integrated this information into his plans.

His first target was Nova Carthago (modern Cartagena). Scipio had realized that the enemy armies were too far away to prevent a sudden attack on this, their main supply base. Scipio informed his men that Neptune had promised his assistance in a dream – they believed him because Scipio was a mystic character who spent hours in prayer, communing with the gods.

Emporiae (Ampurias, Spain), was used by the Romans as a base for their Spanish campaigns. Scipio landed there in 210 BC, aged just 25, at the head of an army consisting of 10,000 infantry, 1,000 cavalry and 30 quinqueremes.

Masinissa, king of Numidia, obverse of a bronze coin. Originally an enemy of Rome, Masinissa changed sides to become an ally of Scipio.

Italica (modern Santiponce, near Seville, Spain), was founded by Scipio as a strategic base in 206 BC. This town later produced the Roman emperors Trajan and Hadrian, and was still an important centre in the time of the Visigoths.

Nova Carthago was captured when some of the Roman soldiers waded across the lagoon in front of the city and seized a strategic gate. Scipio's careful enquiries among the local fishermen had revealed that the lagoon was shallow enough to walk across at low tide. Typically, says Polybius, Scipio had accomplished by intelligence and careful planning what was attributed to fortune and the gods. At Nova Carthago the Scipionic legend was born.

Defeating the Barcids

Next, Scipio paid off a family grudge. In 208 he mauled Hasdrubal Barca's army in a battle at Baecula. The defeated Hasdrubal escaped through Spain, attempting to join his brother Hannibal in Italy. Scipio had the strategic vision to let him go. It removed an enemy army from Spain, and Rome was now strong enough to defeat Hasdrubal in Italy. Not surprisingly, the Romans in Italy were unimpressed. The Roman consul opposing Hannibal was the same Claudius Nero whom Scipio had replaced in Spain. He had to leave the southern front, race up Italy, join his colleague at the River Metaurus, and defeat Hasdrubal. This prevented the two Barcids from uniting their armies and Claudius Nero returned south. The first Hannibal knew of these events was when Hasdrubal's head was thrown into his camp.

Meanwhile, Scipio had defeated the third Barcid brother, Mago, at the battle of Ilipa (just north of Seville) in 206. Except for a few mopping-up operations, Spain was now in Roman hands. About this time Scipio met Masinissa, the African king whose cavalry had been instrumental in his father's death. The meeting began Masinissa's conversion from an enemy of Rome to a valued ally.

The defeat of Carthage

Scipio returned to Rome in triumph. He campaigned for the consulship by promising to carry the war to the Carthaginians in Africa. Fabius 'the Delayer' bitterly opposed him, pointing to the fate of Regulus who had lost an army in Africa. Even success would only bring Hannibal and his army down on Scipio. Consequently, when Scipio was elected consul for 205, the senate did not give him any levies. Scipio was told that he could invade Africa but his troops would have to be volunteers.

Scipio had no trouble in finding men and thus the Roman counter-

The Continence of Scipio by Nicolas Poussin (1640). This story, quoted from Frontinus on p. 102, was a very popular subject in art, and over a dozen paintings have been produced on the theme.

attack began. On landing in Africa Scipio besieged Utica. A Carthaginian general (also called Hasdrubal) came to meet him, accompanied by the young African king Syphax. It was his rival's loyalty to Carthage that finally swayed Masinissa to the Romans. Scipio met the Carthaginians at the battle of the Great Plains, and defeated them. He was now just 75 miles (120 km) from Carthage.

He took Tunis, but the Carthaginian fleet destroyed his transports in a surprise attack. Perhaps with Regulus in mind, Scipio entertained Carthaginian peace overtures. A proposed armistice was presented to the senate in Rome, and accepted. Possibly this truce was a ruse to allow Hannibal safe passage back to Africa. On his arrival, the Carthaginians attacked Scipio's ships. The envoys Scipio sent to protest were attacked too. In 202 the war recommenced.

The final confrontation came at Zama. Hannibal's veterans met the army of Scipio, and with the help of Masinissa, Rome triumphed. Carthage sued for peace and paid a heavy indemnity. Scipio took the cognomen Africanus, and returned to the adulation of the people and the envy of his peers. Hannibal survived the battle and in fact advised that the Carthaginians accept the Roman terms.

Scipio in the East

Scipio was censor in 199, and consul again in 194. He wanted Greece as his proconsular command to build on Roman achievements there, but instead he received north Italy, where he campaigned against the Alpine tribes with no lasting result. In 193 he was called on to mediate between Masinissa and Carthage, but his intervention came to nothing, perhaps because Scipio's protégé was evidently in the wrong.

In 190 Scipio achieved his ambition to campaign in the East, against King Antiochus III of Syria. He was legate to his brother, Lucius. Unluckily for Scipio, Antiochus captured his son, but released him. Either from a sense of obligation, or through genuine illness, Scipio did not take part in

King of one of the Numidian tribes, Syphax originally tried to remain neutral between Rome and Carthage. The Carthaginians won his allegiance by giving him the beautiful Sophonisba as a wife, which in turn brought his enemy Masinissa over to the Roman side.

Plan of the Battle of Zama, 202 BC. Scipio left spaces between his cohorts so that Hannibal's elephants could be diverted through these, while others were pushed to the flanks where they disorganized Hannibal's cavalry. The battle was eventually won when the Roman cavalry drove off the Carthaginian horse and charged into the rear of the Carthaginian battle line.

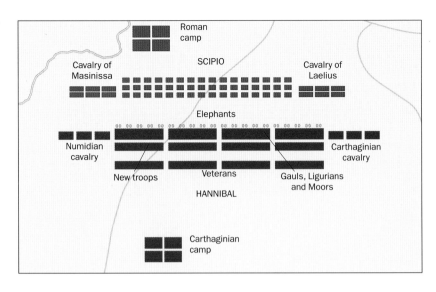

Antiochus' defeat at Magnesia. Instead he chose to return to Rome with news of the victory. While both Scipio brothers were out of Rome, their enemies, led by Cato the Censor, had been gathering strength. Now they struck, bringing the two Scipios to trial on obscure bribery charges. Though not actually condemned (partly through the intervention of Sempronius Gracchus), Scipio was forced into exile at Liternum in Campania, where he died the following year.

Scipio's legacy

Our principal source for Scipio is Polybius, who was the client of his grandson, Scipio Aemilianus. Polybius is unfailingly complimentary about Africanus, whose faults are carefully brushed away. To Scipio's credit, there was much to be complimentary about. He was highly intelligent, humane (by the standard of his times) and cultured. While a mystic, he believed that the gods helped those who helped themselves, and his campaigns were both planned minutely and based on sound intelligence.

Scipio was one of the first Romans to be captivated by Greek civilization. This love of things Greek was inherited by his daughter Cornelia, who was at the forefront of those aristocrats who spread Hellenization in Rome. Cornelia married Scipio's ally, Sempronius Gracchus, and was the mother of the Republic's two most controversial figures – Tiberius and Gaius Gracchus (pp. 126–38).

Roman temple and forum at Liternum. The colony was new (founded in 194 BC) when Scipio retired there in exile. It was later abandoned because of the prevalence of malaria in the area.

Titus Quinctius Flamininus
(c. 229–174 BC)

Marcus Porcius Cato
(237–149 BC)

Aemilius Paullus
(229–160 BC)

Head of Titus Quinctius Flamininus, c. 180 BC, from Delphi. Flamininus' role in liberating Greece from the Macedonians made him deeply revered by the Greeks.

TITUS QUINCTIUS FLAMININUS	
Born c. 229 BC *Famous ancestors* Quinctius Capitolinus, Cincinnatus *Mother* Unknown *Father* Quinctius *Positions held* Consul 198; Censor 189	*Achievements* Victor at Battle of Cynoscephalae; Triumphator *Children* Son: Titus (augur 167) *Death* Illness 174 BC

TITUS QUINCTIUS FLAMININUS

After the games were over they nearly killed Flamininus by their expressions of joy and gratitude. For some of them, longing to look him in the face and call him their saviour, others in their anxiety to grasp his hand, and the greater number threw crowns and floral wreathes on him, and so they all but tore the man in pieces.

Flamininus returns the Greek states to liberty: Polybius, *The Rise of Rome* 14.46

ROME HAD CHANGED MUCH since the days when Lucius Quinctius Cincinnatus (pp. 58–60) was called from the plough to save the state. His descendant was to fight in southern Italy, and across the Adriatic Sea in Greece.

Young and ambitious

Titus Quinctius Flamininus was born around 229. Even as a boy he thirsted for distinction. Plutarch remarks 'he was always more friendly to those who needed his help than he was to those who could help him – these last were competition.'

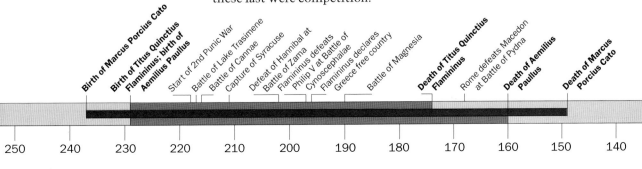

Birth of Marcus Porcius Cato
Birth of Titus Quinctius Flamininus; birth of Aemilius Paullus
Start of 2nd Punic War
Battle of Lake Trasimene
Battle of Cannae
Capture of Syracuse
Defeat of Hannibal at Battle of Zama
Flamininus defeats Philip V at Battle of Cynoscephalae
Flamininus declares Greece free country
Battle of Magnesia
Death of Titus Quinctius Flamininus
Rome defeats Macedon at Battle of Pydna
Death of Aemilius Paullus
Death of Marcus Porcius Cato

| 250 | 240 | 230 | 220 | 210 | 200 | 190 | 180 | 170 | 160 | 150 | 140 |

(*Above*) Philip V of Macedon: a silver coin of *c.* 190–180 BC. Notwithstanding their military confrontation, Philip and Rome treated each other with a degree of respect. 'He acted like a true king, not forgetting his duty even in the hour of disaster' says Polybius.

(*Below*) The starting line for the Isthmian games, where Flamininus proclaimed Greece a free country. The games were administered by Corinth, but open to all Greeks and were held in honour of Poseidon. Events included athletics, chariot races and musical contests.

During the Punic wars, Flamininus was military tribune to Claudius Marcellus (pp. 99–101). He became governor of Tarentum following its recapture by Fabius the Delayer (pp. 96–99), and led Roman colonists to occupy strategic central Italian cities, including one whose name became famous in a very different context – Narnia. He gained a reputation for deft administration, and decided to attempt the consulship of 198, even though he had never been more than quaestor. The people decided to give this headstrong youth a chance, and elected a consul almost a decade younger than most who gained that honour.

Unlike his predecessors, Flamininus did not stay in Rome for half the year. Accompanied by his brother Lucius he instead set out for Greece. Here Rome was fighting a desultory war with Philip V of Macedon which had begun almost the moment the Carthaginian war had ended.

Flamininus detached the Achaean League (a confederation of Greek states) from Macedonian control. Philip still refused to abandon control of Greece, so Flamininus asked his friends in the senate to campaign for his command to be extended for another year. If the command was transferred (Scipio Africanus was lobbying for the job), then Flamininus' friends should urge the senate to make peace with Philip, giving Flamininus the honour of finishing the war.

Flamininus got his extended command, and justified the senate's confidence by defeating Philip in 197 at Cynoscephalae (a hill resembling a dog's head, the meaning of the name in Greek). In part the victory was won when one of Flamininus' lieutenants, Claudius Nero, saw a chance to outmanoeuvre the cumbersome Macedonian phalanx and did so on his own initiative.

The freedom of Greece

With war imminent with the Seleucid king Antiochus III, Flamininus had the strategic vision to consolidate Rome's position in Greece. He attended the Isthmian games, and there, in 196, he proclaimed Greece a free country. By getting the Greeks completely on his side, as Plutarch rather neatly puts it, Flamininus gave Rome a breathing space between Philip's last hopes of victory and Antiochus' first.

Flamininus suggested that Antiochus abandon all claims in Europe in return for undisturbed possession of Asia. When Antiochus' ambassadors replied with lists of the king's lancers, pikemen, spearmen and bowmen, Flamininus remarked that the army reminded him of a dinner which was all pork, but cooked in different ways.

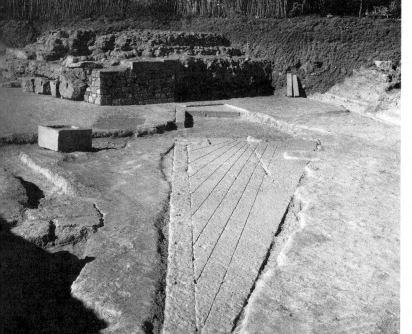

Coin of Antiochus III: modern research has shown that the menace of Rome on his western borders was just one of many threats to Antiochus' beleaguered kingdom, but by energetic and ceaseless campaigning, Antiochus managed to reconstitute the declining Seleucid empire.

There followed several years of intense political and military manoeuvring, in which Flamininus allied himself with the Greek general Philopoemen and crushed the Spartan king Nabis. Flamininus was one of the first Roman generals to establish client-patron relationships with the cities under him, giving them his protection in exchange for their support.

It helped that Flamininus was a cultured philhellene, able to match the Greeks in oratory and trickery. Once he visited Thebes, and the inhabitants – allies of Philip, but not belligerents – came out of the city to greet him. Flamininus accompanied the city fathers back to the city. To the councillors' discomfort, there was no suitable moment to break into Flamininus' smooth discourse until everyone was back within the walls, including a substantial part of the Roman army. After that, the Thebans had to submit to occupation with as good a grace as they could muster.

The end of Hannibal

Returning to Rome, Flamininus became censor in 189 with the son of Claudius Marcellus as his colleague. He later returned to Greece, and took it on himself to demand that Prusias, king of Bithynia (in modern Turkey), hand over Rome's old enemy, Hannibal, who committed suicide rather than be taken.

This mean-spirited action cost Flamininus political support just as he launched into a bitter battle with Cato the Censor. Cato had removed Flamininus' brother Lucius from the senate, and when challenged, cited Lucius' scandalous behaviour with a catamite. Flamininus failed to get his brother reinstated, and died soon after, in 174.

MARCUS PORCIUS CATO, 'THE CENSOR'

'I shall speak about those Greeks in their proper place, son Marcus.... They are a depraved and unruly people, and I prophesy that when that nation gives us its literature, it will corrupt everything. All the more so if it sends doctors here. They have conspired to kill all barbarians with their medicine, and they even charge us for doing so! They regularly call us barbarians and hurl more filth at us ... by calling us Opici [an Oscan tribe].'

Cato quoted by Pliny, *Natural History* 29.7.14

Coin celebrating the defeat of the Macedonians: a Macedonian helmet is shown beneath the horse's tail. Despite the representation on the coin, the Battle of Cynoscephalae was won by infantry rather than cavalry, although it was the cavalry who inflicted the greater casualties on the fleeing enemy.

CATO USED TO SAY THAT HIS FAMILY was old and distinguished – it just didn't happen to be from Rome. He was in fact from Tusculum, a city near Rome and one of Rome's oldest allies. When his father died, Cato inherited a small farm in the Sabine country and moved there and became a farmer.

War and farming

Cato's first military campaign was in 217. Cato was a remorseless self-propagandist, and his claims that he was 17 at the time do not square

ROMAN FARMS

Despite the relatively huge size of Rome, most Roman citizens lived in the country. The soils of the region were light, rainfall fickle, and crops were subject to a host of diseases and parasites.

Even surpluses tended to be dissipated by poor storage and primitive transport systems which prevented agricultural produce being moved to other regions.

The principal crops were barley, wheat, olives and wine. Most farms combined these with a smattering of livestock, including pigs and poultry, with sheep grazing the upland regions where ploughing was impossible. Cash crops were rare, and most agricultural produce was consumed on the farm where it was grown, or at most went as far as the local market.

The Romans made a conscious effort to preserve the small farms which were the source of their citizen armies. The area outside the towns was broken up into small square plots of land which are a distinctive feature of Roman settlement, and which still determine the street pattern of some Italian suburbs.

Towards the end of the Republic so-called villa estates developed. They were about 180 acres (73 ha) in size, and as well as the staple crops they produced fruit and vegetables for the Roman market. The stability of the *pax Romana* steadily improved agricultural efficiency and increased the amount of land under cultivation.

It has been estimated that the level of agricultural development and urbanization which resulted was not matched for the next millennium and a half. Not all this was due to the huge agricultural estates of south Italy (*latifundia*), farmed by chain gangs of slaves and owned by absentee landlords. Archaeological discoveries in the past few decades show that the death of the small farmer has been greatly exaggerated, and much of the farming in the Republic continued to be done on small family farms, using a core labour force of slaves, supplemented by the seasonal labour of the rural poor.

A Roman farm estate depicted in a mosaic of the fourth century AD, from Carthage, Tunisia. Around the walled courtyard of the farm buildings (a design still seen in modern Tuscany), the work of the estate takes place. Crops, fruit and hunting testify to the diverse nature of produce from an individual estate, and this was mostly also true of Republican Italy.

with the usually accepted date of his birth in 237. During the Hannibalic war he was befriended by Q. Fabius Maximus, the 'Delayer' (pp. 96–99), and was with him at the recapture of Tarentum. Later, he took part in the defeat of Hasdrubal on the banks of the Metaurus river.

When not campaigning, Cato worked on his farm, sharing the food and conditions of his labourers. His reputation for common-sense wisdom (the meaning of the word Cato) roused the interest of a Valerian called Flaccus who had a nearby estate. Recognizing Cato's political potential, Flaccus brought him to Rome.

MARCUS PORCIUS CATO	
Born	*Achievements*
c. 237 BC	Triumphator; author
Famous ancestors	of *De Re Rustica*
Cato – grandfather	*Wives*
Mother	Licinia; Salonia
Unknown	*Children*
Father	Sons: Marcus
Unknown	Licinianus, Marcus
Positions held	Salonius
Praetor 198; Consul	*Death*
195; Censor 184	Old age 149 BC

Statue of Cato the Censor. Cato did not believe in statues being erected to the unworthy, and once commented 'After I am dead, I would much prefer that people asked why there were no statues of me than that they asked why I had one.'

In 205 Cato was quaestor to Scipio Africanus; he disapproved of Scipio's easy-going ways, his philhellenism and his lax discipline. By one (probably false) account he went so far as to complain to Rome, which led to a commission of enquiry. The commission reported that the preparations for the African invasion were exemplary, but the story illustrates the bad feeling between Cato and his commander.

Not surprisingly, Cato was given no chance to shine in the African campaign. Afterwards, he returned to Rome via Sardinia, picking up Ennius, one of Rome's earliest poets, on his travels.

Cato the administrator

In 199 Cato was aedile, and together with his colleague, he restored the festival of the plebeian games. He was praetor the following year, and took Sicily as his province. As an administrator Cato was frugal with state funds, utterly incorruptible, and totally impartial and pitiless in administering justice.

In 195, when he and his sponsor Valerius Flaccus were consuls together, there was controversy over the repeal of the Oppian Law, imposed in the dark days of 215. By this law women were forbidden to own more than a pound of gold, wear colourful clothing or use horses if less than a mile from the city. With Rome secure and prosperous, the law was an obvious anachronism, but Cato defended it with misogynistic zeal. He was overruled by a more commonsense majority, and went to vent his spleen on the Spaniards.

His Spanish war was a trademark affair, with impeccable generalship, daring and successful initiatives, and callously brutal treatment of the enemy. Cato set up Spain's gold and silver mines to run at a huge profit to the state, and then sold off his warhorse in order to save the cost of bringing it back to Rome. He celebrated a triumph, and paid his men a larger than average bounty. The following year he dedicated a (small) temple to Virgo Victoria for his successes.

The politician

Moving on to Greece, he was legate to Glabrio, the general charged with preventing the Seleucid king Antiochus III from invading the country. In Cato's account (allegedly stirring, but which has not survived), his cunning and daring turned the pass at Thermopylae and he attacked the king's camp at the critical moment, leaving Glabrio overcome with gratitude and admiration. (Glabrio's version was significantly different.)

Back in Rome once more, Cato successfully opposed the claims of his successor in Spain to a triumph. Depending on one's viewpoint, Cato constantly and mean-spiritedly tried to stop others celebrating their military prowess, or he prevented unworthy generals from unjustifiable self-advertisement. He is also believed to have been behind the political destruction of the Scipio brothers (Africanus and Lucius; p. 106) in a long-running feud which was one of the liveliest features of political life in Rome in the years after the Second Punic War.

ROMAN IMPERIALISM

Roman imperialism was once considered to have been a defensive phenomenon. Having conquered and absorbed a dangerous tribe on its borders, the Roman state found an equally dangerous tribe on the new border, and were forced to conquer that one too. This argument achieved its most sophisticated form in the 1850s with the work of the great German historian Theodor Mommsen. It has now been largely overturned by a new generation of historians who refuse to believe that Rome conquered the Mediterranean world through 'mission creep'.

These historians, led by W. V. Harris, point out that for most of the Republic, Rome was a highly militarized society. Not only were the great magistracies also military commands, but social and political advancement was difficult and rare without military success. Rome had a warrior aristocracy and an economy based on continuous territorial expansion. It is difficult to conceive of such a society limiting its activities to the purely defensive.

A Roman commander in his province was both the civil and military authority. In fact, 'province' was not originally a geographical term but a job description for the commander to whom it was allocated. Thus it was perfectly possible for a 'province' to include areas that were not part of the Roman empire, and which were not intended to become so.

Expansion into Greece in the early second century BC saw a change in the nature of Roman imperialism. While Rome had formerly been interested in the direct exercise of power through its armies, it now began to project power more implicitly, through treaties and client states. This did not make its domination less complete, but it did make it more economical, since in most situations, the threat of Roman force was credible enough to ensure that it did not need to be deployed.

In 189 Cato stood for censor against his old commander Glabrio. He tried to discredit Glabrio with charges of corruption and embezzlement, but this alienated the voters and neither man was elected. Cato tried again in 184, and, despite the heartfelt efforts of an 'anyone but Cato' alliance headed by the Scipios, he and Valerius Flaccus were elected.

The censorship and after

Cato's censorship was everything his opponents had feared and his supporters had hoped for. He initiated a huge building and repair programme, squeezing every last drop of value out of the public contractors. Luxury goods were taxed, and statues of people Cato deemed unworthy were removed from public places. He also removed the brother of the hero Flamininus from the senatorial roll, and struck off another man for kissing his wife in front of his daughter (though by another account the man did more than kiss). The Romans of the equestrian centuries in the assembly had horses paid for by the state; Cato took away one man's horse, saying he was too fat to ride it into battle, and deprived Lucius Scipio of his, essentially because he was a Scipio. After his year in office, Cato was voted a statue in recognition of a job well done.

But Cato did not retire from political life. His controversial censorship had stirred up too many enemies. Titus Quinctius Flamininus took him to court and succeeded in getting a two-talent fine imposed. This is the only known occasion when Cato lost a case, though he was involved in some 45 others. It was Cato's belief that a man could be measured by his enemies. If so, he was one of the greatest men in the state. He was a dreaded prosecutor: in 171 he took up the case of Spaniards oppressed by their governors, and the offenders were exiled.

The last time Cato stood trial was in 153. He defended himself successfully, but commented that it was hard for a man of one generation to make his defence to those of the next. At 85 he was still prosecuting. His last victim was also a governor accused of crimes in Spain (Servius Sulpicius Galba, pp. 118–19), though this offender undeservedly got off.

Cato was an opponent of philhellenism. He affected to despise the Greeks, and warned his son to avoid doctors, since they were generally of that nation. (Cato himself had a healthy lifestyle, and no need of doctoring.) Nevertheless, he was struggling against prevailing opinion, and in his old age he too started to study Greek. In other ways he did not change: when a Roman ally from Asia Minor, King Eumenes II, was visiting Rome, Cato refused to meet him, commenting that 'Kings are naturally carnivorous beasts'.

Though old, Cato was sent as part of a commission to Carthage attempting to mediate between the Carthaginians and Masinissa. Cato was alarmed by the size and wealth of Carthage, and decided that this potential threat should be eliminated. Returning to Rome, he brought out fresh figs from his robes to show that Carthage, where they were picked, was only three days' journey away. Thereafter, he finished any

A coin depicting the Basilica Aemilia: the basilica was built in 179 BC while M. Aemilius Lepidus was censor and therefore responsible for public works. It occupied a prominent position in the forum and was used as a law court. Cato built the first known basilica in Rome, the Basilica Porcia, in 184 BC, using his own funds. This was destroyed in a fire in 52 BC (p. 199) and nothing visible survives today.

speech, no matter what the subject, with the words *Delenda est Carthago* – 'Carthage must be destroyed'. A new generation of Scipios opposed him; Scipio Nasica Corculum finished all his speeches with 'leave Carthage alone'. Carthage was indeed destroyed as Cato had advocated (p. 120), but he died soon before it came to pass. Ironically, the Roman commander responsible was another Scipio – Scipio Aemilianus.

A Roman icon

Revered by the Romans, Cato is regarded more ambivalently today. His impartiality, incorruptibility and integrity are undoubted. But he was inhuman to his slaves and merciless to his enemies. His political life had more petty spite than greatness. He was a shrewd businessman, investor and farmer. His guide for farming, the *De Re Rustica*, still partly survives today. His history of Rome, the *Origines*, was the first written in Latin rather than Greek.

Cato was more indulgent to his offspring than might have been expected. He had sons from both his marriages, and these marriages tell us something about him. The first marriage, when he was an aspiring politician, was to a daughter of the highly aristocratic Licinian clan. When she died, Cato was well enough established to choose any wife he wished; and he did, scandalizing Rome by marrying the daughter of his freed slave Salonius.

Even among the colourful characters of the Roman Republic Cato was exceptional. Despite their professed enthusiasm for his high ideals, one suspects that many Romans were secretly grateful for that.

AEMILIUS PAULLUS

Aemilius Paullus on the day before his triumph, and in accordance with ancient custom, gave an account of what he had done to an assembly of the people outside the city. He prayed that if any of the gods should envy his achievements or fortune, they should be angry with him, rather than with Rome. This prayer proved prophetic and costly.

Velleius Paterculus, *Historia* 1.10.5

KING NUMA'S SON MAMERCUS was such an easy speaker that he was nicknamed Aemilius ('smoothie'), and from this the Aemilian clan were named. The consul who died in 216 BC at the battle of Cannae was an Aemilian; his daughter married Scipio Africanus, and this led to close co-operation between the Scipios and the consul's son, also called Aemilius Paullus.

Early campaigns

Paullus joined the élite priesthood of Augurs in 192, and became praetor the following year. He was given command of Further Spain, where he campaigned for three years, initially suffering setbacks, but finishing victorious. The Roman empire was expanding rapidly at this time, and

AEMILIUS PAULLUS	
Born	*Achievements*
c. 229 BC	Augur; Triumphator
Famous ancestors	*Wives*
King Numa (?)	Papiria; unknown
Mother	*Children*
Unknown	Sons: Fabius
Father	Aemilianus, Scipio
Aemilius Paullus	Aemilianus (2 died
Positions held	young); daughters:
Praetor 191; Consul	Aemilia Prima,
182, 168; Censor	Secunda, Tertia
164	*Death*
	Illness 160 BC

Bust of Aemilius Paullus: he was a fine example of Rome's warrior aristocracy, cultured, honest and skilled in war.

A relief scene, probably of the Battle of Pydna, on the victory monument of Aemilius Paullus at Delphi. Originally the monument stood in front of the Temple of Apollo, but only the frieze blocks have survived and these are now in the museum at the site.

Paullus' next task was across the Mediterranean in Asia Minor. He was part of the commission which settled affairs after the defeat of the Seleucid king Antiochus III by Scipio Africanus and his brother Lucius.

As consul in 182 he fought against the Ligurians – a warlike tribe from northeastern Italy (the area is still called Liguria today). Despite being besieged in his camp at one point, Paullus eventually won the campaign.

In 171 he represented the Spanish in their appeals against oppressive Roman governors. He failed to become consul a second time, and decided to content himself with his priesthood, and his growing family. He was, says Plutarch, 'the most affectionate father in Rome'.

This affection did not stop him giving his two oldest sons in adoption, however. He had recently remarried, and the sons from his first marriage were adopted by Fabius Maximus and Publius Cornelius Scipio respectively. The younger adoptee, Scipio Aemilianus, was to live up to the greatness promised by his combined family name (pp. 119–21).

War in Macedon

Ever since his defeat by the Romans at Cynoscephalae in 197, the Macedonian king Philip V had been secretly preparing revenge. He died before his plans came to fruition, but he left a superb war machine in the hands of his successor, Perseus. To meet this threat, the Roman voters returned to the man they had spurned before – Aemilius Paullus.

In the war which followed, the climax was the Battle of Pydna, in Macedonia, in 168. Here the Romans came face to face with the formidable Macedonian phalanx. Paullus later admitted that even years afterwards he would break into a sweat at the memory of the phalanx charging with levelled pikes. The canny Roman commander had delayed

THE INFLUENCE OF GREECE

Graecia capta ferum victorem cepit et artes intulit agresti Latio.
'Captive Greece took captive her savage conqueror, and brought civilization to barbarous Latium.'

Horace, *Epistles* 2.1, 157–58

It is often believed that Hellenization arrived in Rome at about the time of the Second Punic War (218–202 BC), but in fact Rome had long been influenced by Greek culture and ideas.

At first this came at second hand, as the Romans absorbed much of their culture from the Etruscans, who were also influenced by the Greeks. (The story of Tarquin the Elder, descendant of a Greek refugee who came to Rome from an Etruscan city, well reflects this cultural progress.) When the younger Tarquin had need of definitive oracular advice, he sent his sons to Delphi in Greece, and it was to Greece too that the founding fathers of the Republic went for the laws that were to be embodied in the Twelve Tables (p. 65).

As early as 282, when the Roman envoy Postumius addressed the people of the Greek city of Tarentum, he did so in their own language. And it was in Greek that the historian Fabius Pictor wrote the first history of Rome.

However, it was at the time of the Macedonian wars of the early second century that the Latin cultural tradition was exposed fully to a culture that was in many ways richer and more sophisticated. Rome became heavily involved in Greek affairs and the Roman aristocracy seized upon Greek culture. Everything, from education to architecture and music, was to some degree affected.

Roman taste approved of the Greek ideal in writing, which was concise and powerful, and it was not long before the effects were making themselves felt in Latin literature. This reinforced a tradition that had been present for some time – Hellenic influences are strongly

evident in the works of playwrights such as Plautus and Terence.

It has been said, perhaps unfairly, that while the Romans shared the Greeks' love of sculpture they had none of their appreciation, an opinion exemplified by the Roman general Memmius, who, returning from Greece in 146, appropriated a number of priceless statues. He allegedly told the workmen loading them on to ships that they would have to pay for anything they broke.

The Discobolus, a Roman marble copy of an original Greek bronze, c. 450 BC. The original, by Myron, is now lost. Many Greek statues now only survive in Roman copies.

The Romans were slow to take to philosophy until the arrival of Stoicism with the philosopher Panaetius. This austere creed opened the way for other schools of Greek thought, including the Academics (amongst whom Cicero counted himself) and the Epicureans. It would not be an exaggeration to say that by the time of Augustus, the torch of philosophical debate had passed from Greece to Rome, and other philosophers, such as Epictetus and Seneca, were to continue that tradition into the Empire.

Another area strongly influenced by Greek culture was religion, especially the state religion of Rome. Apollo established himself early under his own name (and was entrenched yet more firmly when Octavian claimed him as his patron), and the other gods followed in a process of dualism that identified Jupiter with Zeus, Mars with Ares, Neptune with Poseidon and so on. By the middle of the first century BC the two cultures had essentially the same religion, making it truly Graeco-Roman.

Laocoon, the priest strangled by sea snakes for trying to warn the Trojans about the wooden horse. This statue, of the second century BC or first century AD, was by three sculptors from Rhodes and was found in the ruins of the palace of the emperor Titus in Rome.

Perseus of Macedon taken captive: a denarius commemorating Paullus, c. 55 BC. The coin depicts a *tropaion*, a memorial on the battlefield erected by the victorious army from the armour of the defeated enemy.

fighting until the afternoon sun was shining into the enemy's eyes. The phalanx pushed the legions back, but lost its cohesion in the process. Seeing their advantage, the Romans advanced into the enemy formation, and at close quarters long pikes were no match for short swords. Within an hour the battle became a massacre.

Roman losses amounted to only about a hundred men, in comparison with tens of thousands on the Macedonian side. There was some anxiety about Scipio Aemilianus, who had accompanied his father to war and had gone missing. He turned up towards nightfall, having been carried away in pursuit of the enemy. Cato, son of Cato the Censor, had lost his sword in a tight skirmish; he then persuaded a group of his friends to plunge back into the middle of the fight with him to help search until the weapon was triumphantly recovered. Another famous Scipio, Scipio Nasica Corculum, was also among the distinguished group who fought that day on the Roman side. Later, the young Cato married Paullus' daughter. Given the close connections between Paullus and the Scipios this constituted at least a cease-fire in the feud between the Catos and the Scipios.

The general in retirement

Triumph and tragedy awaited Paullus in Rome. His triumph was magnificent, with massive amounts of booty. Among the prisoners was Perseus, the Macedonian king, whose attempted escape by sea had been foiled by the Roman fleet. But the week before the triumph, one of Paullus' sons died, followed by the other just a week afterwards. With his two earlier sons given in adoption, Paullus, the proud father, had no one to continue the family name.

He became censor in 160, but his health was declining. He lived for three years at the seaside resort of Velia but then decided to return to Rome. This move was fatal for his health, and he died soon afterwards.

Resolutely an *optimate* (one who supported aristocratic privileges), Paullus was also a philhellene and his sons were given a Greek as well as a traditional Roman education. He was famously incorruptible, and though the booty from the defeat of Macedon was sufficient to relieve the Romans from paying any more taxes, he himself only gained the books from Philip's library. At his death he had hardly enough money to repay his wife's dowry.

L·AEMILIVS
L·F·PAVLLVS
COS·II·CENS·INTER·REX·PR·AED
CVR·Q·TR·MIL·TERTIO·AVG
LIGVRIBVS·DOMITIS·PRIORE
CONSVLATV·TRIVMPHAVIT
ITERVM·COS·VT·CVM·REGE
PERSE·BELLVM·GERERET·A·P
SENSE·ACTVS·EST·COPIAS·R
DICEM·DIEBVS·QVIBVS·MAG
EONIAM·ATT···TDEL
RECEM·VM·LIBER

Eulogy to Aemilius Paullus (cast, Arezzo), commemorating his offices and distinctions. The opening line says that he was twice consul, censor and *interrex* – an ancient and honourable post used by the Romans when holding elections.

Servius Sulpicius Galba
(*c.* 190–136 BC)

Scipio Aemilianus
(*c.* 184–129 BC)

Tiberius Sempronius Gracchus
(*c.* 210–150 BC)

Gnaeus Servilius Caepio
(*c.* 181–112 BC)

A bronze bust of Scipio Aemilianus. Scipio was one of the last Roman generals of his era who was able to rely on the loyalty of his soldiers – both to himself and the state. His successors were not as fortunate.

SERVIUS SULPICIUS GALBA

The Roman people ... showed itself an unduly lenient judge ... (when) Galba softened the hearts of the assembly. Doomed as he had been by universal consent, he received hardly a single vote of condemnation. Pity, rather than justice, presided over that trial, because the acquittal he certainly did not deserve was granted to him out of compassion for his children.

Valerius Maximus, *De Viris Illustribus* 8.1.2

SERVIUS SULPICIUS WAS AN ANCESTOR of the Galba who was briefly emperor two centuries later in AD 69. His was an old family, which had obtained recent distinction in the Hannibalic wars. As often happened, this brought a crop of the next generation into office. One Galba became *praetor urbanus*, while another took the priesthood vacated when Quintus Fabius Maximus (pp. 96–99) died.

A greedy man

Servius Sulpicius Galba was military tribune under Aemilius Paullus, and fought in the battle at Pydna in 168. Famously avaricious, Galba

SERVIUS SULPICIUS GALBA	
Born c. 190 BC	*Achievements* Escaped prosecution
Famous ancestors None	*Children* Son: Sulpicius Galba
Mother Unknown	*Death* 136 BC
Father Sulpicius (?)	
Positions held Praetor 151; Consul 144	

Birth of Tiberius Sempronius Gracchus

Battle of Cynoscephalae

Birth of Servius Sulpicius Galba

Birth of Scipio Aemilianus

Birth of Gnaeus Servilius Caepio

Battle of Pydna

Death of Tiberius Sempronius Gracchus

3rd Punic War begins

3rd Punic War ends; Carthage destroyed

Death of Servius Sulpicius Galba

Capture of Numantia

Death of Scipio Aemilianus

Death of Gnaeus Servilius Caepio

20 210 200 190 180 170 160 150 140 130 120 110

bitterly resented the small bounty which Aemilius distributed after the victory. And deeply envious of Aemilius' success, he tried to block his triumph when they returned to Rome in 167. He failed in this, but did manage to create a controversy.

An inability to make friends and influence people meant that Galba came relatively late to his praetorship, in 151. Campaigning against the Lusitanians, a Spanish tribe then in revolt, Galba won an initial engagement but followed up recklessly. The man who had criticized the 'harsh' discipline of Aemilius lost control of his men. The Lusitanians rallied, fell on the tired and disorganized Romans and killed over 7,000 of them. Galba was forced into the nearest fortified city until the Roman general Lucullus rescued him.

In 150 the Lusitanians sued for peace. They found Galba apparently deeply sympathetic. He understood that the Lusitanians were desperate because their land was poor. In return for their surrender, Galba undertook to find them richer lands. Three points were designated from where the tribesmen, their possessions and families were to be taken to their new homes.

A Roman atrocity

On arrival the Spaniards were disarmed and led to an enclosure. They were then massacred in their thousands. Galba is alleged to have kept the possessions of the murdered Spaniards for himself. Even in peacetime, it was said, Galba would lie, cheat and commit perjury for financial gain, though he was already immensely rich. Rome later paid for his treachery, since a shepherd called Viriathus survived the atrocity to become an embittered and very successful guerrilla leader (p. 125). The massacre also led to a general distrust of the Romans which kept the province disturbed for the next 50 years or more.

The tribunes attempted to indict Galba when he returned to Rome in 149. Cato, then aged 88, made his last public speech against the atrocity. But Galba was a great orator himself (though Cicero alleges he was rather old-fashioned in his style), and his money talked even louder. The nobility were paid off, and Galba begged the common people to be merciful

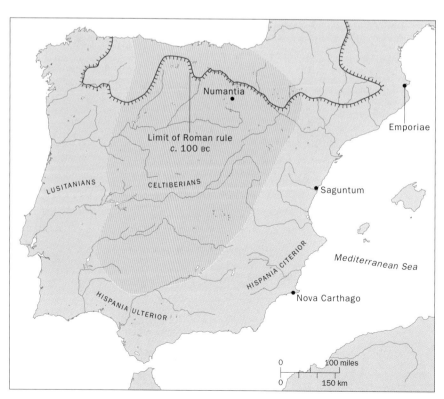

Map of the Iberian peninsula. The difficult terrain and hardy tribespeople made it difficult to conquer, and Roman greed and incompetence made it hard to hold. But once Roman rule took root, Hispania became one of the most peaceful and prosperous parts of the empire.

Numantia

Emporiae

Limit of Roman rule
c. 100 BC

LUSITANIANS

CELTIBERIANS

Saguntum

HISPANIA CITERIOR

Mediterranean Sea

HISPANIA ULTERIOR

Nova Carthago

0   100 miles

0   150 km

for the sake of his sons, whom he displayed with him at his appeal. (One of these sons later became the first priest in Rome ever to be convicted of corruption.)

Galba was acquitted so convincingly that he went on to become consul in 144. He quarrelled with his colleague over which of them should get a command in Spain, allowing Scipio Aemilianus to step in and secure the post for his brother, Fabius Maximus Aemilianus. But Spain had not seen its last Galba. Galba's son later campaigned there when he was praetor.

The last we hear of the unpleasant father is in 138, when he was defending some tax gatherers. Livy comments that he was 'hated and reviled by all', but, in this last case, he was again successful.

SCIPIO AEMILIANUS	
Born	**Positions**
c. 184 BC	Consul 147, 134;
Famous ancestors	Censor 142
King Numa	**Achievements**
(allegedly), Aemilius	Corona Muralis,
Paullus (cos. killed	Corona Graminea;
at Cannae)	Triumphator (twice)
Mother	**Wife**
Papiria	Sempronia
Father	**Death**
Aemilius Paullus	Heart attack or
	murder 129 BC

SCIPIO AEMILIANUS

Who, however, would deny that Scipio's career was most glorious? For unless he chose to covet immortality – a desire which never entered his mind – what of all it is lawful for a man to desire did he fail of obtaining? ... He was made consul twice ... he overthrew two cities, both extremely hostile to this empire, and thus extinguished not only present but also future wars.

Cicero, *De Amicitia 3*

THOUGH ONE OF THE GREATEST OF THE SCIPIOS, Aemilianus was not a Cornelian by blood. Born in 184 (or 185), he was the second son of Aemilius Paullus, the conqueror of Macedon (pp. 113–16). When Paullus remarried, the two sons by his first marriage had been given away in adoption to a Fabius and a Scipio. Such adoptions were not uncommon among Roman aristocrats.

In the Scipionic tradition

Scipio fought in Macedonia at the battle of Pydna, in 168, and had caused alarm by disappearing towards the end of the battle. It turned out that he and his comrades had been chasing King Perseus' fleeing troops and had lost touch with the army. Many thought that because of this Macedonian connection, Scipio would do his early service there – and indeed the Macedonians requested his presence. But Scipio decided to fight as a military tribune in Spain, where he served under Licinius Lucullus and won the *corona muralis*, an award given to the first man on to the wall of an enemy fortification.

He next went to Africa to support an old friend of Scipio Africanus – the Numidian king Masinissa. Scipio attempted to mediate in the feuds between Carthage and Masinissa, but failed because the Roman senate was encouraging Masinissa as a check to Carthage. In 150 Carthaginian patience snapped and they invaded Masinissa's lands. Their invasion was crushed, but the aged king died from his exertions. Scipio saw to it that the land of Masinissa was divided among his heirs as he had wished.

Perseus of Macedon was the eldest son and heir to Philip V. His rivalry with the Roman ally Eumenes II of Pergamum led to his downfall, and he died a captive in Italy.

Punic houses on Byrsa Hill, Carthage.
When the city was refounded as a
Roman colony, this hill was the focus of
the settlement, and most of the remains
of the Punic city were destroyed.

Rome seized on Carthage's attack on an ally as an excuse for war. The senate offered to spare Carthage if the present city was abandoned, and resettled no nearer to the sea than 10 miles. Carthage rejected the terms, and the Third Punic War began. Though outnumbered, the Carthaginians held back the Romans with fanatical tenacity and skill. Scipio served heroically, winning further awards, and distinguished himself politically by persuading a Carthaginian commander to desert.

In 147 Scipio returned to Rome, ostensibly to stand for aedile. But careful preparation of public opinion led to huge popular demand that he be given higher office. Though this was against established procedure, the senate gave way, and Scipio returned to Africa as consul.

The end of Carthage

Scipio was more competent than his predecessors, and in 146 his troops took Carthage after intense house-to-house fighting. The city was plundered and its citizens sold into slavery. Carthage, Rome's persistent adversary for over a century, was razed to the ground and salt was sown on the land to make it infertile. A solemn curse was pronounced on anyone who tried to settle there in the future. Carthage was destroyed, as old Cato had wished.

Scipio celebrated a huge triumph for finally disposing of Rome's ancient and greatest enemy. He then returned to Africa to oversee the settlement of the new province. In 144–143 he toured Asia Minor, apparently as part of an official embassy, though the exact purpose of the embassy is uncertain.

In 142 Scipio was again in Rome, this time to stand for censor. Despite his philhellenic sentiments and Cato's feud with the family, Scipio had been a protégé of Cato, who respected Scipio's courage and high personal morality. Now Scipio attempted a censorship as rigorous as Cato's had been, but the Roman system of colleagues in office was against him. Scipio's fellow censor vetoed his more extreme measures, and mitigated others. This enhanced Scipio's reputation as a severe Roman of the old school, while at the same time preventing him from actually doing anything that would make him enemies – this perhaps was exactly what that consummate politician intended.

Stones at Carthage used by Roman siege
weapons: these were probably thrown by
the *onager*, a torsion catapult. It is
thought that each legion carried 10 of
these weapons, which gets its name
from its savage kick, resembling that
of a wild ass (*onager*).

In fact, the main achievements of Scipio's censorship were the further development of the Capitol as the focal point of Rome and its growing empire, and the repair of the Aemilian bridge. This was the first stone bridge built in Rome, in 179, and repairing it was an act of piety by Scipio to the family he was born into – the Aemilian.

War in Spain

Scipio Aemilianus was already the greatest Roman of his generation, but his career was not finished. War flared up again in Spain. The Roman commander there, C. Hostilius Mancinus, had been entrapped and he made a peace with the Spaniards that allowed his army to escape. Scipio persuaded the senate to repudiate the peace as being dishonourable, and in so doing deeply offended his brother-in-law, Tiberius Gracchus (pp. 126–32), who had been Mancinus' negotiator.

Without even the need for an electoral campaign, Scipio was chosen as consul to avenge the Roman defeat. But Rome was short of manpower at this time and so Scipio took with him an army composed mainly of friends and dependants – something not seen since the ancient days when the Fabian clan fought against Veii. Scipio had an eye for talent and many of his officers became the leaders of the next generation.

The campaign was brutal and it ended with the siege of Numantia, where some 4,000 Celtiberian die-hards held out in terrible hardship against vastly superior Roman forces. Scipio surrounded the city with a wall, and finally broke the will of its inhabitants through starvation. After this campaign he added the unofficial *cognomen* of Numantinus to his title of Africanus.

Scipio and the Gracchi

Scipio seems to have been calm, stoical and peaceable. He was allegedly the first Roman to shave daily, a habit which later became almost universal. He was a close friend of the historian Polybius, who had been brought from Greece to Rome, and believed Polybius' theory that Rome must remain balanced between its monarchical element, embodied in the consuls, its aristocratic element, represented by the senate, and its democratic element, represented by the tribunes. He was torn between family loyalties and principle when his brother-in-law Tiberius Gracchus seemed to be setting the people against the state. When Tiberius was murdered, he could not bring himself to condemn the act, making him unpopular with the people. Many of Tiberius' supporters were new citizens or freedmen, and Scipio once faced down a crowd of them, saying, 'I, who have seen Rome's enemies in their full power in the field, am not going to be cowed by you, stepchildren of Rome.'

Soon after, Scipio died suddenly in his sleep. It was suspected that he had been murdered by his wife, Sempronia, who was Tiberius' sister. Even Scipio's enemies admitted that Rome had lost an outstanding general and politician, whom Cicero would later call the ideal Roman statesman.

A relief thought to be of Polybius, from a site in Arcadia. This is the region of Greece where Polybius was born in about 208 BC, at Megalopolis. Polybius was brought to Rome by Aemilius Paullus and became tutor to his sons, one of whom was Scipio Aemilianus.

TIBERIUS SEMPRONIUS GRACCHUS	
Born c. 210 BC *Famous ancestors* Sempronius (cos. 215) *Mother* Unknown *Father* Sempronius *Positions held* Praetor 180; Consul 177, 163; Censor 169	*Achievements* Triumphator *Wife* Cornelia *Children* Sons: Tiberius, Gaius (others died young); daughter: Sempronia *Death* Curse c. 150 BC

TIBERIUS SEMPRONIUS GRACCHUS

He was censor once, and he twice was raised to the consulship. Twice he celebrated a triumph for his victories. Yet despite all these honours, he was even more renowned for his integrity.

Plutarch, *Life of Tiberius Gracchus*

THE SEMPRONIANS WERE AN ANCIENT plebeian family. The Gracchan branch of Tiberius Sempronius had fought with distinction in the Hannibalic war.

Relations with the Scipios

This Sempronius Gracchus was born in about 210. He had served with Lucius Scipio, brother of Scipio Africanus, against the Seleucid king Antiochus III (p. 105), beginning a lifelong association with the Scipios. Although Sempronius claimed to be the enemy of Scipio Africanus, he helped Scipio to the best of his ability in 187 when Cato and his minions hounded the Scipios to trial.

Friends of Scipio Africanus once asked him if he had chosen a husband for his daughter Cornelia. Scipio had not, and was asked who he would choose. Suddenly an idle conversation turned serious, and Scipio had to tell his wife that he had arranged their daughter's betrothal. She, an Aemilian of the family of Paullus, said bitterly that she had been scheming to get Cornelia someone like Sempronius Gracchus; the relieved Scipio explained that he was the prospective bridegroom.

Sempronius Gracchus became an aedile in 182. This office required heavy expenditure on building and games, and Sempronius was not rich. He squeezed the money from clients and subject peoples so effectively that the senate afterwards restricted the amount that aediles should spend. The upwardly mobile Sempronius then became praetor in 180. Given his experience in Asia Minor, he might have hoped for a posting there. Instead, his command was against the Celtiberians in Spain. Sempronius competently pacified this region of hardy warriors. He claimed the surrender of some 300 towns, though the historian Posidonius comments that some of these were single castles or fortified hilltops. Sempronius next stunned the Spaniards, accustomed to Roman greed and treachery, by establishing a peace so equitable that it lasted for 25 years.

Claudian allies

After triumphing in 177, Sempronius became consul. His patrician colleague, C. Claudius Pulcher, soon became a close family ally and his daughter, Claudia, later married Sempronius' son Tiberius. Sempronia, Sempronius' daughter, married Scipio Aemilianus (pp. 119–21), thus consolidating another dynastic alliance.

Sempronius campaigned in Sardinia in his consular year, pacifying the island in two quick and ruthless campaigns. He took so many Sardinian slaves that the market was saturated: the expression *Sardi venales*

Tiberius Gracchus by the workshop of Luca Signorelli (*c.* 1450–1523), one of a series commemorating men who had behaved chivalrously towards women. Tiberius sacrificed his life so that his wife Cornelia might live. The snakes of the omen (p. 124) are visible under his feet.

Torralba, Sardinia: Roman buildings (first century BC) near the Nuraghe Sant'Antine. The Nuraghe – stone towers built from square blocks – are a typical feature of ancient Sardinian architecture.

('Sardinians for sale') entered the Roman idiom for the modern 'two a penny'. (As another linguistic aside, the Sardinians poisoned elderly relatives who became a burden. This poison twisted the faces of the deceased into a rictus which was the original 'sardonic grin'.)

A list to commemorate Sempronius Gracchus' military campaigns existed in a temple near Rome's cattle market for later generations to see. Meanwhile, his campaigns had become political. He was censor, with Claudius Pulcher again, in 169. The pair severely pruned the roll of knights and reined back the tendency of the *publicani* (see box p. 137) to operate through bribes and backhanders. Sempronius bought the grounds where the house of Scipio Africanus had once stood, added some neighbouring properties, and constructed the Basilica Sempronia, a lasting contribution to the city's architecture.

THE CELTIBERIANS

The Celtiberians were a warrior people from the area around the Ebro valley in Spain. There were in fact a number of distinct tribes in the region, but the Romans lumped them under a common name because of their distinctive language and dress.

As the name suggests, there was a strong Celtic influence in their writing and religion. Archaeology shows that they shared the Gallic love of semi-abstract imagery, and a tradition of richly ornamented clothing and weapons.

The Celtiberians had few towns. Mostly they lived in fortified settlements on hilltops, a lifestyle well suited to the turbulent times. They were ferocious fighters – lightly armoured, they used single-edged slightly curved swords and a heavy throwing spear as their main armament.

After first meeting the Romans in the early second century, the Celtiberians developed an aptitude for guerrilla warfare which, combined with the ineptitude of various Roman governors, prevented the Romans from totally subduing the region for

the next 200 years. When they were finally absorbed into the Roman empire, the Celtiberians helped to make Spain peaceful and prosperous.

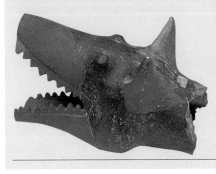

Mouth of a Celtic war horn in the form of a wolf head. The complete horns were over 6 ft (1.8 m) long.

Iberian warrior relief, from Osuna. These are probably Caetrati, lightly armed warriors who carried small round shields and wore helmets made from dried sinew.

When Sempronius and Claudius left office they were attacked by a vindictive host of people who had suffered from their reforms. The battle was fought in the courts and on the Rostra. Sempronius refused to abandon his former colleague, although Sempronius was popular with the people, and Claudius, like many Claudians, was not.

Rituals and portents

Sempronius Gracchus was consul again in 163, a term of office made most famous when he left it. Sempronius disapproved of his successors and a few weeks after they had taken office, he 'remembered' omitting part of the ritual of transferring the consulship, so forcing his luckless successors to resign for fresh elections.

Sempronius finally returned to Asia Minor in a series of semi-official embassies in which he cultivated the friendship and support of the wealthy monarchs of the area. After Sempronius' death, a Ptolemy of Egypt (it is uncertain which one) offered to marry his widow Cornelia, on the strength of his relationship with her husband.

The circumstances of his death were strange. Legend has it that Sempronius found two snakes in his children's room. As this was evidently an omen, he consulted soothsayers. They told him that if both snakes escaped or were killed then disaster would strike his entire family. But if the male snake died, so would he, while if the female snake was killed, Cornelia would die. Sempronius ordered that the female snake be allowed to escape, and killed the male. As predicted, he died soon after.

Though as ruthless as most Roman aristocrats, Sempronius was also honest and fair. Even if untrue, the legend of the snakes says much about Sempronius the family man. Sempronius the politician left a huge stock of political capital for his sons. How they spent that patrimony has been controversial ever since.

GNAEUS SERVILIUS CAEPIO

GNAEUS SERVILIUS CAEPIO	
Born	*Achievements*
c. 181 BC	Defeated the
Famous ancestors	Lusitanians
None	*Children*
Mother	Son: Servilius
Unknown	Caepio (cos. 106)
Father	*Death*
Servilius Caepio	112 BC
(cos. 169)	
Positions held	
Consul 140	

Caepio was unable significantly to harm the enemy, but he caused his own men a number of injuries, and in turn he came near to being killed by them. For he treated them all, but particularly the cavalry, so harshly and with such cruelty that a great number of disreputable jokes were told about him during the nights.

Cassius Dio, *History* 22.78

THE APPOINTMENT OF SERVILIUS CAEPIO to command the army in Lusitania well illustrates the closeness and complexity of the Roman aristocracy.

A family affair

In 144 the influential Scipio Aemilianus procured the Spanish command for his brother Fabius Maximus Aemilianus. Though born to the Aemilian family, the brothers Aemilianus had been adopted by Scipio and Fabius Maximus respectively. In due course Fabius Maximus Aemilianus

A view of the theatre at Saguntum, near Valencia, Spain, built in the third century AD. Saguntum always played an important part in Roman wars in Spain. It was besieged by Hannibal, featured in Caepio's campaign against Viriathus and was later occupied by Quintus Sertorius until he was driven from there by Metellus Pius (pp. 171–74).

The Death of Viriathus, by Federico de Madrazo (1815–94). Madrazo was reared on tales of Spanish guerrillas' resistance to Napoleon, and indirectly paid his homage to them by this depiction of an earlier great guerrilla leader of Spain.

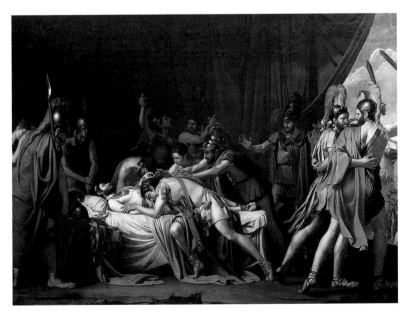

was replaced in Spain by Fabius Maximus Servilianus, another son adopted by Fabius Maximus, this time from the Servilian clan. In 140 Servilianus was replaced by his brother Gnaeus Servilius Caepio, who, as the form of his name shows – it is Servilius rather than Servilianus – had remained in the family of his birth.

The opponent of all these commanders was Viriathus, the Lusitanian shepherd who had escaped the massacre of Servius Galba (p. 118) to become a formidable war leader. Fabius Aemilianus had a mixed campaign against him, and Fabius Servilianus a disastrous one. He was surrounded, outnumbered and facing massacre when, incredibly, Viriathus made peace instead, being recognized as an ally of Rome.

Without honour

That the brother of the defeated general was sent in his place made it clear that Rome wanted revenge. Caepio tried to provoke a war, first covertly then ever more openly, until finally the Spaniard's patience forced Caepio to declare war himself. Still Viriathus tried to negotiate, sending two trusted lieutenants to talk with the Romans. Instead, Caepio talked to the envoys with such success that on their return to Viriathus they killed him while he was sleeping in his tent.

The treacherous envoys were inspired by the promise of a massive bribe, which, in the best tradition of Roman dishonour in Spain, Caepio then refused to pay. The Lusitanians were repulsed from Saguntum, and were pursued by Caepio until they sued for peace. Caepio did not make Galba's mistake. He disarmed the Lusitanians, but kept his promise to settle them on land which was rich enough to ensure that they did not have to live by banditry.

Caepio was heartily hated by his troops for his brutal severity, and on one occasion came very close to being killed by his own cavalry. On his return to Rome, Caepio became well known in the law courts. Barely an adequate orator, he obtained his results through his influence and connections. His son also campaigned in Spain; this Caepio is best known as the general whose arrogance and lust for glory led to a massive Roman defeat at the hands of the Cimbri.

Tiberius Gracchus

(c. 163–133 BC)

TIBERIUS GRACCHUS	
Born	*Achievements*
c. 163 BC	Won *corona*
Famous ancestors	*muralis*; land
Sempronius (cos.	legislation; Augur
215)	*Wife*
Mother	Claudia
Cornelia	*Children*
Father	Son: L. Equitus (?)
Sempronius	*Death*
Gracchus	Killed in a riot
Positions held	133 BC
Tribune 133	

He [Tiberius Gracchus] was a man – in all other respects – of blameless life, he had a brilliant intellect, honest intentions, and was, in short, blessed with the highest virtues of which a man is capable, given the advantages of his nature, and the excellence of his training.

Velleius Paterculus, *Historia* 2.2.1

WHILE TIBERIUS GRACCHUS WAS A BOY, Rome became the Mediterranean superpower, and did not do so graciously. The city of Carthage was destroyed in 146 simply because it was recovering its strength faster than the Romans liked; the ancient city of Corinth in Greece was pillaged in the same year to show Roman impatience with Greek intrigues. But perhaps the best example of Roman arrogance had occurred when the Seleucid king Antiochus IV attacked Egypt in 168. Rome sent an embassy telling the king to withdraw. When the king asked for time to consider this, the Roman ambassador, Popillius Laenas, drew a circle in the sand about the king, and told him he could leave it once he had decided. The king considered the implications of this original 'line in the sand', and backed down.

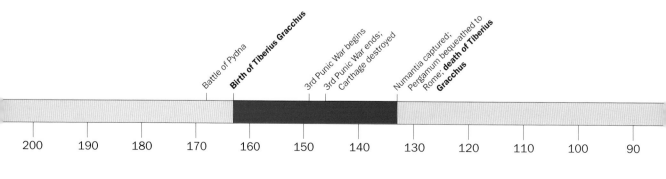

Battle of Pydna

Birth of Tiberius Gracchus

3rd Punic War begins

3rd Punic War ends; Carthage destroyed

Numantia captured; Pergamum bequeathed to Rome; **death of Tiberius Gracchus**

| 200 | 190 | 180 | 170 | 160 | 150 | 140 | 130 | 120 | 110 | 100 | 90 |

A new world order

Tiberius' tutors reflected Rome's new cosmopolitan outlook. They included Diophorus of Mytilene, who taught oratory, and Blossius of Cumae, the Stoic philosopher. In fact Cornelia, the daughter of the great Scipio Africanus, raised Tiberius and his brother Gaius with such care that later generations erected a statue to her, the inscription on the base reading 'Cornelia, mother of the Gracchi'.

Tiberius was a quiet and thoughtful youth. Frugal and neat in his personal habits, he was a cool and precise person, a fact reflected in his oratory, which was calm, reasoned and very convincing. But he was also a Roman, and so possessed in abundance the national characteristics of bravery and bloody-minded stubbornness.

While still in his mid-teens, Tiberius joined the prestigious college of Augurs, following in his father's footsteps. He also continued his father's close ties with the Scipios, serving under Scipio Aemilianus in the final defeat of Carthage, where he won a mural crown for being among the first to ascend the doomed city's walls.

Mancinus and the Celtiberians

His next spell of military service was with the consul C. Hostilius Mancinus who replaced Pompeius (a forebear of the triumvir Pompey) in Spain. (One effect of this Spanish war endures today – to allow the consuls to reach the field early in the campaigning season, the new year was brought forward to 1 January.)

Mancinus' campaign against the formidable Celtiberians went badly. Once, he tried to shift his camp at night while deep in enemy territory, with the result that his army of 20,000 men was trapped and faced obliteration (p. 121). The only possibility was to negotiate a peace. After years of broken promises and Roman treachery the Celtiberians were not interested until they heard that the son of Sempronius Gracchus was in the Roman force. They agreed to negotiate, but only with him.

Tiberius negotiated an equitable peace which allowed the Romans to escape with their lives, if not their equipment. Among the lost items were Tiberius' account books containing the record of his financial dealings as the quaestor of Mancinus. Tiberius went to Numantia, the Celtiberian capital, to retrieve them, finding both the books and a warm and generous welcome.

His reception in Rome was completely different. That Tiberius had saved a Roman army counted for nothing with a people accustomed to total victory. The peace was repudiated, and Mancinus condemned to be delivered up to the Spaniards. (Who, to their credit, refused to accept him.) Scipio Aemilianus led those who pressed for the Celtiberian question to be settled once and for all. He took command of

This statue of Cornelia and the Gracchi, by Pierre-Jules Cavelier (1814–94), reflects the tale that Cornelia told her sons that she wanted to be renowned, not as the daughter of Scipio, but as the mother of Tiberius and Gaius.

an army which set off for Spain, eventually to destroy the Celtiberians as a nation.

Scipio may have felt that he had done his duty in ensuring that his kinsman Tiberius was acquitted of all charges against him. Tiberius, unsurprisingly, felt otherwise. Not only had his reputation suffered in the military defeat, but his personal honour was in tatters. The promises which the Romans were now callously breaking were his, and the peace he had personally guaranteed had survived less than a year. This débâcle, the ancient historians agree, changed Tiberius' life, and with it the course of Roman history.

Tiberius' allies

Numantia was destroyed in 133, the year Tiberius Gracchus stood for election as tribune of the plebs. As tribune, Tiberius was very definitely first among equals. He was the son of the illustrious Tiberius Sempronius Gracchus, and grandson of Scipio Africanus. It is possible he was supported by Servius Sulpicius Galba, the consul of 144, and he certainly was by M. Fulvius Flaccus, another ex-consul. Also among his backers were the brothers Scaevola, of the ancient and powerful Mucian clan, and a Catonian, C. Porcius Cato.

Then there was Appius Claudius Pulcher, son of the colleague of Sempronius Gracchus, and the ex-consul of 143. Like all Claudians, he was a formidable character. Forbidden to triumph after his campaign against the Gallic tribes in the Alps, he celebrated one anyway. His daughter, a Vestal Virgin, rode in the chariot with him, and as Vestal Virgins were sacred, no one dared oppose him.

Another supporter was P. Licinius Crassus (an ancestor of the triumvir Crassus; pp. 175–80). One of the first tribunes ever to hold office in Rome had been a Licinius, and the family traditionally defended the people's rights. It was another Licinius, at an unknown time in the past, who had passed a law that no Roman could own more than 500 acres (200 ha) of public land. By the time of Tiberius Gracchus this law was completely ignored – Tiberius now proposed not just to restore it but actually to extend it.

Land reform in fact was long overdue in Rome. Since the Hannibalic war Roman peasants were conscripted into the army for ever longer periods. Their landholdings were taken by wealthy aristocrats using theft, coercion or cash payment. The huge estates of these aristocrats, called *latifundia*, were worked by slaves, who were cheap and did not have to do military service. The aristocrats had also encroached deep into the public land, the *ager publicus*. For generations they had treated this land as private property, developing it, and giving and receiving it in loans and dowries. Archaeology shows that peasant farmers were by no means extinct, however. From pottery findings, it seems that smallholdings were common in Veii and other parts of Italy. But the fact remains that the reserve of peasant farmers with whom Rome stocked her armies was dangerously depleted.

Land reform

Tiberius proposed giving dispossessed Romans land from the *ager publicus* and from confiscations under the Licinian Law. This land, some 30 acres (*iugera* in Latin) per family, was to be inalienable, meaning that it could not be sold, or the title transferred in any other way. It would be removed from the hands of the rich forever, and would rebuild Rome's stock of small farmers.

Thus, Tiberius would do inestimable good for Rome, and not incidentally both take revenge on the senate for betraying his Spanish peace and upstage Scipio's victory. But the historian Appian felt that Tiberius was mainly moved by genuine idealism. He quotes Tiberius himself: 'Even the savage beasts of Italy have dens in which to lay their heads. But the men who fight and die for Italy have no part of it except the air and the sunshine … they are called masters of the world, who do not possess a clod of earth that they can call their own.'

Tiberius' proposals were impeccably drafted, as might be expected since the brothers Scaevola were famous jurists. One of them was consul for 133 as colleague of the conservative Piso Frugi. Tiberius was proposing sound legislation, he had moral and legal justification – and powerful supporters. It seemed that nothing could stop his measure being carried. The bill's opponents had only their selfish interests to defend, and no credible arguments.

Tiberius against Octavius

But when the bill was read to the assembly, one tribune, Marcus Octavius, vetoed it. This act by a tribune – whose role in the Roman constitution was defined by Polybius as 'to do whatsoever as the people decree' – clearly shows how far the tribunate had been captured by the Roman oligarchy.

Arguably, Tiberius should have accepted defeat and plotted to try again another day, or he should have abandoned the issue, and gone on with the long and illustrious career that undoubtedly awaited him. However, this reverse, on the back of his humiliation in Spain, just made Tiberius more stubborn. He increased the stakes by withdrawing his offer of compensation for confiscated lands. (Though he did offer to compensate Octavius from his own pocket – a ploy which highlighted Octavius' interest in the affair.)

If his opponents could use the tribunican veto, Tiberius could too. He vetoed every piece of official business in Rome, bringing to a halt the public finances, law-making and courts. But Octavius as stubbornly refused to rescind his veto. Finally Tiberius called another assembly and presented his ultimatum – either Octavius removed his veto from the legislation, or the plebs would remove Octavius from office.

Tribe after tribe voted in favour of the motion, and with only one tribe still remaining in order to reach an absolute majority, Tiberius again appealed to Octavius to relent. Octavius would not, and he was duly removed from office.

The Great Altar of Pergamum once stood on the acropolis of that city, now in modern Turkey. The frieze depicted the battle between the Greek gods and giants, an allegory for the struggles of the kingdom of Pergamum against the Galatians, a Celtic tribe. In 1879 the altar was excavated by German archaeologists and transported to a museum in Berlin.

This was unprecedented, and possibly illegal. Cicero calls it 'a seditious act'. Even Tiberius' supporters had reservations, and his opponents talked darkly of prosecution as soon as he left office. The original land legislation was now voted through without opposition, though the senate refused to pay for the commission which was to redistribute the land.

Tiberius was opposed by another Scipio – the ex-consul of 138, Scipio Nasica. Nasica held a huge amount of public land, and wanted to keep it. Famously arrogant, he once lost an election because he shook hands with a ploughman, and, feeling his calluses, enquired if the man walked on his hands.

The cause falters

Matters were inadvertently exacerbated by Attalus, king of Pergamum, a small but prosperous kingdom in Asia Minor. When Attalus died he bequeathed his kingdom to the Roman people. Tiberius promptly legislated for money from Pergamum to fund his land commission. The senate were outraged that a tribune was now dictating Roman foreign policy. It did not help that the Pergamene ambassador had brought the news directly to Tiberius' house when he arrived in Rome. This was natural enough, as Attalus had been a friend of Tiberius Sempronius Gracchus. But rumour insisted that the ambassador had also brought a purple cloak and a diadem for Tiberius to declare himself king of Rome.

To avoid prosecution on leaving office, Tiberius needed time to consolidate. Accordingly he stood for re-election. This was against tradition, and lost Tiberius much of the support he had left. Worse, it was late July and the majority of his supporters were outside Rome, working on the land. Tiberius went about Rome dressed in black, tearfully asking the people to care for his mother and two young sons if his enemies triumphed and he failed to be elected tribune.

The election broke up in confusion over a procedural debate, but Tiberius had plainly lost the support of the other tribunes. He spent the rest of the day, and most of the night, rallying his supporters. The omens the next day were so unpropitious that Tiberius (himself an augur) almost turned back, but matters had reached a climax. In the senate, Scipio Nasica urged that Tiberius be stopped, but the pro-Gracchan consul, Mucius Scaevola, argued that the senate could not interfere in the affairs of the plebs.

A bloody ending

At this Scipio stood, and pulled his toga over his head in the manner of a priest going to sacrifice. By this act, as chief pontiff, he explicitly condoned violence. With his followers, he set out for the Capitoline where Tiberius was holding an assembly. A violent riot followed. After hundreds of years of settling internal disputes by negotiation and debate, the Romans settled this one with blood.

THE CAPITOLINE HILL

The Capitol, where Tiberius Gracchus held his last assembly, was a religious site even before the foundation of Rome – a fact mentioned in the ancient sources and confirmed by archaeology, which has found traces of Bronze Age settlements on the hill.

The Tarquins confirmed the Capitol as the religious focus of Rome by building on it the massive temple to Jupiter Optimus Maximus – the Best and Greatest. This temple was burned down in 83 BC and was rebuilt by Lutatius Catulus, a descendant of the admiral who brought the first Carthaginian war to a successful conclusion. The foundations of the temple can be seen today, though the Catulan temple was also destroyed, this time in fighting during the year of the four emperors in AD 69.

In the first year of the Republic the Capitol was made sacred to the three deities, known today as the Capitoline Triad – Jupiter, Juno and Minerva. Roman colonies reproduced both temple and triad across the Mediterranean.

The Capitoline is the smallest of the fabled seven hills of Rome. It has two separate peaks, the Capitolium and the Arx. In the saddle between,

Romulus supposedly built the temple of Asylum. The Tarpeian Rock, on the side of the Capitol facing the Forum of the Romans, was situated above a steep drop; from here criminals were hurled to their doom. A primitive ancient hut also stood on the hill, where priests went to seek the auguries.

It was on the Capitol that the new year started when the consuls sacrificed, and here Roman governors swore their oaths before they went to their provinces. If the governors were successful in war, it was here that their triumphal procession ended with a final sacrifice.

If the Palatine, where the emperors lived, was the focal point of the Roman Empire, then the Capitol was the focal point of the Republic, and it was

probably for that reason that the Romans insisted that it did not fall in the Gallic sack of Rome. It probably did; though if any one hill was suitable for a stand, it was the Capitol, so the matter is by no means certain.

The emperor Marcus Aurelius making a sacrifice in front of the Temple of Capitoline Jove. Although the temple had changed (the Republican temple was destroyed in AD 69), the ritual of sacrifice on the Capitoline remained unaltered for almost a millennium.

THE ROMAN TOGA

Perhaps nothing distinguished Roman citizens from other peoples as much as the peculiar garment known as the toga. Yet despite this, we do not have any real idea of how often it was actually worn.

There can be no doubt that the Romans wore their togas on formal occasions, which is why we see so many statues of togate Romans. But for any kind of manual activity, togas were completely unsuitable as they had no fastenings of any kind and the elaborately folded mass had to be held in place by keeping the left arm bent.

The toga itself was made of wool; it was not dyed, except under special circumstances. A man standing for political office might whiten his toga to indicate the fact – and the *toga candida* he wore for the occasion gives us the modern word 'candidate'. A general celebrating a triumph would wear a toga dyed purple, and for certain office holders, a toga with a purple border was permitted as a sign of rank.

The Romans also had togas made of undyed dark wool, but these were only worn to indicate mourning or distress. Thus Romans might wear dark togas if on trial or during a national disaster, and, of course, after a death in the family.

Togas were worn only by freeborn Roman males. Evidence suggests that the toga, or something very much like it, originated among the Etruscans and was worn by men and women.

The toga was a single piece of woven wool in the shape of a semicircle and was not small, measuring almost 20 ft (6 m) across the circumference. The wearer started with the mass of material at his feet, then threw one end over his left shoulder, across his back and around his body. From there it finished in an elaborate series of drapes, all held in place by the crooked left arm.

We know that by the later Empire the toga was hardly used, and even at the end of the Republic, Augustus reproached his fellow citizens for so rarely appearing in the national costume. But the fact was that for most purposes a simple tunic was generally more appropriate, and while the woollen mass of a toga might have a purpose in winter, it must have been torture in midsummer.

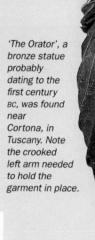

'The Orator', a bronze statue probably dating to the first century BC, was found near Cortona, in Tuscany. Note the crooked left arm needed to hold the garment in place.

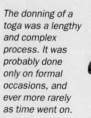

The donning of a toga was a lengthy and complex process. It was probably done only on formal occasions, and ever more rarely as time went on.

Scipio was victorious, and over 100 Gracchan supporters were killed; among them Tiberius himself. His body, like the others, was thrown into the Tiber like a common criminal's.

Though the oligarchs had won, the price was high. Thereafter the Roman people were split. You were either for the Gracchi, or against them. All eyes turned to Gaius Gracchus, the younger brother of Tiberius. Would he take the fate of his brother as a warning, or as a challenge?

Gaius Gracchus

(*c.* 153–121 BC)

GAIUS GRACCHUS	
Born	*Achievements*
c. 153 BC	Substantial
Famous ancestors	legislation
Sempronius (cos.	*Wives*
215)	Junia(?), Licinia
Mother	*Children*
Cornelia	At least 2, no
Father	details
Sempronius	*Death*
Gracchus	Suicide 121 BC
Positions held	
Tribune 123, 122	

If I ask you one favour, that you let me live a quiet life in these troubled times, because my family is of the highest nobility, and I have already lost a brother in your cause, and now no one remains of the line of Scipio Africanus and Tiberius Gracchus but myself and one small boy, if, so that our line might not perish utterly. If I were to ask that one favour of you....

From a speech of Gaius Gracchus

THE DEATH OF TIBERIUS GRACCHUS left Rome on the edge of civil war. To conciliate the outraged plebs, the senate did not now oppose Tiberius' proposed land legislation.

The legacy of Tiberius

One commentator observed 'The senate punished the tribune, but preserved his law'. By great good fortune several marker stones of the land commission instituted by that law have survived. They are generally in the form of stone pillars and bear the names C. (Gaius) Sempronius (Gracchus), Ap. Claudius and P. Licinius (Crassus).

In 132 the consuls embarked on a barbaric witch hunt of Gracchan supporters. One man was killed by being thrust into a cage of poisonous

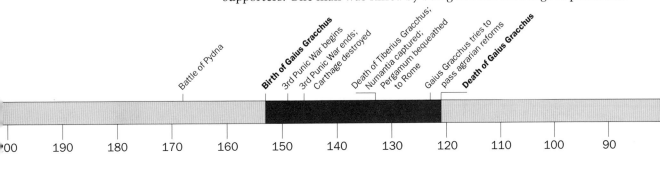

Battle of Pydna · Birth of Gaius Gracchus · 3rd Punic War begins · 3rd Punic War ends; Carthage destroyed · Death of Tiberius Gracchus; Numantia captured; Pergamum bequeathed to Rome · Gaius Gracchus tries to pass agrarian reforms · Death of Gaius Gracchus

'00   190   180   170   160   150   140   130   120   110   100   90

snakes. Another, called Vettius, faced the death sentence, but was reprieved after a passionate defence by Tiberius' younger brother Gaius, then in his early twenties.

Gaius had joined the army at the earliest possible age, probably 16. He served with his relative Scipio Aemilianus in the Numantian campaign and was quaestor in 126. In the family tradition he was an exceptional soldier, with high standards of honesty and good behaviour. Later, he married a Licinia, the daughter of the Gracchan supporter Crassus. (Licinia was later to marry a Brutus – a man of a totally different political complexion but the same moral standards.)

Some thought Gaius' quiet, reclusive life was a result of his brother's fate, but in a speech in 131 he gave clear warning of his intentions. 'You villains, who killed Tiberius, the best of brothers, watch, and see how I will repay you in the same way.'

Preparing for power

Gaius decided that his brother had lacked a solid core of supporters, so he turned to the Equites (knights) and the peoples of the Italian peninsula. The latter had become restive under the arrogance and oppression of the Romans. Fregellae, a town in the Liris valley, once one of Rome's strongest supporters, had been pushed to open revolt, and then mercilessly destroyed by the praetor Opimius. (Archaeologists have excavated a second-century BC sanctuary of Asclepius which was demolished at that time.)

As Gaius was preparing to stand for tribune, the horrified senate seized on a device to keep him out of the way. Gaius was serving with the army in Sicily when the senate voted to keep the commander of the army there at his post. His junior officers, including Gaius, therefore had to remain with him. Gaius defiantly returned to Rome. Impeached before the censors, he pointed to his 12 years of military service (only 10 were required). Also, his present posting had been for three years, while the law only required one.

Gaius' election to the tribunate in 124 was a formality. The new tribune was very different in character from his brother Tiberius. Tiberius had been cool and reasoned, Gaius was fiery and passionate. But where Tiberius had been impulsive and obstinate, Gaius was calculating. He had a quick temper and such magnificent oratorical ability that Cicero, no friend of the brothers Gracchus, called his death a 'massive loss' to Latin literature. Gaius was not always refined. When someone spoke slightingly about his mother, he responded viciously 'How dare you speak of her in that way? You are a man, yet my mother has kept off men for longer than you have.'

He employed a slave with a flute to sound a warning note when his passionate nature made him too heated. In private he was earnest and persuasive, though some contemporaries mention a love of *la dolce vita* that had him returning noisily home long after decent Romans were tucked up in bed.

A Gracchan boundary marker stone (cast), recording C. Sempronius, Ap. Claudius and P. Licinius, *c*. 132/1 BC. Stones such as these testify to the Gracchan land reforms, showing that the brothers did, on the whole, achieve the objectives for which they gave their lives.

Measuring out grain: a floor mosaic in the Piazzale delle Corporazioni, Ostia, second century AD. At the time of the Gracchi, Rome had a population of about 250,000, and had to import most of its food. Gaius established the *frumentatio*, which allowed the sale of grain at an equitable price.

Putting Rome to rights

Late nights did not interfere with sheer hard work. Showing tremendous administrative ability, Gaius reorganized whole sections of the Roman state from top to bottom, with both meticulous attention to detail and a broad grasp of the issues. He had quite probably spent the previous decade planning the programme that he now put into place.

Vengeance came first, and a warning to the senate. Gaius made it illegal to put Roman citizens to death without trial before the people. The law was retroactive and it forced Popillius, one of the consuls in 132, into exile. Another law – that those removed from office by the people could not hold any subsequent office – was clearly aimed at Octavius, but Gaius withdrew it at the request of his mother Cornelia.

Rome was dependent on grain from abroad, and the price could fluctuate wildly according to the harvest, slave revolts or, in one case, a plague of locusts. Gaius stabilized the price of grain at an affordable level, a measure decried by Cicero as 'a great bribe'. This strengthened Gaius' position with the people but was opposed by senators concerned about Rome's finances. Their leader was one Piso Frugi, so Gaius was surprised to find this man queuing for subsidized grain. Piso explained 'if you stole my property and distributed it among the Roman people, you would also find me here, queuing to get some of my own back again.'

Despite Piso's fears, Rome's finances were secure. Gaius had ensured this by exploiting Rome's control of the immense wealth of Asia Minor. He set up the system whereby vast corporations bid to collect provincial taxes in return for a percentage of the profits. This system, called tax farming, continued through the life of the Republic. Senators were forbidden membership of these corporations, which were controlled by knights.

Gaius drove another wedge between these two groups with a law excluding senators from sitting on juries in extortion cases. The knights alone, therefore, judged the conduct of provincial governors. As every ambitious senator wanted to govern a province, the enmity of the knights could be fatal. For the first time in Roman history, the senate's monopoly of power was broken. The senate bitterly opposed the idea, which was passed into law by a majority of one tribe. A commentator remarked 'In return for supporting the tribunes, the knights obtained whatever they wanted, and the senators were terrified.'

Some of this legislation, or at least legislation based on it, is preserved on the brass Tablet of Bembo, which is named after the medieval cardinal who once owned it. Ninety lines of Latin, though far from intact, relate Gaius' proposals on extortion cases in immense detail.

THE GRACCHI

So when Tiberius and Gaius Gracchus, men whose ancestors had done much in the Punic war and other wars to increase the power of Rome, tried to establish the liberty of the common people, and expose the crimes of the aristocracy, the guilty nobles became frightened, and opposed what they were doing by every means at their disposal, using now the Italian allies, and Latin communities, and now the equestrian order, whom they had seduced from the people's cause, while offering them the hope of being allowed to share the privileges which the aristocracy enjoyed. First Tiberius was butchered, while he was actually a tribune. Because he tried to follow his brother's example Gaius suffered the same fate a few years later.

Sallust, writing on the Gracchi 90 years later: *War with Jugurtha 42*

Gaius Gracchus weeping before his father's statue, engraving by B. Barlocini, 1849. The father of the Gracchus brothers left his sons with a web of political alliances, money and clients. The brothers spent these resources freely in their battles with the Roman establishment.

The senate becomes more hostile

The senate was further restricted by another measure – that the senate choose the tasks of the consuls before they were elected. This meant that the senate could decide what was to be done, but the electorate chose who did it.

So large was his programme that it became apparent that the 31-year-old tribune needed another year, despite his energy. But Gaius made it plain that he would not stand for re-election; he did, however, campaign for his closest supporter, Fulvius Flaccus. In another reversal of precedent, Flaccus was standing for tribune despite having already been consul.

Gaius was elected even though he was not standing as a candidate; according to Plutarch this was achieved 'without his seeking or petitioning for it, but at the voluntary motion of the people'. The main proposals of Gaius' second tribunate were the founding of a large Roman colony on the site of Carthage and the enfranchisement of the Italian citizens. Both measures were hugely controversial. Gaius went himself to see the Carthaginian colony settled, and the senate smelled a chance for revenge. As Hannibal had discovered, and as Julius Caesar was later to find out, no one held grudges like the Roman senate.

The senate's demagogue

To separate the Roman people from Gaius, the senate endorsed another tribune, Livius Drusus. Drusus was a noble, possibly a great-grandson of the Aemilius Paullus who died at Cannae. Drusus took all that Gaius had promised the people, and offered more. He attacked the enfranchisement of the Italians, pointing out that more for everyone meant less for those who already had it. So, posing as a popular champion, Drusus vetoed Gaius' proposals.

In Carthage, the omens for the refounded city were terrible (doubtless because of some non-divine intervention). People recalled that Carthage had been formally cursed, and support began to ebb away. The consuls ordered all non-voters out of Rome before the coming elections. A weakened Gaius was unable to veto this, or even protect those who defied the edict. Not only was Gaius not re-elected, but the next year's consuls were a Fabius and Opimius, the grim destroyer of Fregellae's revolt.

For his remaining term in office, Gaius worked hard on an extensive programme of impressive public buildings and road construction and improvement throughout Italy. Everyone knew that when Gaius laid down his office, the senate would strike.

The expected provocation was a proposal to revoke the colonization of Carthage. Gaius had to oppose this, and he did. His supporters were determined to protect him at all costs. So when Gaius pushed away a senatorial supporter who pressed too close, his supporters over-reacted, and stabbed the man to death. Gaius tried promptly to distance himself from the event, but the damage was done.

PUBLICANI

At its greatest extent, the territory of the Roman Republic stretched from the Atlantic Ocean to the shores of the Black Sea. To administer this vast empire, the Republic employed about the same number of staff as the council of a single medium-sized modern city.

This amazing feat was achieved by the delegation of almost all state functions to private individuals, or to corporations of private individuals, called *publicani*. The *publicani* were controlled by the senate, particularly by the censors, who were responsible for the contracts by which the state employed them. They provided public works (such as roads and aqueducts), supplies (such as horses and armour) and services (particularly tax collection), in return for a cash payment from the state.

Contracts were awarded by public auction, with the contract going to the company which accepted the lowest offer. Sometimes companies accepted too little for their services, and attempted to renegotiate terms once they had the contract. (They tried this with Cato the Censor, and got short shrift.)

The *publicani* were crucial in supplying Rome with ordnance during the wars against Carthage, though they caused several scandals by profiteering and supplying sub-standard goods. After the Carthaginian wars, the *publicani* re-organized the Spanish silver mines to make huge profits for themselves and the state but at the expense of hellish conditions for the unfortunate slaves who worked them.

As the Republic grew more prosperous, there was a move towards indirect taxation, with the *publicani* forming corporations to collect harbour dues and road tolls.

Gaius Gracchus' legislation, which gave them the right to collect the tithes of Asia, raised the *publicani* to a new status. Asia was far wealthier than the rest of the empire and the tax companies made huge profits. Naturally, most of these profits came at the expense of the natives of these provinces, for it was in the interests of the *publicani* to collect as much in taxes as possible.

The *publicani* rapidly dominated the equestrian class from which they came (senators were forbidden to engage in commerce). The knights were also in charge of the courts which investigated corruption, particularly of provincial governors. Thus a provincial governor who tried to rein in their exploitation ran the risk of being found guilty in a kangaroo court. One victim was Rutilius Rufus, who tried to restrain the *publicani* in his province and ended up being exiled from Rome on trumped-up corruption charges. He was exiled and retired to live as a hero among the very people he had been found guilty of exploiting.

The letters of Cicero reveal that he made great efforts to balance the demands of the *publicani* with the welfare of the people he was governing. Many governors did not even attempt to do this, or happily collaborated in looting the provinces they were meant to govern. (In fact, abuses by governors were generally on a greater scale than those of the *publicani*.)

The civil wars which ended the Republic were a disaster for the *publicani*. Their revenues were expropriated by the warlords, and many of the richer members were proscribed for their wealth. The *publicani* entered the Imperial period as shadows of their former greatness, and the tasks they had performed in the Republic were gradually taken over by the state.

A relief showing knights on the way to a sacrifice, second–first century BC, Volterra. The legislation of Gaius Gracchus drove a wedge into the social cohesion of the knights and senators. It set the knights, who were often engaged in commerce in the provinces of the empire, against the senators, who were responsible for government.

The *Senatus Consultum Ultimum*

The senate met in emergency session and interpreted their supporter's death as a presage of impending chaos, though Gaius had in fact acted promptly to suppress further violence. The senate passed the *Senatus Consultum Ultimum* – the famous 'Last Decree'. This decree simply ordered the consuls to ensure that the state came to no harm. Unofficially it gave a senatorial endorsement to whatever action the consuls took towards that end.

Consequently, it was highly alarming for Gaius and Fulvius Flaccus to receive a summons to appear before the consuls the next morning. Gaius felt that he should go. He had a strong case, and had done nothing illegal. Fulvius was less sanguine, and he persuaded Gaius to reject the summons. They went to the Aventine hill, to the Temple of Diana, sending the son of Fulvius down to negotiate. The consul Opimius would have none of it. The Gracchans had been given their chance and now the matter would end in blood.

The struggle was short and one-sided. Gaius did not fight with any great enthusiasm, and when all was lost his supporters persuaded him to flee. They fought a desperate rearguard action for him, ironically enough on the same Sublician bridge that Horatius once held against the Etruscans. Their sacrifice was in vain. Gaius reached a sacred grove, and there, aided by a trusted servant, he took his own life. Some 250 of his supporters died that day, and more in the purges that followed.

In a travesty of restoring the social order, Opimius rebuilt the Temple of Concord, which legend said had been first constructed by Furius Camillus to celebrate the cessation of strife between the social classes. The rebuilt temple was one of the first to use concrete on a large scale and its foundations survive to this day. The triumph of the senate was much more fleeting.

(*Above*) A bronze coin struck under the emperor Tiberius between AD 34 and 37, showing the Temple of Concord. Originally built in 367 BC, the temple was rebuilt in 121 BC after the death of Gaius Gracchus. Cicero gave one of his speeches against Catiline from here. The emperor Tiberius ordered considerable renovation of the building, which is situated at the foot of the Capitol.

(*Right*) Remains of the Temple of Concord, seen from the west. In its prime the temple was packed with magnificent works of art, and was sometimes used for meetings of the senate. The consul Opimius, who ordered the temple to be rebuilt after Gaius' death, also built the nearby Basilica Opimia, which is now completely destroyed.

Marcus Aemilius Scaurus

(*c.* 163–89 BC)

Quintus Caecilius Metellus Numidicus

(*c.* 150–91 BC)

MARCUS AEMILIUS SCAURUS	
Born	*Achievements*
c. 163 BC	Triumphator; built
Famous ancestors	Via Aemilia Scauri
King Numa (?)	*Wife*
Mother	Metella
Unknown	*Children*
Father	Son: Marcus
Unknown	Scaurus (praetor
Positions held	56)
Consul 115; Censor	*Death*
109	Old age 89 BC

MARCUS AEMILIUS SCAURUS

Aemilius Scaurus was an enterprising nobleman, a political intriguer with a lust for money, power and advancement; but he had enough cunning to hide his faults.... Jugurtha's bribery was so open and shameless that it was certain to arouse popular resentment. So for once, Scaurus controlled his natural greed.

Sallust, *War with Jugurtha* 15

THE AEMILIANS WERE ONE OF ROME'S great patrician clans, but not all branches enjoyed the same fortune. As Aemilius Paullus rose to fame, the Scaurus side of the family was in decline. Marcus Aemilius Scaurus later claimed in his autobiography – the first of that genre in Rome – that he had to struggle as hard as any *novus homo* (those who were the first in their families to reach the senate).

A master politician

Scaurus was cunning and unscrupulous, and made sure he was never associated with a losing cause. His allies were the newly ascendant Caecilii Metelli, a family with a long history in Rome but one which remained

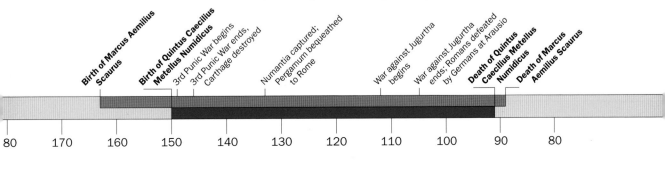

Birth of Marcus Aemilius Scaurus

Birth of Quintus Caecilius Metellus Numidicus

3rd Punic War begins

3rd Punic War ends, Carthage destroyed

Numantia captured; Pergamum bequeathed to Rome

War against Jugurtha begins

War against Jugurtha ends; Romans defeated by Germans at Arausio

Death of Quintus Caecilius Metellus Numidicus

Death of Marcus Aemilius Scaurus

80   170   160   150   140   130   120   110   100   90   80

Coin showing the Temple of Vesta, with the curule chair, the official chair of consuls, praetors, censors and aediles, which was something like a folding camp-stool. The coin also depicts a voting urn and the letters AC (*absolvo/condemno* – 'I acquit/convict'); denarius of Q. Cassius, *c.* 55 BC.

obscure until the end of the second century. He married Caecilia Metella – a lady, it seems, with a taste for fallen aristocrats made good, as she later married the up-and-coming Cornelius Sulla (pp. 164–71).

Scaurus became wealthy (though our sources suggest that his riches were less than honestly gained), and ascended the political ladder until the year 115 saw him as a consul of Rome, with M. Caecilius Metellus. Many nobles looked down their patrician noses at Scaurus' money grubbing, and he was sensitive to this. When the praetor P. Decius failed to stand when Scaurus passed by, the new consul stormed over to Decius and ordered him to do so. Then Scaurus ripped Decius' clothes and smashed his official chair. He later passed an edict forbidding litigants to appear in Decius' court.

This tantrum aside, while in office Scaurus passed a sumptuary law forbidding flagrant displays of wealth and amended the voting rights of those freed from slavery. He campaigned against Rome's long-standing enemies in the western Alps, the Ligurians, and celebrated a triumph. Scaurus' lasting memorial was a road, the Via Aemilia Scauri, which linked the great highways of the Via Postumia and the Via Aurelia.

In 109 Scaurus became censor with M. Livius Drusus – the same Drusus who had been the senate's puppet in the campaign against Gaius Gracchus (p. 136). To Scaurus' annoyance, Drusus died, and tradition obliged Scaurus to step down. He did so with the greatest reluctance, and only when the tribunes threatened to arrest him if he did not comply.

As some compensation, Scaurus later received the honorary and honourable position of *Princeps Senatus* (chief senator) from the censor of the day – a Metellus, as it happened. He then cynically used his influence to take over from Appuleius Saturninus (pp. 146–49) as curator of the grain supply (*cura annonae*) in 105 – an office which was a route to popular favour. The embittered Saturninus became a revolutionary tribune in the Gracchan style, and he later died the same way – and it was Scaurus himself who moved the Last Decree in the senate against him.

Scaurus went on embassies to Africa and Asia, and had a huge network of clients and dependants. Cicero was to say of him that 'the whole world was ruled, almost by his nod'. He also became a confidant of Livius Drusus (pp. 159–63), the son of his former censorial colleague.

Scaurus on trial

Scaurus was often indicted, but never condemned in court. His greatest peril came when peace was made with King Jugurtha of Numidia in Africa – Scaurus had been an advocate of peace, not least because Rome faced a terrifying threat from hordes of migratory German tribes to the north (p. 152). Jugurtha benefited mightily from the settlement, and bribery was suspected to have played a part. The Numidian king was promised immunity if he came to Rome to testify exactly whom he had bribed. But before Jugurtha was able to give his testimony, a tribune (no doubt bribed himself) vetoed the process. War resumed and when Rome suffered a humiliating defeat a witch hunt was started for

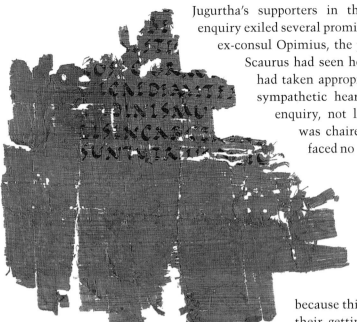

The oldest surviving fragment of Sallust's *War with Jugurtha*, papyrus, fourth century AD. Though thousands of ancient papyri survive, this is one of the handful which was written in Latin. Other existing fragments include some of the work of Cicero and an epitome of Livy.

Jugurtha's supporters in the senate. A commission of enquiry exiled several prominent Romans, among them the ex-consul Opimius, the persecutor of Gaius Gracchus. Scaurus had seen how the wind was blowing and had taken appropriate steps. He received a very sympathetic hearing from the commission of enquiry, not least because the commission was chaired by Scaurus himself, and he faced no charges.

At the age of 72 Scaurus was indicted again, on a charge that he had encouraged the younger Livius Drusus in his sympathy for the Italian cause. A Roman of Spanish origin, Q. Varius, alleged that the Italian allies rebelled because this sympathy had not resulted in their getting the vote, and that Scaurus had thus indirectly incited the revolt.

Scaurus' defence was short, and totally irrefutable. 'The Spaniard, Q. Varius, accuses the *Princeps Senatus*, M. Aemilius Scaurus, of inciting the allies to revolt. The *Princeps Senatus*, M. Aemilius Scaurus, denies the charge. There are no witnesses. Which of the two, people of Rome, do you choose to believe?'

Scaurus was acquitted, but had taken offence. Q. Varius was brought before his own court to face the same charges which he had levelled at Scaurus. He was found guilty and condemned. It is uncertain when Scaurus died, but it was probably in 89, as his wife re-married soon after.

QUINTUS CAECILIUS METELLUS NUMIDICUS

When I was a boy I heard my father say that when Quintus Metellus, the son of Lucius, was prosecuted for extortion and peculation … when he was before the court, and when his account-books were being carried round to the judges that they might see the entry of one item, there was not one judge who did not avert his eyes, or turn himself completely away, in case any one of them should appear to have doubted what such a man had entered in his public accounts.

Cicero, *Pro Balbo* 11

QUINTUS CAECILIUS METELLUS	
Born	*Achievements*
c. 150 BC	Triumphator
Famous ancestors	*Wife*
L. Metellus (cos. 251)	Unknown
Mother	*Children*
Unknown	Son: Metellus Pius
Father	*Death*
Metellus Calvus	Old age/poisoned
Positions held	91 BC
Consul 109; Censor 102	

THE FAMILY OF CAECILIUS METELLUS had no earlier distinction than a consul of 251 who campaigned successfully against the Carthaginians in Sicily in the First Punic War, but after 133 they exploded on to the political scene. The consul of 142, Metellus Calvus, had two sons, Delmaticus and Numidicus, each of whom became consul and censor. Delmaticus' four sons in turn each became consul, as did the two sons of Numidicus.

A respected aristocrat

Numidicus was the most respected of this formidable political dynasty. He was an unswerving optimate – a supporter of the aristocratic cause – but even the common people respected his honesty and integrity.

He was consul in 109, with Numidia in North Africa as his province. At this time the Romans were at war with the troublesome Jugurtha, the Numidian king. Jugurtha had stayed ahead of the Romans in the conflict by a mixture of cunning, political skill and ruthless exploitation of the ineptitude and cupidity of the generals sent against him.

Numidicus' predecessor, Albinus, had left the army in a shocking state. His under-trained and poorly disciplined soldiers preferred oppressing the areas under their control to fighting the enemy. Numidicus leavened this rabble with soldiers brought over to Africa with him, and forbade luxuries within the Roman camps. He then toughened the troops by taking them on long route marches into the desert.

Jugurtha was alarmed. Faced with a competent opponent whom he could not bribe, he tried to make peace. Numidicus appeared interested, but was in fact using the Numidian king's own tactics against him. Jugurtha often offered peace negotiations to delay and mislead his enemies while he prepared for war.

A major battle followed at the River Muthul – it was a confused and bloody affair, but it convinced Jugurtha that he stood little chance in the open field. Thereafter he fought a guerrilla campaign, while Numidicus tried to take his towns and cities.

Numidicus and Marius

Numidicus had a competent lieutenant called Marius (pp. 149–59). That Marius had higher ambitions soon became abundantly clear. He asked Numidicus for leave to campaign for the consulship in Rome. For over a century the consulship had been the exclusive preserve of the Roman aristocracy and 'new men' were kept out of their tightly closed ranks. Metellus pointed this out, and said 'If you must stand for the consulship, wait until my son is old enough to stand as your colleague.'

Perhaps Numidicus intended to be helpful. A co-candidacy with a Metellus would certainly aid Marius; but Marius chose to regard it as an insulting quip – the son of Numidicus was 20 years away from being eligible for the consulship, and Marius was 48.

Marius spread rumours in Rome that Numidicus was prolonging the war for his own glory, and that only he could bring it to a swift end. Helpfully, Jugurtha retook the town of Vaga by treachery, and Numidicus was forced to put the commander of Vaga's garrison to death, as guilty of either treason or gross negligence.

Marius' tactics worked, and the African command was transferred to him in 107. In a fury, Numidicus left for Rome early, leaving the handover to his aide, Rutilius Rufus. Numidicus expected a difficult reception in Rome from Marius' supporters, but he was welcomed warmly by people and aristocracy alike. In 102 he received the honour of the censorship.

Silver denarius of a triumph of Q. Caecilius Metellus, c. 125–120 BC, showing him crowned by victory as he rides in a chariot drawn by elephants. Though they replaced him with Marius for the African campaign, Metellus remained popular with the Roman people.

Opposing Saturninus

As censor he opposed the rising power of Saturninus (pp. 146–49), a tribune in the Gracchan mould. Saturninus produced a man called Equitius whom he tried to pass off as the son of Tiberius Gracchus. Numidicus refused to enrol this man on the list of citizens; an act which caused him some unpopularity until Sempronia, the sister of the Gracchus brothers, came forward to swear that the man was an impostor.

Numidicus then tried to expel both Saturninus and his confederate Glaucia from the senate, but Numidicus' own colleague and cousin, Metellus Caprarius, vetoed him. In Rome, the veto of one magistrate always overrode the act of his colleague, so the attempt failed. It was not long before Saturninus fought back, and in 100 he proposed agrarian legislation. Those who did not swear to accept it were to face a huge fine.

This was clearly aimed at Numidicus, whose honour would not permit him to swear such an oath. It was very probably Marius' idea, as Saturninus' approach was rather less subtle – he had earlier tried to persuade the mob to stone Numidicus to death. Naturally, Numidicus refused to swear any oath instigated by Saturninus. He was tried for treason and exiled from Rome. Some senators planned armed violence to prevent this, but Numidicus dissuaded them.

Exile and return

He took his exile stoically, perhaps in a very literal sense, spending much of his time reading the work of the philosophers and hearing presentations from them. His son campaigned for his return so fiercely that his efforts earned him the *cognomen* 'Pius'.

Fragment of a marble tablet recording the achievements of the Metelli. The words 'cos' (consul) and 'pro.cos' appear very often – a reflection of the degree to which the Metelli dominated these offices at the end of the Republic.

Saturninus and Marius did not long remain allies, and Saturninus died at the hands of an avenging senate. Marius tried hard to prevent Numidicus from being recalled to Rome, but the growing influence of the Metellus clan was a match for his efforts. In late 99 the tribune Calidus passed legislation allowing Numidicus to return, which he did to a hero's welcome.

Thereafter, Numidicus took less interest in politics, preferring to cultivate the arts and his friendship with the poet Archias. When he stirred himself to it, he remained an articulate and moving orator. He died just before the Social, or Italian, War (see box p. 155), perhaps poisoned by his enemies, as some claimed, but more probably from natural causes.

L. Appuleius Saturninus
(c. 138–100 BC)

Gaius Marius
(157–86 BC)

Livius Drusus
(c. 128–91 BC)

Lucius Cornelius Sulla Felix
(138–78 BC)

Metellus Pius
(c. 130–c. 64 BC)

Quintus Sertorius
(c. 126–73 BC)

Marcus Licinius Crassus Dives
(c. 115–53 BC)

Gnaeus Pompey, the Great
(106–48 BC)

Licinius Lucullus
(c. 110–57 BC)

Cato the Stoic
(95–46 BC)

Publius Clodius Pulcher
(c. 95–52 BC)

Julius Caesar
(100–44 BC)

Marcus Iunius Brutus
(85–42 BC)

Marcus Tullius Cicero
(106–43 BC)

Mark Antony
(83–30 BC)

Marcus Aemilius Lepidus
(c. 90–c. 13 BC)

Sextus Pompey
(c. 67–36 BC)

Octavian
(63 BC – AD 14)

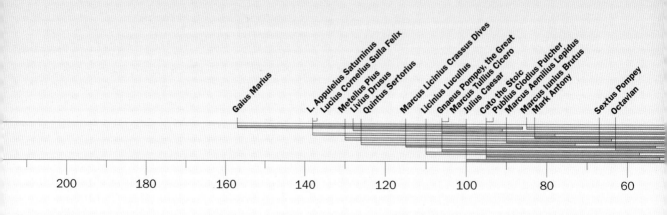

Sulla Felix

Gnaeus Pompey

Julius Caesar

Mark Antony

THE LAST REPUBLICANS
100–31 BC

ROME IN THE LATE REPUBLIC was a dysfunctional state. The Roman failure to face reform in the second century BC led to a revolt by the oppressed non-Roman peoples of Italy at the start of the first century.

This war, too, the Romans won, but only by conceding the principal demand of the Italian rebels – that they be allowed into the state as full citizens. As such, the Italian people also entered the Roman legions, at a time when the nature of military service was changing. No longer was the Roman legionary a peasant farmer who completed his term of military service and retired to the family farm. More often he was a landless man who joined the eagles to make his fortune. So the Roman legions now contained a large number of soldiers who had recently been fighting against Rome, and a similar proportion who had the least investment in the status quo.

The power struggles among the Roman élite regularly produced losers who in the past had nowhere to turn. Now they found a soldiery ready to take up their cause, and to win for them by arms what they had failed to achieve politically.

Sulla set the pattern for the late Republic – defeated by mob violence in Rome, he led his army against the city, and conquered it. For the next fifty years, Rome was torn between the wreckers, who did not care what happened as long as they achieved their personal ends, and those who strove, for altruistic or selfish reasons, to preserve the Republic.

L. Appuleius Saturninus
(*c.* 138–100 BC)

Gaius Marius
(157–86 BC)

Livius Drusus
(*c.* 128–91 BC)

A first-century BC marble bust thought to represent Gaius Marius; it is a good example of Republican Roman portraiture, in which vigorous realism is favoured rather than idealized subjects.

L. APPULEIUS SATURNINUS	
Born	*Positions held*
c. 138 BC	Tribune 103, 100, 99
Famous ancestors	*Achievements*
None	Land legislation
Mother	*Death*
Unknown	Stoned to death
Father	100 BC
Unknown	

L. APPULEIUS SATURNINUS

The madness of Glaucia and Appuleius Saturninus, who were ripping apart the Republic by continually holding office, and who broke up elections with the sword, these men the consul restrained, and caused to be put to death in the Roman Senate house.

Velleius Paterculus, *Historia* 2.12.6

AFTER THE GRACCHANS, ROME WAS TO FACE a series of turbulent tribunes, as other aristocrats came to realize how the office could be used to further their careers. The next in the line was Saturninus, a man who shared Tiberius Gracchus' antipathy for the Roman aristocracy, but who had none of Tiberius' nobility.

Falling out with the senate

The Appuleians were a moderately distinguished clan of praetorian rank, and in 105 Appuleius Saturninus was quaestor for the *cura annonae* in Ostia – the official in charge of importing grain for Rome. (Rome had long passed the size where it could feed itself from the local area.) Because of its crucial importance to the Roman plebs, good management of the grain

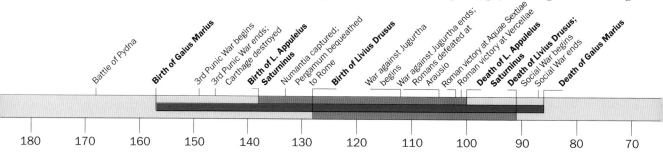

Battle of Pydna

Birth of Gaius Marius

3rd Punic War begins

3rd Punic War ends; Carthage destroyed

Birth of L. Appuleius Saturninus

Numantia captured; Pergamum bequeathed to Rome

Birth of Livius Drusus

War against Jugurtha begins

War against Jugurtha ends; Romans defeated at Arausio

Roman victory at Aquae Sextiae

Roman victory at Vercellae

Death of L. Appuleius Saturninus

Death of Livius Drusus; Social War begins

Social War ends

Death of Gaius Marius

| 180 | 170 | 160 | 150 | 140 | 130 | 120 | 110 | 100 | 90 | 80 | 70 |

supply was a vote-winner and a useful office for any ambitious politician to hold. So Aemilius Scaurus (pp. 139–41) had taken advantage of a slight rise in the price of grain to oust Saturninus and replace him. This act is generally believed to have turned Saturninus against the nobility.

Whatever the cause, Saturninus was a thorough demagogue by the time he became tribune of the plebs for 103. He allied himself with another firebrand tribune, C. Norbanus, to attack the incompetent Roman generals who had been defeated by the Germans (p. 152). One of them, a Q. Servilius Caepio, was first imprisoned and later driven into exile. To achieve his purpose, Saturninus brought into being the *Lex Appuleia de Maiestate*, a charge which accused the defendant of bringing the Roman people into disrepute. (Literally, 'diminishing the majesty of the Roman people'.) This was not the first time such a charge had been levelled, but Saturninus went a step further by setting up a permanent court to try accusations.

In his assault on the nobility, Saturninus found a natural ally in Gaius Marius (pp. 149–59), and one piece of his legislation concerned the distribution of land grants to Marius' veterans of the African campaign. Marius' men, having been recruited from the *capite censi*, would have had no land of their own to settle on after their discharge.

After his period as tribune, Saturninus remained popular. He was a gifted speaker, and had found another ally in one Servilius Glaucia, an ambitious and rising politician. The censor of the time, Metellus Numidicus (pp. 141–43), decided that the two were an unhealthy influence on the state and wanted them struck from the rolls, but Numidicus was blocked in his attempt by his colleague, Metellus Caprarius.

The pair also offered a candidate for the tribuneship, whose name was Equitius. According to them, he was the son of the great reforming tribune Tiberius Gracchus. According to others, including the censor Numidicus, he was a runaway slave, and Sempronia, the sister of the Gracchi, settled the debate when she firmly refused to recognize him, despite the imprecations and threats of the Saturninans.

Land legislation

In 100 Saturninus was tribune again. He immediately brought forward another ambitious programme of land legislation, again to find land for Marian veterans. This time it was the victors of the war against the Germans (p. 153), and Saturninus proposed to settle the bulk of them in Transalpine Gaul, which had now been absorbed into the Roman state. Those senators who had been eyeing the new lands themselves were not pleased, but Saturninus upset them much more with his proposals for a radical land redistribution bill.

Also controversial were his ambitious plans to settle colonists in Greece, Asia and Africa, as well as in different parts of Italy. Some of the colonies were to be for non-citizens, a far-sighted and unpopular move that was probably proposed by Marius, who was also given the right to enfranchise some non-Roman colonists. The legislation was not popular,

Voters cross a gangway and are handed a tally on their way to the ballot box. Silver denarius of P. Licinius Nerva, c. 113/112 BC. Marius had the voting procedure changed to make these votes secret.

especially with the nobility, but Saturninus forced it through. He added a *sanctio*, a rider that said that anyone who did not swear to support the law was liable to heavy penalties.

Marius himself was unhappy. He wanted another consulship, and for this he needed, if not senatorial support, then at least a senate that was not actively hostile. One story alleges that while Marius was planning the settlement of his veterans with Saturninus' envoys a party of anti-Saturninan nobles arrived. Desperate not to offend either group, Marius feigned a stomach disorder, and rushed from one group to the other for the evening.

Nor were the Roman plebs enthusiastic about new legislation that might dilute their privileges. In the end, Marius' veterans entered the forum, and strong-armed the legislation through, though a significant proportion of the crowd shouted that they could hear thunder, which automatically nullified legislation as it signified the displeasure of Jupiter.

Marius got around the *sanctio* attached to Saturninus' land legislation by swearing that he would obey the law, as far as it was a law. Metellus Numidicus, as expected, refused to swear however it was qualified. Saturninus not only enforced the *sanctio* against Metellus, but went further and had him exiled. Marius' equivocation was seen as a deep political plot to get rid of his old opponent, and it resulted in him being politically weakened. And now that his veterans had got their land, Saturninus had become a political liability to Marius.

Standing for re-election

Aware that the nobility wanted his blood, Saturninus now stood for re-election, hoping that tribunician immunity would protect him. He was opposed by one Nonius, who was set upon by a gang of knife-wielding thugs. The unfortunate candidate was chased into an inn where he was stabbed to death.

Glaucia was a sitting praetor at this time. He had passed the *Lex Servilia De Repetundis*, a law allowing the compensation of money illegally seized by Roman officials abroad. Since the officials in question were senators, this measure too did nothing to endear Saturninus and his cronies to the senate. Glaucia wanted to be consul in 99 – quite illegally, as a praetor in office could not be a candidate.

When Marius disallowed Glaucia's candidacy, Saturninus turned to the mob. It had already helped him in 101, when he was accused of molesting the ambassadors of an Asian king – a charge which carried the death penalty because some very serious negotiations were disrupted. The rabble had terrorized the jurors into an acquittal and through their support Saturninus did indeed now get Glaucia recognized as a candidate. But Glaucia faced strong opposition in the election. One consulship would certainly go to the noble Marcus Antonius, and the other probably to a man called C. Memmius. Not waiting for the electorate to choose, as the voters were gathering a group of men with clubs fell upon Memmius and beat him to death.

Marius against Saturninus

Glaucia and Saturninus, who had just been elected tribune for the third time, were evidently behind this brutal killing, and now Aemilius Scaurus moved a *Senatus Consultum Ultimum*, the infamous Last Decree, which forced Marius to take action. Saturninus and Glaucia, together with the radical quaestor Saufeius, fled to the Capitol. The veteran general Marius simply cut off their water supply and waited for thirst to force their surrender.

Saturninus only surrendered after receiving an official pledge of safety. He and his supporters were locked in the senate house but were then abandoned to a mob of young nobles and their supporters who stoned them to death with tiles torn from the roof of the building. That day saw a tribune, a quaestor and a praetor, still in their robes of office, killed by the people of Rome while the consuls did nothing.

Most of the legislation of Saturninus was repealed as being passed *per vim* – by force. The proposed colonies were never founded, but the work of land distribution went ahead, at least to some extent. We know this because one of the supervising commissioners was the praetor of 91, Julius Caesar, father of Julius Caesar the triumvir and dictator.

GAIUS MARIUS

'If they look down on me they do the same to their own ancestors, for they, like me, had no nobility – until we earned it. And if they envy my honours, they should envy the labour, and the danger, by which I earned those honours.'

Speech of Marius in Sallust's *War with Jugurtha* 85.28

GAIUS MARIUS FIRST SAVED THE ROMAN REPUBLIC, and then helped to destroy it. Had he not existed, others would have delivered the state from harm, but only a man of Marius' character could have done the damage he did. In the tragedy of the late Roman Republic, Marius is, on balance, a villain.

'Humble' beginnings

Marius was born in the year 157. The social standing of the family has been confused by propaganda from pro- and anti-Marians. Some say that the family were so poor that they hired themselves out as common labourers, while others claim that Marius was of a local equestrian family. Modern historians tend towards the latter opinion, since Marius never seemed to lack funds during his political career. Also, he married into an old aristocratic family, which would have been impossible for a day labourer. But he was certainly not of the Roman aristocracy, with whom his relations varied between cool and poisonous.

Marius prided himself on being a simple Roman countryman. He never bothered to learn Greek, nor took up the decadent ways of the capital – he applauded when his cousin was killed for making indecent

A bust thought to be of Gaius Marius. The attribution of marble busts of the Republican era needs to be treated with caution, as Victorian amateur archaeologists sometimes simply appended the name of a famous Roman to their discovery.

GAIUS MARIUS

Born	*Achievements*
157 BC	Augur; Triumphator
Famous ancestors	*Wife*
None	Julia
Mother	*Children*
Fulcinia	Son: Marius
Father	(adopted)
C. Marius	*Death*
Positions held	Stroke(?) 86 BC
Tribune 119;	
Praetor 115; Consul	
107, 104–100, 86	

advances to a young man. Once Marius decided to have an operation to remove the numerous unsightly growths that disfigured his legs. He lay uncomplaining while the surgeon cut out the growths on one leg, but stopped the operation when the surgeon moved on to the other leg, remarking that the pain was not worth the reward.

Perhaps sponsored by a noble called Herennius, whose family were traditional patrons of the Marius clan, Marius' career began well. He was among the distinguished group with Scipio Aemilianus (pp. 119–21) at Numantia, and when some flatterer asked the great general where Rome would find another like him, Scipio indicated Marius and commented, 'Here, perhaps'. (Another who was also serving with Scipio Aemilanus with some distinction was a young African soldier called Jugurtha, who went on to trouble the careers of Aemilius Scaurus, Metellus Numidicus and others.)

Against the senate

When Marius became quaestor in 123, the powerful Metellus clan took an interest in his career. Probably with their help, he was elected tribune of the plebs for 119, when he was 38 years old. But the new tribune was nobody's lapdog. He brought forward legislation making it more difficult for the nobility to intimidate voters, much to the pique of the senate which promptly vetoed it. Marius was summoned before the consul to explain himself.

The presumptuous tribune was uncowed. The senate's decree was unlawful, and Marius threatened to arrest the consul unless it was withdrawn. In consternation, the consul called for his colleague, a Metellus, to bring 'his' man to heel. Marius promptly offered to arrest Metellus as well. This was an appalling breach of *fides*, the ties of good faith that joined client with patron, and the incident marked the first breach between Marius and the nobles, while at the same time greatly boosting Marius' popularity with the people. That popularity waned somewhat when Marius vetoed the distribution of cheap grain, though it was grudgingly accepted that he had acted in the public interest. It was also perhaps this veto that reconciled the Metellans to their wayward protégé.

Other senators were less forgiving, and they sabotaged Marius' attempt to become an aedile. The post of aedile had two grades, one more prestigious than the other. When Marius saw that he was unlikely to gain the aedileship he sought, he aimed for the humbler position. But he failed even in this, a humiliation which he was to remember.

Praetor and propraetor

Marius' enemies intervened again when he stood for praetor, probably for 115. This time they were unable to keep him out; Marius scraped in with the lowest votes awarded to any successful candidate. In response, the senate prosecuted him on the grounds that he had bribed his way into office. The prosecution failed, perhaps because Marius still enjoyed the backing of the Metellans, and perhaps because he was already cultivating the Julian clan. At this time Julians were an ancient, though not particularly distinguished, family. Marius later married Julia, the aunt of Julius Caesar, the man who overthrew the Republic.

Marius had very little talent for civil administration, so his term as *praetor urbanus* was remarkable not for any great achievement, but rather for the fact that he avoided making any seriously bad decisions. Militarily, Marius proved his competence as propraetor in further Spain, where he cleared the countryside of bandits and established the Spanish silver mines on a sound footing. (And quite possibly on very good financial terms for himself.)

In 109 he was in Africa as the legate of Quintus Metellus Numidicus (pp. 141–43), campaigning against his former colleague Jugurtha, now the rogue king of Numidia. Marius was very well regarded by the men, but it was only a matter of time before he fell out with Numidicus. Legend has it that a soothsayer in Utica prophesied that Marius was certain to succeed, no matter how high his ambitions. How high these were was soon revealed. Marius asked permission to return to Rome to stand for consul in 107.

Metellus' advice that Marius should be a co-candidate with his son in the distant future may have been well-intentioned; but Marius chose to interpret it as a deadly insult – perhaps not least because such an insult would release him from any ties of obligation to the Metellan clan.

Becoming consul

In a whispering campaign Marius claimed that Metellus was prolonging the war for his own glory, while in Rome the sentiment was growing that Marius and Marius only could defeat Jugurtha. With these attitudes spreading also among Numidicus' own soldiers, the commander saw good reason to be rid of Marius, and allowed him to leave for Rome, probably hoping that the release would do Marius little good – only 12 days remained to the election.

But Marius had prepared his popular support carefully and he was elected by a triumphant majority. He balefully rubbed the nobility's collective nose in the fact that he – a *novus homo* from a family which had never before held the consulship – now ranked higher than the proudest aristocrat.

He immediately set about recruiting an army, and it was one that was different from any other ever raised in Rome. The men Marius enlisted were from the *capite censi* – those Romans too indigent to afford their own armour or weapons and who were lumped into a single century in the voting assembly of the people. This act proved to be unwise for a number of reasons. Even Marius, who was not good at thinking through the long-term consequences of his actions, may have regretted this one when it rebounded on him later.

For the present, however, he was more interested in getting his troops to Africa to finish off Jugurtha. Metellus snubbed him by leaving the handover of his army to his legate, Rutilius Rufus, but worse was to come. Jugurtha was eventually captured, and was delivered to the Romans by his father-in-law Bocchus. The Roman people gave the credit to Marius, but the aristocrats pointed out that it was a rising nobleman of the Cornelian family who had secured the capture by his astute diplomacy. They argued that Numidicus had finished Jugurtha in the field, and Cornelius Sulla (pp. 164–71) had effected the capture of the man himself, so Marius' involvement had been minimal.

The German threat

The people were unconvinced, and they voted unanimously to make Marius consul again for 104. This was unconstitutional, since Marius was not even in Rome for the election, but the threat now facing Rome was so great that it was felt there was no other choice. A huge army composed of two Germanic tribes, the Cimbri and the Teutones, was descending on Italy from the north.

This Germanic force, estimated to be about 300,000 men strong, had already defeated Papirius Carbo in Illyria in 113, and cut to pieces the army of M. Iunius Silanus in 109. The consul L. Cassius Longinus had been killed in a battle near Lake Geneva in 107 and the Roman leader M. Aurelius Scaurus was later taken prisoner. Finally, in 105, the Roman army had gone out to meet the enemy in the great battle of Arausio (Orange); it was a huge defeat – of an army of 80,000 men, only two were reported to have survived.

It was in these circumstances that Marius entered Rome and celebrated a triumph for his African war, and afterwards he entered the senate, still dressed in his purple triumphator's robe. The senators' disgust at this presumptuousness sent him scurrying off to change, but one suspects that Marius was only at ease again when he hastened north to meet this new threat. As it turned out, he need not have hurried. The barbarian horde had turned off towards Spain, and remained there plundering the country.

In 103 Marius was consul yet again. He and Rutilius Rufus based themselves in southern Gaul and trained their troops for the inevitable confrontation with the Germanic tribes. They adjusted the Roman battle array to resist the barbarian assault, and the Roman throwing spear, the *pilum*, was weakened so that after it struck a shield it sagged, making the shield a useless encumbrance.

Two years of war

Still the enemy did not come, and Marius' long tenure of power was beginning to make people restless. But with the help of the deeply

(Above) Marius celebrating a triumph over the Cimbri and Teutones: coin of C. Fundanius, 101 BC. The victory was the high point of Marius' career – admirers proclaimed him the saviour of Rome.

(Below) Map showing the routes of the Cimbri and Teutones – had they not first plundered Spain, and so given the Romans time to prepare for their onslaught, history might have been very different.

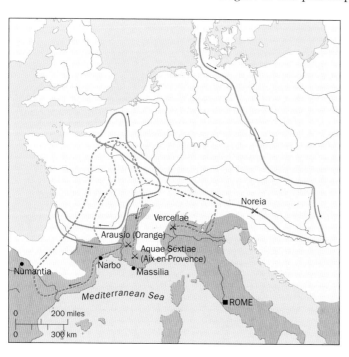

A terracotta head of a barbarian, possibly of the Cimbri, first century BC. Unlike later Romans, the Republicans did not possess superior weapons to the tribes they conquered, who were therefore a real threat to their existence.

The Triumph of Marius (below left; 1729) and the *Battle of Vercellae* (below right; c. 1728–29), by Tiepolo. The flawed grandeur of Marius appealed to Tiepolo.

unsavoury politician Saturninus, Marius was made consul again, and now, in 102, the Cimbri finally did arrive.

Though they had divided their army, it still took six days for the Teutones' troops to pass Marius' camp. Marius did not come out to fight – allegedly so that his men could get used to the appearance of these tall invaders. The invaders themselves were unimpressed with this lack of spirit, and as they passed the fortifications they jokingly asked the soldiers within for messages to pass on to the wives and daughters they would soon be ravishing.

Once the huge Germanic army had passed, Marius followed and the two sides met in battle at Aquae Sextae (Aix-en-Provence). Marius had taken a favourable position, and as he turned the first assault on his lines, his aide, a Marcellus of the Claudian clan, ambushed the enemy rear. The Germans lost an estimated 100,000 troops in the battle, and even more afterwards, while many of their wives committed suicide.

After this victory Marius was elected consul for a fifth time. There was still a huge enemy army of Cimbri in Italy, and it had pushed the other Roman commander, Q. Lutatius Catulus, back across the river Po. On 30 July, 101, in the heat of the summer, the combined Roman armies met the enemy at a place called Campi Raudii, near Vercellae, west of Milan, and defeated them utterly. Plutarch gives much of the credit to Catulus, but to the Roman people, Marius was a hero, the third founder of Rome after Romulus and Furius Camillus.

This was the peak of Marius' career, and as Plutarch comments, if he had died then, he would have done so in undiluted glory. For this point marks the end of Marius the saviour, and the beginning of Marius the public menace.

L. Cornelius Sulla Felix, obverse of a denarius, posthumously minted, 54 BC. The coin shows Sulla's famously blond hair artistically arranged. Sulla enjoyed the good things in life, and this depiction perhaps reveals the beginning of a double chin.

Marius, Saturninus and Sulla

Marius wanted to exceed the record of Valerius Corvus (pp. 69–70), who had been consul six times. To achieve this, Marius had to work even more closely with Saturninus, who could bring out the popular vote for him despite the strong sentiment that it was now time for a change of consul. Marius also needed Saturninus to pass legislation granting land to his troops from the *capite censi* who were now awaiting disbandment. This was one failing of Marius' recruitment policy – his veterans had no lands to go back to. If they were not provided, large bodies of highly trained and disaffected men would be let loose in Italy.

Though Saturninus was a flawed instrument, Marius used him in a discreditable plot to have Metellus Numidicus exiled. But eventually Marius had to choose between the radical Saturninus and the senate. With great distaste he chose the latter, and abandoned his former ally. In short, Marius' year as a civilian consul spent his political credit so thoroughly that he was unable to prevent Numidicus being recalled at the end of the year. Marius did not stand for censor afterwards, so certain was he of being defeated.

Instead he took himself on a tour of Asia, ostensibly to fulfil a vow. For his diplomacy in absenting himself he was given the consolation of election to the élite priestly college of Augurs. Returning to Rome, Marius found his star eclipsed by the rising Sulla – he was incensed with jealousy when he heard of a statuary group depicting Sulla's leading role in the capture of Jugurtha. Violence was only averted by the rebellion of Rome's allies in the Social War in 90 BC.

The Social War

In this dangerous and bitter war Marius commanded the northern front. Now aged 67, he was cautious, and slower than the vigorous Sulla. On one occasion, Marius was challenged by the enemy in his camp: 'If you are such a great general, come out and fight us'. To which Marius replied 'If you think you are any good, why don't you try to make me?' He did come out, in his own time, and inflicted two stinging defeats on the Marsi, the most dangerous of Rome's former allies. He then waited expectantly to be given supreme command of all Rome's armies. When this did not occur, Marius retired, sulking, to Rome, and took no further part in the war.

But even by the year 88 he still had hopes of command. He wanted to lead an army against Mithridates, an Asian king who was defying Rome. To the embarrassment of the nation, he insisted on going to the Campus Martius and training with the young men, though he was approaching 70 and had grown fat. He was devastated when he did not get the job. Even worse, it went to Sulla.

Marius immediately conspired with the tribune Sulpicius who passed a law transferring the Asian command to Marius. The consuls promptly declared a *iustitium* (an adjournment of business for religious reasons), suspending the laws passed in that day and preventing the passing of

The Social War

The Social War (also sometimes called the Marsic or Italian war) gets its name from the Latin word *socii* which means 'allies'. As the name suggests, the war was fought against rebel states who were formerly allies of Rome. This was one of the most desperate wars ever fought by the Romans, because they were fighting against a part of their own military machine.

For most of the history of the Roman army, the legions of Rome were supported by lighter troops called *auxilia*. These were supplied by allies and subject peoples of Rome. Poor communities supplied archers or slingers, but some of the Italiot tribes were rich and powerful enough to supply troops who were armed in much the same way as the legions themselves.

Rome once had a policy of inclusiveness. Subject peoples were made citizens of the Republic, and in a few generations were as Roman as the Romans. But in about 170 BC the Romans stopped absorbing new peoples in this way. Clear-sighted reformers such as the Gracchi, Livius Drusus, and even Marius in his own way, realized that this policy was building up a reservoir of resentment, but their efforts to give the citizenship to the people of Italy were frustrated by conservative reactionaries.

When Livius Drusus was assassinated in 91 (p. 163), the dam broke. The revolt at first centred on tribes close to Rome (the Marsi, Ferentini, Picentines and Samnites), but later spread through Apulia and Umbria. The Italians formed a separate state with a capital at Bovianum (the former Samnite capital).

The main part of the war lasted until 87, with most of the fighting taking place in 90 to 89. The Romans were shocked at the depth of the widespread antipathy towards them, and hastily made amends, promising citizenship to those states which came to terms. Some tribes did not accept this, however, wanting instead the total destruction of Rome.

The war was slowly going in the Romans' favour when the struggle between Marius and Sulla broke out, and fighting gradually became subsumed in this civil war. Thus it might be fairly said that the final battle of the Social War was at the Colline gate in 82 when Sulla and Crassus destroyed their enemies, among them the last remnants of the Italian separatists.

A coin issued by the insurgents during the Social War. On the obverse is the head of personified Italia, while the reverse shows eight warriors swearing an oath, probably representing the eight peoples who formed the core of the rebellion. Another coin of this period showed the Italian bull goring the Roman wolf.

further laws. The political temperature rose. Marius led armed men into the forum demanding that the *iustitium* be lifted. In the subsequent confusion, one of the consul's sons was killed. Sulla only saved himself by fleeing to Marius' house (which was built near the forum to attract more clients). And so, at swordpoint, Marius got the command he wanted.

But Marius had overlooked another aspect of recruiting men from the *capite censi* – they looked to their commander for rewards, and they obeyed him, rather than the state. Marius had created the client army, but the client army he was now trying to lead regarded Sulla as its patron. The military tribunes whom Marius sent to his new army were murdered, and when Sulla arrived, the army marched with him to Rome to 'restore order'.

No one, least of all Marius, had believed that a Roman army would ever march on Rome. The discredit for the fact that one was now doing so is undoubtedly Sulla's. But Marius' blundering attempts to be a politician precipitated the crisis, and he and Sulpicius now fled for their lives as condemned criminals and traitors.

THE ROMANS AT HOME

Many Romans, even quite well-off ones, had little need for extensive accommodation. Many of the domestic functions we associate with a home were carried out in municipal buildings. Public latrines and baths took care of hygiene, and numerous small establishments provided food and drink. Thus, for many a Roman bachelor, a small room for sleeping – a *cubiculum* – was sufficient.

Once he married and acquired a household, however, our bachelor might look for something more traditional. Roman houses were conventionally arranged around the hearth, a central space open to the sky to allow the smoke from cooking fires to escape. The hearthstone was black (*ater*), hence the word atrium, and, like a modern atrium, the atrium in a wealthy household could be quite a substantial area, with greenery and running water. The atrium was central in a more than physical way, as here were located the household gods – the *lares* – and the funeral masks and insignia of distinguished ancestors.

The rooms arranged around the hearth were flexible in their function, serving as bedrooms, and offices or workrooms. (The idea of 'going to work' is modern – most ancient people lived where they worked.) The *vestibulum*, named from the cloaks, boots and other outdoor gear that was kept there, was the room which opened to the street, and one other room would be the *triclinium*, where the family dined or entertained guests.

(Above) Detail of a wallpainting from Room M of the villa of P Fannius Synistor at Boscoreale, 40s BC. Many rooms, even in large Roman houses, were rather cramped by modern standards. Panoramas, either cityscapes or landscapes, were a common theme for frescoes, helping to increase the sensation of space.

(Right) A cutaway reconstruction of a Roman house. The rooms were grouped around a central space, and housed not only the immediate family, but also a host of slaves and relatives. The frontage might be let out for shops.

(Left) Bronze bed of the late first century BC from Amiterno in Abruzzo (the wooden parts are reconstructions). Among the ruins of Pompeii archaeologists found a bed with the wooden parts only slightly charred, allowing accurate reconstructions to be made.

Roman households were complex communities in their own right. Apart from the father, together with his wife and children, there would be slaves and servants, and their children. Given the uncertainties of life in the ancient world, death and remarriage involved frequent family restructurings, and every household had a crop of relatives on the premises.

In addition, many larger households rented out their street frontage to shopkeepers, and had upper floors converted into the ancient equivalent of 'granny flats'. Lack of space meant that slaves often shared tiny rooms, sometimes under the floors of the main house.

The person who made the whole household work was the *materfamilias*, who was supposed to arrange the domestic duties of the slaves, organize the clothing and feeding of all those under her roof, and also arbitrate in various domestic squabbles which inevitably blew up. The last word, though, rested (at least in theory) with the

paterfamilias, who was enshrined in law as the absolute master of the household. In reality, many women were less subordinate, and men less dominant, than the legal picture makes out.

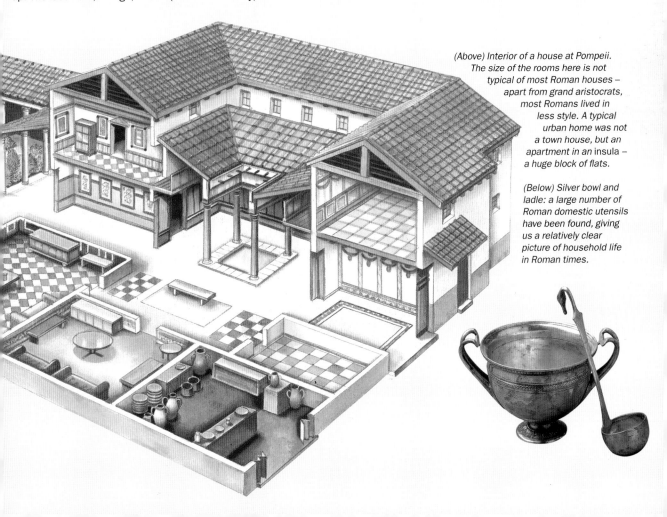

(Above) Interior of a house at Pompeii. The size of the rooms here is not typical of most Roman houses – apart from grand aristocrats, most Romans lived in less style. A typical urban home was not a town house, but an apartment in an insula *– a huge block of flats.*

(Below) Silver bowl and ladle: a large number of Roman domestic utensils have been found, giving us a relatively clear picture of household life in Roman times.

Marius at Minturnae, a painting by Jean-Germain Drouais (1786). Marius stretches out an arm to the German slave sent to kill him, who was unable to commit this act. This is an interesting choice of subject for a pre-Revolutionary French painter, and presages the extent to which politics were to influence art in the coming decades.

Flight and return

An entire body of legend grew up about Marius' flight from Italy, and it is impossible at this distance to tell fact from fiction. Marius remained confident, saying that when young he had once caught an eagle's nest as it dropped from the heavens, and within there were seven eagle chicks. This portended that he would be consul seven times; and so far he had only held that office six times.

But the chase closed in, and Marius was caught trying to hide in the muddiest part of a swamp. The townsfolk decided to execute their prisoner and sent a huge German warrior to do the deed. The man came out of the room moments later, and exclaimed 'I cannot kill Gaius Marius!' The townsfolk realized that none of them could do so either, and so they helped Marius to Africa, where he was eventually reunited with his son.

Meanwhile, in Rome, the situation had changed. Sulla had taken his army to Asia, leaving Rome under the consuls Cinna and Gnaeus Octavius. Both men had professed to support Sulla's ideas for strengthening the senate and curbing the powers of the tribunes. Octavius' support was sincere but Cinna showed himself with increasing openness to be a *popularis* – one who supported the tribunes and the people. It was inevitable that the two men would fall out. Octavius forced Cinna from Rome and installed one of Rome's chief priests as consul in his place.

Seeing his chance, Marius put himself at the service of the deposed Cinna. They were joined by a competent young man called Quintus Sertorius (pp. 172–74). Marius cut off Rome's grain supply and sacked the port of Ostia. This brought the general Pompeius Strabo (father of the triumvir Pompey) to the side of Octavius after months of wavering. No sooner had Octavius welcomed his support, than Pompeius deserted him by dying. The last hope of the Sullans was the son of Numidicus, Metellus Pius (pp. 171–72). Octavius' troops came over to him en masse, and begged him to lead them. When the indignant Metellus told them to return to the consul's command, they went over instead to the enemy. Metellus, correctly judging the situation to be hopeless, left Rome.

The Sullans had no choice but to negotiate. Cinna was conciliatory, but Marius stood behind his chair and said nothing. He had not cut his beard since being expelled from Rome, and he had refused the proconsular dignity Cinna had offered him.

A bloody end

In fact Marius would not enter Rome once it surrendered to Cinna. He first wanted the people to vote for his return. The assembly obediently began voting, but less than halfway through, Marius tired of the farce and entered Rome anyway. He was accompanied by a huge gang of fanatically loyal freed slaves. These took their signal from him, and if Marius did not return the greeting of someone he met as he walked through the city, the ex-slaves killed the unfortunate person on the spot.

Over the following weeks Marius systematically took his revenge on the senatorial class. Anyone who had insulted or slighted him now paid the price. Even his old colleague Lutatius Catulus received no mercy. Marius told those who came to intercede for him 'He must die'. And he did, but by his own hand, committing suicide by closing himself into a smoke-filled room. Marius' retinue of ex-slaves were free to rob and rape unhindered until Quintus Sertorius had their encampment surrounded in the night, and every one of them was killed.

Marius did not long survive them. In 86 he and Cinna were made consuls without the formality of an election, but Marius' aged body had been pushed too far. He died a few weeks later, having held more consulships than any other Roman, yet feared and unloved. Sulla later had his ashes thrown into the River Anio.

LIVIUS DRUSUS	
Born	*Achievements*
c. 128 BC	Social legislation
Famous ancestors	*Wife*
Aemilius Paullus (?),	Servilia
Livius Salinator	*Children*
Mother	Son: Livius Drusus
Cornelia	Claudianus
Father	(adopted?)
Livius Drusus	*Death*
Positions held	Assassinated
Tribune 91	91 BC

Livius Drusus

And so it came about that though they were still at odds with each other, the senators and the knights were united in their hatred of Livius Drusus. Only the common people were happy.... It was for the Italians, above all, that Drusus followed the course he did, yet they too were apprehensive.

Appian, *Roman History* 1.36

In the Roman Republic, a few men rose to greatness through their own efforts. Others, as Cicero rather bitterly put it, were 'made consuls in their cradles'. Livius Drusus was one of the latter.

A noble lineage

Drusus' mother was a Cornelia, and his father was the Livius Drusus who played so large a part in the defeat of Gaius Gracchus in 121 (p. 136). His uncle was Rutilius Rufus, consul of 105, who had served with Metellus Numidicus in Africa and who is credited with training the Roman army which defeated the German invasions under the command of Marius.

Livius Drusus was energetic, highly competent and arrogant. (He once did not wear his official insignia in Asia, claiming 'I am my own insignia'.) He was a fervent supporter of the rights of the senate – so much so that he seems to have inherited his father's title of *Patronus Senatus* – but he was prepared to use the tools of demagoguery for his own purposes. His character was severe, and his lifestyle modest. He purchased a house near the forum, and the architect he hired offered to ensure Drusus complete privacy by some judicious rebuilding. 'On the contrary', Drusus assured him, 'I want you to arrange the house so that everything I do is open to everybody.'

TRADE AND THE ROMAN ARISTOCRACY

For many years it was thought that the Roman élite had little interest in trade. According to this view, they believed it to be vastly inferior to agriculture, which was the only means by which a gentleman could build up his fortune. Modern research, however, is beginning to show that there was more trade going on than could be explained by the activities of a 'middle class' of traders.

With staples such as wine, olive oil, garum (a kind of piquant fish paste), grain and pottery, there can be no doubt that large quantities of material were transported over great distances. Most goods were packed in pottery vases called *amphorae*, which were especially useful for liquids such as wines or oils. In modern Rome a huge mound of discarded *amphorae* still exists today. It is called the Monte Testaccio, and most of the *amphorae* in the mound are from Spain – it is estimated that the Romans imported over 5 million kilos of oil from that country every year.

This kind of trade involves serious money, and it is most probable that the Roman aristocracy were deeply involved. In fact, the people of Rome were so worried that matters affecting their trading interests would affect the foreign policy of senators that by 100 there were laws in place forbidding Roman senators to engage in trade, or even to own boats with a serious trading capacity.

Senators got around these laws by using *negotiators*, middlemen financed by them. In return for seed capital the *negotiators* would trade under their own names, and assume most of the risks, while the senators could look forward to a healthy return on capital if their investment paid off.

Most trade in the ancient world was by sea, since moving goods by land was slow and expensive. One indicator of the amount of trade in a particular period can be measured by the number of shipwrecks found dating to that time. Thus archaeologists are able to confirm that by 100 BC trade in the Mediterranean was approaching levels that would not be seen again until the Renaissance.

Further, the modern historian W. V. Harris has made a study of oil lamps, the principal form of lighting in the Mediterranean world. He has shown that these lamps were made by a few firms and were exported across Rome's growing empire. The lamps would have been sold at the regular markets (*nundinae*) which were a feature of all ancient cities, and which continue to be held in many modern Mediterranean cities today.

In addition to trade within the empire, there were long-distance routes. Given the enormous cost of moving goods along these routes, the goods transported were luxury items, such as ivory, spices and silk.

(Top and above) One of the most significant discoveries in marine archaeology of recent years is a group of boats found in Pisa, dating between the second century BC and the fifth century AD. The trading boats sank in a lagoon which later silted up, preserving them almost perfectly in the mud, along with their contents, such as these pottery vessels. Some of the amphorae contained fruit, including cherries and plums, as well as nuts, and staples such as olives, wine and oil.

(Left) A mosaic from a shipping office at Ostia. Much of Rome's grain went through Ostia, and a number of shipping companies based in the city had 'advertisements' outside their offices.

In his early life he was a close friend of Servilius Caepio, of the family of the Caepio encountered earlier (pp. 124–25). Drusus married Caepio's sister, and his own sister married Caepio. The two men later became bitter enemies; the historian Pliny says that it was a dispute over a ring, but family matters might have been involved.

One event which made an early impression on Drusus was the condemnation of his uncle Rutilius Rufus for extortion (p. 135). While Rufus was the legate of a Mucius Scaevola in Asia Minor he protected the local people against the exorbitant demands of the *publicani* – associations of tax gatherers (see box, p. 137) – and thus earned the enmity of the knights (equites) who controlled the associations. Since the legislation of Gaius Gracchus, the knights had also been in charge of the law courts. So on Rutilius' return to Rome, he was falsely charged with extortion and exiled by a kangaroo court. This sorry episode illustrates the partisanship and corruption with which the knights performed as jurors.

Powerful supporters

Among those who supported Drusus in his bid to become tribune in 91 were the ageing but formidable Aemilius Scaurus (pp. 139–41) and the gifted orator Licinius Crassus. Both men felt that Drusus could rein in the over-mighty equites and restore balance to the state. The support of Crassus was probably disinterested, but the past of Aemilius Scaurus had left him vulnerable to charges of extortion – and therefore to the same fate as Rutilius Rufus.

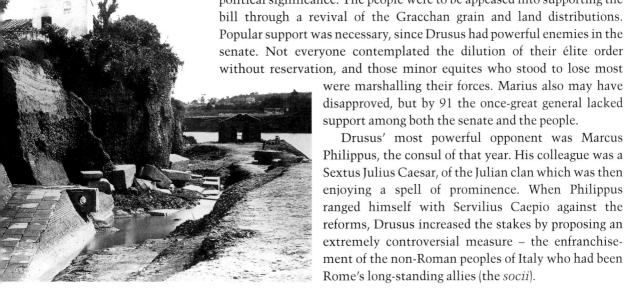

Riverside port facilities on the Tiber. Though it was possible for medium-sized ships to bring their cargoes directly to Rome, the large grain carriers, the supertankers of their day, had their cargo transhipped from Ostia to Rome by barge. Grain distribution to the people was key to the popularity and success of many policies of Republican leaders.

Drusus was duly elected. There is some confusion about his proposed legislation, but he appears to have tried to offer something to everyone. The basis of his scheme was that control of the courts should be handed back to the senate. In return, the senate would be greatly expanded, with 300 of the top equites elevated to the rank of senator. This would align the most powerful equites with the senate, while stripping the others of their political significance. The people were to be appeased into supporting the bill through a revival of the Gracchan grain and land distributions. Popular support was necessary, since Drusus had powerful enemies in the senate. Not everyone contemplated the dilution of their élite order without reservation, and those minor equites who stood to lose most were marshalling their forces. Marius also may have disapproved, but by 91 the once-great general lacked support among both the senate and the people.

Drusus' most powerful opponent was Marcus Philippus, the consul of that year. His colleague was a Sextus Julius Caesar, of the Julian clan which was then enjoying a spell of prominence. When Philippus ranged himself with Servilius Caepio against the reforms, Drusus increased the stakes by proposing an extremely controversial measure – the enfranchisement of the non-Roman peoples of Italy who had been Rome's long-standing allies (the *socii*).

A ROMAN ARMY CAMP

One of the reasons why the Roman army was so hard to beat was that it was difficult to attack. While in the field, a Roman army would make camp whenever it was going to stop for more than a few hours. As one might expect of the Romans, this involved more than a matter of simply pitching tents. There was a complex process to be gone through, one which had been honed to maximum efficiency in centuries of warfare.

The job of finding a suitable camp site was given to an experienced centurion and one of the military tribunes. It had to be relatively flat, command a good view of the surrounding terrain, be about 2,625 ft (800 m) square, and be near water. The ground should be soil, so that the arriving army could dig in.

When the army arrived there was no confusion. Each unit knew exactly where it was to be camped in relation to the commander's tent – the *praetorium* – and the two principal streets of the camp – the *via Principalis* and the *via Praetoria*. The 'streets' of the camp were marked out with spears, and each unit shared the same neighbours as they had in their previous camp. They also had the same defensive duties, and knew where to go to get food, water and supplies. There was even an area set aside (the *forum*) for a market.

After setting down their gear, the soldiers proceeded directly to their next duty – preparing the walls. If there was an enemy presence in the immediate vicinity, half the army would stand to in arms while their colleagues worked on the ditch and ramparts. If the threat was more distant – or if there was no perceived threat – the whole army would work on the defences. These usually consisted of a ditch, about 3 ft (1 m) deep, and a wall of at least a corresponding height. Into this wall were thrust the sharpened stakes that the soldiers had carried with them. There was then a wide space within the walls in front of the soldiers' tents. These tents were made of leather, and usually eight men slept in each one.

At sundown a member of each squad went to the captain of the guard and was given the watchword for the night. After the sentries had been given their duties, they were handed a wooden ticket, called a *tessera*. During the night, a captain came around and collected the ticket. All the tickets were handed to the commander of the guard in the morning. By this method the soldiers knew that their guards would be awake, and that they were being checked regularly. Such an elaborate procedure proved its worth because even with diligent scouting it was possible for armies to come upon each other unexpectedly, and the chances of this were greatly increased if either one was moving at night.

Roman soldiers work on the ditch and rampart of a camp while their companions stand in battle array to fend off any sudden attacks.

Votes for the Italians

Drusus' motives in bringing forward this proposal have been hotly debated. Some claim that he did it simply because he had many good friends among the Italians. (Among them was Q. Poppaedius Silo, leader of the formidable tribe of the Marsi.) According to this opinion, Drusus appreciated that the pressure for enfranchisement had been growing since the time of the Gracchi, and unless something was done, an explosion would surely follow. Others argue that Drusus could see that enfranchisement of the Italians was inevitable, and he wanted to arrange it on terms which gave the senate maximum patronage over the new citizens. Yet others believe that Drusus could see that the Italians were becoming restless because the continual distributions of land by the Romans were impinging on parts of the *ager publicus* – the public land – farmed by the Italians. In some cases this was because although Rome had claimed the lands of some tribes by conquest, up till now it had never actually taken them, and in other cases the Italians, like many Romans, had themselves encroached on public land, and after generations of this liberty had come to feel they had a claim on it.

The Roman people, always jealous of their privileges, were torn between supporting Drusus' generous programme of grain and land distribution, and opposing his support for the Italians. It did not help that Drusus himself was an uncompromising character. When, on one occasion, he felt that Marcus Philippus had gone too far in a condemnatory speech, he ordered the consul to be seized (or seized him himself, according to some accounts). The sudden attack caused a prodigious nosebleed, but Drusus dismissed any sympathy for the consul with the comment 'Blood? That's thrush gravy!' Philippus was a noted gastronome.

Drusus' programme was expensive – he had to debase the currency to pay for it, and he himself remarked that he had nothing left to give away but earth and air. There was also considerable unease about his project: when Drusus gave an acquaintance the common Roman greeting '*Quid agis?*' ('What are you doing these days?'), the reply was a heartfelt 'No, Drusus, in heaven's name, what are *you* doing?'.

The plan fails

Then Philippus struck. He was not only consul, but a reasonable lawyer too. He overturned much of the legislation that Drusus had already passed because it violated a law forbidding different types of legislation being put on to the same bill, and it is possible that some laws had been passed too soon after they were proposed. Politically weakened, Drusus soldiered on and conducted himself honourably. One report has it that he warned Philippus of a planned assassination by the Italians, since he was, first and foremost, a Roman senator.

The compliment was not returned – or perhaps the Italians felt Drusus knew too much. Days later, while Drusus was surrounded by clients and friends at home, he was stabbed in the groin with a shoemaker's knife. The assassin was never found, and shortly afterwards everyone's attention was turned to other things – on the death of Drusus the Italians rose in revolt against Rome (see box, p. 155).

The ensuing war was fought by two arms of the world's finest military machine turned against each other. It was a grim and close-run affair. All that saved the Romans was that they now freely gave Roman citizenship to the Italians, as Drusus and Gaius Gracchus had argued they should. The shades of those murdered tribunes must have been grimly amused.

Lucius Cornelius Sulla Felix
(138–78 BC)

Metellus Pius
(c. 130–64 BC)

Quintus Sertorius
(c. 126–73 BC)

As a young man, Sulla was considered handsome, though Plutarch adds 'his blue eyes, of themselves extremely keen and glaring, were rendered all the more forbidding and terrible by the complexion of his face'.

LUCIUS CORNELIUS SULLA FELIX	
Born 138 BC *Famous ancestors* Rufinus Sulla *Mother* Unknown *Father* Unknown *Positions held* Praetor 97; Consul 88, 80; Dictator 82, 81, 80 *Achievements* Triumphator	*Wives* Ilia; Aelia(?), Cloelia, Metella, Valeria *Children* Sons: Faustus, Cornelius; daughters: Cornelia, Fausta; stepdaughter: Aemilia *Death* Illness 78 BC

LUCIUS CORNELIUS SULLA FELIX

In his youthful obscure years he would converse freely with players and professional jesters, and join them in all their low pleasures. And when supreme master of all, he would often gather together the most impudent players and stage-followers of the town, and drink and joke with them without regard to his age or the dignity of his place.

Plutarch, *Life of Sulla*

LUCIUS CORNELIUS SULLA RANKS HIGH on any list of those Romans most responsible for the death of the Roman Republic. Yet for much of Sulla's early life it did not seem as though he would go into politics at all. The Sullan branch of the Cornelian family had been in decline for centuries, since the time when a Sullan called Rufinus was found to own more than ten pounds of silver plate. This contravened a law against ostentatious luxury and he was expelled from the senate.

A historical accident (the trial of one of his neighbours) has preserved for posterity the fact that Sulla lived in an apartment block as a young man, and paid only slightly more rent than the freed slave who lived upstairs from him.

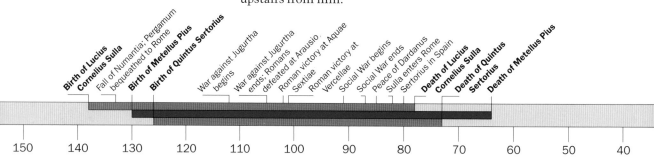

Birth of Lucius Cornelius Sulla | Fall of Numantia; Pergamum bequeathed to Rome | Birth of Metellus Pius | Birth of Quintus Sertorius | War against Jugurtha begins | War against Jugurtha ends; Romans defeated at Arausio | Roman victory at Aquae Sextiae | Roman victory at Vercellae | Social War begins | Social War ends | Peace of Dardanus | Sulla enters Rome | Sertorius in Spain | Death of Lucius Cornelius Sulla | Death of Quintus Sertorius | Death of Metellus Pius

| 150 | 140 | 130 | 120 | 110 | 100 | 90 | 80 | 70 | 60 | 50 | 40 |

A decadent aristocrat

He was a dissolute youth, who possessed brilliant blue eyes and a mane of golden hair. His good looks were somewhat let down by his complexion, which did not take to the sun and tended to go red and blotchy – something the Athenians were later to satirize as 'mulberries sprinkled with flour'. All his life he was fond of good food and the company of actors and dancers. He also possessed great personal charm, and acquired a wealthy mistress whom we know only by the name of Nicopolis.

Sulla's stepmother died, leaving him her money; soon afterwards Nicopolis also died, making Sulla her heir. Suddenly Sulla found himself with enough money to embark on a political career. (There were rumours, at the time and afterwards, that Sulla had a hand in these fortuitous outbreaks of mortality, but the case against him is unproven.)

Service with Marius

Sulla was elected to the office of quaestor and found service with the rising *novus homo* Marius. In Africa he secured the capture of the troublesome Jugurtha by inducing the Numidian king's father-in-law to betray him. This incident piqued Marius' jealousy, but Sulla remained with him in the campaign against the Germans in 104 and 103. Towards the end of this time, these two powerful personalities may have begun to clash – Sulla left Marius and took service with Lutatius Catulus instead.

Sulla served the full campaign against the Germans, and he decided on the strength of this not to bother with the office of aedile but to go straight for the post of praetor instead. He was relying on the electorate to remember and reward his military prowess, but instead they remembered that aediles were responsible for putting on the shows in the arena. Sulla's African connections should have guaranteed some magnificent animals being displayed, and the voters were angry at being denied such a spectacle. Sulla was not elected.

Mosaic showing a writer, perhaps a dramatist, as the mask of an actor sits on the table beside his right elbow. Note the basket of scrolls in the bottom corner. Sulla enjoyed the company of actors and even wrote plays himself.

(*Top*) Sulla, with Bocchus kneeling before him holding an olive branch and Jugurtha bound behind him: a silver denarius of L. Cornelius Sulla, *c.* 63–62 BC. The word 'Felix' on the coin illustrates Sulla's claim to be one of Fortune's favourites.

(*Above*) Golden aureus of L. Cornelius Sulla celebrating a triumph. This coin was probably struck by L. Manlius Torquatus who was proquaestor to Sulla during the Mithridatic War, after which Sulla celebrated the triumph shown here.

Sulla tried again in 98, and was elected *praetor urbanus* for the following year. This time, he had taken the precaution of depositing large bribes in the right places. Consequently, when he threatened to use his praetorian authority against one of the Julii Caesares, the man retorted 'Your authority? I suppose it is your authority, seeing that you paid for it.'

Sulla the commander

As propraetor, Sulla was assigned the province of Cappadocia in Asia Minor. He was given the task of restoring a young king, Ariobarzanes, to the throne of a neighbouring kingdom, and he did this with a minimum of fuss, using mainly levies of native troops raised on the spot. On this eastern trip, Sulla became the first Roman official to encounter the rising power of Parthia, which had grown up from the eastern parts of Alexander the Great's old empire. It was also on this trip that a soothsayer handed Sulla a prophecy which had a profound effect on him. Apparently Sulla was fated to become the greatest of men, and to die at the height of his power and happiness.

When Sulla returned to Rome in 92, he faced prosecution for extortion from a man called Censorinus. The exact nature of the charge is unknown. Also unknown is what pressure Sulla applied behind the scenes, for on the date of the trial Censorinus failed to show up, and the case was abandoned.

Soon after this, it was suggested that a statuary group be raised in Rome depicting Sulla's capture of Jugurtha. Marius was frantically jealous, and violence might have erupted between the two men had not the revolt of the Italian allies pushed other conflicts aside. Sulla acquitted himself well as a commander in the war – his energy and initiative were seen to advantage against the caution and slowness of Marius. He did enjoy several strokes of luck in his campaigns, but rather than claim that his skill helped in these happy developments, he attributed his entire success to fortune. Indeed, he went so far as to add to his name the nickname 'Felix', or 'fortunate'.

On the death of Marcus Aemilius Scaurus (pp. 139–41), Sulla married his widow Caecilia Metella. In 88 Sulla became consul with Quintus Pompeius, probably with the support of the Metellan clan. His daughter then married the son of his consular colleague. Sulla must have felt dangerously close to that foretold height of power and happiness. He was rich, powerful, well connected, and held one of the highest offices of state. Furthermore, he commanded the army which was to go east and defeat King Mithridates, who had wrested much of Asia Minor and even part of Greece from the Romans.

The march on Rome

Then came the turning point of Sulla's life. Marius conspired with the tribune Sulpicius to have Sulla removed from the command of the eastern army and Marius put in his place. Not unnaturally, Sulla as consul resisted this, and declared the law unconstitutional. Rufus and

Marius responded by using mob tactics to push through their legislation. In scenes of disorder, the son of Pompeius was killed and Sulla was forced to flee for his life, finally taking refuge in the house of Marius, perhaps the one place where the mob would not follow.

Not only did Marius take Sulla's command, he also took Sulla's army. Many in that army were veterans of Sulla's forces from the Social War, and it was very likely that Marius would exchange these for his own veterans, both to boost the loyalty of his army and to give his own followers a chance to enjoy the booty that a successful campaign would bring. But Sulla's men were mutinous, and they stoned to death the military tribunes sent out in Marius' name.

At this point Sulla himself arrived. He outlined the wrongs done to him, and pointed out that Rome was in the grip of mob rule. As consul, Sulla was in charge of the state, and as consul, Sulla decided to lead the army into Rome to restore order. Sulla's officers saw it differently. Never before had a Roman army marched to conquer Rome, and they were having none of it. All except one of his officers, a relative called Licinius Lucullus (pp. 191–94), deserted.

Two praetors, a Brutus and a Servilius, came to reason with Sulla, but were sent back to the city with their robes of office ripped off and their official staves broken. There was nothing now to stop Sulla taking Rome, and he did. He reasoned that he had restored order so that normal political life could carry on, and he was therefore unable to do much when a political opponent, Cinna, was elected consul the following year. He did make Cinna swear an oath that he would not act against Sulla or his interests, but it rapidly became evident that Cinna had no intention of abiding by that oath.

Public opinion was very much against what Sulla had done, and before he was able to set off to Asia Minor with his army, he was summoned to stand trial for his misdeeds. Sulla responded by ignoring the summons, confident that no one could stop him. He set off, a Roman consul at the head of his troops, or an outlaw leading a rebel army, depending on one's point of view.

Relief celebrating one of Sulla's victories, possibly at Chaeronea against Mithridates in 86 BC; the Roman eagle in the centre is flanked by winged victories. Winged Victory has survived as a motif to modern times, one example being the statue outside Buckingham Palace in London.

Sulla in Asia

Sulla began by evicting Mithridates' general Archelaus from Greece. The campaigning was sometimes confused and indecisive, not least because the Greeks were uncertain whom to support. Athens, under the tyrant Ariston, resisted Sulla, but he took the city after a brutal siege. He sacked the port of Piraeus, and much of Athens itself, saying that he had only spared any part of the place because of its former glory.

One military tactic that served Sulla well was to dig ditches and earthworks on each side of his army, forcing the enemy to meet him head on and preventing their larger numbers swirling about his flanks. At Orchomenus, in Greece, he was hard-pressed by the sheer numbers of the enemy. Seizing a standard, Sulla rallied his retreating men by shouting 'I am prepared to get the glory of fighting and dying here. As for you men, when they ask you where you betrayed your general, remember this place and say Orchomenus.'

Another army came from Rome, commanded by a Valerius called Flaccus, who fortunately realized that the common enemy was more important than internal disagreements. But Valerius was murdered by one of his officers, called Fimbria. Despite his crime this man was a competent soldier, and he began to make considerable progress against Mithridates in Asia. By now Sulla had crossed the Hellespont, but he was distracted by reports of events in Rome.

Marius, who had fled for his life from Sulla, had returned to the city and had joined with Cinna when that man fell out with his fellow consul Octavius. After a brief and savage civil war, Marius and Cinna were now masters of Rome and were massacring Sulla's supporters. Sulla's wife Metella had escaped from the city and joined him, with the news that his house had been burned down and his lands confiscated.

In 85 Sulla decided to return to Rome. He summoned Mithridates and forced a settlement on him at the Peace of Dardanus. Though Mithridates agreed to give up all his conquests and pay an indemnity, Sulla's men were outraged. Mithridates had ordered the massacre of tens of thousands of Romans in his conquest of Asia, and now he was being allowed to escape with not only his life, but also his kingdom of Pontus. Nevertheless, Sulla managed to get his men to assent to this, and he then marched on Fimbria's camp, persuading them to defect. Fimbria committed suicide.

Sulla returns

Another death, that of Cinna, saw power in Rome fall to the son of Marius, who was as tyrannical and bloodthirsty as his father had been at the end. Sulla abandoned his negotiations with the government in Rome and now became an outright rebel. He left the greater part of his army in the cities of Asia, which were bled almost dry by the demands of the soldiers. Even that part of his army which he took to Italy Sulla could hardly afford to pay – in fact his soldiers once offered to meet his expenses by collecting money among themselves.

His arrival at Brundisium in 83 brought several leading nobles over to him at once, including Metellus Pius, Appius Claudius, Licinius Crassus and Pompey. (These last two were to spend their lives in an uneasy alliance, first as Sullan supporters, and later as Triumvirs with Julius Caesar.) With much of his army still in Asia, Sulla was short of men, but he fought with a mixture of

The Tabularium (record office), Rome, built during Sulla's dictatorship. The Romans were among the most assiduous record keepers in the ancient world. One effect of this was that those who informed on Sulla's enemies for money could later be tracked down and forced to pay it back.

savagery and cunning which inspired his opponent Carbo to say that Sulla was sometimes a lion, sometimes a fox, and he feared the fox more.

The Italians, who had won the right to be counted as Roman citizens after the Social War (p. 155), were uneasy about Sulla, fearing that he might revoke their privileges. Sulla promised to uphold their rights, but massacred those who continued to resist him. Within a year he had fought his way to within sight of Rome. The final battle was outside the Colline gate of the city, against an army composed largely of Samnites who supported the Marian cause; it was a hard fight, and among the fallen was Appius Claudius. Sulla, commanding the centre, was beaten back into his camp. He was grimly contemplating the consequences of defeat when a messenger arrived from Crassus on the right wing. Crassus had routed the enemy and completely mastered his part of the battlefield. He wanted to know if it was all right to stand his men down and have supper.

The realization that the day was mostly won inspired the Sullans as it discouraged their enemies. The Samnites fled or surrendered, and in a complete reversal of fortune Sulla found himself the master of Rome. The position was soon made official when the senate made him dictator – the first in Rome for 120 years. Sulla began as he meant to go on. On the day he took control of Rome he addressed the senate. While he was speaking, terrible screams arose from the Circus Maximus where the prisoners from the battle of the Colline gate were being massacred. Sulla merely said calmly that he was having some malefactors dealt with.

Sulla the dictator

It soon became apparent that Sulla was planning a complete purge of Rome. Senator after senator was killed on his orders. Finally, Metellus persuaded him to post a list of those he wanted killed, in order to free the rest from uncertainty. The list was published over three days and had some 500 names on it. Some were innocent, their names added by lackeys of Sulla who wanted their money or their property. One man, seeing his name on the list, commented ironically 'Ah, I see that my Alban farm has informed on me.'

A relief from the funerary monument of Lusius Storax, Chieti, showing a gathering of magistrates. Sulla increased the number of both Roman senators and magistrates, a reform made necessary by the increasing size of Rome's dominions. Sulla also took this opportunity to pack the senate with his own supporters.

Once the terror was over, it became clear that Sulla did not intend to set up a tyranny. Instead, he set about putting Rome on a stable footing – as far as this was possible. The numbers of the senate had been terribly depleted from the usual 300 senators by the recent troubles. Sulla not only chose new senators from the equites to fill the gaps, but he went ahead with the proposal of Livius Drusus and increased their number to 600, rewarding those who had supported him.

He also created more magistrates; raising the number of quaestors to 20 and praetors to 8. He made tenure of a quaestorship an

The Tomb of Caecilia Metella, wife of Crassus, on the via Appia, outside Rome. Just as the Caecilian menfolk occupied the highest political positions, the women married the top members of the Roman élite. The drum shape of this tomb is similar to that built later, and on a grander scale, by the emperor Hadrian.

automatic qualification for membership of the senate, thus ensuring that its numbers were topped up by 20 new senators per year. The increase in numbers of praetors partly reflected the growing size of Rome's empire – and partly Sulla's idea that a long command in one province allowed the governor to build a dangerous power base.

Sulla crippled the tribunes by ordering that any legislation they proposed had to be ratified by the senate. He also placed restrictions on the use of the veto, and, as a finishing touch, he decreed that persons who had been tribune were henceforth ineligible for any other office. This meant that the tribunate would no longer launch the careers of the politically ambitious. Sulla also increased the number and scope of the standing courts. Then, believing that further tenure of the dictatorship would create dangerous resentment, in 80 BC he returned Rome to civil administration. He and Metellus Pius were the new consuls. At the end of his second consulship, Sulla stepped down from office and became a private citizen.

The prophesied end

Sometime during this period, Sulla's wife Metella gave birth to twins, a boy and a girl, whom he called Faustus and Fausta. Perhaps weakened by the birth, Metella died of the plague shortly after. Sulla was soon remarried, to a daughter of the Valerian house.

Rome was restored. Sulla's veterans were settled in farms in Campania and Etruria. He had a beautiful young wife and healthy children. Beyond question, Sulla was at the peak of his power and happiness. Ever mindful of the prophecy, he set about putting his affairs in order. He died two days after completing his memoirs (which have not survived).

The day of his funeral was suitably overcast. There were worries that rain would hold up the cremation, but a strong wind whipped up the fire, and only after the last ashes had stopped smouldering did a heavy rain start to fall. Sulla was fortunate to the last.

Sulla might claim to have restored Rome, but he had fatally undermined the Republic. It was now apparent that any general who could get enough soldiers behind him had a chance at power. Over the following decades a number of desperate or deluded individuals were to try, and it was only a matter of time before someone succeeded.

'Sulla did it – why can't I?' This catchphrase entered the Latin language, and it sums up Sulla's true legacy to the Republic.

METELLUS PIUS	
Born	*Achievements*
c. 130 BC	Triumphator;
Famous ancestors	Pontifex Maximus
L. Metellus (cos.	*Children*
251)	Son: Metellus
Mother	Scipio (adopted)
Unknown	*Death*
Father	64 BC
Metellus Numidicus	
Positions held	
Praetor 89; Consul	
80; Pontifex	
Maximus	

METELLUS PIUS

What was Metellus Pius doing, when he, the leading man of his day, allowed his hosts to greet him with altars and incense? When he gazed happily at walls covered with cloth of gold? ... so completely had the rigours of his father's war in Numidia faded from his mind. We can see from this how quickly the love of luxury flowed into Rome – Metellus' youth saw the old morality, his old age began the new.

Valerius Maximus, *De Viris Illustribus* 9.1.5

AS WITH MANY ROMANS, WE DO NOT KNOW exactly when Metellus Pius was born. He was about 20 years old in 109 when he accompanied his father, Metellus Numidicus (pp. 141–43), to campaign in Africa. It was Numidicus' suggestion that Marius wait until his son was old enough to stand for the consulship that started the feud between the two men.

A devoted son

This feud continued years later in Rome, and Numidicus was exiled, partly through Marius' involvement. One of the defining moments of the young Metellus' life came in 99 when he abjectly begged the people to permit his father to return – a display of devotion that earned him the nickname 'Pius', which means 'devoted and reverent', though not necessarily in the religious sense of 'pious' today.

Metellus was praetor in 89, and campaigned against the Marsi, the leading tribe in the revolt of the allies against Rome which had raged since 90. A sound general, he defeated and killed Q. Poppaedius Silo, the Marsic leader. He was still campaigning in 87 when Octavius, the consul, fell out with his consular colleague, the pro-Marian Cinna.

Metellus then returned to Rome to assist with the defence of the city against the Marians. As the capital's defenders had little faith in

Coin of Quintus Metellus. The elephant on the coin is neither an Indian nor an African elephant of today, but a now-extinct species which lived in North Africa in Roman times.

Octavius, they appealed to Metellus to take supreme command. But, with a strong sense of propriety, Metellus firmly refused. At this rebuff, the soldiers deserted to Marius *en masse*.

Metellus retired to Africa, where he was joined by the future triumvir, Crassus (pp. 175–80). The two men soon quarrelled, however, and separated. Metellus was then forced to leave Africa after an unsuccessful action against the pro-Marian governor, C. Fabius.

A loyal follower

When Sulla returned from the East in 83, Metellus was among the first to join him, lending the rebel leader the public support of the *nobiles*. In the war which followed, Metellus proved himself a very successful general. He reversed his bad experience of 87, with Marian soldiers frequently deserting to him.

As his reward for standing by Sulla, he was made Pontifex Maximus, one of the chief priests in Rome. When Sulla laid down his dictatorship, it was with Metellus that he shared his first civilian consulship in 80. Metellus took this opportunity to repay the tribune Calidus, who had been instrumental in getting his father recalled from exile, rewarding the man with a praetorship.

As proconsul, Metellus fought to eliminate the rebel leader Sertorius in Spain. Over the course of the next eight years Metellus founded the city of Metellinum (modern Medellin), was challenged to single combat by Sertorius (but declined) and was wounded in the thigh in battle. Neither Metellus nor Sertorius could gain any advantage over the other – no mean feat since Sertorius (though himself a Roman) is rated with Spartacus and Hannibal as one of the best generals to challenge Rome. Pompey was sent to help Metellus, bringing with him a reputation as a promising commander. He promptly suffered an embarrassing and costly defeat.

Metellus finally won a victory of sorts over Sertorius, and was voted a triumph for it, but the war was far from over. In fact it only ended in 72 when Sertorius was murdered by his own men. Metellus returned to Rome in 71, disbanded his men and retired. He died in 63 or just before then, since in that year his office of Pontifex Maximus was taken over by the young Julius Caesar.

QUINTUS SERTORIUS	
Born	*Positions held*
c. 126 BC	Praetor 85
Famous ancestors	*Achievements*
None	Guerrilla leader
Mother	*Children*
Unknown	None
Father	*Death*
Unknown	Assassinated 73 BC

QUINTUS SERTORIUS

When Sertorius' men took the Roman colony of Lauro [in Spain], a woman tore out the eyes of a soldier with her fingers, because he had insulted her and was trying to commit an outrage on her. When Sertorius heard of this, he assumed this soldier's whole cohort was addicted to such brutality, and he had them put to death, notwithstanding that these troops were Romans.

Appian, *The Civil Wars* 1.110

QUINTUS SERTORIUS WAS A SABINE of equestrian stock, born some time around 126 in the city of Nursia. He began his career – as did most noble Romans – as a soldier. He fought against the Cimbri, and was wounded while campaigning under Servilius Caepio. When the Cimbri moved away from the Roman frontiers, Sertorius followed them, disguised as a Celt, keeping Marius informed of their activities. After the final defeat of the Cimbri he served in Spain.

A war hero

Sertorius was a quaestor when the Roman allies revolted (p. 155), and he fought in the war with great energy and courage, losing an eye in action. This was not altogether a bad thing, he commented later, since other men had to put their awards for bravery aside sometime, while he wore his permanently. He seemed certain to rise to the tribunate in 88, but was a casualty of the frenetic politics of that year. His candidature was blocked by Sulla for reasons now lost to us.

Sertorius thenceforth supported Cinna against the Sullans. This did not make him a Marian, since he opposed the suggestion that the old general join the Cinnan side. He was disgusted by the bloody tyranny of Marius when he took Rome, and he did not try personally to pay off any old scores.

However, 4,000 people were killed by the direct orders of Sertorius. These were the ex-slaves of Marius' bodyguard – the most extreme and brutal of his followers who had treated Rome as a conquered city, and their liberty as liberty to rob and rape. Sertorius had their camp surrounded in the night, and the occupants were butchered to a man. It seems clear that Sertorius suffered no consequences for this, since he was made a praetor, probably for 85.

When Sulla returned to Rome in 83, Sertorius' ideas of how to campaign against him were at variance with those of more senior generals. Realizing the anti-Sullan cause in Italy was doomed, he went to Spain. In 81, he was driven from there too, and ended up in Mauretania, in Africa, an exile under sentence of death.

Sertorius in Spain

When the Romans in Spain began to act with the mixture of greed and brutality which characterized their occupation of that country, the Lusitanians called on Sertorius to return. He did so in 80, with a tiny army of 2,600 men 'called Romans for honour's sake' (but probably not, for the most part). Against him in Spain were four Roman armies of about 35,000 men each, including thousands of cavalry, and several thousand auxiliary troops besides.

Sertorius was a brilliant guerrilla leader. He struck the demoralized Roman armies hard and then seemed to vanish to strike again elsewhere. The Spanish flocked to his cause. By 78 Sertorius held much of the country, and his troops treated him as a demi-god. Sertorius kept a white fawn which he claimed was divinely inspired and which gave him warning of

A vaulted substructure in the city of Coimbra, Roman Aeminium, in the ancient territory of the Lusitanians. The nearby ruins of Conimbriga constitute the largest excavated Roman site in Portugal, and provide a vivid picture of a prosperous Roman city.

enemy movements and foretold victory. He treated the Spanish kindly, kept taxes low and ensured his soldiers were well behaved.

Sertorius himself behaved always as a Roman proconsul rather than a Spanish warlord. He opened a school for the children of the Spanish chieftains where the children dressed in togas and learned Greek (and not incidentally provided Sertorius with useful hostages).

After Marcus Aemilius Lepidus had tried to emulate Sulla's march on Rome and was resoundingly defeated (p. 183), the remnants of his army fled to Spain bringing Sertorius 53 cohorts, and a gaggle of Roman nobility led by one Perpenna. Sertorius promptly went on the offensive against Pompey, who had been sent to reinforce Metellus Pius in Spain. Pompey desperately wanted a victory before Metellus arrived to share it, and engaged Sertorius. Only the arrival of Metellus prevented Pompey's complete rout. 'If the old woman had not arrived, I would have whipped the boy back to Rome,' commented Sertorius sourly afterward.

The tide turns

Sertorius had much to be bitter about. The highly bred Perpenna resented having a mere ex-praetor as his commander, and the senate in Rome was finally giving serious attention to the Spanish war. While Sertorius was still a match for the Romans, his lieutenants were not. He spent much of his time retrieving situations they had lost, and became increasingly savage and despotic.

In 73 Perpenna decided that he could do better, and assassinated Sertorius at a dinner. Within days Pompey had defeated his army and taken Perpenna prisoner. He was executed, which could be seen as a rather ungrateful act. Perpenna had after all achieved what numerous Roman armies had failed to do for almost a decade – dispose of Sertorius and bring Spain back under Roman control.

A mounted Roman soldier in battle, relief from a sarcophagus of the second century BC. The soldier is riding without a saddle – stirrups were unknown in the ancient world, which made the cavalry a less effective instrument of war.

Marcus Licinius Crassus Dives
(*c.* 115–53 BC)

MARCUS LICINIUS CRASSUS DIVES	
Born	Triumvir from 60
c. 115 BC	*Achievements*
Famous ancestors	Ovatio
Licinius Crassus	*Wife*
(cos. 205)	Tertulla
Mother	*Children*
Unknown	Sons: Publius,
Father	Marcus
Publius Licinius	*Death*
Crassus	Killed in battle
Positions held	53 BC
Praetor 72; Consul	
70, 55; Censor 65;	

In later life Crassus was charged with romantic intimacy with a Vestal Virgin called Licinia … this lady had a beautiful house in the suburbs, and Crassus wanted to buy it cheaply. It was for this reason he was so attentive to her, and which had caused the scandal. So his avarice served to acquit him of the charge; and nor did he leave the lady until he had got the estate.

Plutarch, *Life of Crassus*

MARCUS LICINIUS CRASSUS, was of the Licinian clan, one of the older established houses of Rome. Crassus inherited the family nickname of *dives* which means 'rich'; it was a name he certainly lived up to.

Victims of Marius

We have only a vague idea of when Crassus was born. We know that he was older than Pompey, and was in his 60s when he died, so a date of about 115 seems probable. He was the younger of two sons of Publius Licinius Crassus, a man of censorial rank who had campaigned with one of the Julii Caesares in the war with the allies in 90. He had supported Sulla against the Marians, and when Marius returned to Rome in 87, the older Crassus anticipated his fate by stabbing himself to death. The

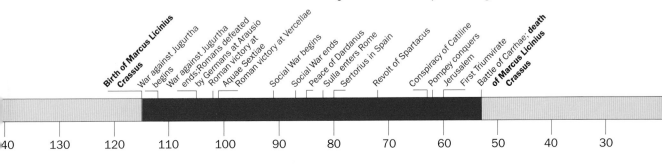

Marians killed the elder of his sons, but spared Marcus, thinking him too young to be a danger.

Not trusting in the continuing good-will of his enemies, Crassus fled to Spain, where he sheltered in a cave. The owner of the land that the cave was on made supplies of food available. As Crassus' stay continued, the landowner decided that some entertainment was also in order, and sent him two female slaves. Plutarch confirms that a contemporary, Fenestella, 'saw one of them, then very old, and he often heard her speak of the time and repeat the story with pleasure'.

The Sullan general

Eventually Crassus escaped to Africa where he joined Metellus Pius (pp. 171–72). The two men did not get on, and in 83 Crassus made his way back to Italy and the army of Sulla. Sulla set him the dangerous task of raising troops among the Marsi, a tribe of formidable fighters who had recently rebelled against Rome. When Crassus asked for a bodyguard, Sulla told him 'I give you the shades of your murdered father and brother. Go now and avenge them.' Stung by his dismissal Crassus went, and performed his perilous task exceptionally well.

He gained considerable credit as a general in the war that followed and his success in the final battle outside Rome secured victory for the Sullan cause. Sadly, Crassus' besetting sin of avarice lost him the favour of Sulla soon afterwards when he added to the proscription lists the name of a man whose property he wanted. Sulla discovered this, and never trusted Crassus again.

Making money

At this time Crassus was worth some 300 talents. For a man of his station, this was a reasonable, but not great sum. He set about adding to it with vigour. He was a capitalist in an age which had hardly grasped the concept. He purchased run-down houses and farms (legend has it he bought houses while they were burning down) and then sent in a horde of highly trained artisans who restored the property to prime condition to lease at a profit. The artisans were slaves, bought and often trained by Crassus himself, and these too he leased or sold for a profit.

At one point Crassus allegedly owned most of the building stock in Rome. He also owned much of the political class. Political life in Rome was extremely expensive, and Crassus was always ready to help a needy or ambitious senator – knowing that the favour would be returned in time. He was popular with the Roman people. Unlike Pompey, who was

(*Opposite*) Remains of the amphitheatre at Santa Maria Capua Vetere, where there was a famous gladiatorial school and where the revolt of Spartacus began.

Gladiators provided the core of Spartacus' forces for his revolt. Highly trained, they formed a formidable enemy but were defeated by Crassus and most were crucified. The figurine is from Tarentum and the relief, early first century AD, is from Santa Marinella.

aloof and uneasy with crowds, Crassus was friendly and familiar, returning greetings, doing small favours, and taking cases in the law courts that Pompey, Caesar and even Cicero disdained. (Many élite Romans acted as legal advocates.)

Spartacus in revolt

In 72 a revolt of slave gladiators broke out. At first this seemed trivial, but their leader, Spartacus, achieved the incredible feat of converting a slave rabble into a disciplined fighting force capable of destroying whole Roman armies. And this it did, including a veteran army under the capable generalship of a Cassius (a member of a family with which Crassus had close links).

Not trusting the consuls to defeat Spartacus, the Roman people turned to Crassus, who went against him with six legions and the rank of propraetor. When a part of his forces, under Memmius, engaged the enemy and were badly defeated, popular legend claims that Crassus decimated the whole army as a punishment. (Decimation was a traditional punishment involving the killing of one man in ten.) In fact, Crassus decimated the first 500 to flee, so some 50 men were executed in all. With the rest, he was more typically Crassan: he made them pay a deposit on their swords and shields, and assured them that this would be lost if they discarded their gear on the battlefield.

Spartacus retreated before the Romans and was trapped in the toe of Italy. He made an agreement with Cilician pirates to ferry his men to Sicily, where he hoped to instigate another slave revolt, but the pirates betrayed him and sailed off. Hoping to contain Spartacus, Crassus built a wall across the peninsula. Spartacus breached it, and headed north once more. Crassus was desperate to finish the war as Pompey was now coming from the north with his army, and, being Pompey, would take sole credit for any victory. Spartacus was forced to fight by his over-confident army. In the battle he made straight for Crassus but was brought down before he reached him.

With the slave army broken, Crassus made a ghastly example of the prisoners, crucifying some 6,000 of them at regular intervals along the Via Appia from Rome to Capua. After mopping up some fleeing survivors, Pompey bombastically announced to the senate that though Crassus had defeated the enemy, he had torn up the revolt by the roots.

Crassus as consul

Any bad feeling between the two was submerged in their common desire to become consul, and Pompey campaigned for Crassus almost as enthusiastically as for himself, saying that a victory was valueless unless shared with Crassus. Nevertheless their consulship in 70 was not a great success. The pair undid much of Sulla's political settlement by restoring the rights of the tribunes, but spent much of their time in

A statue of Hercules, found in Rome. During the last years of the Republic this demi-god became fashionable – Crassus offered one-tenth of his possessions to Hercules and Mark Antony adopted him as an ancestor.

TRIUMVIRS

The term 'triumvir' comes from *tres* ('three') and *vir* ('man'). This construction is often seen describing the number of Romans working together in some official capacity (e.g. 'decemvir'). Because the first triumvirate was an unofficial arrangement, the term was not applied at the time, and is a convention used by modern historians. Contemporary Romans had different terms to describe the triumvirate, many of them unprintable.

office bickering. Once, when told that Pompey the Great was coming, Crassus smiled and asked 'Oh, how big is he?'.

At this time Crassus made an offering of one-tenth of his very considerable possessions to Hercules. His sacrifice had a populist flavour in that he gave each citizen three months' grain and treated them to a public feast. However, the religious aspect should not be overlooked. Crassus was a god-fearing citizen, and unlike many of his contemporaries, his private life was scandal-free. He had a happy marriage (to his brother's widow, a not uncommon practice) and a devoted son. His entertainments were not lavish, but Plutarch says that 'good taste and kindness' made them more enjoyable than richer affairs.

In 65 Crassus was censor. His ambitious plans to enfranchise the Transpadanes (people living in Italy north of the river Po) were foiled by his more conservative colleague Lutatius Catulus. Admitting irrevocable differences, the pair did the honourable thing and resigned.

Crassus the politician

Crassus the politician worked through backroom deals and influence, a mode of operation that leaves little mark in the public record. What is noticeable is that attacks on Crassus were markedly absent – unusual in the rough-and-tumble politics of the day. Both the fiery Clodius and the radical tribune Cornelius steered clear of him, the latter comparing Crassus to a dangerous bull. When someone suggested that Crassus was involved in the Catilinarian conspiracy (p. 213), the accuser was shouted down in the senate and died mysteriously a few days later.

One aspiring politician who benefited from his patronage was the young Julius Caesar. Caesar could only take up his first post in Spain because Crassus stood surety for the 830 talents he owed. (At this time Crassus was worth about 2,000 talents.)

Crassus' political potency ensured his inclusion in the first triumvirate. It is evident why Caesar and Pompey needed the alliance – they realized Crassus would be a dangerous enemy if left out – but how Crassus benefited is less clear. He may have wanted some legislation to help Asian tax collectors; he was not needed for his money – at this time Pompey was even richer, thanks to his Asian conquests.

Nevertheless, the military glory of his partners rankled with Crassus. He literally had more money than he could spend, he was an ex-consul and censor, and he had about half the senate in his pocket. He wanted new worlds to conquer, and he intended to find them over the Euphrates. A conference was called at Lucca, in which the triumvirs patched up their fraying alliance.

The Parthian war

The deal was as follows – Pompey and Crassus were to be consuls together once more. Pompey would take Spain for five years as his command; Caesar's command in Gaul would be renewed for five years; and Crassus would have command in Syria for five years. Gaining the consulate was a formality. The opposition of Cato and Domitius Aheno-barbus was brushed aside, and Crassus began his second consulate with the expressed aim of going to war with Parthia – an eastern kingdom which until then had co-existed peacefully with Rome.

Not everyone approved – the tribune Capito tried to arrest Crassus for breaking faith with Parthia. When that failed, as consul and army departed from Rome, the tribune cursed them with the ancient equivalent of bell, book and candle. (He was later prosecuted for this, having been too successful.)

Crassus took with him seven legions and C. Cassius Longinus (later famous as an assassin of Caesar). In 54 he arrived in Asia, and his early campaigns met with modest success. During the winter break in campaigning, he extorted huge sums from the cities of Asia Minor. Perhaps this was to pay for his campaign, though several ancient sources believe he simply could not let a money-making opportunity pass by. However, the suggestion that he went several hundred miles out of his way to sack what little Pompey had left of the temple in Jerusalem is probably fiction.

In 53 Crassus crossed the Euphrates, intending to take the most direct route through the desert to Seleucia, capital of the old Seleucid empire. His soldiers were plagued by heat and thirst, and it is alleged that their Arab guides led them astray. The Surenas, as the Parthian general was entitled, waited until Crassus and his men were in open country near the town of Carrhae, and then attacked. The Parthians fought at long range, using archers, and the legions were unable to engage their more mobile opponents. When Crassus' son Publius led the cavalry against the horse archers, he was surrounded and killed.

Crassus tried to rally his men, saying that as a father he had lost a son, but as a general he had lost but another soldier, but this did not raise the flagging morale of the troops. They were waiting for the enemy to run out of arrows, and they buckled when they saw that the Parthians had a supply train of camels to keep their bows reloaded.

Crassus defeated

Crassus withdrew to a nearby hill, but his position was untenable. He refused an offer to negotiate, knowing full well it was a trap. But his men, scenting a way out, forced him to go. Reluctantly, Crassus met the Parthians. There was a scuffle and he was killed almost immediately. The Parthians then closed with the Roman army and destroyed it in a confused series of engagements.

The débâcle cost Rome 20,000 men. Cassius Longinus, who had abandoned what he saw as a lost cause early on, escaped to Syria, which he defended ably against the Parthian counter-attack. The head

Personification of Parthia on a marble plinth, AD 145. In one hand the figure carries a phallus – a symbol of good fortune and fertility in the ancient world – and in the other an arrow. During their various excursions into Parthia the Romans learned that the Parthians were expert and lethal bowmen.

PARTHIA

The great enemy of Rome in the late Republic and early Empire was the state of Parthia. It was founded at the relatively late period of the mid-third century BC from the remains of the Alexandrian satrapy of Seleucia. The western border of Parthia proper was the Euphrates, and the state extended to the River Indus in the east. However, Parthia was often able to project its power beyond these boundaries, and was occasionally a threat to the Roman province of Syria. The capital and royal seat of the empire was the city of Ctesiphon.

For many years historians felt that the culture of the Parthian state was derived from the older Classical civilizations of Greece and Rome to the west. More recent archaeological findings reveal a different picture, showing that Parthia had its own rich culture, and the 'Hellenism' of the Parthian kings was in part put on for the benefit of the subject Greek colonies which were an important part of the empire.

Most of what is known about the structure of the state is based on a find of administrative documents dated to the third century AD, and it is uncertain how closely they reflect Parthia in the late Republican period. The little we do know suggests that there was a constant tension between the Parthian king and his nobles, many of whom owned lands extensive enough to amount to small kingdoms in their own right, and who were powerful enough to resent the constraints of centralized rule.

The Parthians adopted the ancient fire religion of Zoroastrianism, which was born in the more ancient empire of Persia. In warfare they relied on peasant levies and heavily armoured knights. The Romans found particularly infuriating the Parthian mounted archers, who would harass them with bowfire, flee from cavalry sent to chase them off, and return as soon as the cavalry retired. Even in flight these archers were deadly, as they could turn in the saddle and shoot at their pursuers with the original 'Parthian shot'.

(Above) A Parthian mounted bowman: these agile archers on their ponies were able to elude the Roman cavalry and constantly tormented the Roman armies sent against them.

Map of the eastern part of the Roman empire and western Parthia. At its greatest extent the Parthian empire stretched as far east as the River Indus.

of Crassus was taken to the Parthian king, and used as a prop in a theatrical production staged for the king's amusement. It was an ignominious end for one of Rome's most distinguished citizens. But at least Crassus died fighting while trying to extend Rome's frontiers. Neither of his fellow triumvirs managed as much. Without Crassus to restrain them, Pompey and Caesar tumbled inevitably into internecine strife. At Carrhae the Roman Republic itself was fatally wounded.

Gnaeus Pompey, the Great

(106–48 BC)

Marble bust of Pompey the Great: this shows Pompey in later life, when he had lost most of his youthful good looks which once caused him to be compared to the young Alexander.

GNAEUS POMPEY	
Born 106 BC	*Achievements* Triumphator three times
Famous ancestors None	*Wives* Antistia, Aemilia,
Mother Unknown	Mucia, Julia, Cornelia
Father Pompeius Strabo	*Children* Sons: Gnaeus,
Positions held Consul 70, 55, 52; Triumvir from 60	Sextus *Death* Assassinated 48 BC

'I have not failed, and I never will fail to fight for you and by your side. I give you my services as a soldier and as a general. I pray to the gods that if I have any experience of war, if through good fortune I have been unbeaten to this day, then may that blessing be continued in our present need.'

Pompey rallies the senate against Caesar, Appian, *The Civil Wars* 2.51

GNAEUS POMPEIUS, KNOWN AS POMPEY THE GREAT, was the first of those Romans to dominate the Republic to the degree to which they almost achieved the status of kings. These towering figures of the late Republic are called the 'dynasts', and the era of the late Republic is sometimes called the Dynastic period.

A precarious youth

Pompey's father, Pompeius Strabo, switched sides between Marius and his opponents as his personal advantage dictated. For this behaviour, Rutilius Rufus called Pompeius 'the vilest man alive'. The people of Rome agreed, and when Pompeius died of the plague, they dragged his body from its bier and desecrated it. Pompey had served with his father and was with him at the taking of the city of Asculum in 89. After his

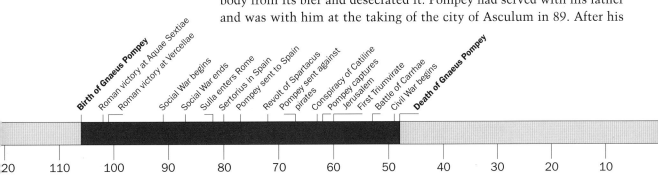

Birth of Gnaeus Pompey · Roman victory at Aquae Sextiae · Roman victory at Vercellae · Social War begins · Social War ends · Sulla enters Rome · Sertorius in Spain · Pompey sent to Spain · Revolt of Spartacus · Pompey sent against pirates · Conspiracy of Catiline · Pompey captures Jerusalem · First Triumvirate · Battle of Carrhae · Civil War begins · Death of Gnaeus Pompey

120 110 100 90 80 70 60 50 40 30 20 10

father's death he was accused of helping himself to the spoils of the town and was put on trial. The praetor presiding over the court had a daughter called Antistia, and during the trial her ambitious father betrothed her to Pompey. The secret got out, and on the predictable 'Not Guilty' verdict, jury and spectators broke into shouts of *Talasio* – the Roman equivalent of 'here comes the bride'.

When strife erupted in 87 between the Sullan consul, Octavius, and his populist rival Cinna, who was a supporter of Marius (pp. 149–59), Pompey went over to Cinna, but his enemies had got there first. The atmosphere in camp was so poisonous that Pompey discreetly withdrew – so discreetly it was rumoured that Cinna had murdered him. This did no good to Cinna's cause, as Pompey was in fact a popular youth. He was helped by his appearance – fine features, golden hair and large, limpid eyes. In later life flatterers compared him with Alexander the Great.

Pompey withdrew to his ancestral estates in Picenum in eastern Italy. When Sulla returned to the peninsula in 83, Pompey brought the town over to him, and on his own initiative raised three legions of soldiers for the cause. One tragic consequence of this was that the Marians in Rome murdered Antistius, Pompey's father-in-law, believing him in league with Pompey.

Sulla's supporter

Sulla greeted Pompey with full honours, and had him hailed as *imperator* (which in the Republic meant 'conquering general'). His early successes against a Brutus and a Scipio perhaps justified the title, though the enemy troops he faced were demoralized and mutinous.

With the fall of Rome to Sulla, Pompey was sent to Sicily as propraetor to defeat the Marian general Carbo. Pompey fulfilled this with commendable promptness, capturing Carbo and executing him after a show trial, an act which gained him the name of 'butcher boy'. Nevertheless, Pompey was moderate in other ways. He ordered his men to refrain from spoiling the country as they passed through, and to ensure that his orders were obeyed, he had the soldiers' swords sealed in their scabbards.

He crossed over from Sicily to Africa, and there took on another Marian, G. Domitius Ahenobarbus, and his African allies. Domitius (an ancestor of the emperor Nero) died in battle, and Pompey returned to Rome. In response to his request for a triumph for his achievements, Sulla pointed out that triumphs were for appointed magistrates, and Pompey had not yet held any office. Anyway, triumphs for victories over Roman citizens were in bad taste. Pompey insisted, saying ominously that men looked to the rising rather than the setting sun – implying that Sulla's era was almost over.

Marriages and alliances

Pompey won his triumph on 12 March, 81. Farcically, his chariot, pulled by elephants, was unable to get through the city gates, and the conquering general had to use more conventional transport. Thereafter, to bind

Pompey closer to him, Sulla ordered Pompey to divorce Antistia and marry Aemilia (the daughter of Sulla's wife Metella and Aemilius Scaurus).

Unlike Julius Caesar, who refused to give up his wife in similar circumstances, Pompey agreed – even though Aemilia had to be divorced from her current husband for the event. Aemilia was not only married, but pregnant, and the whole affair was made tragically pointless when she died in childbirth. Still, Pompey seems to have been taken with the idea of a Metellan marriage, and he married Mucia Tertia, a close relative of the Metelli, who bore him a son in 79.

In 78 Pompey was again at the side of an Aemilian – Marcus Aemilius Lepidus, whose candidature for the consulship Pompey was supporting. Sulla was unhappy with Lepidus, who opposed his policies and was dangerously unstable. In reproach, he cut Pompey out of his will. The old dictator's judgment was sound, for the following year Lepidus attempted to emulate Sulla's march on Rome. He was met and defeated by the other consul, the able and competent Lutatius Catulus.

Commands abroad

Catulus dispatched Pompey to Gaul where he vanquished and killed Lepidus' confederate, Brutus (the father of the man who assassinated Julius Caesar). For the rest of the year, using one excuse or another, Pompey avoided disbanding his army. Finally, in 77, Marcus Philippus proposed that Pompey take this army to Spain to assist Metellus Pius against the Marian leader Sertorius (pp. 172–74). Pompey and Sertorius promptly engaged in battle – united, as Plutarch remarks dryly, by the mutual fear that Metellus Pius should arrive before the battle was decided.

Metellus did indeed arrive in time – fortunately for Pompey – and Sertorius was the disappointed party. Pompey had to be rescued by the man whose glory he had hoped to steal. Chastened, Pompey campaigned thereafter with more circumspection until Sertorius' second-in-command Perpenna did Rome the favour of assassinating its most competent opponent. As a general Perpenna was no Sertorius, and Pompey defeated and captured him within weeks of the assassination.

Perpenna revealed that Sertorius had been in secret correspondence with top-ranking senators, and he offered Pompey the letters in exchange for his life. In a remarkable display of political wisdom, Pompey burned the letters unread, sparing Rome a further civil convulsion. Though the more cynical may wonder whether he did destroy *all* the letters, and whether certain parties in Rome decided to support him in case he had not. Certainly, Pompey enjoyed better relations with the senate for some time thereafter.

The returning hero

Pompey returned to Rome in 71, just in time to finish off the remnants of the slave army of Spartacus which had been largely destroyed by Crassus

Marker stone of Domitius Ahenobarbus from Gaul. The Domitii were one of the oldest families of the Republic. One Ahenobarbus opposed Pompey in Africa and was killed in battle against him.

Les Cluses (Pyrenees), Col de Panissars, with a Roman road over the pass looking north. The rock-cut foundation of the trophy of Pompey of 71 BC is visible on the right. Pompey's Spanish campaign against Sertorius revealed that Pompey could be outmatched on the battlefield by a top-class general. Although Pompey left Spain in triumph, he never overcame this weakness.

(p. 177). He killed some 5,000 of the rebel slaves and typically tried to steal the credit for ending the war, despite the achievement of Crassus. He was awarded a triumph for his Spanish exploits, finally disbanded his army (to general relief) and stood for the consulship. Whether the matter of the Sertorius letters assisted him cannot be said for certain, but until then Pompey had not been so much as quaestor. Now he intended to start the *cursus honorum* at the top.

He succeeded, and he and Crassus were consuls for 70. The partnership was not a success, however. Pompey tended to be populist, whereas Crassus favoured the senate. The major legislation of their year in office rescinded Sulla's restrictions on the tribunate.

During Pompey's consular year the ceremony of discharging those who had completed their military service was held in the forum in front of the censors. The censors were amazed and gratified to find that among those awaiting discharge was the consul, in full regalia and with his public horse. When asked how many campaigns he had served, and under which commander, Pompey enumerated his campaigns, adding that he had always served under himself. After this, the nickname *Magnus*, 'the Great', which he had assumed since 81, became his accepted appellation.

The pirates

Despite this piece of theatre, Pompey was soon seeking another command. The pirates of Cilicia (on the south coast of modern Turkey) had become a real menace. Disruptions in the East had displaced large numbers of skilled soldiery, and the Roman tradition of naval incompetence had allowed them to take to the sea and prosper to the point where they captured whole cities and seriously threatened the grain supply of Rome. The last straw came when they captured two Roman praetors and began marauding inland, even in Italy itself. In 67, the tribune Gabinius proposed that Pompey be given extraordinary powers, superseding those of all other provincial governors up to 50 miles (80 km) from the sea.

Pompey now had almost imperial powers, since the decree covered most of the empire. Many in the senate were horrified, but could not oppose popular pressure. The young Julius Caesar (pp. 200–08) was among those senators who supported the bill. On assuming command, Pompey divided the Mediterranean into sections, allocated each to a particular commander, and swept from west to east in 40 days, bottling the pirates up in Cilicia.

He stormed their stronghold, capturing some 20,000 men, 90 ships, and a mass of treasure. Realizing that many of his prisoners had been driven to piracy by extreme poverty, he settled some in the depopulated cities of Asia Minor, and others in an uninhabited part of Greece. In typical fashion he then rather tarnished his startling achievement by ordering Metellus Creticus to cease operations against the pirate bases in Crete. Pompey wanted the glory of the victory, but Metellus' soldiers ignored him, and brushed aside the men whom had Pompey stationed to guard the pirates until he could get to them.

Another extraordinary command

Still, the people in Rome were deeply grateful, not least for the reduced price of grain. Therefore they responded enthusiastically when the *Leges Manilia* were proposed, giving Pompey command in Asia Minor under almost the same terms as he had been given over the pirates. The intention was that Pompey should defeat Mithridates once and for all. Among the backers of the law was the young Cicero (pp. 211–15), who supported Pompey loyally in the years which followed.

Lucullus (pp. 191–94), the commander of the Romans against Mithridates, had almost won the war when his troops mutinied and refused to go any further. His handover to Pompey did not go smoothly: the two men got into a furious argument and almost came to blows. Pompey pointedly reversed almost every decree that Lucullus had made for the settlement of Asia up to that point, and led the army out on campaign.

There was not a lot of campaigning left to do. Pompey defeated Mithridates as the king attempted to withdraw, and went on to attack Tigranes the Great of Armenia. Tigranes surrendered and paid a massive ransom, so Pompey went on to annex Syria and conquer Judaea. It was pointed out that he was not, in fact, doing much campaigning against Mithridates. However, Pompey had decided that Lucullus was wrong to follow the old king around his territories while his army grew ever more tired of the chase. Instead he made it diplomatically impossible for

Two of the enemies of Rome: (*Top*) Silver tetradrachm of Mithridates VI of Pontus. (*Above*) Coin of Tigranes I, showing his characteristic headdress and tiara. Many of the coins of the 'Asiatic' monarchies are in the Greek style as the kingdoms contained a large number of Greek cities, which had spread from Asia Minor almost to modern Iran.

Pompey the Great: obverse of a denarius struck in Sicily 42–38 BC, at a time when Sicily came under the control of Sextus Pompey, the son of the great general.

Coin of 46–45 BC showing the Pompeians in Spain. After Pompey's death in 48 his sons fled to Spain. This coin is a part of their propaganda attempt to revive old loyalties to the Pompeians in the province.

Mithridates to gather allies or find any place to rest. In the end, Mithridates' own son rebelled against him and Tigranes put a price on his head. Realizing the game was up, Rome's oldest enemy took his own life in the Crimea in 63.

Pompey the politician

An immensely wealthy Pompey returned to Rome in 62 to celebrate a third triumph. His first had been for victory in Africa and the second for victory in Europe; the third, for the conquest of Asia, took several days to pass through the streets of Rome. He disbanded his armies and took his place in the senate, but he got off to a bad start. One of his first actions on arriving in Italy was to divorce Mucia Tertia for infidelity – a move that further alienated the Metellans, already upset by Pompey's treatment of Metellus Creticus. With Cato and Lucullus firmly in the anti-Pompeian camp, Pompey was facing political defeat. He attempted to use Lucullus' enemy Clodius, and in 58 even allowed his supporter Cicero to be exiled at Clodius' instigation. But Clodius was nobody's tool, and he soon turned against Pompey, leaving him worse off than before.

In 59, his Asian settlement still unratified and his veterans without land, Pompey needed allies. He found them in Crassus and Caesar. The three men formed what a contemporary called the 'three-headed monster', known today as the first triumvirate. Caesar got the consulship he wanted, and pushed through the legislation that Pompey needed. The alliance was sealed by Pompey's marriage to Caesar's daughter, Julia.

The compact was renewed at Lucca in 55 (p. 178), mainly because Crassus wanted to campaign against the Parthians and he and Pompey were elected consuls for the year. Pompey took command of Spain for five years but did not go there in person, ruling instead through legates. The dangerous Cato almost became praetor in the same election, but Pompey had the voting called off on a religious pretext.

The triumvirate collapses

In 54 Julia died. She and Pompey seem to have genuinely loved each other, creating a bond between Pompey and Caesar. Then in 53 came the news that Crassus had been killed by the Parthians at Carrhae, and his army destroyed. In the fevered atmosphere that resulted, it was proposed that Pompey be sole consul for 52. Even Pompey's enemies, such as Cato and the ex-consul Bibulus, agreed.

As consul, Pompey supported Metellus Pius Scipio, the adopted Cornelian son of Metellus Pius. Pompey's influence rescued Metellus Scipio from a tricky lawsuit, and Pompey then married Cornelia, the daughter of Metellus Scipio and the widow of Publius, son of Crassus. Re-elected after his sole consulship, Pompey took Metellus Scipio as his colleague.

The question now was what to do with Caesar, who had been winning victories in Gaul even as his political credit ran out in Rome. By 49 Caesar's options were political oblivion or outright rebellion. He chose the latter, and the first of the great civil wars began. The consul, a

GLADIATORS

Gladiatorial combat was a tradition more ancient than Rome. It originated in Etruria, where it was part of the ritual to appease the gods performed at funerals. When the tradition first spread to Rome, it retained the same context.

Until the very end of the Republic, the reason (or pretext) for gladiatorial combat was as part of the funeral rites for a deceased male relative of the person staging the fights. And until the late Republic, the role of gladiators in Roman life was not significant.

The first known combats took place in 264 BC at the funeral of one of the Iunian line named Pera. There was no special venue for these combats; they sometimes took place in private houses and even in the forum. Generally fewer than a dozen gladiators took part, and fights were not invariably to the death.

In the late Republic, staging gladiatorial fights became a means of displaying wealth. It took a lot of money to acquire and train a gladiator (the name comes from *gladius*, or sword), and the owner risked losing everything if his acquisition was killed in a fight. In addition to taking part in formal combat, gladiators served another function as bodyguards, enforcers and shock troops in electoral riots.

Most gladiators were either slaves or prisoners of war. The most famous gladiator of all, Spartacus (whom Pompey helped defeat), was exceptional in that he had served in the Roman army as an auxiliary. Only

A bronze gladiator's helmet for a murmillo, first century AD. The name of this type of gladiator means 'fish' and probably comes from the distinctive 'fin' on the back of the helmet.

at the time. Most of his army were German and Gallic slaves freed from the huge farms worked by slave labour (called *latifundia*) and many were shepherds, or even free men from the rural poor.

a few of those who fought with Spartacus against the Romans were originally gladiators, since it is unlikely there were more than around a thousand full-time gladiators in Italy

A relief showing gladiators, first century BC. The round shields of the gladiators depicted here suggest that these are hoplomachi, the traditional opponents of the murmillo (above). The gladiators may be wearing either chainmail (standard in the Roman army of the time) or scaled armour. To the left are musicians playing long trumpets.

Claudius Marcellus, gave command of the Republic's forces to Pompey, who had once boasted 'if I stamp my foot, Italy will rise in my support'. In the event, a shortage of manpower forced him to withdraw to Greece without a fight, and muster his forces there.

The Pharsalus campaign

Caesar followed, and discovered that Pompey was a master of logistics. Caesar's army was cornered and half-starved, while Pompey commanded the sea lanes and land communications. However, Pompey had his

ENTERTAINMENT

As might be expected of a lively, sociable people, the Romans enjoyed a great variety of games and entertainments. Activities such as wrestling and ball games were indulged in by adults as much as children. Indeed, playing some form of ball game was one means by which a Roman gentleman might work up an appetite for dinner.

Dinner was itself often a social occasion. Meals were eaten reclining on couches (though more modest ladies preferred to sit on a chair), and often in the company of family and friends. We have an epigram of Martial in which he invites a friend to join him in a plain sort of meal, but in the company of good friends. After the meal, games might be played with dice (Augustus was fond of this diversion), or if it was a larger, more formal dinner, professional entertainers might be brought in. Banquets were popular, for they allowed the ostentatious display of luxury that might encourage allies or clients. In fact, expenditure at banquets was regulated for this reason, and an ancestor of Cornelius Sulla (pp. 164–71) was punished for having more than the permitted maximum of gold plates.

Theatre had a long history in Rome, though the first semi-permanent theatre was built by Pompey only in 55 BC. Before this time theatres were temporary structures, often without seats – Roman sentiment at the time was that taking one's entertainment seated during the day was a sign of decadence.

Plays were performed at the great Roman games – the *ludi Romani* and the *ludi Plebei* – at which the Roman playwright Plautus saw his play *Stichus* performed in 200 BC. Even formal plays were enacted with few props, and the writers had a preference for outdoor scenes which meant that they could be staged with any nearby building as a backdrop. Gladiatorial combats (p. 187) feature more in the modern imagination than they did in the entertainments of the Romans of the Republic. Until the very end of the Republic, gladiatorial combats were staged only at private functions, often as a part of the funerary rites of the deceased.

(Above) A banquet depicted in a wallpainting from Pompeii. In this scene the guests can be seen reclining on couches while being attended to by servant boys. Both men and women took part in banquets which were an important aspect of Roman social life.

Plan of Pompey's theatre, Rome, on an ancient plan of the city of Rome called the Forma Urbis Romae which was once attached to a wall in the Temple of Peace. Sadly only fragments of this amazing map survive.

(Centre) Mosaic of new comedy characters, first century BC, signed by Dioscurides of Samos and from the 'Villa of Cicero', Pompeii. Cicero is indeed known to have owned property in Pompeii, but it is by no means certain that he owned the villa that now bears his name.

A more popular entertainment was the *ludi Circenses*, the chariot races, held first at the Campus Martius, and later at the Circus Maximus, the great arena to the south of the Palatine which could hold 150,000 spectators. Admission for spectators to public spectacles was free. There were special seats for senators, and women and slaves probably had separate seats for themselves (at least this was the case in the Imperial period).

On a less formal level board games were popular enough to be etched into city pavements. The two favourites were 'twelve lines', which seems to have been a form of backgammon, and 'robbers', a game in which pieces were moved and taken, rather as in chess.

(Right) Relief showing a chariot race: the Romans supported various teams with passionate enthusiasm. The races were keenly contested and often included some spectacular crashes.

(Below) This drawing of women playing dice is from Herculaneum, first century AD, executed in encaustic on marble. Dice games were popular with all social groups and classes – the emperor Augustus was fond of this entertainment.

limitations as a general. Against Sertorius much of the work had been done by Metellus Pius, against Mithridates by Lucullus. Perhaps aware of this, Pompey opted to starve Caesar into submission.

The other senators would have none of this. They saw an enemy on the ropes, and were impatient for the final blow. (Indeed this could have been delivered a few days previously, when Pompey inexplicably passed up an opportunity to storm Caesar's camp.) Finally, the senate forced Pompey to stake everything that he had fought and campaigned for in his life on a single battle. It was fought at Pharsalus in 48, and Pompey lost. This, despite the fact that his men outnumbered Caesar's two to one. In the words of a modern historian, 'Frankly, he panicked'.

Flight and death

With Caesar master of the Roman empire, there was only one possible refuge for Pompey. Egypt was the last great Mediterranean power that had not fallen to Rome, so Pompey and his wife Cornelia fled there in a commandeered merchant boat. The Egyptians were less than happy with the dilemma posed by Pompey's arrival. It was decided that it would be better if Pompey did not disembark in Egypt at all, and he was assassinated while transferring from his ship to a boat to take him ashore.

It was a sad and humiliating end for the man who had conquered on every known continent, and extended the frontiers of Rome further than any man before him. He was, as Caesar admitted, 'of good character, clean life, and serious principle'. His grieving wife carried his ashes back to Italy where they were interred.

The Head of Pompey Presented to Caesar, by Bonifacio de' Pitati (1487–1553). The Egyptians assassinated Pompey immediately on his arrival in Alexandria. Among the many anachronisms in this picture are the turbaned heads of the Egyptians, and the medieval appearance of the camp and weaponry.

Licinius Lucullus
(c. 110–57 BC)

Cato the Stoic
(95–46 BC)

Publius Clodius Pulcher
(c. 95–52 BC)

Bronze head of Cato the Stoic, from Volubilis (Morocco). In his adamant resistance to the triumvirate, and his choice of death rather than submission to Caesar, Cato became the symbol of obdurate Republicanism.

LICINIUS LUCULLUS	
Born	*Achievements*
c. 110 BC	Triumphator
Famous ancestors	*Wives*
Licinius Lucullus	Clodia; Servilia
(cos. 151)	*Children*
Mother	Son: Licinius
Caecilia	Lucullus
Father	*Death*
Lucullus	Illness 57 BC
Positions held	
Praetor 78; Consul	
74	

LICINIUS LUCULLUS

That he did not put an end to the war [with Mithridates] was due, you might say, more to a lack of inclination than of ability. In all other ways, he was a man of truly praiseworthy character. He had hardly ever been defeated in war, yet he fell victim to his love of money.

Velleius Paterculus, *Historia* 2.33.1

LICINIUS LUCULLUS WAS BORN IN ABOUT 110 BC. He was the nephew of Metellus Numidicus through his mother, a Caecilia Metella. His father had been conducting a successful military campaign in Sicily when a Servilius got himself appointed to replace him. In a rage, the older Lucullus destroyed his military stores, leaving nothing for his successor. He was prosecuted for this by another Servilius, nicknamed Servilius the Augur, and since his guilt was obvious, he was exiled from Rome while Lucullus was still an infant.

Starting in politics

The first action of the younger Lucullus in public life was to have Servilius the Augur brought to court (the charge is unknown). Servilius only

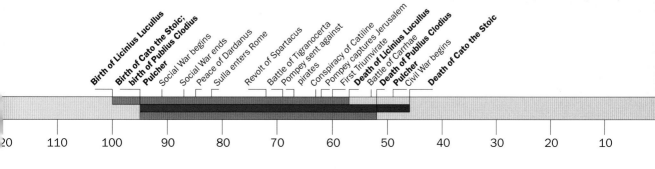

Birth of Licinius Lucullus
Birth of Cato the Stoic; birth of Publius Clodius Pulcher
Social War begins
Social War ends
Peace of Dardanus
Sulla enters Rome
Revolt of Spartacus
Battle of Tigranocerta
Pompey sent against pirates
Conspiracy of Catiline
Pompey captures Jerusalem
First Triumvirate
Death of Licinius Lucullus
Battle of Carrhae
Death of Publius Clodius Pulcher
Civil War begins
Death of Cato the Stoic

120 110 100 90 80 70 60 50 40 30 20 10

just got off, amid scenes of public disorder. This action gained Lucullus some public repute, and it probably helped him to a quaestorship with Sulla, to whom he was also related. Lucullus had served under Sulla in the war with the Italian allies (p. 155), and it is probable that he showed his loyalty again by being the one officer who reputedly stayed with the Sullan army on its march on Rome.

As Lucullus had gone with Sulla to Asia, he escaped the Marian purges. While in Asia he raised a fleet from among Rome's allies to support the land army. It transpired, however, that it also gave him the perfect opportunity to capture Mithridates, the enemy king, who was caught between the army of the renegade Roman commander Fimbria and the sea. Lucullus, to his discredit, stood off and allowed Mithridates to escape rather than allow Fimbria to share in the glory of the capture.

Gaining influence

Lucullus did not return immediately to Italy with Sulla, remaining in Asia to extract badly needed funds, and consequently he avoided being associated with the Sullan proscriptions. When he did return to Rome it was to become aedile in 79. He had waited to hold the post until then because he wanted to hold it together with his brother, and the pair staged magnificent games which gained them great public credit.

Lucullus was erudite in both Greek and philosophy, and no one was surprised when Sulla made him his literary executor, entrusting him with his memoirs. People were surprised, however, when Sulla made Lucullus guardian of his child Faustus Sulla, much to young Pompey's consternation, since he had expected that honour.

As consul in 74, Lucullus proposed giving M. Antonius, the father of Mark Antony, a command against the Cilician pirates who were ravaging the eastern Mediterranean. He also thwarted attempts by the demagogic L. Quinctius to overthrow the Sullan constitution. But much of his time was spent manoeuvring to get a command in the east, where the war with Mithridates was rekindling. He finally got this by shamelessly cultivating the mistress of Cethegus, a Sullan supporter who had great influence in the senate.

Command in Asia

Lucullus' military experience so far had been in administration rather than command, and not much was expected of him. However, he took over the troops of Fimbria after their leader's suicide, and with these and his own men he engaged Mithridates with considerable success. The campaign was fought across western Asia Minor, and by the end of 70 Mithridates had been driven into the mountains of Armenia.

Here Mithridates joined forces with Tigranes the Great, who styled himself the 'King of Kings'. At first Tigranes refused to believe that Lucullus would have the temerity to advance on him, but Lucullus did just that, and defeated him in battle and sacked Tigranocerta, Tigranes' new capital. A decisive battle followed soon after. The Romans were

Head of Mithridates in a lionskin cap. Of all the enemies of Rome, Mithridates lasted longest, having clashed with Sulla, Lucullus and finally Pompey. Mithridates died in 63 BC after valiantly opposing the power of Rome for almost 30 years.

A RENOWNED GARDEN

Of his sumptuous buildings, porticos and baths, still less to his paintings and sculptures, and all his industry about these rare things which he collected at vast expense, lavishly endowing them with all the treasure won in his wars, I can give no higher a name than that, even now, with all the advance in luxury, the Lucullan gardens are reckoned as the noblest the emperor has.

Plutarch, *Life of Lucullus*

vastly outnumbered, so they made their way to one flank of the enemy army and proceeded to fight their way across it to the centre. The enemy broke before they got there.

Lucullus wanted to continue, but his men were weary of campaigning and had been getting steadily more mutinous. Finally they flatly refused to go on. Matters were not helped by Publius Clodius Pulcher (pp. 198–99), a Claudian and Lucullus' brother-in-law. Clodius stirred up the troops, arguing that Lucullus was prolonging the war for his own enrichment and glory.

With his army inactive, Lucullus could only watch in impotent fury as Mithridates reclaimed his old conquests. The senate in Rome also took a dim view of events, and sent Pompey to replace Lucullus. Through the machinations of his enemies, three years were to pass before Lucullus was allowed to triumph after his return to Rome – though he did so splendidly in 63. In the interim Lucullus revenged himself on Clodius by divorcing Clodia, claiming – probably justifiably – that she had been unfaithful. Soon after, he married the half-sister of his political ally Cato.

The good life

Thereafter Lucullus took little part in politics, though his enmity towards Pompey extended to his blocking Pompey's Asian settlement when the province was reconquered. It was to overcome this opposition that Pompey allied himself with Julius Caesar and Crassus to form the first triumvirate.

Lucullus' lifestyle became famous for its luxury. The gardens he laid out in Rome were renowned even centuries later, and we still refer to lavish feasts as being of 'Lucullan proportions'. He is said to have once reproved his butler for a more modest meal than usual. When the butler said he had prepared a simple meal because Lucullus was not entertaining, his master replied severely, 'tonight Lucullus dines with Lucullus'.

In his declining years Lucullus lost control of his faculties and his property was managed by his brother. On his death a sudden surge of affection on the part of the people led to a demand that he be buried on the Campus Martius, as was Sulla, but Lucullus' brother persuaded the people to let him take the body back to his family estate.

A 'Lucullan-style' banquet. Modern ideas of Roman morality are often deceived by the frankness of ancient art. In reality, most Romans would have considered modern western morality considerably more depraved than the mores of their own society.

Even after his death (probably in 57), his lifestyle was a byword. One hypocritical young senator was reproved for 'making money like Crassus, living like Lucullus, yet talking like Cato'. Perhaps unfairly, Lucullus' achievements in the East never achieved the same renown.

CATO THE STOIC

Cato's return with the royal treasure of Cyprus is worth remembering. As he left the ship, the consuls, the other magistrates and the entire senate and people of Rome were there to greet him, rejoicing not because the ships had brought a mass of gold and silver, but because they had brought Cato, safe and well.

Valerius Maximus, *De Viris Illustribus* 8.15.10

MARCUS PORCIUS CATO SALONIUS (or perhaps Salonianus) was born in 95 BC, a direct descendant of Cato the Censor and his second wife Salonia. Orphaned soon after his birth, Cato was raised by his maternal uncle, Livius Drusus (pp. 159–63). His childhood companion was Servilius Caepio, his half-brother.

A stubborn character

A frequent family visitor was Q. Poppaedius Silo, who led the Italians in rebellion against Rome. Once Poppaedius jokingly asked Cato to intercede for him with Drusus, which he stubbornly refused to do, even when Silo dragged him to a window and pretended he would throw him out. Cato was a slow student, but what he learned was never forgotten. His contemporaries also discovered that he was slow to anger, but incandescent once aroused. He was so respected that when the youths were playing the 'Troy Game' (the exact nature of which is now unknown), one side repudiated the son of Pompey as leader in favour of Cato.

Cato's inheritance of 120 talents was no great sum for a Roman aristocrat in his day. But it was plenty for the modest lifestyle of Cato, who had now completely embraced the Stoic doctrine (see box, p. 196). He went bareheaded in summer and winter, and travelled on foot when his contemporaries went on horseback.

He volunteered for the campaign against Spartacus in 72, mainly to be with Caepio who was a military tribune. Cato later refused an official commendation for his part in the campaign, saying he had done nothing to deserve it. His own military tribuneship was spent in Macedonia, where he became popular for sharing the hardships of his troops. Then Cato received the news that his half-brother, on his way out to Asia, was dying in Greece. Cato hurried to Caepio's deathbed, but arrived too late. He was frantic with grief, and spared no expense on the funeral.

Cato in office

Returning to Rome, Cato was elected quaestor. He shocked the clerks under him by actually knowing how the treasury of Rome should be run.

CATO THE STOIC	
Born	*Achievements*
95 BC	Opposed Caesar
Famous ancestors	*Wives*
Cato the Censor	Atilia, Marcia
Mother	*Children*
Livia	Son: Marcus
Father	Porcius Cato;
Marcus Porcius	daughters: Porciae
Cato	Prima, Secunda (?)
Positions held	*Death*
Tribune 62; Praetor 54	Suicide 46 BC

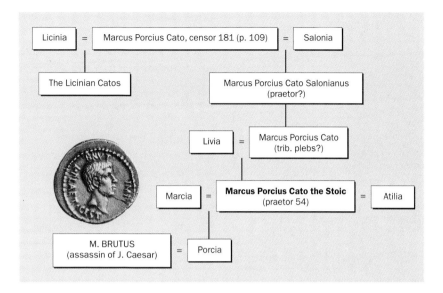

Sharp practice made traditional over the centuries was abolished, and the treasury returned to running by the rules. Cato checked the records, and forced those informers whom Sulla had rewarded from the treasury to pay the money back. At the end of the year he left office to resounding public applause.

Cato was coolly received by Pompey when he went to Asia, and on his return to Rome Cato showed his feelings by throwing his weight behind the petition for a triumph for Pompey's enemy Lucullus. The petition having succeeded, Cato went on to stand for tribune against Metellus Nepos, a Pompeian supporter, who had returned from Asia for that express purpose. Pompey wanted a tame tribune to smooth his political path in Rome, and Cato was determined to resist this. He and Metellus were both elected.

As tribune, Cato promptly prosecuted the consul of 62, L. Licinius Murena for bribery. Cato was a formidable accuser because he was known to be completely objective. As juror or witness, his opinion was decisive. Murena escaped only through the efforts of Cicero (pp. 211–15) and Hortensius, the two greatest advocates of their day.

An enemy of Caesar

Cato was a bitter and lifelong enemy of Caesar, whom he justly considered as a threat to the Republic. Relations were further strained by Caesar's affair with Servilia, Cato's half-sister (and the mother of Marcus Brutus). Cato accused Caesar of involvement in the conspiracy of Catiline (see box, p. 213), and his case was helped when Caesar opposed the death penalty which Cato and Cicero demanded for the conspirators.

Once Caesar received a note while in the senate. Cato, suspecting a communication from a conspirator, forced Caesar to reveal the contents of the note, which turned out to be from Servilia, suggesting an assignation. Furious, Cato threw it at Caesar, saying 'take it, you drunkard!' (an

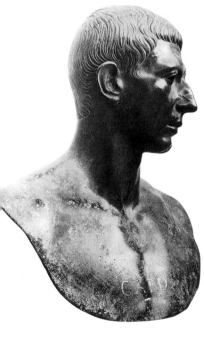

Cato the Stoic, late first-century BC bronze bust from Volubilis, a Roman colony in North Africa. Since Cato died while he was in North Africa, there is a good chance that this bust represents Cato's actual appearance at the time of his death.

interesting accusation, as Caesar was noted for his sobriety, while Cato drank heavily).

Cato had some revenge later when Caesar returned from Spain seeking both a triumph and to stand for consul. This required special dispensation from the senate, and Cato filibustered it by speaking until the senate adjourned without passing a resolution. (Forced to choose between triumph and consulship, Caesar opted for the latter.)

Clodius (pp. 198–99), while he was tribune, arranged to have Cato sent on a mission to Cyprus, which Rome had expropriated. Indeed, the expropriation may have been partly to remove Cato from Rome for a while. Cato returned in 56, having fulfilled his mission in every detail. He was met with a request for a marriage alliance with the orator Hortensius. But Cato was already married to Marcia, the daughter of Marcus Philippus (the enemy of Livius Drusus), and had no one in his household suitable to wed the orator. So in an extraordinary arrangement, he passed Marcia on to Hortensius, reclaiming her when the orator died in 50 BC. In less bizarre fashion, Cato also arranged politically advantageous marriages for other members of his family. However, he did turn down a marriage alliance with Pompey on the grounds that his family would be morally contaminated.

Civil war looms

In 55 Cato opposed the election of Crassus and Pompey to the consulship, and was himself elected praetor for 54. His own bid for the consulship failed in 53, and he announced that he would not stand again.

STOICISM

Stoicism was originally a Greek philosophy, founded in Athens by Zeno of Citium, Cyprus, around 313 BC. Zeno chose to teach in a *stoa* – an open colonnade – in Athens, hence the name Stoic. The doctrine of Stoicism is holistic, meaning it is difficult to explain one part in isolation – the philosophy must be understood as a whole. In essence, however, it stressed the importance of remaining true to oneself no matter what the external circumstances.

The philosophy was brought to Rome during the second century BC, in the course of Rome's interaction with the Hellenistic world, and it found fertile soil there. It might be said that the Romans were natural Stoics – they believed, as did Stoic philosophy, that it was the ability to

Bust of Zeno. Zeno's philosophy was developed after studying the great philosophical schools of Athens. His ideas were to influence Roman thinking more than those of any of his contemporaries.

reason that separated man from the beasts, and therefore to act irrationally was to be inhuman.

Stoicism stressed that each man should be morally responsible for his actions, and that true happiness was to be found in virtue, no matter what the external circumstances. For Romans brought up in a tradition of unswerving self-sacrifice for the state, this too was easy to understand.

The Stoic was a free man, because he chose to be free. It was argued that it was impossible to enslave a man against his will – he had to consent to be a slave. Otherwise he might be imprisoned, tortured and punished, but he was still free.

Thus Cato the Stoic decided that surrender to Caesar would be slavery, and true to the teachings of his doctrine, he chose to die a free man.

The ruins of Utica, in present-day Tunisia, where Cato met his death. The site now lies some 7 miles (11 km) from the sea because of changes in the Mediterranean coastline, but ancient Utica was an important port in the Carthaginian and Roman eras.

When Crassus died in the disaster at Carrhae in 53, Cato accepted Pompey's sole consulship as necessary to save the state. When civil war broke out in 49, Cato was devastated. Very reluctantly, he joined the Pompeian camp.

He was given command of Sicily, but when superior Caesarian forces arrived he quit the island without a fight. His lack of combativeness was noted and he was left in command of the camp when the Pompeians engaged in the fatal battle of Pharsalus. Cato escaped the ensuing rout to join Metellus Scipio in Africa. The army there wanted Cato to command them, but he yielded to the higher rank of Metellus Scipio, an ex-consul.

Cato took command of the strategic city of Utica. Metellus Scipio suggested that he put the townspeople to the sword, but Cato ignored this advice and offered a suggestion of his own – that Metellus avoid battle with Caesar. Events proved the soldiers were right in wanting Cato in charge. The people of Utica did not turn traitor as Metellus Scipio had feared, and Metellus engaged Caesar in battle and was utterly defeated.

Freedom or death

No longer able to oppose Caesar, yet determined not to surrender to him, Cato followed his Stoic doctrine and opted for suicide. His friends discovered his attempt when he accidentally knocked over an abacus. They bandaged his wounds, but Cato tore them open and died.

On hearing the news, Caesar said angrily 'I grudge him his death, for he would not allow me to let him live'.

The Death of Cato of Utica, by Pierre-Narcisse Guerin (detail). This painting won the Prix de Rome in 1797, the year that this art competition in France was re-established after being discontinued by the Revolution of 1789. The choice of subject by the judges shows that Cato still strongly represented the ideals of Republicanism centuries after his death.

Cato became an icon of obdurate Republicanism, and inspired many who opposed Caesar and his heirs. For all the words which ancient authors have attributed to him, we have only one text which is almost certainly from Cato himself: Cicero wanted to be given a triumph, and Cato politely refused Cicero's request for support.

PUBLIUS CLODIUS PULCHER

The death of Publius Clodius is more criminal because he was slain on the Appian road among the monuments of his ancestors – this is constantly said by his supporters; as if, I suppose, that illustrious Appius Claudius Caecus made that road, not that the nation might have a road to use, but that his own descendants might have a place in which to rob with impunity.

Cicero, *Pro Milone* 17

PUBLIUS CLODIUS PULCHER	
Born	*Positions held*
c. 95 BC	Tribune 58
Famous ancestors	*Achievements*
Attus Clausus,	Exiled Cicero
Appius Claudius the	*Wife*
Decemvir, Appius	Fulvia
the Censor	*Children*
Mother	Son: Clodius;
Unknown	daughter: Clodia
Father	*Death*
Appius Claudius	Killed in a fight 52 BC

ALTHOUGH HE ADOPTED THE POPULAR SPELLING of his family name, Clodius was a pedigree Claudian. His grandfather was the Appius Claudius who was father-in-law to the ill-fated Tiberius Gracchus; his father was expelled from Rome by the Cinnans and returned with Sulla in 83. His mother was from the Metellus family.

A wild youth

Clodius was born in about 95, the youngest of a large family. Lucullus was a brother-in-law, and Clodius joined his army in 70 hoping for advancement, and above all profit. (Clodius was in need of money throughout his life, and was not fussy about how he acquired it.) But Lucullus was unhelpful, so Clodius took revenge by stirring the army to mutiny. Then another brother-in-law, Marcius Rex, gave Clodius a naval command. He was no more fortunate this time, being captured by Cilician pirates, who released him unharmed.

In 62 Clodius was back in Rome. In fact he was in the house of the Pontifex Maximus, Julius Caesar, intent on seducing his wife. Caesar had left the house that night, since it was the venue of the all-female rite of the Bona Dea (Good Goddess). Clodius' plans to blend in as a female musician failed disastrously. He escaped, but his alibi was exploded by Cicero, perhaps because he was feuding with Clodius' sister, whom he later accused of incest with her brother.

Cicero's enemy

While quaestor in 61, Clodius was tried for his impiety, but the Claudian family bribed and intimidated the jury into an acquittal. After this, Clodius decided on his next career move – the tribunate of 58. This office was only open to plebeians, and Clodius was from the cream of the patricians. He got around this by being adopted into a plebeian house, with the connivance of the triumvirs, who were becoming irritated by Cicero.

As tribune, Clodius had Cicero exiled, then destroyed his house, and consecrated the ground to the goddess Libertas. He also passed a law giving free grain to the plebs.

Making more enemies

Thereafter, Clodius maintained his political influence by bands of heavily armed supporters. At one point he even had Pompey confined within his house. This was too much for the triumvir, who had Cicero restored from exile and promoted the tribune Milo as a counter-force to Clodius.

In 56 Clodius was aedile. He continued to skirmish with Cicero, and though the two later worked together to secure the acquittal of an M. Aemilius Scaurus, they were never friendly. Once, at a crowded political meeting, Clodius remarked, 'there's hardly room to stand here'. Cicero snarled back 'Well go and lie with your sister!'

Clodius stood for praetor in 53, the same year his enemy Milo stood for consul. Clashes between them kept Rome in turmoil until Clodius went away to his country house. Returning to the city, he encountered Milo near the town of Bovillae. A violent brawl resulted, and Clodius was killed.

In Rome, Clodius received a funeral in keeping with his life. The mob took him from his bier to the senate house, and made a funeral pyre from the benches within. The senate house, and the nearby Basilica Porcia of Cato the Censor, were burned to the ground.

The obverse of a coin of 54 BC, issued by Marcus Brutus, showing the goddess Libertas. This coin was issued ten years before the same Brutus assassinated Caesar, and commemorated the achievement of his ancestor Lucius Iunius Brutus in freeing Rome of the kings. For the reverse of the same coin, see p. 211.

Julius Caesar
(100–44 BC)

Caesar was a brilliant general, and a great orator and writer. He was also ruthless, unscrupulous and vain (he was considerably more bald than his statues admit). Caesar's political ambition caused the death of hundreds of thousands of people and wrecked the Roman Republic.

GAIUS JULIUS CAESAR

Born	*Achievements*
100 BC	Triumphator twice;
Famous ancestors	Pater Patriae;
Venus (?), Aeneas	destroyed Roman
Mother	Republic
Aurelia	*Wives*
Father	Cossutia, Cornelia,
G. Julius Caesar	Pompeia, Calpurnia
Positions held	*Children*
Aedile 65; Praetor	Son: Caesarion (by
62; Consul 59, 48,	Cleopatra), Octavian
46; Dictator 3	(adopted);
times; Triumvir from	daughter: Julia
60; Pontifex	*Death*
Maximus from 63	Assassinated 44 BC

Gaul was brought to shame by Caesar: by King Nicomedes, he.
Here comes Caesar, wreathed in triumph for his Gallic victory!
Nicomedes wears no laurels – though the greatest of the three.
Home we bring our bald whoremonger; Romans, lock your wives away!
All the bags of gold you lent him, his Gallic tarts received as pay.

Marching song of the Roman legions, from Suetonius *Life of Caesar*

THE MAN WHO DID MORE TO DESTROY the Roman Republic than Hannibal and Pyrrhus combined came from its oldest and most aristocratic family. The Julians may never have achieved the prestige of the Valerians of the early Republic, but the family was older than even the Claudians and claimed descent from Aeneas – which made the Julians older than Rome itself – and the goddess Venus. The family enjoyed something of a renaissance in the first century BC and Julius Caesar's uncle was consul in 91. The origin of the name Caesar is uncertain, but is probably derived from the Old Latin for 'curly'.

An unpromising start

Gaius Julius Caesar was born in 100. His father suffered from poor health and died when Caesar was 15. Since his aunt was married to Marius,

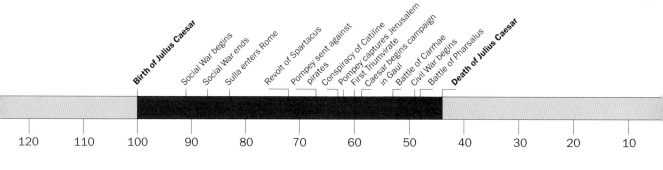

Birth of Julius Caesar | Social War begins | Social War ends | Sulla enters Rome | Revolt of Spartacus | Pompey sent against pirates | Conspiracy of Catiline | Pompey captures Jerusalem | First Triumvirate | Caesar begins campaign in Gaul | Battle of Carrhae | Civil War begins | Battle of Pharsalus | Death of Julius Caesar

120   110   100   90   80   70   60   50   40   30   20   10

Caesar was a Marian supporter, and he was married to Cornelia, daughter of the Marian leader Cinna. Cinna made him Flamen Dialis, an obscure but very senior priesthood surrounded by so many religious restrictions that it effectively disqualified Caesar from other political offices. Perhaps Cinna felt that the young man, lacking money and connections, would be content with his lot.

The return of Sulla changed everything. He annulled Cinna's acts, thereby depriving Caesar of his priesthood, and he took Cornelia's dowry, ordering Caesar to divorce her. Caesar refused, and went on the run, even though he was ill with fever. Tracked down, Caesar was saved from execution by his famous name and connections. Titled aristocrats begged Sulla to reconsider, until finally the old dictator relented with the prescient comment 'You are going to find many Mariuses in that boy'.

The character of Caesar

Caesar began the career of a young Roman aristocrat. In appearance, he was tall and slim. He had huge dark eyes, and a reputation as a ladies' man (according to his enemies, he was anybody's man, as will be seen), but his fair hair caused him great embarrassment in later life by receding to leave him very bald. He was a dandy, elegantly dressed, his tunic fashionably fringed and his clothes loosely worn. He drank sparingly, had an iron constitution, and was no gourmet. Once when served rancid food by mistake, he helped himself to an extra-large portion. He had very occasional epileptic fits, and suffered from nightmares.

The Curia, or Roman senate house, in the Roman Forum. The Roman senate did not meet only in this building – any sacred building in Rome could be used for the purpose. The old Curia had been burned down in the fire following the death of Clodius and the present one was part of Caesar's plans for his new forum.

Caesar in Asia

This was the young man who went to Asia, and served there with military distinction. He visited the court of King Nicomedes of Bithynia, where he stayed so long he was accused of having a homosexual relationship with the king. When he returned to Rome Cicero remarked, 'We all know what he gave – and what you gave him'. Caesar next attempted the prosecution of two Sullan supporters; he failed, but gained a reputation as an orator. Even the master, Cicero himself, conceded of his later oratory 'most people could not even approach him, even if they gave their lives over to the study of rhetoric'.

While returning to Asia, Caesar was captured by pirates. Having been ransomed for 50 talents, he tracked down his captors and crucified them. According to legend, he had sworn to do this while a prisoner, though it is difficult to know who was in a position to report this, apart from Caesar – and he was a ruthless self-propagandist.

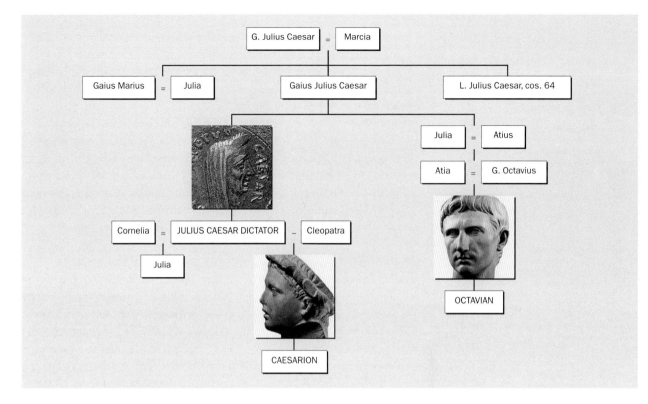

Simplified family tree showing the relationship between Julius Caesar and his protégé Octavian. The complexity of the family trees of the late Republican aristocracy is compounded by serial marriages, adoptions and the degree to which everyone was related.

Caesar the priest

By 73 Caesar regained some of his priestly honours, becoming a pontifex, and in 69 he was quaestor. In this year he suffered a double blow when both his aunt Julia and his wife Cornelia died. He was not above using their funerals to make a political point. He exhibited images of Marius in Julia's funeral parade, much to the disapproval of the Sullan establishment. In his aunt's valediction he called her the descendant of gods (Venus) and kings (there was a link with Ancus Marcius). Implicit was the claim that her nephew, Caesar, had the same forebears.

To conciliate the Sullans, he took Pompeia, Sulla's grand-daughter, as his next wife. He also became a protégé of Crassus (pp. 175–80), who gave him money to restore the Via Appia when he became its curator. Crassus may well have bankrolled Caesar's campaign to become aedile, which he did in 65. One of his acts as aedile was to restore the statues of Marius thrown down by the victorious Sullans.

The post of Pontifex Maximus became vacant in 63 with the death of Metellus Pius. This office was the crown of a distinguished career, given to retired censors and well-regarded ex-consuls – people, in fact, like Lutatius Catulus, the favoured candidate. Caesar, who had risen no further than aedile, had the temerity to stand against him. His latest outrage against the establishment was completed when he was elected through massive bribery. It was a considerable risk. On the morning of the election, Caesar said goodbye to his mother with the remark 'You will next see me as Pontifex Maximus, or not at all'.

Political setbacks

Caesar had already made serious enemies and was experiencing difficulties with his political career. Looking for support through a marriage alliance, he divorced Pompeia, allegedly because of a suspected dalliance with the wild young Claudian, Publius Clodius Pulcher (pp. 198–99), but in reality because her family lacked potent political connections.

In 62 Caesar became praetor. He allied himself with the Pompeian supporter, the tribune Metellus Nepos, and agitated for the recall of Pompey to deal with the Catiline menace (see below). Seeing a chance to take this conceited praetor down a peg, the senate suspended him from office. Caesar meekly accepted the senate's punishment, and told a mob that had gathered outside his house to disperse quietly. As a reward for playing by the rules, Caesar was re-instated in office.

Catiline

Caesar's deference to the senate reflected his acute political vulnerability. Deeply in debt, he had become embroiled in the schemes of the dissolute nobleman Sergius Catiline (see box, p. 213). The Sergians were an ancient family in terminal decline and Catiline hoped to revive the fortunes of his house by leading a popular campaign for the cancellation of debts. This alienated the senate, whose leaders were mostly creditors. By degrees, and partly pushed by Cicero, Catiline moved from radical to revolutionary, and launched an unsuccessful bid to overthrow the Republic.

Caesar made his own position worse by appealing for clemency for the captured conspirators, putting him in physical danger from some of the younger senators and knights. He judged it healthier to avoid the senate house thereafter. Fortunately, as propraetor, he had a military command in Spain, but his creditors obtained an injunction to stop him leaving. Caesar's career might have halted at that point had not Crassus stood surety for Caesar's (massive) debts.

In Spain, Caesar spent little time in administration. He campaigned relentlessly against hostile tribes and did his best to antagonize friendly ones into hostility. He developed a bad reputation for sacking cities after they had surrendered, but a year of plunder and pillage eased the burden of his debts, and he returned to Rome to seek a triumph and the consulship.

Charter of Julius Caesar's colony at Urso (modern Osuna) in Spain, founded in 44 BC. This charter, known formally as the Charter of Colonia Genetiva Julia, was written on four bronze tablets and is perhaps the most complete document of its kind. The tablets were found in the nineteenth century near the modern town.

Caesar's consulship

As a potential *triumphator*, and therefore a general under arms, he was forbidden to enter the city, and as candidate he needed dispensation from the senate to campaign *in absentia*. Cato made sure that the dispensation was not forthcoming, so Caesar laid down his command and abandoned his triumph. Most of the senators loathed Caesar. To prevent a repeat of his

EGYPT AND CLEOPATRA

After the death of Alexander the Great in 323 BC, Egypt came under the rule of a single family – the Ptolemies, descendants of one of Alexander's generals who had seized the country. The capital was Alexandria, a city founded by Alexander, and as well as the Nile Valley, the kingdom included Cyprus and at times much of Syria.

The élite of the kingdom were Greek, and Greeks had higher privileges and social status than the native Egyptians. However, there are strong indications that 'Greeks' were defined not by blood, but by education and employment. Alexandria was one of the cultural centres of the world. It had one of the Seven Wonders, in the great lighthouse of Pharos, and a library that came close to being the eighth. Another wonder – the pyramids of Giza – was also in Egypt.

The seasonal floods of the Nile gave Egypt some of the most fertile fields in the ancient world, and the rule of the Ptolemies combined sophisticated administration with respect for native tradition. As a result Egypt was a rich and influential state. However, as the shadow of Rome fell over the eastern

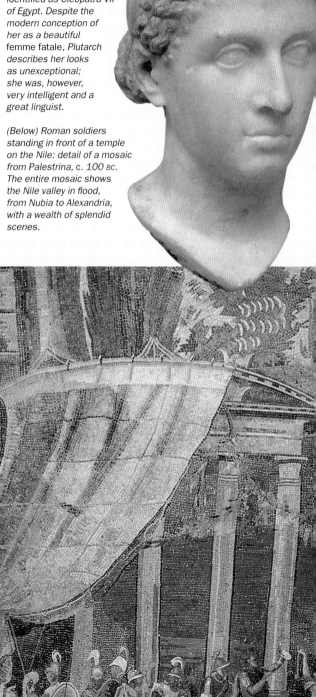

(Right) A marble bust identified as Cleopatra VII of Egypt. Despite the modern conception of her as a beautiful femme fatale, Plutarch describes her looks as unexceptional; she was, however, very intelligent and a great linguist.

(Below) Roman soldiers standing in front of a temple on the Nile: detail of a mosaic from Palestrina, c. 100 BC. The entire mosaic shows the Nile valley in flood, from Nubia to Alexandria, with a wealth of splendid scenes.

Mediterranean, the kings of Egypt had constantly to take into consideration the opinions of their mighty neighbour. They did not engage in foreign policy adventures of the kind attempted by the other successor kingdoms of Alexander's empire, and consequently never threatened Rome. However, Rome first advanced into Palestine and Syria (at times both once parts of the Ptolemaic kingdom) and then directly annexed Cyprus. It was perhaps inevitable that the rest of the Egyptian kingdom would eventually fall into Roman hands.

Cleopatra

The woman known today simply as Cleopatra was in fact the seventh queen of Egypt of that name. Egypt was at that time in a troubled state, with tensions between the Greek north and the more native Egyptian south. Rome was also a

constant presence in foreign affairs and murderous palace intrigues at home.

Cleopatra became queen on the death of her father, Ptolemy XII ('the flute-player'), in 51, but political pressure forced her to accept her brother, Ptolemy XIII, as a joint ruler. When Caesar arrived in Egypt in the course of the civil war in 48–47, her brother opposed him, but Cleopatra came over to his side, according to legend, by being smuggled to him rolled up inside a carpet.

Her alliance with Caesar was so close that it produced a son, whom Cleopatra named Caesarion. After

(Above) Relief showing Cleopatra and Caesarion, her son by Julius Caesar, on a wall of the Temple of Hathor at Dendera, Egypt. In this way Cleopatra attempted to present her son in a traditional Egyptian manner as the future king, and also as the founder of a great dynasty. Caesarion would only have been around eight years old when this relief was carved, but is portrayed as equal in stature to his mother.

(Right) Portrait herm probably depicting Caesarion (47–30 BC). He ruled jointly with his mother as Ptolemy XIV but did not long outlive her: Octavian, the future emperor Augustus, had him put to death.

Caesar's victory, she followed him to Rome, remaining there from 46 to 44, much to the dictator's embarrassment.

On Caesar's assassination, she supported the Caesarian side, eventually joining forces with Antony in a colourful meeting at Tarsus. Antony, no less than Caesar, was captivated by the Egyptian queen. Such statues as have been found of Cleopatra do not show a great beauty, but she possessed a lively intelligence and character.

She had three children by Antony, twins called Cleopatra and Alexander, born in 40, and another son called Ptolemy Philadelphus in 36. At first Cleopatra benefited politically from her alliances with the dynasts. Cyprus was restored to Egypt by Caesar, and Antony took her side in her efforts to expand the kingdom at the expense of the Jewish kingdom of Herod. However, Octavian used fear of Egyptian wealth and culture to make his civil war against Antony into a crusade for Rome, and when Cleopatra and Antony were defeated at the battle of Actium in 31 BC Egyptian independence came to an end. Octavian hoped to keep Cleopatra alive, but she was fully aware that his concern was limited to wanting a star exhibit at his triumph in Rome. She killed herself, according to tradition, by the bite of an asp which she held to her breast. She was 39 when she died, but the manner of her life and death have made her a legend ever since.

(*Top*) Coin possibly showing a Gaul, once thought to be Vercingetorix, and (*above*) a coin issued by Caesar to commemorate his victories in Gaul. (*Below*) Figure of a Gaulish warrior, with long hair and moustache, from a frieze at Civita Alba, second century BC.

Spanish command, they voted to make the job of the proconsuls to rid the fields and forests of Italy of bandits. This was disastrous for Caesar's ambitions. He persuaded Crassus and Pompey to abandon their old rivalry and become allies with him, creating what one contemporary called the 'three-headed monster' – the triumvirate. The threesome co-opted the tribune Vatinius. This gave them the combined executive powers of consul and tribune, allied with the political connections of Crassus, the military power of Pompey and bottomless financial reserves (Pompey and Crassus were the two richest men in Rome).

The combination was irresistible. The other consul, Bibulus, was unable to stop Caesar voting land for Pompey's veterans and having his settlement in the East ratified. Having done his bit for Pompey, Caesar awarded himself a proconsular command in Gaul.

Caesar in Gaul

In Gaul, Caesar launched a ten-year campaign of conquest which he described in his own words in *The Gallic War*, a priceless description of a Roman army on campaign written by its commander. Caesar's writing was so pellucid that his notes, allegedly for use by future historians, were impossible to improve upon. Even today, many students begin the study of Latin literature with the book's opening words: *Gallia in tres partes divisa est* ('Gaul is divided into three parts').

The Gallic War is a work of propaganda. It masks the war's horrendous cost in human life and suffering (one historian describes it as the greatest human and social disaster until the settlement of the Americas). It also hides the fact that the war was fought for Caesar's enrichment and glory. Contemporary Romans were well aware of this, and there was a movement in Rome to hand Caesar to the Gauls as a war criminal.

Domitius Ahenobarbus was planning Caesar's recall and prosecution, but the triumvirate met at Lucca and instead of his being recalled, Caesar's command was renewed for five years. Then in 53 Crassus died at Carrhae; Caesar's daughter Julia had died in 54. Pompey, her former husband, married the daughter of Metellus Scipio. Caesar's political position was deteriorating fast.

The break with the senate

Bribery had secured Caesar a senatorial following, but his enemies were too rich or too highly motivated to be swayed. Their plan was to prosecute Caesar on his return, and have him exiled at least.

Caesar tried to negotiate out of the impasse, but in vain. His last hope was to be made consul on his return in 48, and thus have a year to defuse the situation. The senate would not permit his candidacy, and when the tribune Mark Antony and his colleagues tried to force the senate to change its mind, the tribunes were driven from Rome.

Caesar had failed politically, but he could still triumph militarily. His army of veterans, it was claimed, 'could storm the heavens'. In 49 BC he led this army across the limit of his province – a stream called the

THE GAULS

They lived in villages without walls, and their houses had no superfluous furniture. They slept on beds of reeds, and ate meat. They were interested only in war and agriculture, their lives were very simple, and they knew nothing whatsoever of any art or science. Their possessions consisted of cattle and gold because these were the only things they could carry about with them everywhere, and move to whatever place is best suited to the circumstances. For them friendship was of the greatest importance, and the most feared and powerful of them were those who were thought to have the largest number of attendants and associates.

Polybius, *The Rise of Rome* 2.17

Aerial view of Alesia, a hill fort in Gaul captured by Caesar in 52 BC during his Gallic campaign. According to Suetonius 'Alesia [in the territory of the Mandubii] was regarded as impregnable because of the size and strength of its walls and the great number of its defenders. Caesar besieged it, however ... and it affords more examples of his daring and skill than any other struggle in which he was engaged' (*Life of Caesar* 27).

Rubicon. From that moment there was no turning back – he was no longer a rogue politician, but a rebel in arms. (And his action made the term 'to cross the Rubicon' a metaphor for an irrevocable action.)

Civil war

Caesar took Italy without much resistance. Pompey was slow to raise his levies and wisely decided that they would not stand against Caesar's seasoned troops. Caesar entered Rome. When a Metellus tried to bar his way to the treasury, Caesar restrained his soldiers and grimly informed the man 'at this moment, it is much easier for me to kill you than to keep you alive'. Understandably Metellus gave way.

Pompey was in Greece and Caesar followed him there, but his campaign did not go smoothly. At one point his men were forced to eat bread made from grass, so perilous was their supply situation. On another occasion, Pompey missed an opportunity to storm Caesar's camp, prompting Caesar's comment 'this man does not know how to win wars'. At the battle of Pharsalus in 48, Caesar's soldiers were heavily outnumbered. Despite this Caesar led them to an overwhelming victory. Towards the end of the battle he rode back and forth, urging his men not to kill fellow Roman citizens unnecessarily and extended his clemency towards the senate's leaders. Under Caesar there would be no purges or proscriptions.

Caesar followed Pompey to Egypt. When he left, he had installed Cleopatra as queen, and he also left her with a son whom she called Ptolemy Caesar, or Caesarion.

Master of Rome

In 47 Caesar was absolute master of Rome. He held a triumph for his many victories, which included a lightning campaign against Pharnaces II, king of Pontus, in Asia, summarized by the now famous words *veni, vidi, vici* – 'I came, I saw, I conquered'.

Campaigns followed in Africa and Spain to put an end to the last remnants of senatorial opposition. In a burst of legislative activity, Caesar rearranged the calendar (renaming one month after himself – July), increased the number of patricians and priests, and sent out many colonies of citizens, especially to Spain.

In 44 he declared himself 'perpetual dictator for the restoration of the commonwealth' – dictator for life, if he so chose. He also promoted the career of his great-nephew – a young man called Octavius. Caesar adopted the dress of Rome's ancient kings, but refused the title. He refused few of the honours the senate heaped on him, perhaps in morbid fascination to see how much Caesar would accept. One senator even proposed to exempt Caesar from all laws, and allow him access to any woman he pleased 'for the purpose of creating children'.

The Death of Caesar by Jean-Léon Gérôme (1867). Caesar is shown correctly with his head covered, lying at the feet of a statue of his old adversary Pompey. It is uncertain where the event took place – possibly at the site known today as Temple B in the Largo Argentina (see p. 24). The striking bust (*below*), probably of Caesar, is carved from green basanite, a stone from Egypt.

The Ides of March

Caesar acted through expediency, not because he desired radical reform. He made no fundamental social, economic or political changes, and intended going to war again, this time against Parthia. If Caesar was to be removed, it must be before this campaign. A conspiracy formed about the descendant of the former liberator of Rome, Lucius Iunius Brutus (pp. 43–45), with C. Cassius Longinus a close confederate. Although their plot was almost discovered, the assassins struck on 15 March, 44 BC – the infamous Ides of March.

Caesar had allegedly been warned by a soothsayer to beware that date. Meeting the soothsayer in the morning Caesar observed that the Ides had come, and he remained healthy. The soothsayer replied ominously 'But the Ides have not yet gone'. Caesar, who had always despised a bodyguard, was killed at the feet of a statue of Pompey. Ancient reports say he fought at first, then seeing the inevitability of death, covered his head with a toga. This makes it unlikely that he uttered the words '*et tu, Brute*' when, at the last, he was stabbed by his former protégé.

History has been kinder to Caesar than he deserves. Caesar replaced an elected constitutional government – however imperfect – with a military dictatorship. Over a million Gauls died to further his ambitions, and about another million were enslaved. Caesar left Rome to face another bout of internecine warfare, followed by the establishment of autocratic government. A century after Caesar's death, his biographer Suetonius delivered his verdict: 'He deserved assassination'.

Marcus Iunius Brutus
(c. 85–42 BC)

Marcus Tullius Cicero
(106–43 BC)

Mark Antony
(c. 83–30 BC)

A bust of Mark Antony. A competent soldier and an able politician, Antony was a poor administrator with a weakness for the good life.

Gold aureus of Marcus Iunius Brutus, minted in 43 when the senate gave him *imperium* (command) in the eastern provinces. The coin was probably minted from taxes wrung mercilessly from subject communities to pay for the coming clash with the heirs of Caesar.

MARCUS IUNIUS BRUTUS

The noble Brutus has told you Caesar was ambitious; If it were so, it was a grievous fault, and grievously has Caesar answered it, here, under leave of Brutus and the rest. For Brutus is an honourable man; so are they all, all honourable men.

Mark Antony, in Shakespeare's *Julius Caesar* Act 3, Scene 2

MARCUS BRUTUS, LEADER OF CAESAR'S ASSASSINS, descendant of Brutus the Liberator (pp. 43–45), was born in about 85. His father, tribune of the plebs in 83, supported Marcus Lepidus in a failed military coup and had to flee to Gaul. He later surrendered to Pompey on condition his life was spared. Pompey had him executed.

Young Brutus was raised by his mother Servilia and the man who was probably his uncle, Quintus Servilius Caepio. Caepio adopted Brutus in 59, just as the young man was starting his political career. Like many Romans of his day, Brutus was well educated in the arts and was a sympathetic companion to others of his class. Also like many of his contemporaries, he treated the subject peoples of the empire with callous disregard.

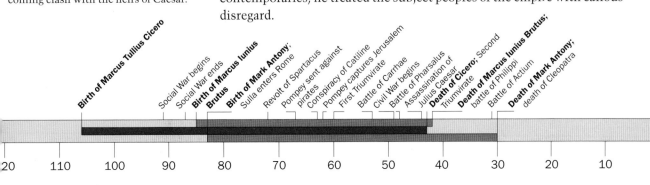

Birth of Marcus Tullius Cicero
Social War begins
Social War ends
Birth of Marcus Iunius Brutus
Birth of Mark Antony; Sulla enters Rome
Revolt of Spartacus
Pompey sent against pirates
Conspiracy of Catiline
Pompey captures Jerusalem
First Triumvirate
Battle of Carrhae
Civil War begins
Battle of Pharsalus
Assassination of Julius Caesar
Death of Cicero; Second Triumvirate
Death of Marcus Iunius Brutus; battle of Philippi
Battle of Actium
Death of Mark Antony; death of Cleopatra

20 110 100 90 80 70 60 50 40 30 20 10

MARCUS IUNIUS BRUTUS	
Born	*Positions held*
c. 85 BC	Quaestor 53;
Famous ancestors	Praetor 44
Lucius Iunius	*Achievements*
Brutus (the	Assassinated
Liberator)	Caesar
Mother	*Wives*
Servilia	Claudia; Porcia
Father	*Death*
Brutus (Tribune 83)	Suicide 42 BC

Accompanying Cato on his mission to Cyprus in 58 (p. 196), he loaned a substantial sum to the people of the city of Salamis, and demanded interest at 48 per cent per annum. Forcing loans on subject cities at usurious interest rates was forbidden by the *Lex Gabinia*, but Brutus had contacts in the senate who got him an exemption. Repayments were enforced brutally. When Cicero was governor of Cilicia he found that Brutus' agent had been made an officer in the cavalry, the better to extort money, and that five members of the Salamis city council had already been killed.

Brutus and Caesar

Brutus was quaestor in 53, and he married Claudia, the daughter of Appius Claudius Pulcher, the brother of Clodius (pp. 198–99). With civil war looming, Brutus abandoned his life-long feud with Pompey for killing his father. After Pompey's defeat at Pharsalus, Caesar spared Brutus – in this case with particular pleasure because of his relationship with Brutus' mother Servilia. (There were rumours that Caesar had corrupted Servilia's daughter Tertia too. When Servilia was given some land by Caesar at a knock-down price, Cicero commented 'It's cheaper than you think – a third (Tertia) has been discounted'.) It may be that Caesar's relationship with his family had inclined Brutus towards assassination.

Brutus hardly tried to hide his loyalties. Caesar made him a pontifex and sent him to govern Gaul. In response, Brutus wrote a eulogy for Cato, and divorced Claudia to marry Porcia, Cato's daughter.

Assassination

As city praetor in 44, Brutus was well-placed to manage the conspiracy to assassinate Caesar. His main collaborator was Cassius Longinus, who had accompanied Crassus to Parthia and had escaped from the disaster at Carrhae in 53. In 51 Cassius had successfully defended Syria against the Parthian counter-attack, and was now, like Brutus, a praetor.

Marble head, thought to be of Cassius Longinus. Cassius was a better general and politician than Brutus, but lacked Brutus' moral authority.

Coin of the liberators, showing the cap of liberty (given to freed slaves) and daggers, with the date of Caesar's assassination below.

Brutus provided the ideological backbone to the conspiracy. He was famously puritanical, and consciously imitated the old Roman virtues. He was motivated not by greed or ambition, but by the desire to emulate his famous ancestor and liberate Rome. Cassius was more practical. He was competent, efficient, ruthless and deeply disinclined to suffer fools gladly. He suffered from poor eyesight, which may have been a family trait – a descendant who lived in the time of Vespasian and was the leading lawyer of his day also had poor eyesight and eventually became blind.

Cassius thought that Mark Antony (pp. 216–22) should die with his leader. Brutus, however, could countenance but one killing – that of Caesar. Cicero lamented that Antony escaped death: 'the act of men, but the policy of children – to kill the leader, yet leave his successor alive. What stupidity!' Antony survived to rouse the Roman people against the assassins so effectively that Brutus and Cassius were forced to leave Rome for the East.

View of the site of Philippi in Greece. This city, named after Philip II of Macedon, dominates the plain on which it stands, and the strategically important Via Egnatia ran through it. Brutus fought the Caesarians outside the city walls in 42 BC, and the city became a Roman colony thereafter.

Coin showing a consul walking ahead of lictors; denarius of Brutus, to commemorate his ancestor Lucius Iunius Brutus. Note the heads of the axes are visible midway down the fasces carried by the lictors. A consul was usually accompanied by more lictors than are shown on this coin.

The senate granted them *maius imperium*, giving them authority over provincial governors there. Confrontation with Antony and his new ally, Caesar's heir Octavian, was inevitable. Brutus and Cassius commandeered the supplies Caesar had prepared for his assault on Parthia, squeezed every last drop of tax revenue from their subject peoples, and mustered an army. When Antony's brother fell into the pair's hands, he was executed.

The Battle of Philippi

The decisive battle was fought at Philippi. Brutus defeated Octavian, but on the other wing Cassius was beaten by Antony. Cassius sheltered on a rocky outcrop, believing the battle to be lost. Thinking that their army had been scattered, he assumed the worst when he saw an organized squad of cavalry heading his way. It was in fact Brutus' men come to announce their success, but Cassius was hindered by his bad eyesight. Not realizing that the troops were friendly, he committed suicide.

This was a blow to the morale of the army, and Cassius' organizational competence was sorely missed. When the two sides clashed again, Brutus' soldiers mostly deserted or fled (among them was a soldier called Horace, later to become one of Rome's greatest poets). His cause defeated, Brutus killed himself.

Antony treated the body with honour. Perhaps even then he realized that the times were such that he too might die in action, and it was tempting fate to despoil the corpse of an enemy.

MARCUS TULLIUS CICERO

'He was fortunate both in his achievements and his rewards for achievement; he enjoyed a long-continued good fortune and a prolonged state of prosperity, yet from time to time suffered severe blows, his exile, the downfall of the party he represented, the death of his daughter, and his own sad and bitter end. He behaved in an unworthy manner, except when facing death himself.'

Asinius Pollio, in Seneca's *Suasoriae* 6.17

ONCE, WHEN CICERO WAS ADDRESSING THE SENATE, Metellus Nepos interrupted him, saying 'Who was your father, Cicero?' Cicero's father, as the highly bred Metellus certainly knew, had been a well-regarded, but little-known and relatively humble, equestrian from the town of Arpinum.

MARCUS TULLIUS CICERO	
Born	*Achievements*
106 BC	*Pater Patriae*;
Famous ancestors	Augur; greatest
None	Latin writer
Mother	*Wives*
Julia	Terentia; Publilia
Father	*Children*
M. Tullius	Son: Marcus Tullius;
Positions held	daughter: Tullia
Quaestor 75;	*Death*
Praetor 66; Consul	Killed by triumvirs
63	43 BC

Marble statue of Cicero. Apart from the Caesars, few Romans have been so frequently depicted in stone: later Roman aristocrats liked to show their cultural pretensions by having a bust or statue of the great orator in their libraries.

Turning on Metellus, Cicero retorted 'I am afraid that in your case, your mother has made it harder for you to answer the same question.'

The man from Arpinum

This story shows at once the strength and weakness of Cicero's position. He had no ancestral record, no mass of family clients and relatively little money. But he did have the intelligence and eloquence to be one of Rome's greatest citizens. In fact, some historians refer to the end of the Republic as 'the age of Cicero'. This is appropriate, since he has deeply influenced our perception of the period.

He was born in Arpinum in 106. This small country town already had one famous son – the six-times consul, Marius. In fact, Marius and Cicero were distantly related through Cicero's grandmother Gratidia. Cicero's father was intelligent and had connections – L. Licinius Crassus encouraged him to consider a political career for Cicero and his younger brother, Quintus. The boys' education took them from Rome to Greece, and if Plutarch is to be believed, Cicero showed promise at an early age. When the Social War broke out, he served with Pompeius Strabo; later, Strabo's son Pompey powerfully influenced Cicero's career.

In 81, Cicero defended Sextus Roscius, who was accused of killing his father. Cicero showed that the accusation was false and inspired by a corrupt Sullan henchman. Roscius was acquitted, and Cicero acquired a name as a crusader against Sulla's regime. Sulla had a direct way with opposition, so when Cicero went to Greece soon afterwards 'for his health', it was literally true. Until 77 he studied philosophy in Athens and Rhodes, and visited Metellus Numidicus' former second-in-command, Rutilius Rufus, now in exile.

Cicero in politics

Cicero was quaestor in Sicily in 75, where his task was to send Sicilian grain to alleviate a shortage in Rome. This he did with such political skill that he earned the thanks of the very people from whom he was expropriating the grain. Returning to Rome, he discovered that almost no one there was aware of what he had done, and thenceforth he resolved to remain in Rome at the centre of things.

In 70, he fought a landmark case, charging Verres with extortion against the people of Sicily. Verres had retained the best orator of the day, Q. Hortensius Hortalus, and he had the support of the influential Metellan clan, including the consul-designate for the coming year. The only thing against him was the evidence, as Cicero showed with such devastating skill that Verres went into exile without awaiting the jury's verdict.

Soon after, Cicero married Terentia, of the influential Terentius clan. With their help, he became praetor in 66 at the earliest possible age. So far, Cicero had stayed clear of party politics, but now he threw his weight behind the proposed Manilian Law giving Pompey command against the pirates. Cicero knew he needed a political heavyweight like Pompey to back his next bid – to become the first *novus homo* to be consul since 94.

THE CONSPIRACY OF CATILINE

The Sergians were one of the Republic's long-established clans, and Catiline had been one of Sulla's lieutenants, brave and loyal, but brutal and bloodthirsty. He rose to the praetorship in 68, but the effort may have used up the last of his cash reserves. Consequently, he divorced his wife to marry the heiress Aurelia Orestilla.

He seems to have tried further to enrich himself as the propraetor of Africa in 67. He was followed back to Rome in 66 by a delegation of outraged provincials demanding restitution. Being under indictment for extortion, Catiline was unable to stand for the consulship in 66 or 65. Interestingly, Cicero offered to defend Catiline against the extortion charges, perhaps with a view to a joint consulship.

Catiline refused. He and Gnaeus Piso then allegedly became involved in a plan to kill the consuls and take over the state, but the conspirators procrastinated and the chance was lost. Catiline stood against Cicero for the consulship and was defeated, despite extensive bribery. In 63, Catiline tried again for the consulship, this time on a radically *popularis* manifesto which included the remission of debts, perhaps because he was by now deeply in debt and becoming desperate.

When he was frustrated by Cicero, he turned to insurrection. With members of Rome's leading families in his entourage, he began stockpiling weapons and seeking allies. He approached a Gallic tribe, the Allobroges, who promptly reported him to the authorities. Cicero had already been alerted, since Catiline had been betrayed by his mistress Fulvia.

Cicero delivered several rousing condemnations of Catiline in the senate. These speeches, the *Catilinarian Orations*, are among his finest. Catiline was harried from Rome and joined his army in the field, awarding himself the consular insignia he had been unable to win at the ballot box. His army was composed mainly of disaffected Sullan veterans. Like their commander, they fought bravely, but their cause was futile. While attempting to withdraw to Gaul, Catiline was killed in battle at Pistoia by a senatorial army led by Cicero's co-consul Gaius Antonius, and Quintus Metellus Celer. Those conspirators who remained in Rome were rounded up by Cicero and executed without the benefit of a trial.

Catiline was an unpleasant character driven to desperation by his debts and his hunger for power. At every turn he was blocked and hounded by Cicero. No one doubts the courage and character Cicero showed in saving the state. But there remains an uneasy uncertainty as to whether the major factor that turned Catiline from an unscrupulous and ambitious politician into a desperate revolutionary was nothing other than Cicero himself:

In (Catiline's) bands are all the gamblers, and adulterers, all the unclean and shameless citizenry. His witty, delicate boys have learned not only to love and be loved, but to use a dagger and to administer poison. If they are not driven out; if they don't die; if Catiline does not die; then I warn you, the school of Catiline will take root in our Republic.

Second Oration against Catiline

Cicero in the Senate Accusing Catiline of Conspiracy – *detail from an 1889 fresco by Cesare Maccari. Despite many factual inaccuracies in this picture, it remains the most visually evocative depiction of how Catiline was isolated by Cicero's oratory.*

Catiline's conspiracy

Cicero was duly elected for 63, with a Gaius Antonius as his colleague. Rome was alive with rumours that the dissolute noble Catiline, who had failed to win the consulship, intended to gain supreme power in a less orthodox way. Cicero exposed the plot, accused Catiline, and forced him to flee from Rome. Five of Catiline's fellow conspirators who remained in Rome were arrested, including a praetor of the Cornelian clan.

Realizing that the revolt might flare up at any moment, Cicero had the captured conspirators executed without trial. This was highly questionable, even though the senate had passed the *Senatus Consultum Ultimum*, the famous 'last decree' which ordered the consul to 'see to it that the Republic came to no harm'. Without support in Rome, Catiline took to the field and was defeated. Cicero's handling of the crisis was widely praised, and he was saluted as *Pater Patriae* – the father of his country.

Brave and determined as he had been, the praise unfortunately went to Cicero's head. Always susceptible to flattery, he was never slow to remind others of his achievement. We may be grateful that his poem about it has not survived – antiquity had a low opinion of Cicero the poet.

Cicero and Clodius

Cicero's inflated idea of his strength led him to clash with the Claudian house in the form of Publius Clodius Pulcher, who was accused of blasphemy (p. 191). Cicero destroyed his alibi, but Clodius escaped through bribery so extensive that the presiding judge, Lutatius Catulus, sarcastically asked the jury whether they wanted a guard to keep the money safe on their way home. By siding against the triumvirate, Cicero increased his stock of enemies. Consequently, the threesome allowed Clodius to adopt plebeian status and become tribune. In 58 Cicero was charged by Clodius with putting Roman citizens to death without trial, and was forced to flee into exile in Macedonia.

But Clodius too fell out with the triumvirs, and Cicero was recalled in August 57. When he attempted to show his former independence in 56, the triumvirs brought him sharply to heel. A humiliated Cicero was forced to defend the triumvirate's minions in court, and he showed his disgust by withdrawing from politics and turning to philosophy.

More encouragingly, he was elected to the élite college of Augurs, taking the place of young Crassus, who had died in his father's Parthian expedition. He was less happy when the governorship of Cilicia was forced on him in 51. As an ex-consul, this was Cicero's duty, and he performed it competently – he was a just governor, and even defeated a horde of bandits in a minor battle. Ever egotistical, Cicero wanted a triumph, and hastened to Rome to celebrate it. Instead, he was swept up into Caesar's civil war against the Republic.

Cicero at war

Caesar was a personal friend, so Cicero was reluctant to oppose him. But his sense of duty and his loyalty to Pompey eventually forced him into the Republican camp. Cicero's daughter, Tullia, was married to Cornelius Dollabella, a partisan of Caesar. Pompey once pointedly asked him 'Where is your son-in-law?'. Unintimidated, Cicero retorted 'with your father-in-law!' – a reminder that Pompey had been married to Caesar's daughter Julia.

Cicero was not at the Battle of Pharsalus, and wisely turned down the command of the survivors which Cato offered. He made his peace with Caesar, who received him warmly, and returned to Rome. Because the two men got on well at a personal level, Cicero was not informed of the plot to assassinate Caesar, though when the deed was done in 44, Cicero was delighted.

He was less delighted with Mark Antony. He spoke against Antony's tyranny in the *Philippics* – which rank among the most entertainingly excoriating political invectives ever penned. Cicero cultivated Caesar's heir, the young Octavian, as a counter-balance to Antony. He hoped to exploit the young man's political naivety, and allegedly commented that Octavian was to be 'raised, praised and erased'.

Death of an orator

When Antony was driven from Rome and then defeated in battle, it looked for a moment as though the Republic might be restored. But Octavian, perhaps sensing what Cicero had planned for him in this new Republic, suddenly switched sides and allied himself with Mark Antony.

They were joined by Marcus Aemilius Lepidus, son of the Lepidus who had tried to take Rome after the death of Sulla. But Antony refused to come over to this new triumvirate unless Cicero was proscribed. This was not negotiable. After trying for two days to change Antony's mind. Octavian gave Cicero up on the third day.

Cicero fled from Rome. He considered taking a ship for Greece, but his heart was not in it. The soldiers came for him in one of his seaside villas on 7 December, 43 BC, and he died bravely.

His hand and head, the instruments with which Cicero had insulted Antony so comprehensively, were impaled on the Rostra in the Roman forum. Too late – as one contemporary noted – for Cicero's inspired epithets had blackened Antony's name forever.

Cicero's freed slave Tiro later organized and published Cicero's letters. They give us an insider's view of the crisis of the Republic on almost a day-to-day basis. These, and dozens of orations and philosophical works, have indebted posterity to Cicero more than to any other single Roman.

The Rostra in the forum. This famous speaker's platform was constantly altered, but it remained one of the central features of political life in the Republic. Its total unimportance in the Imperial era is a vivid reminder of how many freedoms died with the Republican cause.

MARK ANTONY	
Born	*Achievements*
c. 83 BC	Triumvir
Famous ancestors	*Wives*
Antonius the Orator	Fadia, Antonia,
(cos. 99)	Fulvia, Octavia,
Mother	Cleopatra
Julia	*Children*
Father	Sons: Antonius,
Antonius Creticus	Iullus, Alexander,
Positions held	Ptolemaeus;
Tribune 49;	daughters: Antoniae
Magister Equitum	Prima, Secunda,
47; Consul 44;	Tertia, Cleopatra
Triumvir from 43	*Death*
	Suicide 30 BC

MARK ANTONY

Everything was on sale at your house in the most infamous traffic; when you confessed that those laws which had never been promulgated, had been passed with reference to you, and by you; when you, being augur, had abolished the auspices, being consul, had taken away the power of interposing the veto; when you were escorted in the most shameful manner by armed guards; when, exhausted with drunkenness and debauchery, you were every day performing all sorts of obscenities....

Mark Antony the politician: Cicero, *Philippics* 2.6

THERE WERE TWO TYPES OF ANTONIUS in Rome. The patrician branch usually adopted a third name of Merenda, while members of the plebeian branch of the family were unusual in not having any third name at all. Mark Antony – the anglicized version of his true name, Marcus Antonius – was of the plebeian branch, though he tried to give his family status by alleging descent from Anton, a son of Hercules.

Family affairs

Mark Antony was born in about 83 to Marcus Antonius Creticus (his last name was bestowed after his attempts to clear pirates from that island); his mother Julia was the sister of L. Julius Caesar, the consul of 64, and so was of the house of Caesar. In a twist of fate this made Antony one of the closest relatives in Rome to young Octavian.

Creticus was an amiable man, but far from wealthy by the standard of the Roman élite. When he died, Antony went to live with a relative, Cornelius Lentulus, who was soon afterwards executed by Cicero for his part in Catiline's conspiracy. From this bad start, relations between Antony and Cicero deteriorated. The young Antony rapidly dissipated what little money he inherited – the beginning of a lifelong reputation for wild living. By 58 he was forced to flee Rome to escape his outraged debtors.

He ended up in Asia, where he joined the army. Antony proved a surprisingly good soldier, and in 54, by now a seasoned campaigner, he was with Caesar in Gaul. The young man's liking for extreme living was to Caesar's taste, and in 53 he sponsored Antony's return to Rome to stand for quaestor. Caesar forced Antony's reconciliation with Cicero, though later, less than a day after Caesar's assassination, the pair were back at each other's throats.

Caesar's supporter

Antony was elected tribune for 49 BC. When the senate stripped Caesar of his command, Antony interposed his tribunician veto, as he was entitled to do. The senate overrode the veto, forcing Antony to flee Rome. This, not coincidentally, gave Caesar his *casus belli* – he claimed that he marched on Rome to restore the rights of the tribunes.

When Caesar swept the Republicans out of Italy and followed them to Greece, he left Antony in charge of Italy and Marcus Amelius Lepidus (pp.

A probable bust of Mark Antony, *c*. 40–30 BC, green basalt, reputedly found in Egypt. Although more refined than the usual picture we have of Antony – he had a reputation for wild living – there are features that can be compared with his images on coins.

OSTIA

Like many ancient peoples with no sea-going tradition, the Romans preferred to build their capital city inland, where pirate fleets could not appear literally from out of the blue. Rome, like London, was built at the 'head of navigation' of its river – the point where sea-going ships cannot proceed easily upriver, and where the river can first be bridged.

Ostia, on the coast, was originally founded less as a port for Rome than to exploit the local salt flats. Its site at the mouth of the Tiber gave Ostia the further function of giving advance warning of any large fleets making their way upriver to Rome.

Reputedly founded in the fourth century by King Ancus Marcius (pp. 30–31), Ostia's growth was slow until the expansion of the Republic. By the time of the Punic wars its strategic importance meant that it was protected by a wall. Its vulnerability from the sea was demonstrated in 67 BC, when pirates attacked and destroyed a Roman fleet in the harbour. This was Ostia's second exposure to the troubles of the late Republic. It was besieged by Marius, entered by treachery and sacked.

With the suppression of the pirate menace, Ostia became a resort for wealthy members of the Roman merchant class. Large villas were built, and visitors today can still wander around the huge *insulae* (apartment blocks), many of which had over half a dozen rooms. Mosaic pavements fronted the merchant guilds, each section of pavement bearing the logo of a trading house.

The remains of the temple to Capitoline Jupiter dominate the town square, and the huge warehouses nearby give a clue to the reason for Ostia's later prosperity – grain. By the first century BC Rome had become too large to feed its population from local agriculture, and the urban poor depended on grain from Sicily or, later, Egypt. Some of the largest grain carriers would stop at Ostia and their cargoes would be transferred to barges for transport upriver to the metropolis.

Much of what is visible at Ostia dates from the Imperial period, though outside the landward gate are many fine tombs from the Republic.

Ostia did not long survive the decline of Rome. Shifting sand dunes blocked the sea lanes (today Ostia is several miles inland from the modern port), and the resulting shallows bred

Aerial view of Ostia, showing the flatness of the land and the proximity of the river. When the river silted up, marshes developed and swarms of malarial mosquitoes forced the site to be abandoned.

swarms of malarial mosquitoes. By the fifth century AD the city was abandoned. The area remained depopulated until almost the present day, preserving Ostia as an archaeological site of the highest importance. Less well-known than Pompeii, in many ways it better preserves the feel of what life was like in an ancient city.

(Left) Mosaic from Piazzale delle Corporazione, with the maritime theme common to many mosaics in Ostia. As well as the dolphins in the foreground, a warship, a merchant ship and a lighthouse are visible.

(Right) Warehouses of Epagathus and Epaphroditus, two eastern freedmen. Grain was imported from overseas and stored in warehouses such as these.

223–25) in charge of Rome. Antony was not interested in lawsuits and administration, and soon followed Caesar to Greece, bringing welcome reinforcements for Caesar's legions. At the fateful battle of Pharsalus in 48 he commanded the left wing, and saw the Republican cause collapse.

Antony in Italy

With Caesar now dictator, Antony was again in charge of Italy while his chief mopped up the Republican resistance in Spain and Africa. Antony the administrator was lazy, unconscientious and more inclined to drunken parties than routine paperwork. He divorced Antonia, who was his second wife – he had earlier married and divorced an heiress called Fadia and was to marry three more times, eliciting scathing remarks about serial polygamy from Cicero. He now shared the cares of his office with an actress called Cytheris.

The party ended when Caesar returned to Rome, and pulled his subordinate sharply into line. Antony had taken over a substantial part of Pompey's property and was caused no little financial embarrassment when Caesar made him pay for what he had usurped. This is perhaps why he married again in 46, to the terrifying Fulvia, former wife of the late Clodius (pp. 198–99). 'She was not one to rule a household when she could rule a consul instead,' says Plutarch tartly, adding that Cleopatra was indebted to Fulvia for accustoming Antony to taking orders from a woman. In 44 Antony repeatedly offered Caesar a crown, urging him to become king in name (as he was already in fact). Caesar, seeing the popular unease at this bit of theatre, pretended to be displeased.

Caesar's death

Antony became consul for 44 and a target for the more practical conspirators planning Caesar's death. Brutus insisted on killing only Caesar, so Antony was engaged in conversation outside the senate while the assassination took place within. There was also a practical reason for this. Antony was a powerful man and a skilled fighter whose intervention would have been significant.

Antony pretended to acquiesce in the killing. But with Caesar's funeral eulogy (dramatically re-written by Shakespeare to begin 'Friends, Romans, countrymen …'), Antony roused the people, showing them Caesar's clothes, bloodstained and cut through by knife stabs. With the mob behind him, Antony forced Cassius and Brutus from Rome.

As Caesar's executor, Antony began to govern on the basis of laws allegedly detailed in the papers that Caesar had left. On the same basis he appointed people to key positions, though cynical Romans called these office holders 'Charonites' after Charon, who ferries the dead over the Styx.

Octavian arrives

Antony was well placed to replace Caesar, until Caesar's heir arrived in Rome. Octavian naturally questioned Antony as to what had happened to Caesar's money. Caesar had left a huge bequest to his former soldiers

Silver coin of Mark Antony: this portrait clearly shows Antony's bull-like features and neck, which gave credibility to his claim to descent from Hercules.

in his will, and Octavian had been forced to meet some of the expense from his own pocket.

After accepting his inheritance, the young man abandoned the name Octavius altogether (he disliked people calling him Octavianus), and styled himself Julius Caesar, son of Julius Caesar. The senate saw Octavian as a counterweight to Antony – especially Cicero, who felt that through him the Republic might be restored.

Antony was sent to Gaul for his proconsular command. While there, the senate declared him a public enemy, and sent the army with the consuls Hirtius and Pansa against him. The consuls defeated him in battle at Mutina in 43, though at the cost of their lives, and Antony fled over the Alps. Despite the hardships of the journey he did not despair, and tried hard to keep up the spirits of those with him. As a near-contemporary remarked, Antony in times of severe crisis was almost a virtuous man.

In Gaul he faced Marcus Aemilius Lepidus (pp. 223–25), a man whose army had at best mixed loyalties. Rather than take the risk of ordering Antony's arrest and imprisonment, Lepidus went over to his side. In a further massive stroke of luck for Antony, Lepidus used his good offices to effect a reconciliation with Octavian. Antony had gone from starving refugee to one of the three most powerful men in the world in a few weeks – they formed an alliance now known as the second triumvirate.

The second triumvirate

Immediately they set about settling scores. Cicero's trenchant insults had put him at the top of Antony's list of those to die. Octavian failed to dissuade Antony from his purpose even when he demanded the death of Antony's own uncle, Lucius, as the price for Cicero's murder. Lucius very sensibly fled to his sister, who kept back the soldiers by saying 'If you want to kill him, you must first step over the body of the mother who gave Antony birth'.

With Italy united under the triumvirs, the three now moved against Brutus and Cassius in Greece. Octavian was almost as bad at fighting as Antony was at government, so Antony led the way, and gets most of the credit for the victory at Philippi (p. 211), where the Republican cause was finally crushed. Antony then summoned those eastern leaders who had supported Brutus and Cassius to submit to his judgment. Among them was Cleopatra of Egypt.

Antony and Cleopatra

Cleopatra came to Tarsus in style, in a gilded boat, and her luxurious decadence instantly captivated the hedonistic Antony. Though their romance was genuine, Cleopatra had solid political reasons for an alliance with Antony, and her support was in turn very useful to him. Antony felt that he deserved a holiday, and with Cleopatra by his side, he took one.

Their idyll was soon interrupted by war. The Parthians had invaded Syria, and in Italy, Antony's wife Fulvia and his brother Lucius had declared war on Octavian. Leaving Syria in the hands of a capable

A coin of Cleopatra VII, *c.* 34 BC. In her dress and hairstyle, Cleopatra is evidently more Romano-Greek than Egyptian. Contemporary commentators praised her manner, conversation and style, and she was a great linguist.

ANTONY AND CLEOPATRA

Nay, but this dotage of our general's
O'erflows the measure: those his
goodly eyes,
That o'er the files and musters of the
war
Have glow'd like plated Mars, now
bend, now turn,
The office and devotion of their view
Upon a tawny front: his captain's
heart,
Which in the scuffles of great fights
hath burst
The buckles on his breast, reneges
all temper,
And is become the bellows and the
fan
To cool a gipsy's lust.

Look where they come:
Take but good note, and you shall see
in him
The triple pillar of the world
transform'd
Into a strumpet's fool: behold and see.

Shakespeare, *Antony and*
Cleopatra Act 1, Scene 1

Cameo of Octavia, wife of Antony. In her goodness and steadfast support for her wayward husband, Octavia was seen as a virtuous, and badly wronged, Roman matron. This lowered Antony's support in Rome, which may or may not have been Octavia's intention.

subordinate, Antony hurried to the larger crisis. Fortunately, by the time he arrived it was already over: Fulvia was dead, and the war ended. The triumvirate sorted out their disagreements, and Antony took Octavian's sister as his new wife. The three divided the Roman world between them, with Lepidus taking Africa, Octavian the west and Antony the provinces east of the Adriatic. They made peace with Sextus, the son of Pompey, who had set himself up as a sort of pirate king with a large fleet (pp. 225–26). He was now given command over Sicily.

In 37 the triumvirate was renewed for a further five years. Antony wanted to invade Parthia, and sent Octavia back to her brother in Italy. But when he began openly to consort with Cleopatra, Octavian seized on this, alleging that Antony had been turned from Rome by Cleopatra, and was planning to make Egypt the centre of the Empire.

The Parthian campaign

Antony's Parthian campaign went badly. The Parthians were well equipped for fighting in the open, waterless terrain, and their archers yet again tormented the Roman legionaries, while their lightly armoured cavalry gave ground before the Roman charges and flowed back when they withdrew. Antony became separated from his siege train and the Parthians destroyed the irreplaceable equipment, making it impossible for him to capture Parthian cities.

Antony was forced to withdraw to the Mediterranean, where Cleopatra received him with supplies for his decimated army. Vindictively, Antony attacked Armenia, whose king had abandoned him at a critical moment. This was not enough for Antony to regain his lost prestige, and sensing weakness in his rival, Octavian declared war.

Octavian's pretext was that Antony had been corrupted by his Egyptian queen, and planned to give his part of the empire to Egypt. In a ceremony in Alexandria, Antony's children had nominally been made rulers of different parts of the East. Furthermore, Antony's will (illegally seized by Octavian from the Vestal Virgins with whom he had deposited it) stipulated he should be buried in Egypt.

War with Octavian

Octavian had learned his lesson, and though titular head of the army he left the actual command to others. Octavian's highly competent admiral Agrippa brought Antony to bay in Greece, and forced him to battle at Actium in September of the year 31. Antony's battle plan is obscure. The armies on the shore saw the two fleets converge, and then, unexpectedly, Cleopatra's ships crowded on sail, broke past the Roman line, and headed for the open sea. Antony had to choose whether to return to land and fight it out with his army, or to follow Cleopatra to Egypt. He followed Cleopatra. Demoralized by their leader's defection, Antony's army surrendered to Octavian soon afterwards.

In Alexandria, Antony was in despair. He and Cleopatra offered each other their mutual commiserations and awaited the arrival of the victori-

THE BATTLE OF ACTIUM

Then came the day of the great conflict, in which Caesar [Octavian] and Antony led out their fleets, and fought – one for the safety of the world, the other for its ruin. The command of the right wing of Caesar's fleet was given to Marcus Lurius while the left was with Arruntius, and Agrippa had full command of the entire conflict on the sea.

Caesar kept himself in reserve for any part of the battle where fortune might call him, and he was present everywhere. Antony's admirals were Publicola and Sosius. So when the battle began one side had everything, commanders, rowers and soldiers, the other side had only soldiers. Cleopatra took the lead in fleeing, and Antony chose to be her companion in flight rather than stay with his fighting soldiers. So the commander whose duty it would have been to deal severely with deserters now deserted from his own army.

Even without their commander, Antony's men long continued to fight bravely, and when they despaired of their victory they fought to the death. Caesar, trying to win by words those whom he could have killed with the sword, kept shouting and telling them that Antony had fled, asking them who they were fighting for, and who they were fighting against. Only very reluctantly, and after a long struggle, did these men surrender their arms and concede Caesar the victory.

Caesar promised them pardon and granted them their lives before they could bring themselves to ask for it. The soldiers had done their part in a

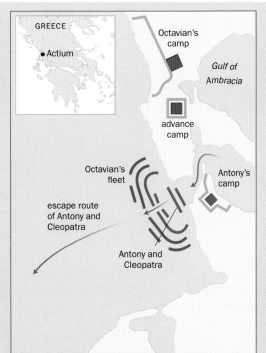

GREECE

● Actium

Octavian's camp

Gulf of Ambracia

advance camp

Octavian's fleet

Antony's camp

escape route of Antony and Cleopatra

Antony and Cleopatra

Plan of the Battle of Actium showing the deployment of the fleets. It remains uncertain whether Antony intended to flee or fight it out with Octavian.

manner worthy of a great commander, and the commander had acted as one who deserves cowardly soldiers. Since by Cleopatra's will he had resorted to flight, one might question whether he would not also have acted according to her orders had he won the victory. Antony's land army likewise surrendered when their commander hurried off to join Antony in flight.

Velleius Paterculus,
Historia 2.85ff

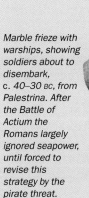

Marble frieze with warships, showing soldiers about to disembark, c. 40–30 BC, from Palestrina. After the Battle of Actium the Romans largely ignored seapower, until forced to revise this strategy by the pirate threat.

ous Octavian. Then, Antony, being Antony, partied quite literally as if there was no tomorrow. His slender hopes of holding off Octavian were dashed when his fleet and cavalry defected on Octavian's arrival.

Final defeat

Antony was defenceless. He was told that Cleopatra was dead, and he despaired, committing suicide by falling on his sword. The rumour was false, but Antony had only hastened the inevitable. Cleopatra was

ROMAN WOMEN

There are very few instances where women in our sources speak with their own words and so what we see of the role of women in Republican Rome is presented to us by their male contemporaries.

To the Roman male, the ideal woman was domestically orientated, quiet and chaste. The ideals of chastity and domesticity are well combined in Lucretia, whose rape brought about the fall of the Tarquins. When she was unexpectedly visited by her fiancé she was at home weaving with the servant women. When Sextus raped her, she first reported the crime to her father and fiancé, and then killed herself through shame.

However, it is not unusual to find women who do not act according to this stereotype. In the story of Lucretia, Sextus was so attracted to her because all the other women he had visited were socializing and enjoying the good life.

Women were excluded from formal political life –

A wallpainting from Pompeii, showing women having their hair dressed by slaves. As in the modern world, hairstyles tended to go in and out of fashion, and as a result they provide additional means of dating frescoes and statues.

Bronze statue of a young girl fastening her robe, from Herculaneum. Roman girls often studied alongside their brothers, and as they married young, had a tendency to outlive their husbands into prosperous widowhood.

they had no vote and could not hold office or propose legislation. But they still exerted considerable political influence. First, women were wives and mothers. As is seen in the case of the Gracchi (pp. 126–38), a mother could have a powerful influence on the development of her children. Also, a Roman did not merely marry a woman, he married into her entire family and was expected to be at least sympathetic to his in-laws' political ideals. Because a Roman matriarch had full control of domestic affairs and Roman politicians tended to work from home, a wife was in a good position to know who her husband was seeing and what political alliances he was cultivating. And because a Roman wife remained a part of her father's family, it was difficult for the husband to work against his father-in-law's interests without it becoming known very quickly.

Legally, most Roman women were *in potestate*, meaning that they were under the tutelage of a father, husband or guardian. In theory this meant that a woman needed their consent before making important decisions, including marriage, divorce or the sale of property. This did not suit many of the strong-willed matrons of Rome, and they took care to choose as guardians men who were in some way under their control.

One instrument of such control was the dowry. When a Roman woman married, she brought with her a dowry, generally considered to be the size of the inheritance she would have received and it could amount to a very substantial sum. Though the husband had control of the money as long as the marriage lasted, on divorce or death, the dowry reverted to the wife or her family. There are numerous examples of Roman aristocrats, such as the heirs of Aemilius Paullus, struggling to find the necessary money to repay a dowry. A divorce thus involved a Roman politician in considerable political and financial expense: political, since a divorce was usually a signal of a rupture of relations with the family, and financial as the dowry had to be repaid.

captured by Octavian. He wanted to keep her alive as an ornament for his triumphal parade, but Cleopatra outwitted him, with her legendary suicide by snakebite. The senate ruled that the name Marcus could not be used again by the Antonian family. But Rome had not seen the last of the line of Antony. His daughter married a Domitius Ahenobarbus, and her grandson was adopted into the Claudian house, to become infamous as the emperor Nero.

Marcus Aemilius Lepidus
(*c.* 90–*c.* 13 BC)

Sextus Pompey
(*c.* 67–36 BC)

Octavian
(63 BC–AD 14)

The young Octavian: when he came to Rome, Octavian called himself Julius Caesar after his adoptive father. Later, when master of the empire, he took the name of Augustus. Octavian is a modern form of the Roman 'Octavianus' – a name he never used.

MARCUS AEMILIUS LEPIDUS	
Born c. 90 BC	Triumvir from 43; Pontifex Maximus from 44
Famous ancestors M. Aemilius Lepidus (cos. 187, 175)	*Achievements* Triumphator
Mother Unknown	*Wife* Junia
Father Marcus Lepidus	*Children* Son: M. Aemilius Lepidus
Positions held Praetor 49; Consul 46, 42; Magister Equitum 47, 45, 44;	*Death* Old age c. 13 BC

Marcus Aemilius Lepidus

Lepidus rejected Antony's first overtures … but Antony showed himself to the soldiers of Lepidus. And since Lepidus was the worst of all generals, and Antony was far his superior – while he was sober – the soldiers of Lepidus broke open their wall and took Antony into the camp.

Velleius Paterculus, *Historia* 2.63

WITH EVEN THE MOST DISTINGUISHED Romans of the Republic, many personal details are scanty. Marcus Aemilius Lepidus was one of the greatest men of his time, yet we do not know when he was born and it is uncertain exactly when he died. Yet at other moments of his life, the evidence is so good that we can track his movements almost day by day.

The family name

Lepidus was the son of the Marcus Aemilius Lepidus who tried to imitate Sulla's march on Rome and was defeated by Lutatius Catulus and Pompey. He was probably a younger son, since his brother Aemilius Paullus received his public offices before him. (The direct line of Aemilius Paullus (pp. 113–16) had recently become extinct, and Lepidus senior

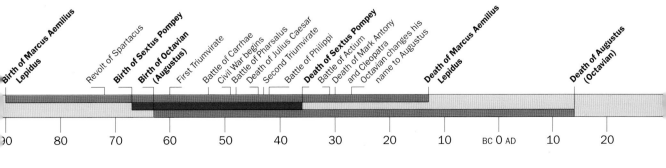

Birth of Marcus Aemilius Lepidus — Revolt of Spartacus — Birth of Sextus Pompey — Birth of Octavian (Augustus) — First Triumvirate — Battle of Carrhae — Civil War begins — Battle of Pharsalus — Death of Julius Caesar — Second Triumvirate — Battle of Philippi — Death of Sextus Pompey — Battle of Actium — Death of Mark Antony and Cleopatra — Octavian changes his name to Augustus — Death of Marcus Aemilius Lepidus — Death of Augustus (Octavian)

90 80 70 60 50 40 30 20 10 BC 0 AD 10 20

took the chance to include the illustrious name of Paullus within his own family, and bestowed his family name on the younger son.)

We first hear of Lepidus in 52 when he was involved in riots instigated by Clodius. In 49, when civil war broke out, he was a praetor. Lepidus opted for the Caesarian side, and was assigned by Caesar to a governorship in Spain. He returned in 46 and celebrated a triumph (though it was unkindly remarked that he had nothing to display except for the money he had robbed from the unfortunate Spaniards); and then became consul for that year.

He was sufficiently trusted by Caesar to be his official second-in-command until Caesar's assassination in 44, and the assassins at one time considered killing Lepidus too. As he had been about to take command in Gaul when Caesar's killers struck, Lepidus had his army ready outside Rome. His support for Antony was therefore crucial.

Lepidus and Antony

Having seen Antony on his way to supreme power, Lepidus retired to Gaul to watch the struggle between Antony and the senate from a distance. Antony then arrived in his province, a bedraggled refugee from his defeat by the senatorial army. Cicero's correspondence has preserved some letters from Lepidus in those crucial days, in which he swears loyalty to the senate, and afterwards says that his soldiers forced him to go over to Antony's side. Neither Cicero nor anyone else believed him.

In the proscriptions of 43, the name at the top of the list was that of Aemilius Paullus, but as with Antony's uncle, Lepidus' brother escaped death. For his acquiescence in the purges, Lepidus was again made consul in 42. He also became Pontifex Maximus in Caesar's place, an office held once before by a direct ancestor – the Aemilius Lepidus who was consul in 187 and 175.

The junior triumvir

Lepidus governed Rome and Italy while his colleagues fought the Philippi campaign, and he also held the provinces of Spain and Gaul. However, his place in the scheme of things was made plain to him when the other two triumvirs removed his command of the two provinces, alleging he was plotting with Sextus Pompey.

When the triumvirate was renewed in 37, Lepidus was barely even consulted. Later, as relations with Antony deteriorated, Octavian tried to make sure of Lepidus' loyalty by giving him Africa to govern. How well Octavian's idea succeeded can be judged by a failed attempt by one of Lepidus' sons to assassinate Octavian five years later.

Lepidus made one last attempt to regain his position in the campaign against Sextus Pompey. When he had conquered most of Sicily he attempted to re-assert his rights as a triumvir against the almost defenceless Octavian,who had been defeated at sea. But Octavian was the adopted son of Caesar, and Lepidus' army simply went over to his rival, leaving him to beg for his life.

Coin of Lepidus. Originally the Romans did not display the heads of living people on their coins, but to the dynasts of the dying Republic the propaganda value of coinage was a weapon they could not afford to ignore.

Octavian contented himself with banishing Lepidus, and later, feeling even that was too severe, he allowed him to return to Rome. Nor did he strip Lepidus of his title of Pontifex Maximus. Rome was firmly under the rule of Octavian, now the emperor Augustus, when Lepidus died in 13 or 12 BC, having at least achieved the distinction of being one of the very few protagonists in the crisis of the Republic to die of natural causes.

SEXTUS POMPEY	
Born	*Positions held*
c. 67 BC	Prefect of the Fleet
Famous ancestors	*Achievements*
Pompey Strabo	Resisted the
(grandfather)	Triumvirs
Mother	*Wife*
Mucia	Scribonia
Father	*Death*
Pompey the Great	Executed 36 BC

SEXTUS POMPEY

Though the restless spirit of Pompey would not rest content with the agreement [at Misenum] one good thing did come out of the meeting. Pompey stipulated that all those who had been proscribed, or all those who had taken refuge with him for any reason, should be granted a safe return to Rome.

Velleius Paterculus, *Historia* 2.78

SEXTUS POMPEY WAS THE YOUNGER SON of Pompey the Great and Tertia Mucia, born in about 67, when Pompey senior's fame was rising to its zenith. His later life was totally dominated by the ultimate failure of his father's cause.

Brothers in arms

Sextus Pompey's older brother Gnaeus fought alongside his father against Caesar, once destroying a convoy of Caesar's transport ships. At the time of the fateful Battle of Pharsalus, Sextus was with his stepmother Cornelia in Greece. There they were joined by the defeated Pompey, and fled with him to Egypt. His father was assassinated, almost before his eyes, and Pompey was separated from his mother. He went to Africa where his brother intended to continue the struggle with the remnants of the Pompeian forces. Later, they crossed to Spain, where they soon gained command of the southern part of the province.

(Above) Sextus Pompeius Magnus Pius, a portrait with an oak wreath on a coin struck in Italy, 42–38 BC. The 'Pius' reflects his loyalty to his father's doomed cause.
(Below) Pompey and his son on a coin struck in Sicily, 42–38 BC.

Caesar campaigned against the pair in person, and Gnaeus Pompey was brought to battle at Munda in 45. Defeated, Gnaeus attempted to flee, but was captured and executed. Sextus was not at the battle, being commander of the garrison at Cordoba. He did not abandon the war, however, and mauled successive generals whom Caesar sent against him. With Caesar's assassination in 44 he came to terms with the Roman senate. Pompey Senior was still fondly remembered in Rome, and at that time Aemilius Lepidus counted as a friend.

The Triumvirs

Distrustful of the political situation, Sextus remained outside Rome. His suspicions were justified, for he was first put in charge of the Roman fleet, and then suddenly outlawed. Taking his fleet south, he occupied Sicily, brushing aside Octavian's attempts to prevent him.

Sextus supported Antony against Octavian in 42, but made his peace with the triumvirate at the Pact of Misenum, which recognized his

occupation of Sicily, and promoted him to the élite priestly college of Augurs. While this peace was being concluded, Sextus invited the triumvirs aboard his ship for a dinner. During the dinner, his captain took him aside and said 'We could, at this moment, slip the anchor, take to the sea, and kill these three. You could be master of the world.'

Sextus thought about this for a long time, then replied. 'If you had done this without telling me, well and good. But now I know of it, I cannot honourably do as you suggest.'

Octavian was less scrupulous. As soon as he saw a chance, he accused Sextus of breaking the pact and attacked him. Two naval battles followed, and Octavian was soundly beaten each time. When Antony's wife Fulvia failed in her rebellion against Octavian, two noteworthy refugees fled to Sextus. One was Livia, grand-daughter of Livius Drusus (pp. 159–63) and Octavian's future wife, and the other was her infant son, the future emperor Tiberius.

The Roman people disapproved of the campaign against Sextus, and ostentatiously cheered statues of Poseidon when they were presented at the games. Sextus had taken to calling himself the son of Poseidon, and the Roman people were pleased to salute him as such.

Agrippa

But Octavian could now match the energetic and skilful Sextus with his admiral Vipsanius Agrippa. In an attack in 36, Octavian's fleet was defeated, but Agrippa won. He followed up his victory with another, and at the same time Aemilius Lepidus invaded Sicily by land. With only a few ships, Sextus fled to the eastern Mediterranean. In the province of Asia he surrendered, and was put to death by the Roman commander there.

Sextus was a worthy son of his father, but his cause was lost from the start. The Caesarians dominated the Roman empire, and even at the height of Sextus' success, the only real question was whether Octavian or Antony would eventually be victorious.

Marcus Vipsanius Agrippa, marble bust from Capri, late first century BC. Agrippa was an exceptional general and administrator. While he was content to remain in the shadow of Octavian, there can be little doubt that his contribution was crucial to the final victory, and he played a large part in the reconstruction of Rome thereafter.

OCTAVIAN	
Born	from 31; Pontifex
63 BC as Gaius	Maximus from 12
Octavius	*Achievements*
Famous ancestors	Pater Patriae;
None	Triumphator
Mother	*Wives*
Atia	Claudia, Scribonia,
Father	Livia
Octavius	*Children*
Positions held	Daughter: Julia
Consul 43, 33,	*Death*
31–23, 2; Triumvir	Old age AD 14
from 43; Emperor	

OCTAVIAN

Those who killed my father, I drove into exile, punishing what they had done by due process of law. Afterwards when they waged war on the Republic, I twice defeated them in battle. I fought wars, both foreign and civil, throughout the world, and when victorious I spared all those citizens who asked for pardon.

Octavian, *Res Gestae* 1.2–3

THE FUTURE MASTER OF THE ROMAN EMPIRE was born as Gaius Octavius on the Palatine hill in Rome in 63 BC – the year of Cicero's consulship and Catiline's conspiracy. In the eyes of the Roman aristocracy, Octavian's origins were modest indeed. His father was a *novus homo*, the first of his line to attain senatorial rank, who rose to the rank of praetor in 61, and was a very successful governor of Macedonia thereafter. Whether he might have risen higher will never be known, since he died before he could attempt the consulship, leaving Octavian and his two sisters fatherless at an early age.

Family background

Octavian's obscure family background allowed Mark Antony to slander him with the claim that his great-grandfather had been a slave and that his father had been a money-changer specializing in the distribution of bribes before he broke into politics. As for his mother, alleged Antony, she was the daughter of a baker.

Apologists for Octavian (and later in his life, naturally, there were many) found more distinguished ancestors. One report has it that the family could be traced back to the time of Tarquin the Elder. Later, the line divided. One section produced the Octavians of Rome, who included praetors and consuls as well as the famous tribune whose expulsion from office helped to ruin Tiberius Gracchus (p. 129). The other section remained equestrian and became leading citizens of the town of Velitrae, until the father of Octavian restored them to senatorial rank.

Antony failed to mention that he and Octavian were quite closely related. Antony's mother was a Julia, the sister of Lucius Caesar. The grandmother of Octavian was another Julia, sister to Julius Caesar. Nor was Octavian's mother of ignoble birth. On her husband's death she married the ex-consul Marcus Philippus.

Caesar's protégé

When just 12 years old, Octavian delivered the funeral oration for his grandmother Julia, a speech which brought him to the notice of Julius Caesar. Octavian was too young to accompany Caesar on his campaign against the Pompeians in Africa, but Caesar awarded him military honours nevertheless. He did join Caesar in his Spanish campaign against the sons of Pompey, at some physical cost to himself. All his life he suffered from ill-health, and he made the journey to Spain when he should have been in his sick-bed.

Caesar awarded the young man a pontificate, but then dispatched him to Apollonia in Dalmatia 'to continue his studies'. Octavian duly went – taking his tutor with him. At Apollonia, Octavian formed a lifelong friendship with Marcus Vipsanius Agrippa. Without Agrippa, there might have been no Augustus, for Agrippa's generalship was crucial to Augustus' rise. Another friend of the time, Maecenas, was to be almost as important politically as Agrippa was militarily.

Caesar's heir

In 44 the dramatic news arrived from Rome: Caesar had been assassinated, and Octavian was his heir. At that moment, Octavian's fate was sealed. Given the political climate, whoever seized supreme power in Rome was unlikely to allow Caesar's heir to grow old. Octavian had either to try for supreme power himself, or perish in the attempt.

A statue of Augustus of the early first century AD. Augustus attempted to promote the wearing of togas as an element of *Romanitas* ('Roman-ness'). Covering the head with a fold of the toga was usually done on religious occasions.

He hurried to Rome and discovered that his first rival would be Antony. Antony had Caesar's money and papers in 'safe-keeping' and was reluctant to hand them over to the new arrival, so Octavian had to meet Caesar's bequests to his soldiers from his own pocket. This nearly bankrupted him but did earn him the loyalty of the soldiers. To build on this, Octavian called himself Julius Caesar, son of Julius Caesar. Normally an adopted son took the name of his adoptive father and added his former family name with a suffix (e.g. Scipio Aemilianus). But Octavian went directly from Octavius to Julius Caesar. The senate, suspicious of Antony, helped Octavian by deifying the murdered dictator, making Octavian officially the son of a god.

The triumvir

Cicero particularly was in favour of Octavian, seeing him as a counterweight to Antony. While Antony was campaigning at Mutina, the senate declared him a public enemy and sent the consuls Pansa and Hirtius against him. Octavian, now given the power of a praetor by the senate, went with them. Antony was defeated in the brief campaign which followed, but both Hirtius and Pansa died. Hirtius in the field, Pansa under circumstances so suspicious that his physician was arrested. Contemporary historians strongly suspected that Octavian engineered both deaths to create a vacancy for the consulship, which he seized on his return to Rome with the army.

Meanwhile, Antony had made common cause with Lepidus, and the pair marched on Italy. Octavian made the cold-blooded decision that he would do better joining the other two than trying to defend the Republic against them, even if this meant abandoning old allies such as Cicero.

As a triumvir, Octavian pursued his enemies mercilessly. At Philippi, in Greece, he and Antony fought the assassins of Caesar, Brutus and Cassius. Octavian had a bad battle. He was defeated, driven from his camp and forced to take shelter with Antony, who won his part of the battle and carried the day. Perhaps in consequence, Octavian was ruthless with the defeated. He refused all pleas for mercy, and when one person asked for at least a decent burial, Octavian told him to 'discuss that with the crows'.

Victory at Philippi left the triumvirs masters of the Roman world. Octavian and Antony wasted no time in putting Lepidus in his place in that world by accusing him of colluding with Sextus Pompey, the last of the Republicans, and depriving him of his provinces. Antony took

The Theatre of Marcellus was part of Augustus' reconstruction of Rome. Originally planned by Julius Caesar, the theatre was finished in about 16 BC. It was used as a fortress in the Middle Ages, and today only the two lower storeys of the original building survive.

Copy of the *Res Gestae* inscribed on the Temple of Augustus, Ankara, Turkey. Written by Augustus himself, this is a description of his life and achievements. A work of propaganda, it shows clearly that being economical with the truth is not a trait confined to modern politicians.

command of the east and Octavian the west of the empire. In theory, Italy was held in common, but as Antony's attention shifted to Cleopatra and Alexandria, Octavian became the *de facto* ruler.

Octavian in trouble

Antony seemed to have made the better choice. His provinces were richer than war-devastated Gaul and Spain, and his alliance with Cleopatra brought with it the wealth of the Ptolemies. The Italians and Romans were restless at being deprived of their accustomed liberty, and the senate was surly and untrustworthy. Sextus Pompey cut off the capital's grain supplies and Octavian got the blame.

The campaign to defeat Sextus Pompey was nearly a débâcle – and worryingly he was more popular in Rome than Octavian. To add to Octavian's troubles, it was at this stage that Fulvia, the wife of Antony, allied herself with Antony's brother Lucius to stage an uprising against him. Octavian fought back doggedly against these setbacks. He knew that he had to finish the war quickly, since Antony was coming with a huge fleet to 'mediate'. If Octavian was in a position of weakness when Antony arrived, his fellow triumvir would seize the chance to finish him off.

Octavian fought with extreme brutality, and put the rebels under siege in the city of Perusia (modern Perugia, in Umbria). When Perusia fell, Fulvia fled. Weakened by the privations of the siege, she died soon after. Antony arrived to find himself without a *casus belli* and agreed to an extension of the triumvirate. To strengthen the partnership, Antony married Octavian's sister Octavia.

More enemies

Octavian had been forced to make peace with Sextus Pompey and cede Sicily to him. Now he felt strong enough to contest the issue again. He and Agrippa commanded a fleet each, and the third triumvir, Lepidus, was recruited to take command of the land campaign.

Octavian's miserable record as a general continued. He was again defeated, perhaps because he was suffering from illness. 'He lay on his back, staring at the sky, and never showed that he was alive until Agrippa had routed the enemy' was Antony's caustic summary of Octavian's contribution. Fortunately, Octavian was better at picking men than leading them. Agrippa defeated the Pompeians at Mylae, and finished them off at Naulochus, Sicily.

Pompey was replaced as a threat by Lepidus. After seizing the legions on the island, Lepidus commanded a huge force. Reckoning that he had found a counter to Octavian's arrogance, he stood up to his colleague, and demanded a fair share of the spoils.

PRAISE FOR OCTAVIAN

But will anyone hesitate to call Octavian a conquering general? Most certainly, his age will not prevent anyone from agreeing with this, since he has gone beyond his age in virtue. And indeed, to me the services of Octavian have always appeared the more thankworthy in proportion, as they were less to have been expected from a man of his age. When we gave him military command, we were in fact encouraging the hope with which his name [of Caesar] inspired us, and now that he has fulfilled these hopes, he has sanctioned the authority of our decree by his exploits. This young man of great mind....

Cicero on Octavian, a few days before Octavian betrayed him, *Philippics* 14.28

Cameo showing Augustus in a chariot drawn by Tritons, made after 27 BC to commemorate the victory at Actium; the gold setting was added later, in 1600. Tritons were the escorts of Venus and so this cameo neatly links Augustus' victory with Caesar's claimed descent from the goddess.

Prow of a ship, found in the bay of Actium, first century BC. Although the right date, it is unlikely that this bronze prow was from a ship that took part in the Battle of Actium, as was once thought.

Winning the west

Whatever Octavian's merits as a general, he did not lack physical courage. He climbed the rampart of Lepidus' camp, and addressed Lepidus' soldiers, reminding them of their allegiance to his 'father' Caesar. His reception was initially so hostile that he received a flesh wound from a missile flung at him. But his appeal had its effect, as Lepidus' men deserted to his camp in ever larger numbers. Finally, Lepidus was forced to follow them to Octavian's camp and beg for his life. Octavian restrained his bloodthirsty nature, and spared Lepidus all but a brief exile.

Only Antony remained between Octavian and supreme power. Octavian's propaganda machine now painted Antony as the besotted slave of Cleopatra. It was alleged that Antony was planning to move his capital to Alexandria, and that he wished to be buried there. This last was confirmed when Octavian illegally obtained a copy of Antony's will, and made it public.

The last battle

Maintaining that his Parthian campaign was consuming all his energies, Antony returned Octavia to Rome, and openly consorted with Cleopatra. Despite this Octavia remained loyal to her husband. She did not move back to the house of Octavian, but remained at Antony's house, handling the Italian side of his affairs with great skill. This loyalty worked against Antony, for it showed the world what a noble wife he had spurned.

Octavian mustered his forces, even as Antony's were squandered on his Parthian campaign. When that campaign finished in ignominious retreat, Octavian showed his hand. He declared war, not on Antony, but on Cleopatra, knowing that Antony would stand by his queen. Antony did, defiantly marrying her before he set off to campaign against Octavian. Finally, in 31, that campaign reached its climax off the promontory of Actium. The fleets of Antony and Cleopatra were defeated, and their army surrendered. As the great modern historian Ronald Syme (no admirer of Octavian) grudgingly conceded, 'he won his war, this Caesar'.

Octavian the man

Octavian the man was very different from Octavian the politician. As a man he stood by his friends and allowed them considerable latitude in their behaviour. Coldly calculating in politics, he would break alliances whenever it suited him.

He divorced his wife Scribonia, the mother of his daughter Julia, allegedly because 'she nagged me too much', but probably because of her connections with Sextus Pompey. He married Livia Drusilla, formerly the wife of Tiberius Nero, while she was still pregnant by him. Octavian and Livia remained happily married for decades, until Octavian's death.

Abstemious in drink and frugal in his expenditure, Octavian nevertheless retained a weakness for other women all his life. A fragment of Antony's reply to Octavian's complaint about his conduct with Cleopatra has survived. 'And you? Have you really been faithful to Livia?

A cameo portrait of Livia, wife of Augustus. Despite numerous suggestions – both modern and ancient – that Livia was a ruthless plotter and poisoner, there is no hard evidence that she was other than a loyal and supportive wife, though she certainly had considerable influence over Augustus.

I congratulate you, if by the time this letter arrives, you have not bedded Tertulla, or Terentilla, or Rufilla, or Salvia Titisenia – or all of them. Does it really matter so much who you screw, or where?'

It helped Octavian's amorous conquests that he was good-looking. He was small, but well-formed, and his expression was clear-eyed and tranquil. His teeth were his least appealing feature – small, carious and badly formed – and his health was weak – in winter he wore multiple layers of clothing and in summer protected his head with a broad-brimmed hat.

It is hard to associate this genial figure, fond of mild gambling and amorous liaisons, with the brutal master of *Realpolitik* who brings this chronicle of the Roman Republic to a close. Octavian was aware of the dichotomy. When dying he asked, 'So, did I play my part well in this farce?', and almost his last words were the traditional lines of an actor departing the stage who asks the audience to show their approval of his act by their applause.

IMPERATOR

Imperator is the origin of the modern word 'emperor'. It originally meant something like 'great commander' and was used by troops to salute their victorious general after a battle. A general who received this salutation might then assume the name until he triumphed, or laid down his command.

It is possible that the first general to be saluted as *imperator* was Scipio Africanus at the end of the second century BC. Certainly the term was common in the first century, when generals began to keep count of the number of times they had received the salutation.

After the victory at Actium, Octavian began to use the title as a *praenomen* (i.e. calling himself *Imperator Caesar* rather than the usual *Caesar Imperator*). Thereafter, as the title came to be associated with the ruler of Rome, it was used less and less frequently by others. However, it did not become the formal title of the emperor until it was adopted by Vespasian in AD 69.

Octavian depicted as a general directing his troops (in reality something which he did with a notable lack of success). The statue was found at Prima Porta, outside Rome, in a villa belonging to Livia.

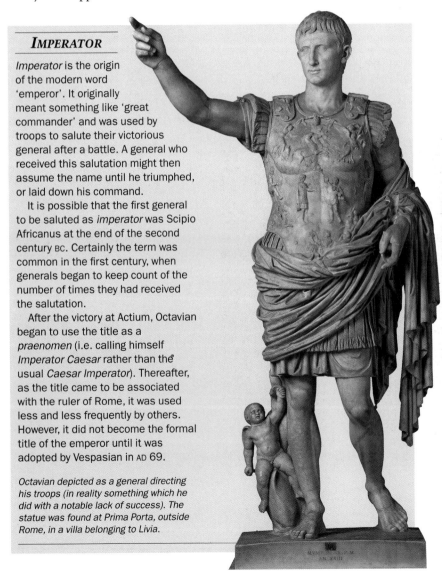

SELECT BIBLIOGRAPHY

Individual ancient sources

All authors are from the Loeb Classical Library (Cambridge MA: Harvard UP) unless stated otherwise; most translations in the book have been adapted by the author.

Appian *Roman History*. Vols I–IV trans. H. White, 1912–13

Augustus *Caesar Res Gestae Divi Augusti. The Achievements of the Divine Augustus* P.A. Brunt and J.M. Moore (eds). Oxford & New York: Oxford UP, 1967

Caesar Vol. I: *Gallic War* trans. H. J. Edwards, 1917

Caesar Vol. II: *Civil Wars* trans. A. G. Peskett, 1914

Caesar/anon. Vol. III: *Alexandrian, African, and Spanish Wars* trans. A. G. Way, 1955

Cassius Dio *Roman History*. Vols III–VI, trans. Herbert B. Foster, 1905–06, revised trans. Earnest Cary, 1914–17

Cato Varro *On Agriculture* trans. W. D. Hooper, H. B. Ash, 1934

Cicero Vol. VIII: *The Verrine Orations*. II: *Against Verres*, Part 2, 3–5, B. *Orations* trans L. H. G. Greenwood, 1935

Cicero Vol. X: *In Catilinam 1–4. Pro Murena. Pro Sulla. Pro Flacco*, B. *Orations* trans C. Macdonald, 1976

Cicero Vol. XI: *Pro Archia. Post Reditum in Senatu. Post Reditum ad Quirites. De Domo Sua. De Haruspicum Responsis. Pro Cn. Plancio*, B. *Orations* trans N. H. Watts, 1923

Cicero Vol. XIV: *Pro Milone. In Pisonem. Pro Scauro. Pro Fonteio. Pro Rabirio Postumo. Pro Marcello. Pro Ligario. Pro Rege Deiotaro*, B. *Orations* trans. N. H. Watts, 1931

Cicero Vol. XV: *Philippics*, B. *Orations* trans Walter C. A. Ker, 1926

Cicero, Vol. XVI: *De Re Publica. De Legibus*, C. *Philosophical Treatises* trans. Clinton W. Keyes, 1928

Cicero Vol. XX: *De Senectute. De Amicitia. De Divinatione*, C. *Philosophical Treatises* trans. W. A. Falconer, 1923

Cicero Vol. XXI: *De Officiis*, C. *Philosophical Treatises* trans. Walter Miller, 1913

Cicero Vols XXII–XXIV. *Letters to Atticus*, D. *Letters* trans. D. R. Shackleton Bailey, 1999

Cicero Vols XXV–XXVII. *Letters to Friends*, D. *Letters* ed. & trans. D. R. Shackleton Bailey, 2001

Cicero Vol. XXVIII: *Letters to His Brother Quintus; Letters to Brutus; Handbook of Electioneering; Letter to Octavian*, D. *Letters* trans W. Glynn Williams, M. Cary, Mary I. Henderson

Cicero Vol. XXIX: *Letters to Atticus*, D. *Letters* trans. D. R. Shackleton Bailey, 1999

Diodorus Siculus *Library of History*, Vol. X, trans. Russel M. Geer, 1954

Diodorus Siculus *Library of History*, Vols XI, XII, trans. Francis R. Walton, 1957, 1967

Dionysius of Halicarnassus, Vols I–VII *Roman Antiquities* trans. Earnest Cary, 1937–50

Frontinius *Stratagems. Aqueducts*, trans C. E. Bennett, Mary B. McElwain, 1925

Livy *History of Rome*. Vols I–V, trans. B. O. Foster, 1919–25

Vols VI–VIII, trans F. G. Moore, 1940–49

Vols IX–XII, trans. Evan T. Sage, 1935–38

Vol. XIII, trans. A. C. Schlesinger, 1951

Vol. XIV, *Summaries. Fragments. Julius Obsequens* trans. A. C. Schlesinger, 1959

Plutarch *Plutarch's Lives*, 'The Dryden Plutarch', revised by Arthur Hugh Clough. Vols 1–3. Everyman's Library. Nos 407–409. London: J. M. Dent, 1962

Polybius *The Histories*, Vols I–VI, trans. W. R. Paton, 1922–27

Sallust *War with Catiline. War with Jugurtha. Selections from the Histories. Doubtful Works*, trans. J. C. Rolfe, 1921

Suetonius *The Lives of the Caesars*. Vol. I. *Julius. Augustus. Tiberius. Gaius. Caligula*, trans. J. C. Rolfe (rev. ed. D. Hurley), 1914

Valerius Maximus Vols I, II, *Memorable Doings and Sayings* ed. & trans. D. R. Shackleton Bailey, 2000

Varro *On the Latin Language*. Vols 1 & II, Books 1–10, Fragments trans. Ronald G. Kent, 1938

Velleius Paterculus *Compendium of Roman History. Res Gestae Divi Augusti*, trans. F. W. Shipley, 1924

Modern references

Alföldi, A., 1965. *Early Rome and the Latins*. Ann Arbor, MI: University of Michigan Press

Astin, A., 1967. *Scipio Aemilianus*. Oxford & New York: Oxford UP

Astin, A., 1978. *Cato the Censor*. Oxford & New York: Oxford UP

Ayres, P., 1997. *Classical Culture and the Idea of Rome in Eighteenth-century England*. Cambridge & New York: Cambridge UP

Badian, E., 1970. 'Titus Quinctius Flamininus: Philhellenism and Realpolitik', in *Lectures in Memory of Louise Saft Semple*, C. G. Boulter et al. (eds). Norman: University of Oklahoma Press for University of Cincinnati

Badian, E., 1970. *Lucius Sulla. The Deadly Reformer*. Sydney: Sydney UP

Badian, E., 1972. *Publicans and Sinners: Private Enterprise in the Service of the Roman Republic*. Dunedin: University of Otago Press; Ithaca, NY: Cornell UP

Barton, I. (ed.), 1989. *Roman Public Buildings*. Exeter: University of Exeter Press

Beard, M. & Crawford, M. H., 1985. *Rome in the Late Republic: Problems and Interpretations*. London: Duckworth; Ithaca, NY: Cornell UP

Bernstein, A., 1978. *Tiberius Sempronius Gracchus: Tradition and Apostasy*. Ithaca, NY: Cornell UP

Blois, L., 1987. *The Roman Army and Politics in the First Century before Christ*. Amsterdam: J.C. Gieben

Boren, H. C., 1977. *Roman Society: A Social, Economic, and Cultural History*. Lexington, MA: D. C. Heath

Bowder, D., 1980. *Who was Who in the Roman World: 753 BC–AD 476*. London: Phaidon; Ithaca, NY: Cornell UP

Bradford, E., 1984. *Julius Caesar: The Pursuit of Power.* London: Hamish Hamilton

Broughton, T., 1984. *The Magistrates of the Roman Republic.* Chico, CA: Scholars Press

Brunt, P., 1987. *Italian Manpower 225 BC–AD 14.* (rev. ed.). Oxford & New York: Oxford UP

Buck, C. D., 1904. *A Grammar of Oscan and Umbrian with a Collection of Inscriptions and a Glossary.* Boston: Ginn & Co.

Cambridge Ancient History, 1923–39. 17 vols. Cambridge: Cambridge UP

Carney, T., 1961. *A Biography of C. Marius.* Salisbury: African Classical Associations

Casson, L., 1984. *Ancient Trade and Society.* Detroit, MI: Wayne State UP

Corey Brennan, T., 2001. *The Praetorship in the Roman Republic.* Oxford & New York: Oxford UP

Cornell, T., 1975. 'Aeneas and the Twins: the development of the Roman foundation legend', *Proceedings of the Cambridge Philological Society n.s.* 21, 1–32

Cornell, T., 1995. *The Beginnings of Rome: Italy and Rome from the Bronze Age to the Punic Wars (c. 1000–264 BC).* London & New York: Routledge

Cornell, T. and Matthews, J., 1982, *Atlas of the Roman World.* Oxford: Phaidon

Crawford, M. H., 1975. *Roman Republican Coinage.* Cambridge & New York: Cambridge UP

Crawford, M. H. (ed.), 1983. *Sources for Ancient History.* Cambridge & New York: Cambridge UP

D'Arms, J. H. & Kopff, E. C. (eds), 1980. *The Seaborne Commerce of Ancient Rome.* Rome: American Academy

David, J., 1997. *The Roman Conquest of Italy.* Oxford & Cambridge MA: Blackwell Publishers

Develin, R., 1979. *Patterns in Office-holding 366–49 BC.* Brussels: Latomus

Develin, R., 1985. *The Practice of Politics at Rome 366–167 BC.* Brussels: Latomus

Dumezil, G., 1980. *Camillus: A Study of Indo-European Religion as Roman History.* Trans. Aronowicz, A. and Bryson, J. Berkeley, CA: University of California Press

Eckstein, A. M., 1987. *Senate and General: Individual Decision-Making and Roman Foreign Relations, 264–194 BC.* Berkeley, CA: University of California Press

Everitt, A., 2001. *Cicero: A Turbulent Life.* London: John Murray; New York: Random House.

Finley, M. I., 1983. *Politics in the Ancient World.* Cambridge & New York: Cambridge UP

Forde, N., 1975. *Cato the Censor.* New York: Twayne

Fox, J., 1990. *Hannibal, Enemy of Rome.* Chicago: Adams

Franzero, C. M., 1961. *The Life and Times of Tarquin the Etruscan.* London: A. Redman; New York: John Day

Gelzer, M., 1968. *Caesar, Politician and Statesman.* Oxford: Blackwell; Cambridge, MA: Harvard UP

Gelzer, M., 1969. *The Roman Nobility.* Oxford: Blackwell; New York: Barnes & Noble

Goldsworthy, A., 2001. *Cannae.* London: Cassell

Grant, M., 1980. *The Etruscans.* London: Weidenfeld & Nicolson

Greenhalgh, P., 1981. *Pompey, The Republican Prince.* London: Weidenfeld & Nicolson; Columbia, MO: University of Missouri Press

Gruen, E., 1968. *Roman Politics and the Criminal Courts, 149–78 BC.* Cambridge, MA: Harvard UP

Gruen, E., 1974. *The Last Generation of the Roman Republic.* Berkeley, CA: University of California Press

Harris, W., 1971. *Rome in Etruria and Umbria.* Oxford: Clarendon Press

Harris, W., 1979. *War and Imperialism in Republican Rome 327–70 BC.* Oxford & New York: Clarendon Press

Holloway, R., 1994. *The Archaeology of Early Rome and Latium.* London & New York: Routledge

Hornblower, S. & Spawforth, A. (eds), 1996. *The Oxford Classical Dictionary.* 3rd ed, Oxford & New York: Oxford UP

Huzar, E., 1978. *Mark Antony, A Biography.* Minneapolis, MN: University of Minnesota Press; London: Croom Helm,1986

Keaveney, A., 1982. *Sulla, the Last Republican.* London: Croom Helm

Keppie, L., 1991. *Understanding Roman Inscriptions.* London: Batsford; Baltimore, MD: Johns Hopkins UP

Kildahl, P., 1968. *Caius Marius.* New York: Twayne Publishers

Kleine Pauly, Der, 1964–75. *Lexicon der Antike.* Munich: Konrad Ziegler & Walther Sontheimer

Kyle, D., 1998. *Spectacles of Death in Ancient Rome.* London & New York: Routledge

Lazenby, J., 1978. *Hannibal's War: A Military History of the Second Punic War.* Warminster: Aris & Phillips; Norman, OK: University of Oklahoma Press

Leach, J., 1978. *Pompey the Great.* London: Croom Helm

Lempriere, J., 1984. *Classical Dictionary of Proper Names Mentioned in Ancient Authors with a Chronological Table.* 3rd ed. London: Routledge & Kegan Paul

Lewis, N. & Reinhold, M., 1990. *Roman Civilization. Selected Readings.* Vol. 1, *The Republic and Augustan Age.* 3rd ed. New York: Columbia UP

Liberati, A. M. and Bourbon, F., 1996. *Splendours of the Roman World.* London: Thames & Hudson

Liddell Hart, B., 1994. *Scipio Africanus; Greater than Napoleon.* New York: Da Capo Press

Lintott, A., 1967. 'P. Clodius Pulcher – Felix Catilina?', *Greece & Rome* 14, 157–69

Lintott, A., 1982. *Violence, Civil Strife and Revolution in the Classical City.* London: Croom Helm; Baltimore, MD: Johns Hopkins UP

Lintott, A., 1999. *The Constitution of the Roman Republic.* Oxford & New York: Clarendon Press

McKay, A., 1975. *Houses, Villas and Palaces in the Roman World.* London: Thames & Hudson; Ithaca, NY: Cornell UP

MacMullen, R., 1974. *Roman Social Relations, 50 BC to AD 284.* New Haven & London: Yale UP

Marshall, B., 1976. *Crassus. A Political Biography.* Amsterdam: Hakkert

Matz, D., 1997. *An Ancient Rome Chronology, 264–27 BC*. Jefferson, NC & London: McFarland & Co.

Meiggs, R., 1973. *Roman Ostia*. 2nd ed., Oxford: Oxford UP

Millar, F. & Segal, E. (eds), 1984. *Caesar Augustus: Seven Aspects*. Oxford: Clarendon Press

Mitchell, T., 1979. *Cicero: The Ascending Years*. New Haven: Yale UP

Mommsen, T. (ed.), 1873. *Corpus Inscriptionum Latinarum*. 16 vols. Berlin: Walter De Gruyter

Oman, C., 1925. *Seven Roman Statesmen of the Later Republic: The Gracchi. Sulla. Crassus. Cato. Pompey. Caesar*. London: E. Arnold

Pinsent, J., 1975. *Military Tribunes and Plebeian Consuls: The Fasti from 444 V to 342 V*. Wiesbaden: Steiner

Raaflaub, K. (ed.), 1986. *Social Struggles in Archaic Rome*. Berkeley & Los Angeles: University of California Press

Rammage, N. & A., 1991. *The Cambridge Illustrated History of Roman Art*. Cambridge: Cambridge UP

Rawson, E., 1983. *Cicero: A Portrait*. Rev. ed. Bristol: Bristol Classical Press; Ithaca, NY: Cornell UP

Reiter, W., 1988. *Aemilius Paullus, Conqueror of Greece*. London & New York: Croom Helm

Richardson, K., 1976. *Daggers in the Forum: The Revolutionary Lives and Violent Deaths of the Gracchus Brothers*. London: Cassell

Rodgers, W., 1964. *Greek and Roman Naval Warfare: A Study of Strategy, Tactics, and Ship Design from Salamis 480 BC to Actium 31 BC*. Annapolis, MD: United States Naval Institute

Scarre, C., 1995. *Chronicle of the Roman Emperors*. London & New York: Thames & Hudson

Scullard, H. H., 1973. *Roman Politics, 220–150 BC*. Oxford: Clarendon Press

Scullard, H. H., 1970. *Scipio Africanus: Soldier and Politician*. London: Thames & Hudson; Ithaca, NY: Cornell UP

Seager, R., 1969. *The Crisis of the Roman Republic*. Cambridge: Heffer; New York: Barnes & Noble

Seager, R., 2002. *Pompey the Great. A Political Biography*. 2nd ed. Oxford: Blackwell

Shackleton Bailey, D., 1991. *Two Studies in Roman Nomenclature*. Atlanta GA: Scholars Press

Shatzman, I., 1975. *Senatorial Wealth and Roman Politics*. Brussels: Latomus

Shelton, J., 1988. *As the Romans Did: A Source Book in Roman Social History*. Oxford & New York: Oxford UP

Sichel, M., 1980. *Costume of the Classical World*. London: Batsford

Smith, R., 1966. *Cicero, the Statesman*. Cambridge: CUP

Smith, W. (ed), 1844–49. *A Dictionary of Greek and Roman Biography and Mythology*. London: Taylor and Walton

Spann, P., 1987. *Quintus Sertorius and the Legacy of Sulla*. Fayetteville: University of Arkansas Press

Stockton, D., 1971. *Cicero, A Political Biography*. London: Oxford UP

Stockton, D., 1979. *The Gracchi*. Oxford & New York: Oxford UP

Stockton, D., 1981. *From the Gracchi to Sulla: Sources for Roman History, 133–80 BC*. London: London Association of Classical Teachers

Syme, R., 1960. *The Roman Revolution*. Oxford & New York: Oxford UP

Syme, R., 1986. *The Augustan Aristocracy*. Oxford: Clarendon Press

Syme, R., 2002. *Sallust*. Berkeley, CA: University of California Press

Szemler, G., 1972. *The Priests of the Roman Republic. A Study of Interactions Between Priesthoods and Magistracies*. Brussels: Latomus

Talbert, R. (ed.), 2000. *Barrington Atlas of the Greek and Roman World*. Princeton, NJ: Princeton

Tatum, W. 1999. *The Patrician Tribune: Publius Clodius Pulcher*. Chapel Hill & London: University of North Carolina Press

Taylor, L., 1949. *Party Politics in the Age of Caesar*. Berkeley, CA: University of California Press

Thomsen, R., 1980. *King Servius Tullius: A Historical Synthesis*. Copenhagen: Gyldendal

Torelli, M. (ed.), 2001. *The Etruscans*. London: Thames & Hudson; New York: Rizzoli

Toynbee, J., 1978. *Roman Historical Portraits*. London: Thames & Hudson; Ithaca, NY: Cornell UP

Treggiari, S., 1993. *Roman Marriage*. New ed. Oxford & New York: Oxford UP

Twyman, B., 1972. 'The Metelli, Pompeius and Prosopography', *Aufstieg und Niedergang der Römischen Welt* I-1, 816–74

Usher, S., 1970. *The Historians of Greece and Rome*. London: Hamish Hamilton; New York: Taplinger Pub. Co.

Ward, A., 1977. *Marcus Crassus and the Late Roman Republic*. Columbia, MO: University of Missouri Press

Weigel, R., 1992. *Lepidus, the Tarnished Triumvir*. London: Routledge

White, K., 1970. *Roman Farming*. London: Thames & Hudson; Ithaca, NY: Cornell University Press

Wiseman, T. P., 1971. *New Men in the Roman Senate (139 BC–AD 14)*, London: Oxford UP

Wiseman, T., 1974. 'Legendary genealogies in late Republican Rome', *Greece & Rome* 21, 153ff.

Wiseman, T., 1979. *Clio's Cosmetics. Three Studies in Graeco-Roman Literature*. Leicester: Leicester UP

Wistrand, E., 1979. *Caesar and Contemporary Roman Society*. Göteborg: Vetenskaps-och Vitterhets-samhället

Zanker, P., 1988. *The Power of Images in the Age of Augustus*. Trans. A. Shapiro. Ann Arbor, MI: University of Michigan Press

Websites

http://www.perseus.tufts.edu/

http://www.thelatinlibrary.com/

http://ccat.sas.upenn.edu/bmcr/

http://www.ukans.edu/history/index/europe/ancient_rome/E/Roman/home.html

http://www.barca.fsnet.co.uk/

ILLUSTRATION CREDITS

a = above, c = centre, b = bottom, l = left, r = right

The following abbreviations are used to identify sources and locate illustrations: BM – © Copyright The British Museum, London; PB – Peter Bull; GC – Giovanni Caselli; DAI – Deutsches Archäologisches Institut, Rome; MD – Michael Duigan; PAC – Peter A. Clayton; RW – Roger Wilson.

1 BM. 3 Capitoline Museums, Rome, photo Araldo De Luca, Rome. 5a–b BM; Staatliche Museen, Berlin; Staatliche Museen, Berlin; Fitzwilliam Museum, Cambridge. 6 Châteaux de Versailles et de Trianon, photo © RMN – R. G. Ojeda/ Le Mage. 7l Metropolitan Museum of Art, New York, Rogers Fund 12.233; r Robert Harding/ © Robert Frerck/Odyssey/Chicago. 8 Museo Nazionale, Naples. 9a Kunsthistorisches Museum, Vienna; b Vatican Museum, Rome, photo Alinari. 10–11 PB. 12a Photo Alinari; b from A. Thevet, *Portraits et vies des hommes illustrés*, 1584. 14l–r BM; PAC; Foto Vasari, Rome; photo Araldo De Luca, Rome. 16 BM. 17a Capitoline Museums, Rome; b Palazzo Publico, Siena, photo Scala. 18 The Bridgeman Art Library. 19a Museo Nazionale di Villa Giulia, Rome; b © M. Bertinetti, White Star; 20 Musée du Louvre, Paris. 21a Museo dei Conservatori, Rome; b Robert Harding/© 2001 K. Gillham. 22 Photo Alinari. 23a Photo Leonard von Matt; b Musée Condé, Chantilly, France/The Bridgeman Art Library. 24a Museo Gregoriano Etrusco, Vaticano, photo Scala; b RW. 25a BM; b PAC. 26 PAC. 27a Musée du Louvre, Paris, photo Giraudon/The Bridgman Art Library; b GC. 28a PB; b BM. 30 PB. 31 Deutsches Museum, Munich. 32 Foto Vasari, Rome. 33 RW. 34l The Archaeological Museum, Zagreb; r Museo di Villa Giulia, Rome, photo Scala. 35a Museo di Villa Giulia, Rome, photo Scala; b Photo AKG London. 36a Museo delle Terme, Rome, photo Alinari; b Gabinetto Nazionale delle Medaglie, Rome. 37 Foto Vasari, Rome. 38 Fototeca Unione, Rome. 39a MD; b Mary Evans Picture Library. 41a, b Photo Alinari. 42 Fitzwilliam Museum, Cambridge. 43 Museo dei Conservatori, Rome, photo Araldo De Luca, Rome. 44 GC. 45 Musée du Louvre, Paris, phoro Alinari. 47l–r Musée des Beaux-Arts, Caen, France, photo Giraudon/The Bridgeman Art Library; Bibliothèque Nationale, Paris; École Nationale Supérieure des Beaux-Arts, Paris. 48 Musée des Beaux-Arts, Caen, France, photo Giraudon/The Bridgeman Art Library; 49l Museo Nazionale, Portogruaro; r DAI. 50a BM; b Museo dei Conservatori, Rome, Fototeca Unione, Rome. 51 Fototeca Unione, Rome. 52 By permission of the Trustees of Dulwich Picture Gallery. 53 Fototeca Unione, Rome. 54 Robert Harding/© 2001 K. Gillham. 55 Musée des Beaux-Arts, Caen, France, photo Giraudon/The Bridgeman Art Library. 56 École Nationale Supérieure des Beaux-Arts, Paris. 57 Fototeca Unione, Rome. 60 École Nationale Supérieure des

Beaux-Arts, Paris. 64 Musée du Louvre, Paris, photo The Bridgeman Art Library/Peter Willi. 67 Museo Nazionale di Villa Giulia, Rome. 68 Fototeca Unione, Rome. 69 Museo Civico Archaeologico, Bologna. 71a GC; b Palazzo Madama, Rome, photo Scala. 72 Museo Nazionale, Naples. 73a PB; b Sonia Halliday Photographs/photo F. H. C. Birch. 74 Museo Nazionale, Naples, photo Alinari. 75a GC; b Vatican Museums, Fototeca Unione, Rome. 76l–r Musée du Louvre, Paris, photo © RMN – R. G Ojeda; Capitoline Museums, Rome, photo Alinari; photo Araldo De Luca, Rome; École Française d'Athènes, P. Collet. 78 Mary Evans Picture Library; 79a Musée du Louvre, Paris, photo © RMN – R. G Ojeda; c DAI; b The Art Archive/ Museo della Civilta Romana, Rome/Dagli Orti. 80a BM; bl MD; br Kunsthistorisches Museum, Vienna. 81 PB. 82 National Museet, Stockholm. 83 from E. Hennebert, *Histoire d'Annibal*, I, 1870–91. 85 RW. 86 British Museum, photo PAC. 87 Museo Aquilano, photo Alinari. 88a Cabinet des Médailles, Bibliothèque Nationale, Paris; c PB; b Casa dei Vettii, Pompeii, photo Scala. 89 Carthage Museum. 90 Capitoline Museums, Rome, photo Alinari. 91 British Museum, photo PAC. 92a RW; b PB. 93a BM; b British Museum, photo PAC. 94 Museo Arqueologico, Madrid, photo AKG London. 95a RW; b Museo Nazionale, Naples, photo AKG London. 96 PB. 97 The Hermitage Museum, St Petersburg. 98l Soprintendenza alle Antichità, Taranto, photo Carrano Gerrano; r PB. 99a BM; b Capitoline Museums, Rome, photo Alinari. 100 from J. C. de Folard, *Histoire de Polybe*, 1727–30. 101 Liebieghaus Frankfurt, Foto Marburg. 102 Photo Araldo De Luca, Rome. 103 RW. 104a BM; b RW. 105a Pushkin Museum, Moscow/The Bridgeman Art Library; b BM; 106a PB; b RW. 107 École Française d'Athènes, P. Collet. 108a Photo Hirmer; b DAI. 109a BM; b British Museum, photo PAC; 110 The Art Archive/Bardo Museum, Tunis/Dagli Orti. 111 Photo Alinari. 113 British Museum, photo PAC. 114a Museo dei Conservatori, Rome; b Delphi Museum, École Française d'Athènes. 115a, b Vatican Museums, Rome. 116a British Museum, photo PAC; b RW. 117 Musée du Louvre, Paris, photo Giraudon/The Bridgeman Art Library. 118 PB. 119 Münzkabinett, Staatliche Museen, Berlin. 120a, b RW. 121 Photo Alinari. 122 The Bridgeman Art Library. 123a RW; bl Museo Arqueologico Nacional, Madrid; br Musée du Louvre, Paris, photo Giraudon/The Bridgeman Art Library. 125a Foto Mas; b Prado, Madrid, photo Scala. 127 Musée d'Orsay, Paris, photo Scala. 130 Staatliche Museen, Berlin. 131 The Art Archive/Museo Capitolino, Rome/Dagli Orti. 132l PB; r Museo Archeologico, Florence, photo Scala. 134 Museo Civico, Rome, RW; 135 Editions Arthaud. 136 The Bridgeman Art Library. 137 BM. 138l Museo Nazionale, Rome; r British Museum, photo PAC. 141 John Rylands University Library, Manchester. 143a BM; b Museo dei Conservatori, Rome. 145l–r Staatliche Antikensammlungen, Munich; Ny Carlsberg Glyptotek, Copenhagen – © Ole Haupt; Museo Pio-Clementino, Vatican, Rome, photo Scala; Kingston Lacy, the Bankes Collection. 146 Staatliche Antikensammlungen, Munich. 148 BM. 149 Staatliche

Antikensammlungen, Munich/Agenzia Fotografica Luisa Ricciarini, Milan. 152a BM; b PB. 153a Vatican Museums, photo DAI; bl and br Metropolitan Museum of Art, New York, Rogers Fund 65.183.1/3. 154 Staatliche Museen, Berlin. 155a, b BM; 156a Metropolitan Museum of Art, New York; b photo Araldo De Luca, Rome. 156–57 PB. 157a Giovanni Lattanzi. 158 Metropolitan Museum of Art, New York. 158 Musée du Louvre, Paris, photo © RMN. 160a, c Giovanni Lattanzi; b PAC. 161 Fototeca Unione, Rome. 162 Photo AKG London/Peter Connolly. 164 Museo Archeologico, Venice, photo Scala. 165 MD. 166a, b British Museum, photo PAC. 167, 168 Fototeca Unione, Rome. 169 Chieti Museum. 170 © M. Bertinetti, White Star. 172 BM. 174a RW; b The Art Archive/Museo Capitolino, Rome/Dagli Orti. 176 Fototeca Unione, Rome. 177a Museo Archeologico Nazionale, Taranto; b Museo Archeologico Nazionale, Civitavecchio. 178 Museo dei Conservatori, Rome, photo DAI. 179 Fototeca Unione, Rome. 180a Museum für Islamische Kunst, Berlin photo © Preussischer Kulturbesitz, Berlin; b PB. 181 Ny Carlsberg Glyptotek, Copenhagen – © Ole Haupt. 183, 184 RW. 185a BM. b BM. 186a Staatliche Museen, Berlin; b British Museum, photo PAC. 187a BM; b Glyptotek, Munich. 188a Museo Nazionale, Naples, photo Scala; b Museo Capitolino, Fototeca Unione, Rome. 188–89 The Art Archive/ Archaeological Museum, Naples/Dagli Orti. 189a MD; b Museo Nazionale, Naples/The Bridgeman Art Library. 190 Collection Berenson, Florence, photo Scala. 191 Rabat Museum, Morocco, photo Roger Wood. 192 MD. 193 Museo Nazionale, Naples, photo Scala. 195l Fototeca Unione, Rome; r Staatliche Museen, Berlin. 196 Museo Nazionale, Rome, photo Alinari. 197 RW. 198 École Nationale Supérieure des Beaux-Arts, Paris. 199 BM. 200 Museo Pio-Clementino, Vatican, Rome, photo Scala. 201 RW. 202l PW; c National Gallery, Oslo; r British Museum, photo Edwin Smith. 203 Museo Arqueologico Nacional, Madrid. 204a Staatliche Museen, Berlin. b RW. 205a MD; b National Gallery, Oslo. 206a Musée des Antiquités Nationales, Saint-Germain-en-Laye, photo © RMN; c BM; b Museo Civico Archeologico, Bologna. 207 Photo © Dr René Goguey. 208a The Walters Art Gallery, Baltimore; b Staatliche Museen, Berlin. 209l PAC; 209r The Art Archive/Museo Capitolino, Rome/Dagli Orti. 210a The Montreal Museum of Fine Arts; b BM. 211a Photo Alison Frantz; b British Museum, photo PAC. 212 Ashmolean Museum, Oxford/ The Bridgeman Art Library. 213 Palazzo del Senato, Rome. 215 RW. 216 Kingston Lacy, The Bankes Collection. 217a © M. Bertinetti, White Star; bl, br PAC. 218 PAC. 219 Fitzwilliam Museum, Cambridge. 220 Cabinet des Médailles, Bibliothèque Nationale, Paris. 221a PB; b Vatican Museums, Rome. 222l Museo Nazionale, Naples; r Museo Nazionale, Naples, photo Scala. 223 British Museum, photo Edwin Smith. 224 BM. 225a Staatliche Museen, Berlin; b BM. 226 BM. 227 Museo Nazionale delle Terme, Rome. 228 RW. 229 DAI. 230a Kunsthistorisches Museum, Vienna; b BM. 231a Kon Penningkabinet, The Hague; b photo Araldo De Luca, Rome.